...LLEGE LIBRARY
SHELF No. 320.968
BRE

CAN SOUTH AFRICA SURVIVE?

WITHDRAWN

Also by John D. Brewer

MOSLEY'S MEN: The British Union of Fascists in the West Midlands
AFTER SOWETO: An Unfinished Journey
*THE POLICE, PUBLIC ORDER AND THE STATE (*with Adrian Guelke, Ian Hume, Edward Moxon-Browne and Rick Wilford*)

**Also published by Macmillan*

Can South Africa Survive?

Five Minutes to Midnight

Edited by

John D. Brewer
Lecturer in Social Studies
The Queen's University of Belfast

MAGDALEN COLLEGE LIBRARY

MACMILLAN
PRESS

© John D. Brewer 1989

All rights reserved. No reproduction, copy or transmission of this publication may be made without written permission.

No paragraph of this publication may be reproduced, copied or transmitted save with written permission or in accordance with the provisions of the Copyright Act 1956 (as amended), or under the terms of any licence permitting limited copying issued by the Copyright Licensing Agency, 33–4 Alfred Place, London WC1E 7DP.

Any person who does any unauthorised act in relation to this publication may be liable to criminal prosecution and civil claims for damages.

First published 1989

Published by
THE MACMILLAN PRESS LTD
Houndmills, Basingstoke, Hampshire RG21 2XS
and London
Companies and representatives
throughout the world

Typeset in Great Britain by
Latimer Trend & Company Ltd
Plymouth
Printed and bound in Great Britain at
The Camelot Press Ltd, Southampton

British Library Cataloguing in Publication Data
Can South Africa survive? : five minutes to midnight
1. South Africa. Politics
I. Brewer, John D.
320.968
ISBN 0–333–47059–1 (hardcase)
ISBN 0–333–47060–5 (paperback)

Contents

List of Figures

List of Tables

List of Abbreviations

AAC	Alexandra Action Committee
ANC	African National Congress
ARB	African Research Bulletin
ASRA	Atteridegeville–Sauskville Residents' Association
AZACTU	Azanian Confederation of Trade Unions
AZAPO	Azanian People's Organisation
AZASO	Azanian Students' Organisation
CI	Christian Institute
CONSAS	Constellation of Southern African States
COSAS	Congress of South African Students
COSATU	Congress of South African Trade Unions
CP	Conservative Party
CUSA	Council of Unions of South Africa
DAC	Defence Advisory Council
EC	European Community
ECC	End Conscription Campaign
ECSC	European Coal and Steel Community
EPC	European Political Cooperation
FOSATU	Federation of South African Trade Unions
GWU	General Workers' Union
HNP	Herstigte Nasionale Party
JMC	Joint Management Centre
MAWU	Metal and Allied Workers' Union
NATO	North Atlantic Treaty Organisation
NECC	National Education Crisis Committee
NIC	Natal Indian Congress
NP	National Party
NPC	Natal Provincial Council
NUM	National Union of Mineworkers
OAU	Organisation of African Unity
PAC	Pan-Africanist Congress
PEBCO	Port Elizabeth Civic Organisation
PEYCO	Port Elizabeth Youth Congress
PFP	Progressive Federal Party
RMC	Release Mandela Committee
RSC	Regional Service Council
SAAWU	South African Allied Workers' Union

SABRA	South African Bureau of Racial Affairs
SACLA	South African Confederation of Labour
SACP	South African Communist Party
SACTU	South African Congress of Trade Unions
SADCC	South African Development Coordination Conference
SADF	South African Defence Force
SAIRR	South African Institute of Race Relations
SAN	South African Navy
SSC	State Security Council
SWAPO	South-West African People's Organisation
SWATE	South-West African Territory Force
TOYCO	Tumahole Youth Congress
TUCSA	Trades Union Council of South Africa
UDF	United Democratic Front
UN	United Nations
UP	United Party
UWUSA	United Workers' Union of South Africa
VVPP	Vukani Vulimehlo People's Party
WCC	World Council of Churches

Notes on the Contributors

G. R. Berridge is Lecturer in Politics at the University of Leicester since 1978, and teaches international relations and South African foreign policy. His principal publications are *Economic Power in Anglo–South African Diplomacy* (1981); *Diplomacy at the UN* (co-editor, 1985); *The Politics of the South African Run* (1987); *International Politics: States, Power and Conflict Since 1945* (1987). He is currently working on South Africa's defence relations with the European colonial powers in the period 1948–64.

Gerald Braun is Research Fellow at the Arnold Bergstraesser Institute and Lecturer in Political Science at the University of Freiburg. He studied economics, political science and sociology in Berlin and Freiburg. Senior Lecturer at the General Staff Academy of the Federal German Defence Forces, Hamburg. He has published on structural and development problems in Southern and East Africa.

John D. Brewer teaches social studies at The Queen's University of Belfast. He previously held lecturing posts at the University of Natal in Durban and the University of East Anglia. He was Visiting Fellow at Yale University in 1989. His previous books reflect wide interests: *Mosley's Men: The BUF in the West Midlands* (1984); *After Soweto: An Unfinished Journey* (1987); *The Police, Public Order and the State* (co-author 1988). He is currently doing a study of the Royal Ulster Constabulary, funded by the Economic and Social Research Council, and writing up his work on the South African Police and the Scottish Enlightenment.

Hermann Giliomee is Professor of Political Studies at the University of Cape Town. He was previously Lecturer in History at the University of Stellenbosch. He has held visiting fellowships at Yale University, the Hebrew University of Jerusalem and the University of Cambridge. He has published in the fields of history and politics. He is co-author of *Ethnic Power Mobilized* (1979) and co-editor of *The Shaping of South African Society 1652–1820* (1979) and *Up Against the Fences: Poverty, Passes and Privilege* (1985). In 1984 he founded Voorbrand Publications, which publishes the radical Afrikaans magazine *Die Suid-Afrikaan*.

Adrian Guelke is a Lecturer in the Department of Political Science at The Queen's University of Belfast. He was educated at the University of Cape Town and the London School of Economics. The main field of his research is conflict in divided societies, such as South Africa and Northern Ireland. He is author of *The Northern Ireland Conflict in an International Perspective* (1988) and a co-author of *The Police, Public Order and the State* (1988).

Martin Holland is Senior Lecturer at the University of Canterbury, New Zealand. He was Jean Monnet Fellow at the European University Institute during 1987. His principal publications are *The European Community and South Africa* (1988); *Candidates for Europe – The British Experience* (1986); co-editor of *The Fourth Labour Government: Radical Politics in New Zealand* (1987). His articles on South Africa have appeared in *Political Studies, World Today, British Journal of Political Science*, and *Political Science.*

Tom Lodge is Senior Lecturer in the Department of Political Studies at the University of the Witwatersrand. Educated in the Department of History and the Centre for Southern African Studies at the University of York. He is author of *Black Politics in South Africa Since 1945* (1983) and editor of *Resistance and Ideology in Settler Societies* (1986). He is currently writing a book on the African National Congress and a two-volume study of the South African Communist Party.

Mark Mitchell is Acting Head and **Dave Russell** is Senior Lecturer in the School of Social and Historical Studies at Portsmouth Polytechnic. For a number of years they have together taught courses on the state and on race in Britain and South Africa. Previously they have written articles together on militarisation, and black trade unionism in South Africa, as well as on the new right and the politics of race in Britain.

T. C. Moll is currently doing doctoral research in economics at St John's College, Cambridge, on structural change and sectoral productivity levels in the postwar South African economy. He studied economics and sociology at the universities of Cape Town and Natal, and has lectured in South Africa and the Irish Republic.

Nicoli Nattrass is a D.Phil student at Magdalen College, Oxford, working on the political economy of South Africa. She has taught at universities in South Africa and the Irish Republic.

Paul B. Rich lectures in the Department of Politics at the University of Warwick and has held previous appointments at the Universities of the Witwatersrand, Cape Town, Aston and Bristol. He has written a number of articles on both South African and British politics. His books include: *White Power and the Liberal Conscience* (1984); *Race and Empire in British Politics* (1986). He is currently writing a series of essays entitled *Prospero's Return: Essays on Race, Class and Culture in Britain.*

Heribert Weiland is Research Fellow and Administrative Director of the Arnold Bergstraesser Institute. He studied economics and political science at the University of Freiburg and the London School of Economics. His publications are primarily on political developments in Africa, especially Southern Africa.

Introduction

'The fate of books', wrote Terentianus Marus in AD 200 'depends on the capacity of the reader.' By this I take it that he meant that some books are hardly ever read, some are read and quickly forgotten, while others create so many resonances for their readers that they survive the vagaries of time and fashion. R. W. Johnson's book *How Long Will South Africa Survive?* was one of the latter.[1] Of course, these resonances derive from many sources – fine prose, illuminating insight and convincing argument among them. Johnson's reviewers found none of these. Many criticised the lack of documentation and citation that could have made his argument more persuasive. They found the style rather journalistic and the insights too few.[2] But the general theme of a book can also give it influence, so that its resonances are to be found in its association with a recurring issue which is of continuing importance. There can be few topics of such universal interest as the survival of apartheid in South Africa, and Johnson's book was the first directly to address this theme, and in many people's minds has been associated with it ever since.

The book had a tremendous impact when it was first published in South Africa, with newspapers carrying extensive reports of Johnson's arguments, which he followed by a popular lecture tour of South Africa's English-speaking universities. The South African Broadcasting Service even devoted an entire current affairs programme to dismissing his claims. These sorts of resonances are quite ephemeral, but beyond the level of popular consciousness the book had a more lasting effect on academics who specialise in the study of South African society and politics. This is attested to by the number of citations it has received over the years in the *Social Science Citation Index*. But even more important, *How Long Will South Africa Survive?* was a catalyst for debate and initiated a round of claim and counter-claim which itself contributed to making apartheid's prospects of survival an issue in the academic literature,[3] over and above whatever effect the conduct of the South African state has on sustaining interest in this theme.

The Johnson thesis can be simply stated: the system of white supremacy in South Africa is under considerable strain but will survive in the short to medium term. The analogy with Russia was employed extensively. Just as the czars weathered sporadic revolutions, so the South African state can survive as long as it avoids an external war, such as proved to be the eventual downfall of Czar Nicholas II. The thesis was controversial at the time because it ran counter to the wishful thinking of many liberals and challenged the almost ubiquitous prediction of imminent revolution. In 1965 Richard Dale warned against foolhardily predicting the future of South Africa, claiming there were too many unknowns and too many variables in the equation,[4] but in the context of regional and domestic circumstances in the late 1960s and early 1970s the overthrow of apartheid in South Africa was thought to be inevitable. Widespread industrial strikes had broken out in South Africa; political mobilisation was taking place again via Black Consciousness groups after the period of quiescence following the banning of the leading organisations in 1960; students were becoming more militant; all this eventually culminated in the 1976 protest in Soweto and elsewhere. Colonial regimes in southern African were also crumbling. In the midst of the euphoria generated by these events, Johnson introduced a depressing element of realism, claiming that the South African state's capacity for survival ensured that the clock was stuck permanently at five minutes to midnight,[5] although he never implied that survival was deserved, as some critics claimed. The metaphor of the motionless clock well sums up Johnson's arguments, for South Africa was a fraction away from revolution but was unlikely in the medium term ever to reach that point; it was a question of how near to the hour yet how so far.

According to Johnson, four factors were bringing South Africa to this juncture – international pressure; the dynamics of internal politics; the fragility of the domestic economy; and hostility from neighbouring black states. But within each there were circumstances which blunted their impact and slowed down the march to midnight. It was Johnson's discussion of these circumstances which gave his book its novelty and controversial character. The superpowers were portrayed as being unwilling if not unable to apply pressure to South Africa. The Soviet Union preferred not to intervene, but to work indirectly and less effectively through regionally-based surrogates, but even here Johnson thought that South Africa's neighbours were unlikely to harbour guerrillas and would seek to normalise their relations with Pretoria rather than provoke military engagement. As for the United States, Johnson argued that it saw its best interests served by not threatening the stability of the regime. Indeed, he claimed that the United States could not afford otherwise because of Pretoria's strategic and economic roles both on a regional and world scale. One of the most interesting insights concerned Kissinger's manipulation of the gold market to apply pressure on South Africa in order to persuade Vorster to influence Smith in Rhodesia; but in the context of what Johnson called 'cold war competition', he thought it unlikely that such manipulation would be used to affect South Africa's domestic relations.

How Long Will South Africa Survive? was remarkable for its account of the internationalisation of southern African conflicts and was rather weak on developments inside South Africa, but where Johnson did discuss internal political dynamics he understood white politics better than black. While recognising that there were traditional conflicts between English-speaking and Afrikaans-speaking whites, which left a residue of suspicion, he felt that the trend was for whites to become more politically unified and thus better able to present a united opposition to black majority rule. White politics would be increasingly characterised by consensus, with politicians from within the two communities agreeing on a strategy whereby apartheid was reformed in order to strengthen white dominance; policies such as the cooption of the black middle classes would be adopted and 'social apartheid' would be abolished. However, while whites recognised that unity is strength, blacks did not, and Johnson predicted that black politics would become moribund as a result of divisions between urban and rural dwellers, rich and poor, and moderates and radicals. The African National Congress (ANC) was thought to be incapable of reasserting itself again inside the country, and no organisations were deemed effective enough to replace it. Moreover, state power was such that black protest would be easily crushed, forcing it to rely increasingly on ineffective and occasional guerrilla insurgency.

One other domestic development Johnson discussed was the country's economy. While it was described as fragile, Johnson argued that it was not in the state of near-collapse which many others claimed. Accordingly, economic considerations were not presented as constituting a source of pressure working in the direction of reform; if anything economic trends would result in the intensification of oppression as the costs of recession were offloaded on to blacks and expenditure on the parastatal sector, such as defence and policing, increased in order to maintain white employment.

A great deal has happened internationally, within the region and inside South Africa since 1977, when these arguments were outlined. South Africa is now the last pigmentocracy in southern Africa, being completely encircled by hostile states, so that the region's diplomatic and strategic resources can be concentrated for the final assault. Pretoria's peaceful accords with some of her neighbours have been ratified by signature but not in practice and have simply failed to deliver compliance with South Africa's interests. Guerrilla bases exist in some neighbouring states and the whole region is being destabilised by South Africa's attempt to obliterate them through military incursions and economic pressure. Aluko and Shaw were exaggerating only slightly when they argued that the 1980s symbolise the shift from 'global to regional determinants'.[6] This is an overstatement because important changes have occurred internationally which affect the Johnson thesis. Selective sanctions have been imposed on South Africa and some Western disinvestment has occurred. Those in the West who oppose sanctions have been placed more on the defensive as sanctions gain wider legitimacy and support. Moreover, the context of international relations is different. At a relatively simple level, the personalities have changed, in some cases with quite crucial differences in style and belief; there is no Kissinger, no Carter, and Reagan and Thatcher dominate the West, while Gorbachev focuses increasingly inward on economic and bureaucratic changes within the Soviet Union. But there are more fundamental changes. The relations between the superpowers have been influenced by such things as nuclear disarmament talks, the Soviet invasion of Afghanistan and tension in the Middle East and Central America, all of which can affect how they perceive their best interests being served in southern Africa.

Changes in the constellation of forces inside South Africa have been as profound. The South African state is a powerful actor in the scenario and shifts in state policy have been considerable, some of which Johnson foresaw. He believed that the 'White establishment' would continue to pursue policies of separate development but would concede changes in 'social apartheid'; he predicted that the regime would introduce policy changes under the banner of 'reform', such as the abolition of 'petty apartheid' and the cooption of the black middle classes, with the intention merely to strengthen white dominance. However, a more extensive range of policy shifts has occurred than Johnson thought, including the legalisation of black trade unions, new constitutional structures, the rise of the 'security establishment' at central and regional levels,[7] the abolition of the pass laws, influx control and discriminatory legislation in the economy, the expansion of black education, economic decentralisation and regional development, and revisions to the Group Areas Act. The state describes these as the abolition of apartheid, but most commentators agree with Johnson's judgement in 1977 that the regime uses reform merely to strengthen the hold whites have on political power, no matter how extensive the shifts.

Hence terms such as 'sham reform', 'deracialisation' or 'neo-apartheid' are used in the literature to accommodate those changes which alter the appearance of apartheid without dismantling the system of white political dominance. But there are limits to this policy of 'reform-from-above' because the state cannot control the unintended consequences of its policies, and many of the changes have simply intensified the pressures on the state.[8]

However, there are other elements in the scenario besides the actions of the state. New forces have arisen inside South Africa which affect Johnson's arguments and were not foreseen by him, some of which originated as an unintended effect of 'government-led reform'. These include the schisms within white politics resulting in the complete fragmentation of white hegemony; the politicisation of black trade unions and black South Africans generally; the re-emergence of the ANC and its links with internal political movements such as the United Democratic Front (UDF), and the associated coordination of guerrilla insurgency and political mobilisation; the intensification of the border war in Namibia with the increase in the loss of young white conscripts; and economic hardship amongst a growing number of whites as a result of the severity of the recession.

In these changed circumstances it seems appropriate to review Johnson's argument about the medium-term stability of the system of white supremacy in South Africa, especially now that, in the light of the new situation, predictions of its imminent overthrow have surfaced again. Intellectual consideration is being given to the nature of the post-apartheid society and economy,[9] and numerous works devote themselves to exploring the dimensions of South Africa's crisis.[10] As exhilarating as it is to imagine a free, non-racial South Africa emerging from the final crisis, it is necessary to reflect on just how unstable the apartheid system has become since Johnson warned us in 1977 of its tenacity and endurance. Richard Hodder-Williams was correct when he once wrote that those who attempt to predict the future are hostages to fortune, but that it is necessary for reputable scholars to use their understanding to clarify the factors which are likely to be significant in delineating the future path of countries like South Africa.[11]

This volume is the outcome of such reflection, and addresses the four aspects of Johnson's thesis which he deemed important to South Africa's future. The international dimension is covered by a chapter on the superpowers (Berridge) and by two chapters which explore different features of the sanctions debate (Braun and Weiland, and Holland), international diplomatic and economic sanctions having become more widely supported and applied since the publication of Johnson's book. The regional dimension is addressed (in a chapter by Braun), along with features of internal political dynamics. The fragmentation of white hegemony is considered in a chapter which explores the effects of splits within Afrikaner politics (Giliomee), and there are two chapters on the growth in black protest (Brewer, and Lodge). The political effects of the South African economy are covered in two chapters (Moll, and Nattrass), one of which explores the constraints imposed also on black politics, in this case the KwaZulu–Natal Indaba. Because a number of important policy changes have been introduced by the South African state since Johnson's book, some chapters address themselves to assessing their effects on the regime's medium-term stability. Two in particular are examined – the legalisation of black trade unions (Mitchell and Russell), and constitutional change (Guelke). 'Government-led reforms' are one means by which it is intended to strengthen the system of white political supremacy, but they have both an ideological and structural dimension, and there are chapters on 'change' as it is conceived at the level of ideological discourse (Rich) and of the state (Mitchell and Russell). The chapter on the state's structural incapacity to reform also explores some of the more repressive ways in which the state seeks to strengthen its position, such as by the development of the state security system, although this also features in other chapters.

The theme of the 'Johnson thesis ten years on' was the subject of a workshop held at the University of Amsterdam in April 1987 with the title 'Change in South Africa and its Regional and International Aspects', organised under the auspices of the European Consortium for Political Research, co-directed by Heribert Weiland and myself. With one or two exceptions, the chapters in this volume are revised versions of papers presented to the workshop. While it has not been possible to include all papers in this volume, the contributions here have benefited from the constructive and friendly interchanges that took place during the workshop, and have been enriched by the comments of all participants. It is also pleasing to express thanks to the European Consortium of Political Research for giving us the opportunity to meet in Amsterdam and to pursue further the ideas that have culminated in this volume.

Notes

* I wish to thank Geoff Berridge and Adrian Guelke for commenting on a first draft, but absolve them from responsibility for the inadequacies of the final version.

1. R. W. Johnson, *How Long Will South Africa Survive?*, London, Macmillan Press, 1977.
2. For a sample of the reviews see: Heribert Adam in the *Canadian Journal of African Studies*, 12, 1978; Valentine Belifiglio, 'How Will Majority Rule Come About in Azania/South Africa?', *Journal of Modern African Studies*, 21,1983; Gwendolen Carter in the *American Political Science Review*, 73, 1979; Simon Clarke in the *Journal of Southern African Studies*, 3–4, 1976–78; Adrian Guelke, 'Change in South African Politics?', *Political Studies*, 31, 1983; Richard Hodder-Williams, 'Well, Will South Africa Survive?', *African Affairs*, 80, 1981; B. Huber in the *Journal of Modern African Studies*, 18, 1980; Luke Malaba in the *Review of African Political Economy*, 10, 1977; M. Midlane, 'The Crisis Facing South Africa: Has The Twelfth Hour Passed?', *Round Table*, 69, 1979; C. Stevens in the *Journal of Commonwealth and Comparative Politics*, 16–17, 1978–79.
3. For the debate see among others: H. Adam and H. Giliomee, *Ethnic Power Mobilized: Can South Africa Change?*, New Haven, Yale University Press, 1979; O. Aluko and T. Shaw (ed.), *Southern Africa in the 1980s*, London, Allen and Unwin, 1985; J. Barber, J. Blumenfeld and C. Hill, *South Africa and the West*, London, Routledge and Kegan Paul, 1982; Gwendolen Carter, *Which Way Is South Africa Going?*, Bloomington, Indiana University Press, 1980; L. H. Gann and Peter Duignan, *South Africa: War? Revolution? Peace?*, Cape Town, Tafelberg, 1979; L. H. Gann and Peter Duignan, *Why South Africa Will Survive*, London, Croom Helm, 1981; C. Legum, *The Western Crisis over Southern Africa*, London, Holmes and Meier, 1979; R. Rotberg, *Suffer The Future*, London, Harvard University Press, 1980.
4. R. Dale, 'South Africa and the International Community', *World Politics*, 18, 1965–66, p.313.
5. *How Long Will South Africa Survive?*, op cit., p. 288.
6. *Southern Africa in the 1980s*, op. cit., p.xii.
7. A term taken from Kenneth Grundy, 'The Rise of the South African Security Establishment', Bradlow Paper no. 1, South African Institute of International Affairs, 1983.
8. For an extended discussion on the limits of 'government-led reform' see J. D. Brewer, *After Soweto: An Unfinished Journey*, Oxford, The Clarendon Press, 1987, pp. 45–50; Sam Nolutshungu, *Changing South Africa*, Manchester, Manchester University Press, 1982.
9. For example, the Centre for Southern African Studies at the University of York held a conference in 1986 on 'The Southern African Economy After Apartheid', and Heribert Adam and Kogila Moodley have written *South Africa Without Apartheid*, Berkeley, University of California Press, 1986.

10. For a selection see: J. Blumenfeld (ed.), *South Africa in Crisis*, London, Croom Helm, 1987; R. Cohen, *Endgame in South Africa*, London, James Currey, 1986; F. Parker, *South Africa: Lost Opportunities*, Aldershot, Gower, 1984; M. Murray, *South Africa: Time of Agony, Time of Destiny*, London, Verso, 1987; J. Saul and S. Gelb, *The Crisis in South Africa*, London, Zed Press, 1986; M. Uhlig (ed.), *Apartheid in Crisis*, Harmondsworth, Penguin, 1986; H. Wolpe, 'Apartheid's Deepening Crisis', *Marxism Today*, January 1983.
11. 'Well, Will South Africa Survive?, op. cit., p.405.

1 The Role of the Superpowers*

G. R. Berridge

INTRODUCTION

Southern Africa is a region in which for long the United States had only very limited interests and in which the Soviet Union had virtually none at all. Britain had been without doubt the paramount external power in the area, with only minor competition from France and Portugal. However, by the mid 1970s British influence had declined considerably, and Portuguese colonial rule in Angola and Mozambique had disintegrated. Against this background, opportunities for Soviet intervention were provided by the civil wars in Rhodesia, Namibia and, above all, in Angola; and the United States was drawn in to stiffen the Western position, albeit hampered by the post-Vietnam anxieties of Congress and the diplomatic drawbacks of being too openly on the same side as the South Africans.

Writing two years after these dramatic developments, R. W. Johnson laid considerable stress on the present and likely future policies of *both* superpowers in support of his thesis that South Africa was likely to survive for much longer than at that time it was usual to suppose. These conclusions were in their turn based on three premises about South Africa itself: first, that the Republic ('possibly the greatest military power in the southern hemisphere'[1]) was the chief arbiter of events in southern Africa; secondly, that it also occupied a critical position in the whole western strategic and economic order;[2] and thirdly, that it remained highly, and increasingly vulnerable to outside pressures precisely because of its advanced integration in the world economy. In the light of these facts, argued Johnson, the United States under the Republicans had come to treat South Africa as the guardian of the Western position throughout the region and even permitted it to become a 'back-door member of NATO',[3] and would be likely to *strengthen* further the stability of the country under its 'White Establishment'.

Washington, Johnson claimed, would certainly continue to use its economic strength (principally in the gold market) to encourage the

South Africans to cooperate with the policy of fostering the emergence of moderate, black states to the north – 'other Zambias'. However, he argued, such a regional policy would help to underpin the external security of the 'White Establishment', while the United States would be likely to provide it with increased internal support as a result of mounting Western anxieties that in its absence southern Africa as a whole would succumb to the remorseless advance of Soviet power. Nevertheless, Johnson conceded, if despite US support South Africa found itself faced with an externally-supported guerrilla war, accompanied by mounting unrest among urban blacks, the leverage over Pretoria which its 'metropolitan' role would provide Washington in such circumstances might be exerted instead in order to *weaken* the apartheid regime. In such conditions 'majority rule' might seem the only alternative to the 'loss' of South Africa.[4]

As for the Soviet Union, Johnson was impressed by the growth of its military and economic strength relative to that of the West, and by the recent expansion of its influence into southern Africa and the Indian Ocean area. However, he thought it unlikely that the Russians, who still had 'very limited means for making their strategic weight felt in southern Africa'[5] and were acutely conscious of the economic weakness of the frontline states, would press them into confrontation with Pretoria; on the contrary, he claimed, all the signs were – especially in regard to Mozambique – that they would encourage the continuation of normal relations with South Africa. Soviet policy, thought Johnson, insofar as its main preoccupation was the immensely difficult task of helping to consolidate the new Marxist regimes which had recently appeared in the region, was only a long-term threat to the stability of the 'White Establishment'.

Ten years on, what is the role of the superpowers in southern Africa, what policies might they adopt henceforth, and what bearing do the answers to these questions have on the present and future stability of the National Party regime? As will become clear, Johnson's analysis of the superpowers was on the whole strikingly prescient.

SOVIET INTERESTS IN SOUTHERN AFRICA

Following the Soviet/Cuban intervention in Angola in 1975, and the associated rise of Moscow's influence in Marxist Mozambique (China's eclipse being assisted by the fact that it had backed the losing side in Angola), a general Soviet presence has become quite marked in southern Africa, even if this is not as great as South African propaganda would have the West believe and has of late begun to diminish. With the exception of Malawi, Swaziland and South Africa itself, all states in the region host Soviet diplomats (a Soviet embassy has even been opened in Zimbabwe despite the fact that Moscow supported Joshua Nkomo in the Rhodesian civil war), and most contain representatives from Eastern Europe, Cuba, Vietnam and North Korea as well. Treaties of Friendship and Cooperation have been signed with Angola and Mozambique by both the Soviet Union and East Germany.[6] Party-to-party agreements have been concluded not only with the Marxist governing parties in these two countries but with the ruling United National Independence Party in Zambia.[7] A limited economic aid programme has been initiated and advisers and technical operatives (such as harbour pilots at Maputo and Beira, together with a shore-based coördinator[8]) have been sent in swarms. Above all, the Soviet Union and its allies have poured into the region (especially into Angola) heavy armaments, military advisers, and 20–30 000 Cuban troops; and the Soviet navy has paid well-publicised visits to Luanda, Beira and Maputo. The implication conveyed by all this in respect of Angola and Mozambique, is that the Soviet Union and its allies will not stand idly by if their regimes come under attack. What interests in southern Africa have prompted the Soviet Union to make its presence felt in these ways, and give such hostages to fortune?

The South African government has ritualistically pronounced that Soviet policy in the region has two overriding purposes: to seize control of its mineral riches (if only to deny them to the West); and to secure mastery of the sea lanes around the Cape of Good Hope. The Soviet Union, however, has made no attempt to use its influence to deny to the West primary products from Angola and Mozambique, countries which, indeed, remain desperate to increase their exports to the capitalist world. Nor does it have any confidence in a change in this attitude since it regards southern Africa as 'entirely at the mercy of international capital'.[9] Furthermore, if only because of Moscow's own anxiety to increase its foreign currency earnings by entering the Western liner trades as a 'conference-minded' member,[10] it is difficult to believe that it would allow a pro-Soviet majority-ruled South Africa to interfere with Western shipping around the Cape in peacetime. In a general war, even assuming a conventional stage, it is just as hard to understand why the Soviet Union would wish to interdict Western shipping as far away from its home ports as the Cape.[11] In short, the official South African view of Soviet policy in the region is not even plausible, any more than it was in the early 1950s when the new National Party government's political generals occasioned unrestrained hilarity in Whitehall (especially in the War Office) by insisting on the necessity of spending huge sums on a radar network for the Rand in order to give early warning of Russian bomber attacks.[12]

Less partisan observers have achieved a rough consensus on the general promptings of Soviet policy in southern Africa which is distinctly at odds with the official South African view, and which has not changed radically since 1977. This begins with the unsurprising proposition that judging by the *relatively* low levels of economic and military aid extended to southern Africa by the Soviet Union in comparison with its disbursements elsewhere in the Third World, Moscow has no vital interests in the region at all.[13] Of these less-than-vital interests the first is probably the *spoiling interest* in undermining the non-economic interests of the West and China in the region and keeping them off balance at relatively low cost. Secondly, there is the *propaganda interest* in promoting leftist change and supporting regimes of 'socialist orientation', for this appears to confirm the claim of the Soviet Union that history is on its side and thus bolsters its prestige. Thirdly, there is the *status interest* in reinforcing the Soviet claim to equality with the United States, with a right to a seat at all conferences aimed at settling major international disputes. (This interest is promoted by the establishment of the Soviet presence in southern Africa partly because of the dramatic geographical reach of Soviet power of which it provides evidence and partly because it gives Moscow an 'interest' in the settlement of problems in the region; were the Russians able to gain a seat at conclusive negotiations on Namibia, for example, it would greatly strengthen their claim to a seat in other regional negotiations of much greater interest to them, most obviously, of course, in the Middle East.) Fourthly, there are *strategic interests* in air and naval facilities (especially in Angola), which provide Moscow with some ability to 'counter US strategic forces, monitor US military activity, and transport assistance to friendly regimes in the region',[14] and in preventing South Africa from contributing to an increase in nuclear weapons proliferation. Fifthly, there are some *economic interests*. These include fishing concessions off the coasts of Angola and Mozambique, arms sales,[15] and sailings for Soviet bloc vessels in the presently West European-dominated liner trades serving the region. Soviet bloc lines are already members of the Europe–East Africa shipping conference (headquartered in London[16]), and are treated as 'tolerated outsiders' by the Europe–South Africa shipping conference (embracing Beira and Maputo as well as South African ports, and also headquartered in London), but because of the wars in Angola and Mozambique are able to lift hardly any of the valuable cargos originating in Central Africa, most of which leave via ports in the Republic. However, if the railways in Angola and Mozambique were to be made to work again, Soviet vessels could well secure a bigger share of this trade. At the moment they are confined to shipping in arms and other military material and returning more or less empty.[17] Finally, there is the *diplomatic interest* in keeping the support of southern African states for Soviet attitudes in international forums, for example on Afghanistan and arms control, by increasing Moscow's visibility in the 'struggle' against South Africa. Altogether, then, it seems fair to say that while none of the Soviet Union's interests in southern Africa is in any sense vital, collectively they make up a moderate stake. Were it to be ousted from the region altogether, this would be a considerable blow to its prestige but it would be no more than a minor material and strategic irritant. It would probably not compare in seriousness to the loss of its influence in Egypt in 1972.

AMERICAN INTERESTS IN SOUTHERN AFRICA

Any discussion of American interests in southern Africa – and many other regions, for that matter – is bedevilled by two problems: the obvious lack of consensus on the question within recent administrations; and the common confusion in secondary analysis between historical accounts of what those interests are and prescriptive statements concerning what they should be. (Johnson's own account did not suffer from this confusion.) Bearing this in mind it is perhaps fair to say that the Reagan Administration has more tangible interests in southern Africa, and especially in South Africa, than does the Soviet Union, and appears to attach more importance to all of its interests, collectively, than Moscow does to its own; furthermore, it seems to believe that they are all vulnerable. Shortly before assuming a prominent role in the Reagan Administration's policy towards southern Africa, Chester A. Crocker described these interests as 'important' and 'exposed',[18] while on 22 July 1986, in his first full-length address on South Africa, which was designed to deflate Congress's mounting enthusiasm for wide-ranging sanctions against the Republic, President Reagan himself stated that the region was of 'vital importance to the West'.[19] However, the margin between the importance attached to their respective interests by the United States and the Soviet Union is probably not vast and the only American interests which are regarded as 'vital' by conservative opinion in Washington are *in fact* relatively invulnerable, in marked contrast to all Soviet interests in the region.

The United States and its allies appear to believe, probably rightly, that they have vital *strategic and economic interests* in the uninterrupted flow of merchant shipping (especially oil tankers) along the 'Cape Route'. And it is certainly true that, following the growth of Soviet naval strength in the Indian Ocean and the rise of Soviet bloc influence in southern Africa in the first half of the 1970s, anxieties on this score were expressed by the US Joint Chiefs of Staff and the Defence Planning Committee of NATO.[20] However, for reasons already mentioned, it is extremely difficult to visualise circumstances in which NATO shipping would be threatened at the Cape, as Johnson himself emphasised. As a result, it is probably as much for this reason as for fear of the diplomatic consequences of closer association with South Africa that no major steps have been taken by the United States to protect the Cape Route, unless development of the Indian Ocean island base of Diego Garcia is included. This is not because US planners have believed that in a crisis they could rely on an important contribution to the defence of the sea lanes from the South African Navy (SAN), the long-range patrolling capacities of which were never worth much, are now worth hardly anything at all, and have indeed been publicly abandoned. (The SAN's 'blue water' force is now represented by three *Daphne* class submarines and one *President* class frigate.[21] Its only cruiser, the *President Kruger*, sank accidentally in 1982.) Having said this, such is the prominence given to the importance *and vulnerability* of the Cape Route in conservative demonology in the United States that this interest serves both as an ingredient of genuine concern over southern Africa, and as a convenient rationalisation to conceal less presentable motives in parts of Congress and the executive branch of government.

The same sort of arguments apply, as Johnson also knew, to the *strategic and economic interests* of America and its allies in continuing access to the undoubted wealth of southern Africa in non-fuel minerals, which a 1980 Senate study described as of 'significant, but not critical, importance to the West'.[22] Thus the Rockefeller Foundation-funded Study Commission on US Policy Toward Southern Africa observed that 'if widespread conflict broke out in southern Africa or if a government hostile to the West took power in South Africa ...

stoppages in exports of these minerals, should they occur, are likely to be partial, intermittent, and short term (less than five years) in duration'. The Commission concluded that 'medium-term (five to ten year) and long term (more than ten-year) interruptions appear unlikely'.[23]

In addition to these important but relatively invulnerable interests, the United States has an important but more exposed interest in relation to southern Africa. This is the *diplomatic and domestic political interest* in avoiding a posture towards issues in the region which in view of the strong feelings of African and (more recently) American blacks on the question of apartheid, is believed likely to lead to a deterioration in American relations with countries of the Organisation of African Unity (OAU) and – probably more importantly – to revive acute racial unrest in the United States itself.[24] (In practice American interests in black Africa have not suffered markedly in those periods when Republican administrations have been accused of providing 'support for South Africa'.[25]) This interest in maintaining some distance between Washington and Pretoria does not necessarily conflict with America's other interests in South Africa, though it does so in the eyes of conservatives since they regard the existing National Party regime as indispensable to their protection.

Among its less important but equally exposed interests in southern Africa the United States has other *economic interests*: investments and trading interests which, while considerably greater than those of the Soviet Union, are nevertheless small in aggregate terms. South Africa itself, the major location of these interests, has accounted annually for only about 1 per cent of US foreign trade and between 1 and 2 per cent of US direct investment overseas since the Second World War,[26] and recently, for a mixture of political and commercial reasons, some major American corporations have been pulling out. Moreover, as is well known, foreign economic transactions are in aggregate terms relatively unimportant to the American economy.

The United States also has a *strategic interest* in access to intelligence on the region and its surrounding oceans (the Indian Ocean is probably of some importance as a prowling zone for American nuclear missile carrying submarines[27]), and this is assiduously supplied by South Africa's Silvermine ground station. However, in view of America's own enormous technical intelligence-gathering capacity, not to mention the increasing redundancy of far-flung and vulnerable ground stations, this can be no more than an interest in a back-up service.[28] Washington has a *strategic interest* as well in discouraging the unambiguous development of South Africa as a nuclear weapons state because of its general interest in the avoidance of nuclear proliferation.

All of the American interests in southern Africa detailed so far – important or less so, invulnerable or more exposed – are local interests. However, probably the most important American interest of all in southern Africa in the view of the Reagan Administration, as in 1977 Johnson predicted it would be, is the *diplomatic, cold war interest* in expelling Soviet influence from the region, in the same way that this was the cardinal US interest in the Middle East during the first Nixon Administration. Chalking up a major cold war victory against Moscow, most dramatically by securing the removal of the Cuban troops from Angola, seems to be the major impulse behind American policy and is seen most obviously in the American attitude over the protracted negotiations for the independence of Namibia. Here the United States, to the great relief of the South Africans, has 'linked' Namibian independence to the withdrawal of the Cubans from Angola. In 1985, also, Congress repealed the Clark Amendment, which in 1976 had been introduced in order to halt American support for UNITA, and subsequently the Reagan Administration has renewed its backing for a military solution to the Angolan civil war. Partly to increase pressure on Angola, the United States has also recently upgraded its military role in the Shaba province of Zaire.[29] In short, as Bowman has noted, the 'globalists' are in the ascendancy over the 'Africanists' in the determination of America's southern Africa policy, and have been so since the second half of the Carter Administration.[30]

COMMON GROUND

Of obvious importance in understanding the present and likely future roles of the superpowers in southern Africa is the degree to which their interests are compatible. For reasons which will by now be self-evident, this is a difficult question to answer, and it is not one which Johnson directly addressed – largely, it is fair to say, because most of the evidence has come to light only since publication of his book. On the face of it, the superpowers seem to possess very few common interests in the region. Further thought, however, suggests five candidates – and perhaps not entirely trivial ones at that. First there is the acknowledged common interest in preventing South Africa from becoming an open nuclear weapons state, which was dramatised by the Soviet revelation in August 1977 of the possibility of a South African nuclear test in the Kalahari desert, and by the subsequent pressure applied on Pretoria by Washington with a view to preventing its occurrence. Secondly, in view of recent Soviet keenness to collaborate with the West against international terrorism, there is the presumed common interest in dissuading the African National Congress (ANC) from resorting to the terrorist method of random attacks on civilians for political ends. Thirdly, there is the acknowledged common interest in Western-financed economic development in the frontline states. This flows on the one hand from the now obvious inability of the Soviet bloc to help in this regard and its hope that Western capital will help to stabilise pro-Soviet regimes (especially those in Angola and Mozambique) at no cost.[31] Conversely, there is the hope of the Americans that Western economic support will lead either to the return of such regimes to the Western fold or to their adoption of a more genuine policy of non-alignment. Fourthly, there is the possible common interest in independence for Namibia. And far from least, there is the certain common interest in the 'abolition of apartheid'.

Independence for Namibia under a government dominated by the South West Africa People's Organisation (SWAPO), *provided this is linked to the departure of Cuban combat troops from Angola as part of a package deal*, was first suggested by the incoming Reagan administration in 1981.[32] Whether or not the Soviet Union were to play a direct hand in events, such an outcome *should* certainly suit the Soviet interest. And this is so even though it is true that this 'linkage' proposal has been condemned by Moscow and widely opposed in Africa as unacceptable interference in Angola's domestic affairs, and inconsistent with Security Council Resolution 435 of 1978 on the procedures for achieving Namibia's independence (on which, incidentally, the Soviet Union abstained). On the one hand, Moscow could claim to have hastened Namibian independence by its long standing support for SWAPO and its general policy in southern Africa, and might well gain a new partner in the region. On the other, the withdrawal of the Cubans would enable it to reduce its substantial subsidy of the Cuban economy and alleviate OAU suspicions of Soviet policy on the African continent. The Cuban troops themselves could be presented as no longer necessary since a major incentive for incursions by the South African Defence Force (SADF) into Angola (the destruction of SWAPO bases) would have been removed and UNITA's lines of supply to South Africa (though not, it is true, to Zaire) would have been cut.[33] In any case, it could be made clear that the Cubans would return – or that an Inter-

MAGDALEN COLLEGE LIBRARY

African Force (of the kind seen after Shaba II) might intervene – if the MPLA regime were to come under renewed threat. It is interesting that Angola itself has accepted the principle of linkage.[34]

The Namibia/Angola linkage is rightly seen as suiting the American interest since through its consummation Washington could claim to have achieved a long-sought and widely approved diplomatic goal (Namibian independence), placed itself in a good position to compete with the Russians for influence in Windhoek, and removed 'the Cuban menace' from southern Africa into the bargain.

It might be supposed that the claim that the superpowers share a perceived interest in the 'abolition of apartheid' is weakened by the vague practical implications of this slogan. However, a paper produced in Moscow in 1986 by Gleb Starushenko of the Soviet Union's Africa Institute, strongly suggests that there may indeed be a great measure of common ground here. The paper by Starushenko, a corresponding member of the USSR Academy of Sciences, is suffused by a fear that regional conflicts might lead to nuclear war, while as for South Africa, it supports negotiations between the ANC and the 'white bourgeoisie' ('which is not tied to the chariot of apartheid'); cautions against 'broad nationalization of capitalist property'; argues that pragmatism is strongly entrenched even among 'middle and lower strata' whites; favours provision by the ANC of 'comprehensive guarantees for the white population' on the models of 'Kenia' (*sic*) and Zimbabwe; suggests a two-chamber parliament ('one formed on the basis of proportional representation and the other, possessing the right of veto, on the basis of equal representation of four communities'); and concludes by indicating a preference for a post-apartheid South Africa having 'a unitary system with autonomous components'.[35] This programme is not exactly a million miles away from the American position!

It might still be said, however, that the pursuit of an agreed superpower policy on the future of South Africa is complicated by the lack of any publicly extant geopolitical *quid pro quo*, comparable to the proposed departure of the Cubans from Angola in the Namibia negotiations, which the Russians could use their influence to hand to the Americans the smooth acceptance of the collapse of National Party power by Washington conservatives. However, the fact that such *quid pro quos* have not yet been publicly canvassed does not mean to say that they could not be contrived. For example, in acknowledgement of the greater American interest in the security of the Cape Route, the Soviet Union could support the idea of a treaty of neutrality for post-apartheid South Africa comparable to the Austrian State Treaty (there is a strong Afrikaner neutralist tradition, as well as a likely disposition to support neutralism on the part of the black population) or treaty-guaranteed rights over facilities at Simonstown and other South African ports for NATO vessels.

PATRON–CLIENT RELATIONS IN THE REGION

Whether or not the superpowers can cooperate to produce solutions in Namibia and South Africa or simply to avoid collision depends to some extent, of course, on the degree to which they can control their clients in the region. And pride of place in this context naturally goes to the relationship between America and South Africa, the only patron–client relationship to which Johnson paid any attention.

The United States has tended to regard South Africa as a 'client' ever since the Nixon Doctrine advanced the idea that the United States should appoint regional 'deputy sheriffs' rather than employ direct force itself outside recognised American spheres of influence. However, it has from time to time been halfhearted, to say the least, in accepting South Africa as a client, and in small degree for this reason has only had very limited success in controlling the Republic's policies, foreign as well as domestic. Such internal changes as have occurred within South Africa are more likely to have been a response to domestic unrest than to American pressure, while the United States has failed to end South African prevarication over Namibia, has failed to halt the Republic's nuclear weapons programme, and has not curbed the ferocity of its regional 'destabilisation' policies, including attacks on the capital of Western-inclined Botswana and American-owned oil installations in northern Angola.

America's inability to manipulate the South African government to any great effect has a variety of sources. Firstly, there is the adequacy of the Republic's military strength relative to the threats which it believes it faces. Unlike Israel, South Africa does not need a constant supply of advanced heavy weapons from the United States or anyone else in order to protect its security. However, it is important to note that this may change before long because, as far as can be told, the South Africans cannot build jet fighters of their own without smuggling in components from abroad,[36] and there is evidence that they are becoming reluctant to commit their ageing squadrons in combat against Angola's modern Soviet-supplied fighters and air defence systems.[37]

Secondly, Pretoria knows that it has powerful friends as well as powerful enemies in Washington, and as a result has every incentive to resist pressure in the hope that the influence of these friends will grow, either as a result of a change of administrations or a change in the international climate. And thirdly, there are other states to which South Africa can turn for commercial, financial and military/technical assistance, such as Israel and Taiwan (though it is true that on 19 March 1987, under pressure from the US Congress, the Israeli government announced that it would enter no *new* military contracts with South Africa).[38]

The Republic also has a well-developed siege economy, which makes it highly resistant to economic coercion, though in this connection two particular weaknesses should be mentioned. Firstly, international bankers – who are vulnerable to a degree of political pressure – have shown over the last few years that they can hurt South Africa badly by withdrawing credit. And secondly, as Johnson went to some pains to show in 1977, Washington possesses leverage over South Africa via the price of gold, still the sheet-anchor of the Republic's economy. This price is artificially supported by the enormous quantity of bullion held out of the market in non-communist central bank reserves, 28 per cent of which is controlled by the US Treasury (about the same as in 1977). Considering the issue of sanctions against South Africa in July 1986 in the light of these facts and the likely ineffectiveness of other sanctions, *The Economist* urged the West to 'go for gold',[39] and at the beginning of the following month the Senate Foreign Relations Committee recommended that Treasury sales of gold should at least be used as part of a sanctions package against South Africa. The credibility of any threat to raid the gold market is widely held to be enhanced by the fact that the other chief sufferer would be the Soviet Union, which is the world's second largest gold producer. In addition, sales from gold stocks would be a useful way for the Federal Reserve to raise revenue, since gold in Fort Knox has a book value of only $42.22 per ounce,[40] which is way under the current market price.

Nevertheless, the gold weapon may not always be easy to use and has more damaging than beneficial side-effects for the United States. It is notable that in 1979, despite unprecedentedly high gold sales by the US Treasury and continuing IMF auctions prompted by the American desire to see gold demonetised, such was the inability of supply to meet the level of speculative and investment demand that the price more than doubled and on 21 January 1980 reached an all-time high of $850.[41] Conditions in the market for gold, still playing its traditional role as a hedge against political and economic uncertainty, remain volatile. As for the damaging side-effects, these are numerous. Firstly, since gold has been predictably resistant to complete demonetisation (it is not only the American central bank which still holds large quantities in its reserves), a swingeing cut in its market value might have unpredictable and damaging effects on an already somewhat precariously balanced international financial system. Secondly, gold producers in the United States itself (accounting for 8 per cent of total non-communist output in 1986, with activities spread throughout Montana, Utah, Nevada, California, Wyoming, Colorado, Arizona, New Mexico, South Dakota, Alaska, Idaho, Missouri, South Carolina, Tennessee, Washington, and Oregon) would also suffer, the more so since their costs are much higher than those in South Africa, and, unlike gold-mining companies in the Republic, they cannot adjust to a dropping price by mining higher grade ore. A severe drop in the price of gold could also make the mining of other minerals in the United States, already a depressed industry, uneconomic, and hit American companies involved in gold-mining in other countries, for example in Australia. Thirdly, important producers amongst America's friends would also be hit, especially Canada, Australia, Brazil, Chile, Mexico and the Philippines. Fourthly, forcing down the price of gold would fly in the face of the administration's attempt to encourage investment in American-minted gold coins, following passage of the American Gold Bullion Coin Act in December 1985. Fifthly, driving down the price of gold tends to strengthen the dollar, which made sense in the mid 1970s but, against the background of America's massive trade deficits in the 1980s, has been contrary to US economic policy. And finally, if the Soviet Union would suffer from a savage drop in the price of gold, so would American farmers, for one of Moscow's chief motives for selling gold is to purchase grain. In the light of these considerations, it is perhaps not surprising that the section in the Congressional Anti-Apartheid Bill[42] containing the threat to use the gold weapon was defeated on the floor of the Senate on 14 August 1986. The campaign to have this section struck from the Bill had been led by Senators from gold-mining states, and Senator Lugar, Chairman of the Foreign Relations Committee, conceded the amendment before the debate. As a result, there was no serious opposition to it.[43]

America's only other obvious client in southern Africa is UNITA, to which 'covert' aid was promised following Congressional repeal in 1985 of the 1976 Clark Amendment. This aid is now apparently being delivered, via Zaire and even South Africa itself.[44] As a result, American influence over UNITA may well have increased relative to that of South Africa, the movement's main backer.[45] At any rate, Washington has recently been successful, in the face of South African opposition, in persuading UNITA to offer the Angolan government talks on the reopening of the Benguela railway.[46]

It should also be noted here that there is a black group within South Africa itself which is a *potential* American client of some importance, Chief Gatsha Buthelezi's powerful Zulu-based Inkatha movement. This group is committed to a negotiated solution to the South African crisis and supports a free market economy; as a result, it is bitterly at odds with the ANC and the leftist umbrella group, the United Democratic Front (UDF). At the same time, Buthelezi has avoided identification with the South African government by refusing to accept 'independence' for KwaZulu and has been a prime mover in discussions concerning multiracial government for Natal. Though the tribal basis of his movement is a handicap, all of this makes Buthelezi a very attractive figure in the West and it is known that his contacts in the United States are good. If South Africa collapses into civil war it is highly likely that Washington will back Buthelezi, especially if he forges an alliance with moderate whites. Renamo, the movement of Mozambique 'contras', is not an American client, being controlled (to the extent that it is controlled by anybody) by the South African military and right-wing Portuguese who fled Mozambique following independence in 1975; its headquarters are in Lisbon.

The Soviet Union's principal clients in southern Africa are the MPLA government of Angola, the FRELIMO government of Mozambique, and the two militarily weak but nevertheless prestigious 'national liberation movements', SWAPO and the ANC.[47] It is important to stress, however, that Soviet control of these 'clients' is far from complete. For example, in February 1984, to the great embarrassment of the Soviet Union, the Angolan government signed a non-aggression pact with South Africa, while in the following month the Mozambique government followed suit in the Nkomati Accord. The fact that these pacts have since crumbled – not through Soviet machinations – is beside the point.

The reasons for the weakness of Soviet control over its clients in the region are not far to seek. First of all, suspicion of Soviet motives on the part of almost all African politicians is at least as deep as suspicion of Western motives, and most of them share a strong attachment to non-alignment, the Angolan and Mozambique governments are stiffened in this regard by neighbouring leaders with high prestige in the non-aligned movement, Kenneth Kaunda of Zambia and Robert Mugabe of Zimbabwe. Secondly, the Soviet bloc has been manifestly incapable of providing the *economic assistance* so badly needed by Angola and Mozambique and both have been turning for this increasingly to the West. (Of course, because neither SWAPO nor the ANC have as yet states to administer and are preoccupied with 'military struggle', the inability of Moscow to provide large-scale economic aid is not a weakness in its present relationship with them.) Thirdly, the Soviet bloc has no monopoly on the supply of military equipment or advice and recently Mozambique has accepted military advisers from Britain and Portugal, while Angola has begun purchasing weapons from Western Europe.[48] Fourthly, it does not have a monopoly on the supply of troops for internal security either; Mozambique, for example, whose need in this respect is particularly urgent in view of the extensive activities of the South African backed Renamo 'bandits' (the Mozambique National Resistance), has since July 1985 come to rely increasingly on the large and well-trained Zimbabwe army (plus a small complement of Tanzanian troops), especially for defence of the vital Beira Corridor; following an agreement of December 1986,[49] defence of the Nacala route by the Chissano government is to be assisted by troops from Malawi. Fifthly, the Soviet Union cannot marshal military and economic power in the region comparable to that of South Africa. And finally, it has no influence over the South African government nor even (since 1956) formal diplomatic relations with it; consequently, it cannot plausibly offer to put pressure on Pretoria in the interests of any of its clients.

As well as clients in southern Africa, however loosely controlled they might be, the Soviet Union has a 'proxy' in the shape of Cuba, with its substantial armed forces stationed in Angola. The degree of control exercised by Moscow over Cuba's Angolan adventure is a vexed question, conservative opinion in Washington naturally holding that Castro plays a compliant role, but other observers being more inclined to allow some independence of action to the Cuban leader and to suggest, indeed, that it was Cuba which prodded a profoundly cautious Soviet leadership into the expedition in the first place.[50] In any case, whatever the circumstances of the initial decision to enter Angola, it seems likely that it reflected a harmony of outlook between Moscow and Cuba; Castro is clearly not an unwilling servant. However, in view of the well-known dependence of Cuba on the Soviet Union for economic, diplomatic and above all military support, it is inconceivable that Castro would attempt to play a lone hand in southern Africa. It is inconceivable, in particular, that he would decide to keep his troops in Angola if Moscow told him to get them out.

THE UNLIKELIHOOD OF SUPERPOWER MILITARY CONFRONTATION

Apart from the risk of escalation, there are many reasons why direct superpower military confrontation in southern Africa in the foreseeable future is extremely unlikely, even if South Africa itself were to collapse into civil war. This was implicit in Johnson's analysis. To take first the Soviet Union, its interests in the region are not of sufficient importance to warrant the undertaking of military risks, and these would be seen as high since it appears to believe (incorrectly) that NATO stands behind the present South African government.[51] In this connection it is interesting to note that the defence provisions of its Treaties of Friendship and Cooperation with Angola and Mozambique are very vaguely worded,[52] and that East Germany – whose treaty with Mozambique is equally guarded[53] – has been delegated responsibility for the southern African interests of the Warsaw Pact's Political Committee precisely in order to avoid provoking a NATO intervention.[54] Moreover, the frontline states themselves have displayed great caution in responding to the kind of Soviet clumsiness which *might* have produced intervention by the Warsaw Pact.[55]

As for the United States, its interests in the frontline states, including the geopolitical interest in the withdrawal of the Cubans from Angola, are similarly not of sufficient importance to justify military intervention, while in South Africa itself America's main interests – minerals and the Cape Route – are rightly regarded as relatively invulnerable by at least some influential bodies of opinion in Washington. Besides, the National Party government is so unpopular in America and among America's allies that military intervention on its behalf would almost certainly provoke major domestic racial turmoil. Indeed, even in the extremely unlikely event that the Soviet Union should assume the role in which the United States cast itself over Korea ('champion of international legality and of aroused world opinion') and proposed to intervene militarily against Pretoria following a UN General Assembly Resolution calling upon members to do just that, it is likely, as Conor Cruise O'Brien has recently suggested, that America's most attractive option would be to side with Moscow rather than against it.[56] Having said this, it is clear that southern Africa is an irritant in superpower relations which might get worse and it is for this reason that the Soviet Union and the United States appear to observe certain tacit rules of crisis-avoidance in the region.

Since the failed South African intervention in Angola in 1975–6 (itself partly a result of the refusal of US support), the United States has sought to restrain the Republic's military sorties into its neighbouring black states and, following the Clark Amendment (only recently repealed), denied 'covert' support to UNITA. Of course, for reasons already advanced, Washington has not been spectacularly successful in restraining the South African military machine but it has manifestly tried and, with the isolated exception of South African-surrounded Lesotho in January 1986, Pretoria has not risked provoking the Americans to the point of bringing down any of the governments of the neighbouring black states, or of creating new buffer states in, say, southern Angola or southern Mozambique, though this has long been easily within its grasp. As a result, the Soviet bloc and Cuban governments have not themselves been provoked into strengthening their military support for their regional clients to a point at which an increase in superpower tension would be inevitable.

For its part, the Soviet bloc has carefully kept its military advisers out of combat roles and ensured that the Cuban troops in Angola are kept behind a defensive line well above the Namibian frontier.[57] Indeed, in 1983 'Castro instructed his troops in Angola not to engage South African forces in the south so as to avoid exacerbating East–West tensions at a particularly critical time in relations between the United States and the Soviet Union'.[58] In the same spirit, in 1977 and 1978, when successive invasions of the Shaba province of Zaire were launched by Katangan exiles based in Angola and reportedly trained and equipped by the Cubans, Castro was at some pains to disown these actions and after the second of them apparently collaborated with the Neto government of Angola to disarm the rebels.[59]

Of course, it cannot be assumed that because both superpowers, together with the Cubans and even in some measure the South Africans, have behaved with reasonable restraint since the Soviet/Cuban/MPLA victory in Angola in 1976 that this is a result of a norm implicitly upholding the regional status quo. For one thing, the United States has probably been more anxious to restrain South African 'destabilisation' tactics in order to preserve its own credentials as a regional mediator with the frontline states, and to show that its policy of 'constructive engagement' with South Africa was working, rather than to avoid the possibility of an increase in tension with the Soviet

Union. For another, not all of P. W. Botha's advisers appear to be convinced that, quite apart from the American reaction, it would be in South Africa's interests to wage an all-out assault on Angola, Zimbabwe and Mozambique, where a combination of economic pressure, transport diplomacy and coercive bargaining has kept Marxist governments in a reasonably passive frame of mind towards the South African 'struggle'.

Nevertheless, in the light of a norm of restraint in more dangerous areas of Third World superpower confrontation (for example in the Middle East), it would be surprising if such a rule was not also operating tacitly in southern Africa. That the United States, at any rate, has been thinking expressly in these terms for some years is also evidenced by Kissinger's (albeit belated and unsuccessful) suggestion to Moscow in late 1975 that the superpowers should not only agree to a withdrawal of Cuban and South African forces from the Angolan civil war but also cease military supplies to their respective clients engaged in the fighting.[60] Subsequently the Carter administration tried – equally unsuccessfully – to persuade the Russians to leave Africa to the Africans, and its UN Ambassador, Andrew Young, somewhat contradictorily, described the Cubans as a 'stabilising' presence in African politics.[61] However, with the 'correlation of forces' now less drastically unbalanced along the Angola–Namibia frontier and turning against it in the rest of southern Africa, the Soviet Union is now probably more amenable to the observance of a regional norm of restraint.

SCRIPTS FOR THE FUTURE

Since the middle of the 1970s it has been American policy in southern Africa to encourage the 'solution' of the region's major problems – Rhodesia, Namibia and apartheid – and thereby remove the opportunities for Soviet/Cuban intervention. During the Carter presidency, as already mentioned, it was hoped that while solutions were being sought, superpower intervention could be minimised by persuading the Russians to agree to a policy of facilitating 'African solutions to African problems'.

However, the idea of a superpower 'no-go zone' as far as southern Africa was concerned overlooked the following: the formal responsibility of America's major NATO ally, Britain, for settling the Rhodesian problem; the disinclination of Moscow (which rightly saw Carter's suggestion as in large measure an attempt to make a virtue out of a necessity) to pass up opportunities for the expansion of its influence; and the enormous disparity of power between South Africa and the frontline states, which meant that Pretoria could not be shifted from its entrenched positions in the absence of external pressure (or internal collapse). As a result, the Carter Administration never abstained from diplomacy in southern Africa itself (though it allowed Britain to take the lead in the Rhodesian negotiations), and under Chester Crocker's direction during the Reagan period the United States has played a very active mediating role in the region. It mediated between South Africa on the one hand and Angola and Mozambique on the other in the non-aggression pacts signed in 1984, and it has been an active member of the Western Five's 'Contact Group' on Namibia. The Soviet Union has been resolutely excluded from this diplomacy by the United States, with the collusion of the frontline states (including Angola and Mozambique),[62] and in any case could not have aspired to a mediating role itself as a result of its absence of diplomatic relations with Pretoria.

Nevertheless, impaled on the contradiction between the requirements of its geopolitical desire to support the present South African regime and its domestically-prompted concern to push it in the direction of racial reform, and hampered by a traditional lack of State Department expertise on 'white Africa',[63] American policy has so far failed. The Namibian independence negotiations are stalled and the Contact Group was disbanded in 1982. Constructive engagement has up to now failed to move the Botha government far enough in the dismantling of apartheid, and in September 1985 constructive engagement was abandoned in favour of minor sanctions which will please no one and, on their own, will not work because they are not remotely commensurate with the stakes at issue. South Africa's low-intensity wars on its frontiers continue and have become possibly more dangerous with the recent military strengthening of Angola by the Soviet Union. Soviet influence itself, while diminishing perceptibly in Mozambique, remains strong in Angola. Moreover, the United States, which made the mistake from the beginning of refusing to recognise the MPLA government in Luanda (this was partly a function of American–Cuban relations[64]), may have now further compromised its ability to play the role of mediator in Angola – and indeed in the wider southern African conflict – by resuming 'covert' aid to UNITA. It thus behoves us to consider whether alternative superpower strategies are necessary or whether it might not be better for the Americans to fine-tune their existing strategy and try again.

The idea of a superpower '*no-go zone*' in southern Africa remains as much a non-starter today as it was when it was floated by President Carter. Unlike Antarctica, the region is too important to ignore and, unlike Iran, not so dangerous that opportunities have to be passed up in order to avoid the risk of swift escalation into direct superpower conflict. In any case, neither is such a proposal advisable since, as already mentioned, the disparity of power between South Africa and the frontline states means that outside pressure on Pretoria is unavoidable if the region's problems are to be either solved or at least brought under control.

The possibility of minimising violence in the region by *arms limitation techniques* is also very low. This is principally because the mandatory UN arms embargo placed on South Africa in 1977 has encouraged the Republic to build up an impressive arms industry (though it is true that it is not as self-sufficient in armaments, especially in aircraft components, as it likes to make out), and also made it impossible for the Americans to offer the Russians any direct *quid pro quo* (other than another cessation of supplies to UNITA) in return for a halt to Soviet arms supplies to its own regional clients.

United Nations intervention in the region sanctioned by the superpowers via the Security Council (either with observer groups or peacekeeping forces in Hammarskjöld's virtually pacifist conception) is obviously inappropriate within South Africa itself and is hardly less so in Namibia. Here, as the Contact Group's protracted and finally abortive negotiations revealed, intervention by the world organisation founders on the rock of the Republic's profound hostility to the UN,[65] its local military supremacy, its determination to exclude effective SWAPO participation from any constituent-assembly elections,[66] and the inability of the United States – under present circumstances – to bring sufficient pressure to bear on it. In Angola and Mozambique none of the disputants would be inclined to take the idea of UN peacekeeping seriously since all believe that they still have a good chance of prevailing with outside help from other sources.

The idea of a *superpower condominium* in southern Africa, in the form of the *military* imposition of solutions in the region by the superpowers acting in concert (preferably under UN auspices), is as appealing as it is unlikely – though it would be unwise to rule it completely impossible. Indeed, such a proposal was canvassed by Conor Cruise O'Brien in early 1986, though he posited its possibility on a degree of South African government brutality towards its black population comparable to that employed by the French Army against the Algerian nationalists in the 1950s.[67] Unlike economic sanctions, a superpower condominium would certainly have the great advantage of going straight to the heart of the matter – the need to destroy the military confidence of Afrikaner nationalism without wrecking the South African economy and what is left of the economies of the frontline states. Unfortunately, O'Brien's precedents – Suez and Katanga – are hardly good ones since superpower intervention in these cases never even approached the military threshold. Moreover, at Suez the stakes were by no means as high for Britain, France and Israel as they are for Afrikaner nationalism today; and in Katanga, Tshombe's army was infinitely weaker than the SADF. Besides, neither of these instances approached anything like the prominence in American domestic politics of the South African problem. An American proposal to intervene by force against a white government involved in a brutal race war, especially if in collaboration with the Russians, would be likely to provoke as violent a white backlash in the United States as a pro-white intervention would a black one.

If ever a joint superpower intervention in southern Africa were to get off the ground, therefore, at a minimum the following conditions would have to be met. Firstly, there would not only have to be a superpower consensus on the need for dramatic action of this kind but a much lower temperature than presently exists in the *overall* relationship between the superpowers; it is inconceivable that the Russians and the Americans could mount a joint military operation against the South Africans while still engaged in 'cold war' activities on other fronts, not least in the competition in nuclear arms. Secondly, Soviet influence throughout southern Africa would need to be considerably greater than it is now, otherwise joint military intervention would entail the United States and its allies making a major and thus politically unacceptable sacrifice to the Soviet Union (unless requited, via 'linkage', in some other area, which would admittedly be possible if the last-mentioned condition existed). Thirdly, there would need to be in office in Washington a *Republican* president who combined enormous popularity with excellent anti-communist credentials and was not looking for a further term in office. And finally, both superpowers would need to be fairly certain that the South Africans would not in some fashion resort to the use of nuclear weapons. In other words, joint superpower military intervention in southern Africa is, to put it mildly, highly unlikely.

For much the same reasons, plus South African resistance, an *international conference* jointly presided over by the superpowers, in the style of that presently being canvassed for the Middle East, is unlikely to get off the ground, though Starushenko has implicitly suggested this by indicating that 'the peaceful settlement of the conflict might be expedited by resorting to the institution of international guarantees, the sides selecting the guarantors by agreement from among prestigious international organizations or individual states'.[68]

CONCLUSION

In the light of all this it seems desirable that there should, as well as likely that there will be a continuation of the present regimen: third-party mediation led by the United States with the assistance of the other Western states with interests in the region (especially Britain, West Germany and France), together with the observance of limited procedural rules designed to minimise superpower antagonisms. So far this has tended to underpin the stability of the 'White Establishment', as Johnson predicted. However, in the last few years the United States has adopted selected sanctions against the Republic, which, in the event of mounting black unrest, Johnson also foresaw. If Washington should follow the logic of its mediator's role, as there is every indication that it will, it will adopt further measures which may weaken the 'White Establishment' relative both to its internal opponents and especially to the frontline states. By fostering a balance of power in the region, this will make negotiated solutions, albeit accompanied by occasional border clashes and periodic outbursts of township violence, more likely. What form should these further measures take?

The United States should improve its mediator's credentials by severely restricting its support for UNITA and opening relations with Luanda (these moves would also help the MPLA to get rid of the Cubans). In addition, Washington, together with its allies, should pour more economic aid into the region – especially via the Southern African Development Coordination Conference (SADCC) – in order to increase its leverage over the frontline states (and thus indirectly over SWAPO and the ANC) *and* make it more difficult for South Africa to destabilise their regimes. The 'linkage' between Namibian independence and the withdrawal of Cuban troops (not civilian personnel) from Angola should be maintained in order to carry along South Africa and conservative opinion in Washington, and a deadline should be set for Pretoria's agreement to this package deal, which a failure to meet would result in the automatic introduction of rapidly escalating economic sanctions tied specifically to the Namibian question. (The threat of severe economic sanctions – secretly delivered – is much more likely to shift the South Africans over Namibia[69] than over the issue of power within the Republic itself, which is the answer to the argument that after sanctions have brought down the National Party regime the Namibia problem will solve itself.) With Namibia independent, probably under a 'pragmatic' SWAPO government, and the Cubans departed from Angola, conservative opinion in the West will have less incentive to support the present government in Pretoria.

Notes

* I am grateful for the comments on this chapter of Jack Spence, John Day, Gareth Winrow and the members of the South Africa Workshop of the European Consortium for Political Research, Amsterdam, April 1987. A different version appears in R. Allison and P. Williams (eds), *Superpower Competition and Crisis Avoidance in the Third World*, Cambridge, Cambridge University Press, forthcoming.

1. R. W. Johnson, *How Long Will South Africa Survive?* London, Macmillan, 1977, p. 173.
2. Ibid., p. 15.
3. Ibid., p. 214.
4. Ibid., p. 326.
5. Ibid., p. 309.
6. The significant role played by the German Democratic Republic in southern Africa is emphasised by Christopher Coker in his *Nato, the Warsaw Pact and Africa*, London, Macmillan, 1985.
7. Peter Clement, 'Moscow and Southern Africa', *Problems of Communism*, 34, March–April 1985, p. 45.
8. Private South African shipping source; information dated 23 December 1986.
9. Coker, *Nato, the Warsaw Pact and Africa*, p. 183.
10. G. R. Berridge, *The Politics of the South Africa Run: European Shipping and Pretoria*, Oxford, The Clarendon Press, 1987, pp. 194–7.
11. Larry Bowman, 'The Strategic Importance of South Africa to the United States: An Appraisal and Policy Analysis', in D. Aluko and T. M. Shaw (eds), *Southern Africa in the 1980s*, London, Allen & Unwin, 1985, pp. 139–40; and K. Booth, *Navies and Foreign Policy*, London, Croom Helm, 1977, p. 173.
12. J. E. Spence and G. R. Berridge, 'South Africa: The Road to Simonstown', in John W. Young (ed.), *The Foreign Policy of Churchill's Peacetime Administration*, Leicester, Leicester University Press, forthcoming.
13. For example, Clement, 'Moscow and Southern Africa', p. 30; R. Legvold, 'The Soviet Threat to Southern Africa', in R. I. Rotberg and others, *South Africa and Its Neighbours: Regional Security and Self-Interest*, Lexington, Mass., Lexington Books, 1985, pp. 27–30; David E. Albright, 'Moscow's

African Policy of the 1970s', in David E. Albright (ed.), *Africa and International Communism*, London, Macmillan, 1980, p. 49; and Kurt M. Campbell, *Soviet Policy Towards South Africa*, London, Macmillan, 1986, p. 165.

14. Clement, 'Moscow and Southern Africa', p. 30.
15. According to John A. Marcum, Angola 'uses upward from 50 percent of its oil revenues of over $2 billion annually to purchase Soviet arms and to maintain Cuban troops and technicians . . .', 'United States Options in Angola', *CSIS Africa Notes*, 52, 20 December 1985, p. 4.
16. Polish Ocean Lines (Gdansk) and Deutsche Seereederei (Rostock) operate the Baltafrica service as members of this Conference. While it is true that the Soviet Baltestafrica service remains in opposition to the East African Conference, negotiations for its entry – which first took place in the second half of the 1970s – are once more in train, though not apparently proving very fruitful. Private London shipping source: information dated 5 March 1987.
17. Private South African shipping source; information dated 23 December 1986.
18. 'South Africa: Strategy for Change', *Foreign Affairs*, 59, Winter 1980–81, p. 346.
19. *Congressional Quarterly Weekly Report*, 44, 30, 26 July 1986, p. 1698.
20. Coker, *Nato, the Warsaw Pact and Africa*, pp. 82–7 and p. 98.
21. *The Military Balance 1985–1986*, London, The International Institute for Strategic Studies, 1985, p. 106.
22. Quoted in Campbell, *Soviet Policy Towards South Africa*, p. 123.
23. *South Africa: Time Running Out*, Report of the Study Commission on US Policy Toward Southern Africa, Berkeley, University of California Press, 1981, p. 392.
24. W. J. Foltz, 'United States Policy toward South Africa: Is One Possible?' in G. J. Bender, J. S. Coleman and R. S. Sklar (eds), *African Crisis Areas and U.S. Foreign Policy*, Berkeley, University of California Press, 1985, pp. 38–42.
25. Ibid., p. 37.
26. Ibid., p. 32.
27. William J. Foltz, 'United States Policy Toward Southern Africa: Economic and Strategic Constraints', *Political Science Quarterly*, 92, 1, Spring 1977, pp. 56–8; and Dieter Braun, *The Indian Ocean: Region of Conflict or 'Peace Zone'*, translated from the German by C. Geldart and K. Llanwarne, London, Hurst, 1983, p. 44; cf. Campbell, *Soviet Policy Towards South Africa*, p. 150.
28. Foltz, 'United States Policy toward South Africa: Is One Possible?', p. 35; and J. T. Richelson and D. Ball, *The Ties That Bind*, London, Allen & Unwin, 1986.
29. *Independent*, 24 March 1987.
30. 'The Strategic Importance of South Africa to the United States', pp. 142–5.
31. Arthur J. Klinghoffer, 'The Soviet Union and Superpower Rivalry in Africa', in B. E. Ardinghaus (ed.), *African Security Issues*, Boulder, Colorado, Westview, 1984, p. 30. Insofar as Soviet bloc concurrence in the

presence of Western multinationals in southern Africa, as opposed to acceptance of Western aid for the region is concerned, this is more readily forthcoming from certain East European countries than from Moscow itself; see Coker, *Nato, the Warsaw Pact and Africa*, pp. 187 and 202.

32. *The Economist*, 30 March 1985, p. 19.
33. This point is oddly overlooked by R. I. Rotberg in his otherwise penetrating analysis of the question: 'Namibia and the Crisis of Constructive Engagement', in G. J. Bender, J. S. Coleman and R. L. Sklar (eds), *African Crisis Areas and US Foreign Policy*.
34. Marcum, 'United States Options in Angola', p. 4.
35. 'Problems of Struggle against Racism, Apartheid and Colonialism in the [*sic*] South Africa', Report presented to the Second Soviet–African conference 'For peace, cooperation and social progress', Moscow, 24–26 June 1986, Moscow, 1986. I am grateful to Peter Shearman for a copy of this document
36. Anthony Sampson, *Black & Gold: Tycoons, Revolutionaries and Apartheid*, London, Hodder & Stoughton, 1987, pp. 101–2.
37. Robert S. Jaster, 'South Africa and its Neighbours: the Dynamics of Regional Conflict', *Adelphi Paper* 209, Summer 1986, p. 66; and Lt-Gen. D. J. Earp (Chief of the SA Air Force), 'The Role of Air Power in Southern Africa', in M. Hough and M. van der Merwe (eds), *Contemporary Air Strategy*, Ad hoc Publication No. 23, Institute for Strategic Studies, University of Pretoria, April 1986, pp. 27–52.
38. *The Economist*, 4 April 1987.
39. Ibid., 19 July, 1986.
40. *Congressional Record*, 132, 102, Proceedings and Debates of the 99th Congress, Second Session, S9926.
41. *Annual Bullion Review 1979*, London, Samuel Montagu & Co. Ltd, March 1980, and *Annual Bullion Review 1980*, March 1981.
42. This was finally passed, over President Reagan's veto, as the 'Comprehensive Anti-Apartheid Act' on 2 October 1986.
43. *Congressional Record*, 132, 113, Proceedings and Debates of the 99th Congress, Second Session, S11639–48.
44. *The Times*, 21 November 1986 and 10 January 1987; *Independent*, 28 March 1987.
45. Much of UNITA's cash, incidentally, has come from Saudi Arabia and other Gulf sources; Marcum, 'United States Options in Angola', p. 2.
46. *Independent*, 29 April 1987.
47. On the history of Soviet backing of the ANC (and the South African Communist Party), see Campbell, *Soviet Policy Towards South Africa*, pp. 41–6.
48. Jaster, 'South Africa and its Neighbours', p. 72.
49. President Chissano, speaking at Chatham House, 7 May 1987.
50. W. J. Foltz, 'Africa in Great-Power Strategy', in W. J. Foltz and H. S. Brewer (eds), *Arms and the Africans*, New Haven, Yale University Press, 1985, pp. 15–16.
51. J. E. Spence, 'Soviet Relations with Africa', *Soviet Jewish Affairs*, 15, 1, 1985, p. 126.
52. The relevant clauses in the Angolan Treaty read as follows:

'VII. In the event of any situation arising that may create a danger to peace or disturb peace, the High Contracting Parties shall immediately establish contact with each other in order to co-ordinate their positions in the interests of removing the danger or restoring peace . . . .
X. In the interests of strengthening the defence capability of the High Contracting Parties, they shall continue to promote co-operation in the military field on the basis of corresponding agreements concluded between them', *Africa Contemporary Record 1976–7*, p. C153.

Similar clauses (IV and IX), with only insignificant differences in wording, appear in the Treaty with Mozambique; see *Africa Contemporary Record 1977–8*, pp. C17–18.

53. Its treaty with Angola has no defence provisions at all; see *Against Racism, Apartheid and Colonialism: Documents published by the GDR 1977–1982*, Dresden, Verlag Zeit im Bild, 1983, pp. 244–6 and 265–6 (Treaty with Mozambique). However, supplementary military agreements appear to have been negotiated by the GDR with both Angola and Mozambique, though their terms remain secret.
54. Coker, *Nato, the Warsaw Pact and Africa*, pp. 200–1.
55. Ibid., pp. 148–9.
56. Conor Cruise O'Brien, 'What Can Become Of South Africa?', *Atlantic Monthly*, March 1986.
57. Jaster, 'South Africa and its Neighbours', p. 65.
58. Coker, *Nato, the Warsaw Pact and Africa*, p. 246.
59. G. Volsky, 'Cuba', in T. H. Henriksen (ed.), *Communist Powers and Sub-Saharan Africa*, Stanford, California, Hoover Institution Press, Stanford University, 1981, p. 68.
60. A. L. George, 'Missed Opportunities for Crisis Prevention: The War of Attrition and Angola', in A. L. George (ed.), *Managing US–Soviet Rivalry: Problems of Crisis Prevention*, Boulder, Colorado, Westview, 1983, pp. 211–19.
61. Volsky, 'Cuba', p. 78.
62. Jaster, 'South Africa and its Neighbours', p. 73.
63. R. E. Bissell, *South Africa and the United States: The Erosion of an Influence Relationship*, New York, Praeger, 1982, p. 31.
64. Klinghoffer, 'The Soviet Union and Superpower Rivalry in Africa', p. 36.
65. On South African attitudes to the UN, see John Barratt, 'South African Diplomacy at the UN', in G. R. Berridge and A. Jennings (eds), *Diplomacy at the UN*, London, Macmillan, 1985
66. See Anthony Verrier, *International Peacekeeping: United Nations Forces in a Troubled World*, Harmondsworth, Penguin Books, 1981, Chapter 8.
67. Conor Cruise O'Brien, 'What Can Become Of South Africa?'.
68. 'Problems of Struggle against Racism, Apartheid and Colonialism in the [*sic*] South Africa'.
69. On the economic and strategic arguments for South African withdrawal to the 'Orange River Line' (from the National Party government's own point of view), see *Africa Contemporary Record 1983–4*, p. B701–7.

2 Sanctions Against South Africa: Punitive Action or Placebo Politics?

Gerald Braun and Heribert Weiland

> However one looks at the problem, though, there is no doubt that the West, if its object is nothing less than the abandonment of White supremacy, will face very considerable difficulties in exercising pressure on South Africa.
>
> R. W. Johnson[1]

INTRODUCTION: THE REDISCOVERY OF SANCTIONS POLICIES

In the nuclear age, in which war can no longer simply be the pursuit of politics by another means, the significance of sanctions as a tool of international politics seems to be growing. Sanctions are regarded as the ultimate non-violent means of economic and political intervention. However, the sanctions debate in recent years has been one-sided, in so far as it has concentrated on the classic nation-state as the sole actor within the international system. Sanctions analyses – often very normative – concentrate almost exclusively on the quantitative economic effects on the target state and pay too little attention to historical experience. In the hope of partially redressing this imbalance, this contribution considers the role of non-state actors as well as non-quantifiable socio-psychological and political aspects. It will consider not only the implications of sanctions for the target country but also two equally important determinants of sanctions policies: the domestic cost-benefit calculations of the Western industrial states, and the imperatives of alliance commitments.

SANCTIONS AGAINST SOUTH AFRICA – A NEVER-ENDING STORY?

The debate on sanctions against South Africa has gone on with fluctuating intensity for almost as long as the worldwide protests against the apartheid policy of the postwar Afrikaner government. One consistent feature is renewed worldwide interest in sanctions against the white minority government whenever the conflict between black and white over equality and black codetermination escalates into open violence. This was the case after the Sharpeville massacre in 1960, after the Soweto uprising in 1976 and during the countrywide strikes and demonstrations during 1984–6.[2] With each new peak of violence, international coverage has been greater and international outrage intenser, provoking an escalation in the calls and proposals for sanctions. Whereas in the aftermath of Sharpeville there were only threats and calls for non-mandatory sanctions, in the aftermath of Soweto the UN imposed a total arms embargo. Finally, since 1984, the major Western industrial states have imposed selective economic sanctions against South Africa. But as Johnson had already pointed out ten years ago, the prospects of successful pressures are limited because of the internal strength of the white apartheid regime and the difficulties of reaching agreement in the international community.

The case for imposing sanctions against South Africa rests essentially on three arguments: the occupation of Namibia in contravention of international law;[3] repeated attempts to destabilise southern Africa through a combination of military counter-insurgency and economic arm-twisting;[4] and the continual violation of universally-accepted human rights[5] through statutory racial discrimination. The current preoccupation with South Africa is conditioned by the latter in particular.

GOALS AND PROSPECTS OF SANCTIONS

Sanctions: ends and means

In modern international law the term 'sanctions' is interpreted as 'a punitive action by one state against another, designed to force a change of policy without resorting to overt aggression'.[6] Sanctions thus presuppose a cause and require: actors or initiators; a target group; non-military punitive instruments; and political objectives which determine the utility, the range, and the limits of sanctions. In the event of international sanctions the *actors* are, as a rule, national governments, supranational communities, or international organisations.

Sanctions against South Africa constitute a special case insofar as the majority of the national states, though actors, are not *initiators*. Public opinion, churches, and other parapolitical groupings – non-state actors – have an important say in the debate.

The *target group* of international sanctions is normally the government and its social power base in the state under sanction. Although the intention, as a rule, is to force change on specific power groups in the target state, sanctions may affect the whole population. In the case of South Africa this conflict is aggravated by the structures of racial discrimination themselves: although the effects of sanctions are supposed to force the white minority to change its behaviour and attitudes, the black majority may be affected as hard or even harder.

The *instruments of sanctions* cover a range of prohibitive and revocative measures. Economic sanctions are generally regarded as the most effective form of coercion short of recourse to violence.

Trade sanctions aim at restricting or stopping imports and exports between the target state and the sanctioning or sender state or group of states, as well as trade relations between the target state and third parties.

Financial sanctions are intended to influence the flow of foreign capital into (and the volume of capital in) the target state. Their aim is to impair both the willingness and the possibility to invest and, above all, reduce the liquidity of the economy as a whole.[7] The two concepts most commonly used in connection with South Africa are disinvestment and divestment. By disinvestment is meant the withdrawal or reduction of all forms of capital already invested in South Africa, the cancellation or non-renewal of credit facilities, and, in particular, the undertaking on the part of companies and banks already active in the country not to make any new investments. By divestment is meant the breaking of economic and financial links with companies which either do business with South Africa (directly or indirectly) or profit from such business. Divestment is achieved through pressure – either boycotts or threats of boycotts – on parent companies or their subsidiaries (for instance in the USA, Europe, and so on).

Sanctions on services are intended to put a strain on international relations. They affect mainly traffic, for instance refusing South African airline companies landing and overflying rights, closing land and sea routes, and restrictions on tourism (visa requirements) as well as restrictions on communication (mail, media, flow of information, and so on).

Sanctions on the transfer of technology are intended to prevent the international exchange of technological knowledge and technical expertise (computer hard- and software, blueprints, know-how, and the like).

Apart from economic sanctions, prohibitive measures can include political and diplomatic sanctions (reducing or breaking off diplomatic relations, refusal of entry), cultural sanctions (restricting or breaking off cultural and sporting relations and academic and scientific exchanges), and military sanctions (arms embargo, abrogation of cooperation agreements, and economic blockade).[8]

The *political objectives* determine the nature and range of sanctions adopted. There is a wide spectrum of possible objectives, ranging from marginal reorientations in government policy through the reversal of important political decisions (for example military intervention in neighbouring states) to fundamental changes in the existing system.

The uniquely problematical nature of sanctions against South Africa lies in the fact that any serious demand for the abolition of apartheid simultaneously implies that the existing regime should dismantle its own structures. Yet, if the minority government is determined on one thing, it is the retention of power. Accordingly, any serious discussion on sanctions must also consider alternative forms of post-apartheid society.

General conditions for the success of sanctions

In the literature on sanctions there is a lot of speculation about their utility and their prospects of success, though comparatively little empirical research on previous sanctions policies. The following is a presentation of general conclusions about the chances of implementation and success, as well as the effects and repercussions of sanctions.[9]

On past experience, the smaller and weaker the target state, the greater prospects sanctions have of success. The same applies to close political and economic relations between the target and sender states. On the other hand, the closer the relations, the higher the potential costs, both political and economic. High costs are a deterrent: a doubtful cost-benefit analysis should caution against sanctions. Economic costs in particular may be relevant to sender-state domestic politics. For, if certain sectors are likely to bear the brunt of economic sanctions the resultant hardship could have internal political consequences.

The more precise the objectives of the sender state and the more calculable their consequences for the target state, the more effective sanctions will be. The more fundamental the objectives and the greater the principle involved (for instance a perceived threat to existence), the greater the likely resistance. The corollary of this is a need for a realistic assessment of what sanctions can achieve politically and economically, both in terms of goals and speed. Protagonists and activists tend to overestimate the efficacy of sanctions. Expectations of success should not be too great: sanctions cannot move all mountains.

Once sanctions have been decided on, success requires proper planning and favourable timing, as well as effective, rapid, and ruthless implementation: sanctions that bite are sanctions that work (though this may conflict with a policy of specific objectives). A policy of slowly turning the screw gives the target state opportunities to develop counterstrategies and gives sceptics in the sender state time for second thoughts.

Whereas past experience is clear on the above points, it is equivocal on the effectiveness of both aspects of comprehensiveness. Comprehensive political, cultural, and possibly paramilitary flanking measures need not improve the prospects of success. For, there is the danger of losing sight of the original objectives, that is, of taking a sledgehammer to crack a nut – the nub of the problem of selective versus comprehensive sanctions – and thereby provoking obduracy. Nor need a greater number of participants mean a more watertight, more effective boycott. Not only are there numerous examples of leaks, but the search for consensus may also become self-defeating. The greater the effort of sender states to reach international agreement, the weaker the sanctions finally decided on: too many cooks spoil the broth.

THEORETICAL CONDITIONS: SOUTH AFRICA AND THE WEST

South Africa – a target state?

We have used these generalised conclusions from past experience to formulate some necessary – if not necessarily sufficient – conditions for the success of sanctions.

Condition 1 The target state should be internally disrupted, economically weak and politically unstable.

South Africa is the regional power in southern Africa and has been regarded as an island of economic and political stability compared to its post-independence neighbours. Although its regional hegemony is unbroken, signs of crisis are increasingly apparent.

The *economy* has been in recession since the early 1980s.[10] The trend of the most important economic indicators has been negative. In this period real per capita income of all population groups has fallen constantly. Export income (in foreign currency) has stagnated, foreign investment has ceased, the rand is worth a quarter of its previous value, inflation is at an historically high level, and unemployment – in particular among the urban blacks – exceeds 25 per cent. In addition, South Africa shows internal structural inequalities typical of all threshold countries: a dual economy, a disproportionately important export sector, and a developed but stagnating domestic market. The structural crisis in the economy is influenced both by the worldwide economic recession and internal political unrest.

The internal *social and political situation* is becoming increasingly precarious. In apartheid society racial distinctions coincide for the most part with crass contrasts between rich and poor. The government faces an almost impossible task in reducing these: to preserve social stability it is necessary to spend billions of rand on creating jobs, improving education, and providing social services for the majority of the population. Yet, increasing amounts of resources are being spent on internal security to contain social unrest instead of on social reform. The declaration of states of emergency is simultaneously a declaration of political bankruptcy: in spite of its economic and military strength the country is internally disrupted and weakened, and therefore not impervious to external pressure.

Condition 2 The target state should maintain close and good relations with the sender states and conduct the major part of its trade in goods and services with them.

South Africa still regards itself culturally, politically, and economically as part of the West and its Christian tradition. Despite the handicap of the apartheid policy, it still maintains very close economic, political, and geostrategic ties with the West. Over 1000 multinational companies have subsidiaries in South Africa and the West has invested more than $50 000 million.[11] South Africa is the principal source of certain raw materials – chrome, vanadium, platinum, rhodium – for which the major Western industrial states would have some difficulty, at least in the short term, in finding alternative suppliers or substitutes. Despite incipient redirection, the greater part of South Africa's trade is still with the West: more than 70 per cent of its export trade and more than 80 per cent of its import trade.[12] The reverse, however, does not hold. Apart from specific raw materials, South Africa is a trading partner of minor importance, accounting for about 1 per cent of the West's total foreign trade.[13] In other words, the trading relationship between South Africa and the West reflects the typical north–south pattern of *asymmetrical dependence*, both in quantitative (trade figures) and in qualitative terms (trade patterns: technology versus raw materials). South Africa is more dependent on the West – that is, the sender or sanctioning states – than vice versa.

Condition 3 The target state should have only limited possibilities of circumventing sanctions or of instituting effective countersanctions.

South Africa's possibilities of circumventing sanctions or of responding with countersanctions are limited, but it does have some.[14]

Firstly, it can threaten to impose countersanctions, that is, refuse to export strategic raw materials desired by the sender states. Secondly, South Africa could impose sanctions against neighbouring states. This could well bring them to the brink of ruin, which would probably compel the West, and possibly the East as well, to act to avert a catastrophe. In this way South Africa could indirectly increase the financial cost of sanctions to the sender states. Finally, South Africa will intensify its search for illegal and semi-legal ways and means of *evading* sanctions. Its experience with the arms boycott and involvement in Rhodesian sanctions-busting will be invaluable in the fields of trade, finance and technology.

However, these countersanctions could well be counterproductive. The West would be able to find other sources as well as substitutes, even if this involves higher costs and temporary bottlenecks. But South Africa's neighbours would not be able to cope as easily with countersanctions – unless the West were prepared to support these countries with special sanctions-neutralising programmes. Yet even sanctions against neighbouring states could be costly for South Africa in terms of lost revenues both from inner-African trade and from inner-African transport (transit dues). Over and above this, such countersanctions could conceivably draw both superpowers into the conflict.

On balance, South Africa is neither an 'ideal target state' for sanctions nor an 'impossible target state', but is an intermediate case.

All in all, on account of its international dependence and internal instability, South Africa is vulnerable to comprehensive economic sanctions. The effects in terms of income, employment, and growth, that is, on the prosperity of the country and its population as a whole, would be significant.[15] At the same time, South Africa is capable of countermeasures, in particular of rolling as great a part as possible of the costs of sanctions on to neighbouring states. But now we must turn to the other side of the coin.

The Western community – incapable of imposing sanctions?

As we have seen, South Africa is not an invulnerable target state, even if its vulnerability is difficult to assess. However, is the West willing and in a position to impose sanctions? This requires the fulfilment of two necessary (but probably insufficient)[16] conditions.

Condition 4 The sender states should have precise objectives which can be achieved within a set period of time.

In recent years a potpourri of measures has been considered within the framework of international sanctions diplomacy. Depending on the actors (international organisations, individual states, and non-governmental organisations) and their time perspectives, the objectives range from the general demand for the abolition of apartheid to specific demands, such as the release of Nelson Mandela, the lifting of the state of emergency, and the recognition of prohibited organisations.

These demands have a number of points in common.[17] Firstly, there is a lack of consensus on details of the objectives: what is excessive for one is cosmetic for another, such as the abolition of apartheid, on the one hand, and the lifting of the state of emergency, on the other; paradoxically, the inability to reach agreement means that both 'utopian' and 'pragmatic' objectives serve to cement the status quo in South Africa. Secondly, there is usually silence about how to deal with Pretoria's reactions, be it agreement to fulfil the demands of the sender states, willingness to negotiate, or the decision to ignore them. Thirdly, there is the lack of an escalation or de-escalation mechanism in terms of either time or content.

In conclusion, the Western sender states have only a very vague (if any) idea of what form sanctions should take, how long they should be enforced, and what they should achieve.

Condition 5 The sender states should impose sanctions which produce the greatest direct effects rapidly in terms of the set objectives and time-limits.

For a quarter of a century South Africa has had time to adjust to the threat and the occasional reality of selective sanctions, with varying degrees of success and at great cost (rerouting flights, oil substitution, arms production, import substitution, development of the domestic market). It has also had time to accustom itself psychologically to its pariah status.

The current sanctions debate in the Western community has gone on since 1984. Thus, there can be no question of rapid decisions, nor of surprise effects. Nor can one speak of specific measures which produce direct effects as quickly as possible. The timespans involved and the spectrum of the respective sanctions are too great. They range from total sanctions (Denmark and Norway) to pinpricks (Israel).[18] The governments of South Africa's major trading partners – the USA, West Germany, the UK, and Japan – seem intent on implementing sanctions which have the fewest direct effects.

On balance, the sender states have not fulfilled the most minimal conditions for successful sanctions. There are neither precise conceptions about the objectives of sanctions or the timespans involved, nor are the measures adopted likely to have any lasting effect. This serves to strengthen the suspicion that the measures adopted belong to the category of '*symbolic or pseudo-policies*',[19] which have relatively little to do with South Africa and relatively much to do with cost-benefit considerations in the domestic politics and alliances of the Western community.

SOFT SANCTIONS: THE HARD RESULT OF COST-BENEFIT CALCULATIONS

Sanctions as a tool of domestic policies

Contrary to conventional wisdom, which defines sanctions as a tool of active government foreign policy, we maintain that in the South African controversy the opposite is the case. Sanctions have been a reaction by governments to non-governmental organisation demands as a means of acquiring domestic political legitimation (and taking allies' interests into account). In other words, we believe that governmental behaviour has been an ad hoc reaction to domestic political pressure and protest. They have tried to close the debate with a decision which offers something for everyone. Nothing less, but nothing more. Let us illustrate this by looking briefly at the sanctions debate in the USA and Europe.

Constructive disengagement: the sanctions policy of the Reagan Administration

The current sanctions debate in the Western community began in the USA.[20] A rapidly growing coalition of black human rights groups inspired by the Atlanta Movement (Trans Africa), anti-apartheid organisations (the Free South Africa Movement), universities, churches, and trade unions demanded comprehensive sanctions, including disinvestment – and began themselves to enforce divestment. The US media supported this temporary alliance, reporting (often sensationally) on South Africa in detail, especially on the repressive reactions to spectacular protests and following the declaration of the state of emergency.

The sanctions movement spread across the nation, from town councils through numerous states[21] and into the conservative camp. The Conservative Opportunity Society began to popularise the US policy towards South Africa as a 'fundamentally moral question' that was contrary to the democratic traditions of American liberty (a stance which was to trip up intransigent Republicans in the Fall 1986 elections). Eventually the movement found prominent spokesmen and widespread support among liberals and conservatives on both sides of Congress.

President Reagan used his veto against Congress's sanctions packet in 1986, but he was overruled by the required two-thirds majority, thanks to a 'Republican revolt'.[22] Against the express will of the Administration the following US sanctions came into force in October 1986: a ban on imports of coal, steel, uranium, aluminium, iron, agricultural products, and textiles; a ban on exports of oil, arms, and munition; and the prohibition of all new US investments in and credits for South Africa.

It is difficult to assess the effects of the US sanctions; they may well be more important psychologically than economically.[23] The US experience can be summarised as follows: thc sanctions campaign was initiated by a broad extra-parliamentary alliance of non-governmental organisations across otherwise ideologically antagonistic camps; the media were crucial to its momentum; over the sanctions question the

Administration lost control – at least temporarily – of US policy towards South Africa; and, finally, parallel to the political measures, US corporations and banks were motivated by economic considerations to institute 'market sanctions'.[24]

The sanctions policy of the European Community: the smallest common denominator

Compared to the US campaign, the debate in the European Community (EC) has been more complex, time-consuming, and diffuse. The explanation lies in structural and procedural factors, and the number of diverging interests is considerably greater at all levels – non-state, national, and supranational.

As a simplification, the national non-state actors can be divided into the relatively influential anti-apartheid and sanctions movements in Denmark, Ireland, the UK, and the Netherlands, and the relatively weak movements in Belgium, West Germany, and Luxembourg. Anti-apartheid groups in France, Italy, Greece, Spain, and Portugal find virtually no public resonance at all. In contrast to the USA, at no time have there been any signs of a broad sanctions alliance between these groups and the 'conservative' economic and security camps, which have consistently opposed sanctions.

Although the European media have given considerable attention to South Africa, this theme has had to compete with issues of domestic political importance (East–West conflict, rearmament, environmental problems, reservations about American foreign policy, and so on).

The European states themselves are divided between traditional 'sanctionists' (Denmark, Ireland, and the Netherlands) and traditional 'hardliners' (the UK, Portugal, and West Germany), in the final instance irrespective of the ideological leanings of the government of the day. Only France has changed its stance in recent years, switching from a 'hardliner' to a hard 'sanctionist'. This diversity is reflected in the dissimultaneous implementation of Community sanctions policies. Whereas France went it alone with unilateral action on 25 July 1985,[25] the 'gang of three' – the UK, Portugal, and West Germany – resisted any sanctions policy for as long as possible.

Hence, it is not surprising that, compared to the USA, the EC debate started with a time-lag, lasted longer and has ended – for the time being – in 'softer' sanctions. After hectic sanctions diplomacy the foreign ministers of the EC agreed on the following measures on 17 September

1986: a ban on imports of iron, steel, and gold coins as well as the prohibition of new investment in South Africa. In contrast to the USA, high-grade steels, gold ingots and – in particular – coal were excluded.[26]

Agreement was reached on the smallest common denominator. 'Soft sanctions', the hard result of sober cost-benefit calculations,[27] was a careful compromise between: *alliance interests* which, despite strenuous denials, required a European gesture recognising the change of course forced on the US Administration in the sanctions question; *European solidarity* – a symbolic demonstration in a relatively marginal political field involving little real cost; and, not least, *domestic political considerations*, which called for a pragmatic balancing act between the pressures from various organised interest groups.

The agreement does not appear to reflect a lack of political will or weak political leadership. Rather, it reflects the structures and composition of pluralistic democratic societies, in which lengthy, complex processes of decision-making are the rule, not the exception. 'The politicians ... will have to adopt a strategy which is acceptable to as many as possible with as few disadvantages as possible. ... the more pluralistic the society, the greater the number of groups to be satisfied, the more incremental and gradual the decision-making process will be.'[28]

In terms of this logic the EC compromise was enough to pacify domestic political interests.[29] Despite condemnation of 'pseudo-policies' and 'hypocrisy', or panegyrics on 'statesmanlike wisdom', the EC compromise could be 'sold' as a victory of idealism over *Realpolitik* in countries with influential anti-apartheid groups (the Netherlands, Denmark, Ireland), and as a victory of realism over idealistic policies in countries with powerful pro-South African lobbies (the UK, Portugal, and West Germany).[30] These are issues which are explored further in the following chapter.

DIFFERENT COUNTRIES – DIFFERENT CUSTOMS: CONJECTURES ON NATIONAL DIFFERENCES AND THE SANCTIONS QUESTION

General phenomena such as the role of non-governmental organisations, the media, and the primacy of domestic politics may adequately explain the EC compromise; but they do not satisfactorily explain the national differences which determine a compromise of this nature. From a theoretical point of view it is necessary to explain exceptions, not the rule, such as the divergent behaviour of France, the United Kingdom, and Portugal. The anti-apartheid lobby in France is comparatively weak – yet the French government dashed ahead. The British government was under considerable pressure from the anti-apartheid movement, the Crown, and the Commonwealth – yet the Prime Minister refused to the last to agree to sanctions. Portugal had a socialist government with a decidedly anti-racist policy and good relations with lusophone Africa – yet Lisbon voted against sanctions.

Of course, each individual case can be explained by unique factors – France's third-world policies[31] are orientated towards francophone Africa; Great Britain's economic interests are manifest; Portugal has 600 000 citizens in South Africa.[32] Models of systems analysis offer a more general, heuristic explanation.[33] We can regard the political system as an input-output system in which the relative factor mix produces political decisions (or non-decisions) that maximise domestic support and legitimacy for the political actors (see Figure 2.1). It is worth elaborating on the relevant factors.

(1) *Economic interest groups and dependencies*
In post-industrial societies the potential of organised economic groups and interests to generate conflict is enough to activate the political and administrative system to protect its own interests, which for political groups means avoiding the loss of voting support, preventing the growth of alternative parties, protecting tax revenues, and averting collective refusals to work; in short preventing 'rebellion'. The larger the potential threat to powerful organised interests from sanctions – loss of jobs, income markets – the more likely sender-state governments will be opposed to sanctions.

The significance of this conflict potential stands in relation to the economic dependencies between South Africa and the sender states. The economic importance of South Africa – defined, say, as South Africa's share of a sender state's total exports and imports and total direct foreign investments and foreign credits – varies from state to state in the Western community (with the UK and Denmark at the extremes). The greater South Africa's economic importance for a sender state (relative to black Africa),[34] the more strongly the respective government will oppose sanctions (for fear of negative effects on growth, employment, and revenues), and vice versa.

(2) *Non-profit interest groups*
The above remarks on economic interest groups apply by analogy to non-profit groups and actors such as churches, anti-apartheid move-

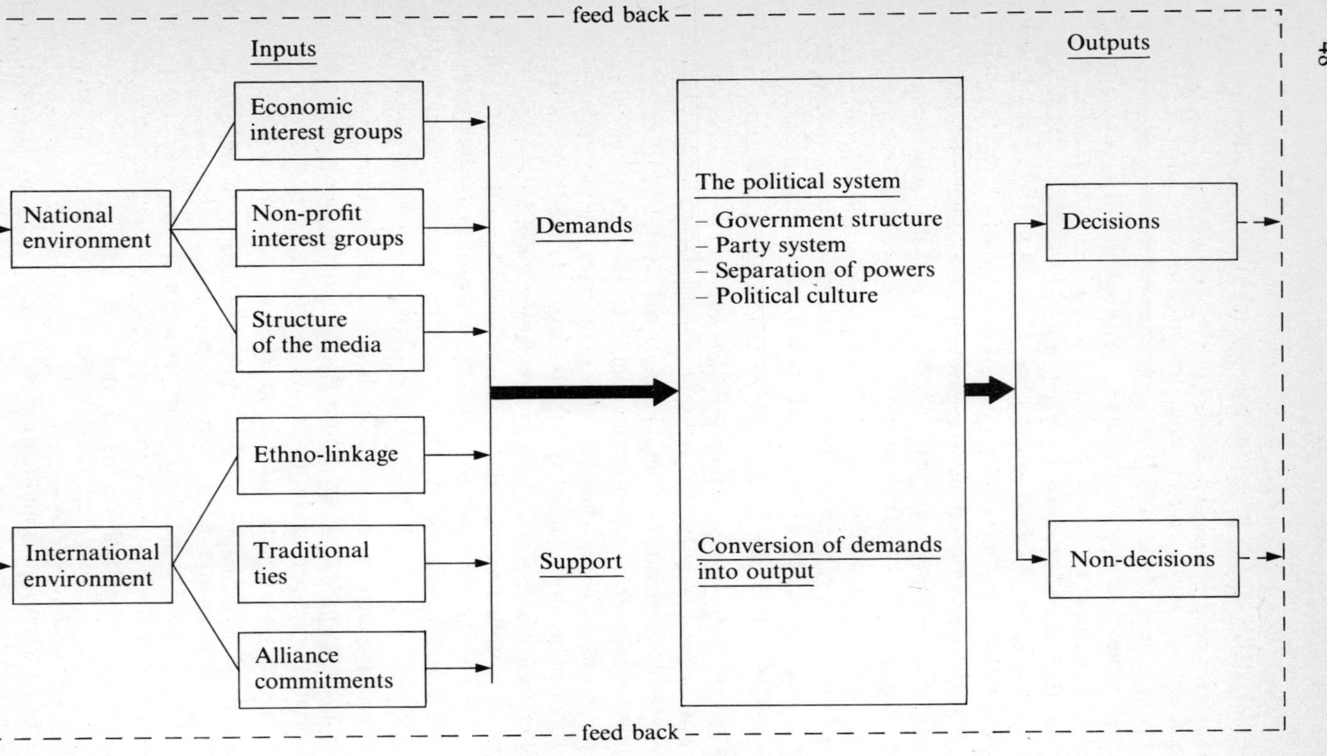

Figure 2.1 A dynamic response model of a political system

Source: Adapted from David Easton, *A Systems Analysis of Political Life*, New York, John Wiley, 1965.

ments, cultural and sporting associations, and so on. Size and conflict capability are necessary as well as sufficient conditions for articulating political protest and exerting pressure: the larger and more powerful the pro-sanctions lobby, the more likely the government concerned will impose sanctions.

(3) *Media*
The extent and intensity with which political protest is articulated depends largely on the structure of the media: the more pluralistic the media are and independent of other economic interests and the state, the better they can publicise 'divergent' political protest and popularise the call for sanctions.

(4) *Ethno-linkage*
The South African population also forms a lobby (that is, an input factor) in the political system of the Western states. Depending on one's point of view, this is either an internal factor (ethno-perspective) or an international factor (perspective of international law). The greater the numbers of the national group (British, Germans, Portuguese, and so on) living in South Africa, the more likely the respective government will intercede in their perceived interest against sanctions.

This reveals a structural asymmetry between the white and black population. Whereas these white groups may be an important political factor in their countries of origin – potential voting behaviour, organisation of powerful, vocal interest groups, access to the media and to the political system in general – this is, with one exception, not the case for blacks (no vote, underprivileged social situation, at best refugee status, and the like). The exception is the ethno-linkage between black South Africans and black US Americans.

(5) *Traditional ties*
The duration and intensity of historical links with South Africa, on the one hand, and with Third World states or associations on the other (the Commonwealth, the OAU, frontline states, francophone Africa) is an important international factor. Although complicated by the question of trade-offs, in general the older and more intensive the links (loyalties) to the Third World, the stronger the support for sanctions.

(6) *Alliance commitments*
The extent and depth of the alliance commitments within the framework of the Western community play a considerable role in decisions concerning the Third World. There are three dimensions: (1) the bilateral relations with the Western great power, the USA, (2) NATO

commitments, and (3) 'European solidarity', especially within the framework of the European Community (which may, of course, involve a conflict of loyalties). Given the nature of alliances per se, the closer and more intensive the relations to the USA or to the EC, the greater the likelihood that the sender state will take the line of the superpower or the EC majority on the respective decision.

(7) *Structure of the political system*
Reaction to political problems and protest also depends on how the political and administrative actors perceive problems and whether they are willing to translate perception into action. This is partly a function of the structural features of the political and administrative system. Apart from the above-mentioned group interests and the organisation of the media, these factors include the system of government (centralised/federal), the separation of powers, and party systems.[35]

Two plausible extreme constellations may illustrate this point. The conjunction of one-party dominance, weakly-organised interest groups, and state-supervised mass media (the French model) potentially serves to smother political protest and pressure. By contrast, majority-vote democracy, strong, organised interest groups, and pluralistic mass media (the British model) can strengthen protest and pressure.

This has consequences for both the level and the direction (that is, pro or contra sanctions) of political protest and pressure. And it presumes that the behaviour of the political actors is reactive, that is, that the political and administrative system does not actively plan in anticipation but reacts ad hoc to political and economic pressure.

(8) *Political culture*
An analysis of political structures does not take account of non-quantifiable 'superstructure' phenomena, in particular the political culture. If one defines it as a subjective dimension of the socio-political system (beliefs, attitudes, values), then differences in political culture may well play a considerable role in the sanctions question. Some countries have produced a beliefs system with a greater affinity for ideal values and norms – such as human rights, anti-racism, international solidarity and so on. In others, greater emphasis is placed on material values – such as the standard of living and achievement. One may distinguish between *conviction-orientated* and *achievement-orientated* cultures.[36] Factors which play an essential role in political culture include, in our opinion, religion, national history, ethnic composition, political socialisation, and democratic traditions. The greater the

emphasis on idealistic and universal values in a country's national political culture the greater the support for sanctions. A discussion of the concept of political culture would go beyond the bounds of the present topic, but certain tendencies are relevant to the sanctions debate. Thus, the Netherlands, the Nordic countries, as well as Ireland, may be classified as conviction-orientated; West Germany and Great Britain are more achievement-orientated.[37] This phenomenon may help explain why certain European countries have concentrated on the letter of the sanctions agreement and others on finding loopholes.

This list of possible explanations for differences in behaviour between states is neither exclusive nor definitive. Nor do the factors constitute watertight analytical categories. Moreover, it may be felt that differences in relative importance, both international and inter-temporal, as well as possible contradictions, make for an unnecessarily complex analysis. However, pluralistic, democratic societies are complex, and, accordingly, their decision-making processes equally so – as the run-up to the EC compromise amply demonstrated.

BACK INTO THE LAAGER

The complexities of the decision-making processes in the Western community have given the South African government time to develop a comprehensive arsenal of countermeasures.

(1) *Control of the media*
By introducing rigorous censorship Pretoria has restricted communication, until then a prime condition for the spread and growing intensity of the sanctions movement in the Western community. As a tangible result, South Africa now receives only erratic mention in the Western media, and seldom on the front page or as first item in news broadcasts. This lack of publicity is one of the major reasons why the sanctions campaign has faltered.

(2) *Counterpropaganda*
Pretoria has participated indirectly, but intensely, in the debate in the Western world through a propaganda counter-offensive. Its arguments are essentially that the 'unrest' is part of a communist conspiracy directed from abroad, that sanctions will worsen the fragile economic situation in the West, and that black South Africans will bear the brunt of sanctions.

(3) *Countermeasures*

South Africa has prepared itself for embargoes and sanctions by: creating a Secretariat for Unconventional Trade, building up stocks, intensifying relations – by product – with non-sanction states (Hong Kong, Singapore, Cape Verde Islands, Oman, Egypt, etc.), and seeking clandestine alliances (especially with other pariah states such as South Korea, Israel and Taiwan).[38]

(4) *Regional countersanctions*

Pretoria has intensified – against some internal resistance – its 'carrot-and-stick' strategy towards the rest of southern Africa. The prime objective of this strategy is to safeguard the social status quo by creating a *cordon sanitaire* of dependent neighbouring states.[39]

Carrots include, *inter alia*, economic and financial aid to 'moderate' states such as Malawi, Lesotho and Swaziland, as well as attractive agreements on transport and water. Sticks include covert and overt military intervention and intimidation, support for guerrilla movements (even in breach of international treaty), the repatriation of migrant labour (especially to Mozambique), and threats of South African embargoes and sanctions. Paradoxically, Pretoria persists in condemning carrots and sticks as 'immoral' or 'terrorist' – whenever they are applied to South Africa.[40]

(5) *Passing on the costs of sanctions*

A proven strategy of relieving the burden of sanctions is to shift the – so far relatively minor – costs on to the black population (in the form of taxes, rent increase, higher charges for services, redundancies, etc.).[41] This may not only cushion many effects of sanctions on the white minority for some time but also ensures that the prophecy of black hardship is fulfilled.

Neighbouring states will probably also have to help through, for instance, increased service charges, and less favourable customs agreements.

(6) *Mobilisation of the white population*

Finally, a pre-condition for approval and support of 'unconventional' measures of government policy is the moral mobilisation of the white population – the appeal to Christian Nationalism, patriotism, total onslaught, and so on. If appearances in the West are not deceptive, this psychological propaganda in South Africa has been successful. The consensus on the necessity of securing white rule and privileges does not appear to have been shaken by the conflicts and disagreements within the white community. Nor are there signs of a white ideological dissident movement.[42]

CONCLUSION

Is time running out? Ten years on, Johnson's statement quoted at the beginning of this chapter – '. . . the West . . . will face very considerable difficulties in exercising pressure on South Africa' – has proved correct. The difficulties in reaching any decisions on sanctions against South Africa have been very considerable indeed. Nevertheless, an agreement to exercise some form of pressure has been reached, and this, ironically, under conservative government leaders, including Reagan, Thatcher, and Kohl, expressly opposed to sanctions. At the same time, the prolonged negotiations required for this decision have enabled the South African regime to partially counter the desired effects by preparing for this eventuality. It has adapted to the new situation with comparative ease, at least in the short run. The noticeable asymmetry between the abilities of the West and South Africa to implement sanctions quickly and effectively is rooted in the qualitative differences between their political systems. Pluralistic, open societies have their price – as, of course, does a racial oligarchy.

Whether the sanctions policy of the West signals the beginning of the end of apartheid in South Africa falls within the realm of political astrology. The road of South African studies is paved with false predictions. However, it is probable that even soft sanctions have markedly raised the cost of defending white privilege. Contrary to conventional wisdom, this cost is reflected less in terms of quantifiable economic effects than in change in the psychological and political climate.

As might be expected in this situation, sanctions have increased the polarisation within the white population: both the trend towards escapism and the retreat into the laager are growing stronger. At present it seems as though the white regime is trying to stop the clock at five to twelve. But how long can time stand still? Bookmakers' odds are as good a guide as any. Minority regimes which hold human rights in contempt can survive for a very long time. But not for ever.

Notes

1. R. W. Johnson, *How Long Will South Africa Survive?*, London, Macmillan, 1977, p. 321.
2. Publications dealing with the respective periods include: Ronald Segal (ed.), *Sanctions against South Africa*, Harmondsworth, Penguin, 1964; Arnt Spandau, *Economic Boycott against South Africa: Normative and Factual Issues*, Cape Town, Juta, 1979; Clyde Ferguson and William R. Cotter, 'South Africa: What is to be done?', *Foreign Affairs*, 57, 1978, pp. 253–74; D. G. Clarke, *Economic Sanctions on South Africa: Past Evidence and Future Potential*, Geneva, International University Exchange Fund, 1980; B. Rogers and B. Bolton, *Sanctions against South Africa: Exploding the Myths*, Manchester, Manchester Free Press, 1981; Richard Moorsom, *The Scope for Sanctions. Economic Measures against South Africa*, Catholic Institute for International Relations, London, 1986; Gerald Braun, Uwe Tonndorf, and Heribert Weiland, *Sanktionen gegen Südafrika. Ziele – Meinungen – Erfolgsaussichten*, Arbeitspapier für die Deutsche Kommission Justitia et Pax, Bonn 1986.
3. In accordance with the decisions of the United Nations (1966) and the International Court of Justice (1971). South Africa also ignores the resolution of the UN Security Council (1978).
4. South Africa has frequently and unilaterally broken the bilateral ceasefire and withdrawal agreements with Angola and Mozambique. Preliminary estimates put the cost of South African destabilisation measures to the Southern African Development Coordination Conference states since 1980 at more than what these states have received in international capital and aid in the same period (approx. $10 000 million).
5. Compare the UN Declaration of Human Rights (1948).
6. R. Scruton, *A Dictionary of Political Thought*, London, Pan, 1983. Also: L. M. Goodrich, 'International Sanctions', in *International Encyclopedia of the Social Sciences*, 14, 1968, p. 5; Wilhelm A. Kewenig und Anton Heim, *Die Anwendung wirtschaftlicher Zwangsmassnahmen im Völkerrecht und im internationalen Privatrecht*, Heidelberg, C. F. Mueller, 1982.
7. Cf. Mark Orkin, *Disinvestment, the Struggle, and the Future. What Black South Africans Really Think*, Johannesburg, Ravan Press, 1986, passim.
8. The ultimate step short of overt aggression is the economic blockade, the use of military means to force unwilling states to comply with internationally imposed sanctions.
9. This summary is based primarily on Gary C. Hufbauer and Jeffrey J. Schott, *Economic Sanctions Reconsidered: History and Current Policy*, Washington, Institute for International Relations, 1985. The authors present a comprehensive systematic analysis of over 100 cases of sanctions. Also see David Leyton-Brown (ed.), *The Utility of International Economic Sanctions*, London, Croom Helm, 1987.
10. Cf. Gerald Braun, Uwe Tonndorf, and Heribert Weiland, *Sanktionen gegen Südafrika*, pp. 15ff.; and Axel Halbach, 'Südafrika unter Druck: Sanktionen und ihre Wirkungen'; *ifo-schnelldienst*, 1987, 3, pp. 21ff.
11. *Die Zeit*, 42/11, 6 March 1987, p. 3; and *Race Relations Survey 1985*, South African Institute of Race Relations, Johannesburg, 1986, p. 121.

12. The figures are for 1984; cf. Richard Moorsom, *The Scope for Sanctions*, p. 98.
13. Joseph Hanlon and Roger Omond, *The Sanctions Handbook*, Harmondsworth, Penguin, 1987, p. 230.
14. Countermeasures are dealt with in greater detail under the heading 'Different countries – different customs' below.
15. Cf. *The Economist*, 304/7512, 22 August 1987, p. 52f.
16. For further conditions see 'General conditions for the success of sanctions' above. Costs to the sender states have two important consequences: (a) political/diplomatic and cultural sanctions are more attractive than economic sanctions, and of the latter, restrictions on imports and finance are more attractive than restrictions on exports; and (b) sanctions should not provoke (political and economic) competitors or adversaries to jump into the breach.
17. The following points list the incongruencies between the demands. The fact that important governments and non-governmental organisations – as a rule influenced by economic interests – regard business as usual as the most effective way of dismantling apartheid is, of course, crucial to the decision-making process.
18. Officially Israel has joined only the international oil and arms boycotts, but still retains close contacts with South Africa in all fields. In September 1987 it announced – apparently under US pressure – that it intends to apply the measures accepted by the EC.
19. See Chapter 3.
20. Compare with the extremely thorough and detailed study by Janice Love, *The U.S. Anti-Apartheid Movement, Local Activism in Global Politics*, New York/London, Praeger, 1985.
21. From the beginning of 1985 to the end of 1986 nineteen states (including California with $11.4 billion), sixty-three cities and 119 universities had introduced divestment measures.
22. *Neue Zürcher Zeitung*, 5 October 1986.
23. It is estimated that the US sanctions affect at most 2 per cent of South Africa's foreign trade.
24. In the two years 1985–6 sixty-five US corporations withdrew their direct involvement in South Africa, though, with the exception of Kodak, they have retained an indirect presence through minority interests, delivery contracts, repurchase agreements, etc.
25. Cf. Chapter 3.
26. 'We estimate that, if the EC, US, and Japanese packages are scrupulously implemented, South African exports in 1987 will be about 5 percent below the level that would otherwise be reached.' *The Economist Intelligence Unit, Country Report. South Africa*, no. 4, 1986, p. 16; cf. also n. 14 above.
27. See for details Gerald Braun, 'Die Burenrepublik: Paria der internationalen Gemeinschaft', *Jahrbuch Dritte Welt 1987*, Munich, Beck, 1987.
28. E. B. Haas, 'Die Einigung Europas', in D. Sidjanski et al. (eds), *Erfolge und Krisen der Integration*, Cologne, Europa-Union Verlag, 1969, p. 61.
29. This proposition seems to be substantiated by the loss of interest in the sanctions controversy on the part of both the media and the informed public in the western community, see page 47: 'Economic interest groups'.

30. The British Prime Minister and the German Chancellor immediately dissociated themselves from their own decisions on the grounds that they were 'inexpedient'.
31. Guy Martin, 'The Historical, Economic and Political Base of France's African Policy', *Journal of Modern African Studies*, 23, 1985, pp. 189–208.
32. Norman MacQueen, 'Portugal and Africa: the Politics of Re-engagement', *The Journal of Modern African Studies*, 23, 1985, pp. 31–51.
33. The model presented here is adapted from David Easton, *A Systems Analysis of Political Life*, New York, John Wiley, 1965.
34. In practice, this is essentially a dynamic cost-benefit calculation between South Africa, on the one hand, and black Africa (above all the states of the Southern African Development Coordination Conference and Nigeria) on the other.
35. Forms of party systems include majority-vote democracy, proportional representation and one-party dominance. See Richard S. Katz, *Party Governments: European and American Experiences*, Berlin/New York, de Gruyter, 1987.
36. Compare with: Hermann W. von der Dunck, 'Holländer und Deutsche. Zwei politische Kulturen', *Beiträge zur Konfliktforschung*, 1986, pp. 59ff.; Desmond Colborne, 'Dutch-Afrikaner Relations: a Case Study in Foreign Perceptions of South Africa', *South Africa Quarterly*, 18, 1987, pp. 48–52.
37. For a detailed discussion see Peter Reichel (ed.), *Politische Kultur in Westeuropa, Bürger und Staaten in der europäischen Gemeinschaft*, Frankfurt/New York, Campus, 1984.
38. Robert M. Price, 'Domestic and International Linkage in South African Policy', *Vierteljahresberichte der Friedrich-Ebert-Stiftung*, no. 106, December 1986, pp. 415ff.
39. Cf. Theodor Hanf, 'Konflikte im südlichen Afrika', in Karl Kaiser and Hans-Peter Schwarz (eds), *Weltpolitik. Strukturen – Akteure - Perspektiven*, Bonn, Bundeszentrale für politische Bildung, 1985, pp. 660ff.; Joseph Hanlon, *Beggar Your Neighbours*, London, Catholic Institute for International Relations, 1986.
40. Gerald Braun, 'Das südliche Afrika zwischen Krieg und Frieden', in Ulrich Fanger (ed.), *Krisenherde in der Dritten Welt*, Freiburg, Rombach, 1986, pp. 17ff.
41. Interestingly, sanctions – too recent to have really taken effect – are now being held partly responsible for long-term structural problems in South Africa (unemployment, dual economy, etc.), and not only in Pretoria's propaganda but also by the pro-South Africa lobby in the West. The first effects of the private disinvestment process seem to be increased concentration in the private sector and a relative weakening of the trade union movement.
42. Only time can tell whether a few independent, ex-National Party politicians and the protests of a body of Stellenbosch professors are really more than storms in a teacup.

3 The European Community and Sanctions Against South Africa

Martin Holland

INTRODUCTION

The analysis of South Africa's international relations from the multilateral perspective of the European Community (EC) has been largely ignored in favour of the examination of bilateral links with Britain and America.[1] During the 1980s the importance of the EC's collective action has grown and, arguably, superseded the existing bilateral relations between the individual countries of Western Europe and South Africa. Independent national foreign policy-making has been constrained by the agreement to consult and cooperate within what is known as the framework for European Political Cooperation (EPC). This chapter addresses the Community's collective relationship with South Africa.

The Community's South African policy only dates from 1977. It developed in tandem with the EC's wider efforts to promote EPC, the closer coordination of foreign policy among the member states. Because of this, EPC and the Community's political relations with South Africa were ignored in Johnson's analysis. He only noted the lessening of South Africa's 'old semi-colonial' dependence on the United Kingdom and the emergence of significant trading relations with the European Community. For Johnson, the importance of the EC was essentially economic, not political, and concerned future access to the British market once Britain became a Community member.[2] In a general sense, Johnson interpreted the West as tantamount to American interests, with the EC very much a minor international actor.

The key to EC–South African relations is EPC. In contrast to the legal competences of the Treaty of Rome, EPC is a pragmatic extra-Treaty activity that has evolved through practice, shared experiences and a consistent, if limited, series of successes. It is primarily an intergovernmental process, and not tantamount to a supranational common European foreign policy. The only commitment on the part of the member states is to consult and exchange views before deciding their own national foreign policies and, where possible, to agree on collective positions. Informality and an absence of legal obligation are its hallmarks. As Wallace notes, 'It expands the reach of national foreign policies, without too sharply constraining them; it offers additional information and the option of common action, but without any binding commitment'.[3]

While there is no obligation under EPC for Community member states to implement a collective foreign policy, agreement on consensus positions have increasingly come to characterise the EC's international relations. However, according to Wallace, foreign policy coordination and cooperation has tended merely to 'unite the participants behind a common position sufficiently loosely defined to allow each to add his own interpretation, so producing some forward movement without confronting the major obstacles ahead'.[4] The characteristic feature of EPC is therefore the juxtaposition of consensual decision-making, and collective action where national diversity clearly exists, and this has shaped the nature of contemporary EC–South African relations.

In the first ten years of multilateral EC–South African relations, three distinct policy periods can be discerned: that of formal policy harmony between 1977 and 1984; the 1985–6 period of dissensus and policy reformulation; and the post-sanctions policy of 1987. The common theme linking these periods has been the tendency for member states to 'issue joint declarations, yet pursue a discernibly individual national interest'.[5] In the context of this historical background, three issues are discussed in this chapter. Firstly, the differing national interests of the member states towards South Africa; secondly, the constraints which consensual decision-making within the EPC imposes on the EC's relations with South Africa; and finally, the likely impact of the Community's policy on South Africa.

FORMAL POLICY HARMONY: 1977–84

The origins of the EC's political cooperation on South Africa were strongly influenced by the United Kingdom: for a decade (1977–86), the British perspective determined the expression of Community policy. Rather than being a strength, this reliance on a single country's interpretation may be seen as a defect in policy formation. The EC–South African policy was not an amalgam of member-state bilateral positions; rather the existing British policy was adopted, marginally adapted, and applied in an EC context. Barber has argued that British policy towards South Africa has been cautious and hesitant, with an absence of 'clear-cut policies based on stands of principle'.[6] It should come as no surprise to find that the Community's 'British' EPC policy has been similarly compromised.

The 1970s witnessed an intensification in the economic ties between South Africa and the EC. As Johnson noted, the Anglo-South African relationship underwent 'an alarming alteration' after British entry into the EC in 1973.[7] Prior to this, South Africa had been essentially a non-issue for the then six member countries: economic, cultural, and historical ties all confirmed the impression that South Africa was a British foreign policy concern. By way of illustration, between 1948 and 1973, 52.6 per cent of all white immigrants to South Africa were of British origin. In 1965, 27.9 per cent of South Africa's imports and 36.7 per cent of exports were with the UK, making South Africa the third largest export market for the United Kingdom; by 1970 the figures were still 22.1 and 27.3 per cent respectively. An innovation indicative of this special association was the introduction in 1974 of a Code of Practice that regulated the employment conditions of British firms operating in South Africa.

The transition from a bilateral to a Community-wide position on South Africa within the framework of EPC occurred during 1976. Understandably, Johnson does not comment on this change. Earlier experience of political cooperation in southern Africa had been disappointing, with the Community in disarray over the independence of Angola and Mozambique in 1975. This example of political cooperation did not suggest that joint Community action could be more easily achieved over the question of South Africa. Despite this, a collective position based on two common objectives was established: the economic liberation for the black states of southern Africa; and the abolition of apartheid. In answer to criticisms that it was vacuous rhetoric rather than substantive policy which characterised the scope of EPC on South Africa, an EC-wide Code of Conduct was introduced on 20 September 1977 for Community firms with subsidiaries operating in South Africa, modelled on the earlier British Code of Practice. Commentators agree that the prime motivation behind the Code was to forestall the post-Soweto tide of protest over British, and now EC, links with South Africa, as well as to protect and maintain those interests.

During the 1977–84 period, the Code of Conduct was the only Community instrument used to promote change in South Africa. The informal and voluntary nature of EPC ensured that collective Community southern African policy was one based on the lowest common denominator. Sanctions or embargoes on normal third-country relations were not employed. The Code's provisions were designed to nullify apartheid legislation with regard to employment, although the operation of the guidelines were constrained by apartheid legislation. From the Community perspective the Code was uniformly applicable (on a voluntary basis) to all EC firms operating in South Africa. Each national government produced annual reports on its application, with the Community presidency compiling periodic summaries. All member states were in agreement that the Code was sufficient: none called for a more demonstrative policy.

Despite the EC's like-mindedness, the Code was far from being a collective policy. As I have demonstrated elsewhere, uniformity was missing from EPC, in all but a superficial sense, and from the Community's application of the Code as a foreign policy instrument.[8] For example, no EC institution was responsible for the central supervision or coordination of the Code, no common reporting format was adopted, and the quality of information often precluded comparative analysis (whether intentionally or otherwise). The reporting responsibility was national, not European, and only one EC member, Britain, submitted reports for each year of the Code's existence. No consistency existed in terms of firms' anonymity and access to information, and the criteria used to determine which firms reported under the Code varied according to national labour legislation. Lastly, the Code was voluntary and no direct Community sanctions for non-compliance existed, other than the possibility of public criticism and lobbying.

The objective of Community policy (the removal of apartheid) and the mechanism for that policy (the Code), raised two fundamental questions. Firstly, could the chosen policy mechanism fulfil the stated policy aims? Secondly, were the EC's policy objectives sincere or feasible? The record shows that the achievements promoted in labour relations by the Code were marginal, and that it was being used beyond its capacity as a foreign policy tool.

While the Code was the only policy on which consensus was possible until 1984, it did not represent a coherent and cohesive policy. The contradictions within the EC's policy precluded a collective policy in any meaningful sense because a uniform and vigorous application of the Code was absent. However, in another sense the Code succeeded admirably as a collective policy, at least until 1986, because it prevented the implementation of sanctions, protected EC business interests in

South Africa, and delayed the anti-apartheid pressure for disinvestment.

DISSENSUS AND POLICY REFORMULATION: 1985–6

In contrast to the 1977–84 period of policy complacency, the events of 1986 led to a critical reappraisal of EC–South African relations, and jeopardised the continuance of foreign policy cooperation. The catalogue of escalating civil unrest inside South Africa, coupled with renewed Western media attention, and intensified anti-apartheid lobbying, forced the Community to address the appropriateness of the Code as an instrument designed to eradicate apartheid.

The Community's initial response to the South African government's state of emergency of 22 July 1985, was to issue a joint declaration, the contents of which reaffirmed previous statements on South Africa. Within three days this seeming unity was disturbed by French unilateral action: the French Ambassador to Pretoria was recalled, new investments in South Africa were prohibited and France formulated a UN resolution calling for comprehensive international sanctions. In a belated attempt to stabilise an evidently floundering policy, and to maintain at least diplomatic unity, all EC Ambassadors were recalled from Pretoria on 31 July. Even this united expression of collective diplomacy appeared vulnerable, with Denmark officially closing its consulate, and the United Kingdom insisting that the recall of its Ambassador was just for 'consultation' and did not imply an alteration in Britain's policy of constructive dialogue. To bolster this shaky facade, a further statement was issued which reiterated the EC's 'total condemnation of the apartheid system in all its forms'.

Although the Community fell short of endorsing economic sanctions, at the Council of Ministers meeting on 9 September 1985 (which Spain and Portugal attended as observers) a joint package was proposed, many items of which were already implemented bilaterally. The new policy called for the following common restrictive measures: the withdrawal of member states' military attachés to Pretoria; the banning of nuclear and military cooperation, and the sale of EC oil and sensitive technology; the freezing of official contacts and international agreements in the sphere of security; an embargo on exports of arms and paramilitary equipment; and all sporting and cultural events were discouraged, 'except where these contribute towards the ending of apartheid'. In addition, a series of positive measures were announced on which it was agreed that the Community should 'harmonise their attitudes'. These included the adaptation of the Code of Conduct, assistance programmes for anti-apartheid organisations, further support for the SADCC states, and an 'intensification of contacts' with, and educational support for, the non-white community.[9]

The United Kingdom was alone in objecting to this proposal, but faced with mounting EC, UN and Commonwealth criticism, Britain subsequently adopted the new Community policy in late September. At this stage Britain's Foreign Secretary, Sir Geoffrey Howe, argued that the United Kingdom would not comply with any form of mandatory sanctions promoted under the auspices of EPC. Collective action was strengthened, however, by the announcement of a revised Code on 19 November 1986. Greater emphasis was placed on relations with black trade unions, and upon providing supplementary benefits, training and promotion, for black workers. Attempts were made to improve coordination in applying the Code, with future reports on its operation being scrutinised by the European Parliament, and the Economic and Social Committee.

Despite these minor policy revisions, by the end of 1985 the widely discredited Code (in its revised form) continued to constitute the substance of EPC towards South Africa. The inertia and vacillation that had typified the Community's earlier history of reactive foreign policy towards such international crises as the Iranian hostages, Afghanistan and Poland, again became the dominant characteristic of political cooperation over South Africa.

Britain's unique membership of both the Commonwealth and the Community, and the former's Eminent Persons Group initiative, essentially suspended the development of the EC's South African policy during the first half of 1986. As the internal South African situation continued to deteriorate, the embarrassing absence of any substantial Community policy revision led to 'acrimonious exchanges' at the June 1986 European Council meeting in The Hague where 'hammering out an EC response proved as tortuous as ever'.[10] A plan to send a troika delegation to South Africa was rejected, in favour of a single envoy of the incoming British presidency, as was any form of immediate EC action. A Dutch proposal to ban agricultural imports was defeated, though the Danish and Irish had already signalled their intention to ban the import of these products independently of the EC. In the final communiqué, the European Council reaffirmed the main goal of Community policy as 'the total abolition of apartheid'. In addition to the familiar calls for dialogue, the unconditional release of all political prisoners, including Nelson Mandela, and the removal of the ban on the ANC and PAC, the communiqué announced that:

> in the next three months the Community will enter into consultations with other industrialized countries on further measures which might be needed, covering in particular a ban on new investments and import of coal, iron, steel and gold from South Africa.[11]

In the interim, acting in his capacity as President of the Council of Foreign Ministers, Sir Geoffrey Howe visited southern Africa in July 1986. Pressured by the negative impact of this visit, and by the Commonwealth communiqué of August, on 15 September 1986 the EC belatedly moved towards 'restrictive measures', while stressing the need for 'more effective coordination of the positive measures being taken to assist the victims of apartheid'.[12]

Despite Danish, Dutch and Irish demands, the package of sanctions agreed at the June meeting in The Hague were not fully adopted. The Community agreed to ban by the end of September the import of certain types of steel and iron through national measures (affecting just 188.3 million ECU worth of goods in 1985), although within the framework of the European Coal and Steel Community, and to investigate Community-wide legislation prohibiting the sale of Krugerrands, and new investment in South Africa. In the cause of preserving the facade of collective policy, West German and Portuguese opposition to the proposed coal embargo was sufficient to forestall the introduction of this sanction. The full Hague package would have affected 19.5 per cent of South Africa's 1985 exports to the Community (1559.8 million ECU); without coal, this fell to 3.5 per cent (330.4 million ECU). The Community imports roughly half of South Africa's total coal exports which, in 1985, were worth R3.2 billion, representing approximately 9 per cent of South Africa's export revenue when excluding bullion.

At the Council of Ministers meeting of 27 October the restrictions on new investments and Krugerrands were clarified. A Council decision limiting new EC direct investments in South Africa was issued but it did not cover those contracts signed before this date, and the measures were to be implemented through national 'guidance', not Community legislation.[13] In contrast, the EC's Foreign Ministers adopted a binding Community Regulation against the import of Krugerrands. A consensus on introducing the coal embargo remained elusive.

The irony of the British position during its third presidential term in 1986 is an excellent example of the constraints of consensus-building on the presidency. As an ordinary member state, the United Kingdom had successfully resisted the call for Community sanctions, either alone or with minority support. However, once in the chair, Britain was unable to exclude the issue from the agenda of the European Council, or advocate such a strong national position, though informal encouragement was given to the German-lusophone anti-sanctions position.[14] As correctly predicted by Helen Wallace, the presidency served to intensify 'the spotlight on British policy and thereby further constrain[s] the room for manoeuvre' over South Africa.[15] Consequently, sanctions (though modest by international standards) were at last introduced, albeit reluctantly, under the auspices of a British presidency.

POST-SANCTIONS POLICY: 1987

As the Community entered 1987, there was a lull in the immediate pressure for sanctions, or at least a general acceptance that there needed to be an interim in which the effects of sanctions could be evaluated. The May election for the white chamber of South Africa's tricameral Parliament also provided the Community with a credible excuse for delaying the formulation of the next policy stage. This breathing-space was welcome. The Community had indicated little knowledge of, and even less enthusiasm for developing substantive policy in a post-sanctions era. In the short-term, the adoption of a sanctions package served an end in itself. Where policy could go from this point seemed less clear.

The nominal effect of the EC's sanctions made them fairly easy for member countries to adopt. As is the case in the application of most trade sanctions, there was a danger that trade in the targeted products would increase in the short term: this tendency was compounded by the EC giving a three-month warning of its intention to invoke sanctions, and the adopted restrictions only then applying to new contracts. In general, these fears proved groundless. As Tables 3.1 and 3.2 demonstrate, the import of Krugerrands has been halted and that of the embargoed iron and steel products significantly reduced. Of course, behind these statistics a variety of sins can be disguised; in particular, the continuation of imports through contracts signed prior to the introduction of the Community ban. Two questions that require further examination are: whether South Africa will use a third country

Table 3.1 EC imports of Krugerrands, 1984–87

Value of Krugerrands imported (ECU '000)					
Year	*EC total*	*Major importers*			
		West Germany	*Belgium*[b]	*Netherlands*	*Denmark*
1984[a]	189 225	135 130	51 503	2316	276
1985	141 968	97 939	43 964	—	65
1986	90 570	71 987	18 583	—	—
Monthly average value					
1984[a]	15 769	11 261	4 292	193	23
1985	11 831	8 162	3 664	—	5
1986					
(Jan–Sept)	8 763	6 708	2 055	—	—
(Oct)	3 344	3 343	1	—	—
(Nov)	7 731	7 914	17	—	—
(Dec)	177	—	—	—	—
1987 (Jan)	1 875	1 875	—	—	—
(Feb)	134	—	—	134	—
(Mar)	3	3	—	—	—
(Apr)	22	14	8	—	—

[a] = excludes Spain and Portugal.
[b] = includes Luxembourg.

Source: Commission of the European Community (1987) *Developments in Trade with South Africa, Sec B7/1575*, 9 October, Brussels, European Community.

to re-route its embargoed exports, and whether the Commission and national governments will be successful in monitoring the sanctions.

The Belgian presidency in the first half of 1987 saw the issue of the Middle East take priority over South African policy within EPC. Any direct presidential dialogue with the Republic along the lines of Howe's ill-fated 1986 endeavour was ruled out. The Belgian presidency inherited from its predecessor the obligation to seek a consensus on the ban of South African coal. No Community agreement proved possible, however, when the issue was again raised in the Council of Ministers in late April 1987. Seeking some measure of policy development, the Belgian presidency shifted Community policy from a directly South African to a regional focus. By doing so, a break from the formerly reactive EPC was heralded. Historically, the less emphasised thrust of the EC's twin policy was the promotion of economic independence for southern Africa, principally through the Southern African Develop-

Table 3.2 EC imports of South African iron and steel products covered by the ECSC Decision Embargo, 1984–87

Value of Embargoed iron and steel imports (ECU '000)

		Major importers						
	EC total	*UK*	*West Germany*	*Italy*	*Belgium*[b]	*Greece*	*Spain*	*Portugal*
1984[a]	85 134	25 968	30 077	2 478	10 196	8 562	*	*
1985	188 304	39 261	36 843	9 535	10 395	27 997	20 886	29 275
1986	174 502	35 978	45 904	7 643	8 483	31 127	15 195	16 008
Monthly average value								
1984[a]	7 094	2 164	2 506	206	850	713	*	*
1985	15 692	3 272	3 070	795	866	2 333	1 740	2 440
1986								
Jan.– Sept.	15 682	3 260	4 222	720	747	2 535	1 410	1 466
Oct.	17 065	3 104	2 483	594	428	6 711	2 036	624
Nov.	8 451	529	3 232	389	1 081	637	42	1 653
Dec.	7 602	3 250	1 625	173	249	1 043	468	521
1987 Jan.	7 419	1 019	2 314	2	262	1 382	1 325	302
Feb.	14 181	2 973	692	1 171	405	3 093	3 501	2 199
Mar.	7 419	933	2 261	1 022	407	1 044	456	479
Apr.	8 704	2 172	3 581	80	221	619	1 030	574
May	7 200	1 533	2 307	67	290	1 295	75	977
Jun.	10 487	4 036	3 138	200	527	*	503	1 403
July	13 284	3 240	4 191	4 131	—	*	567	782

[a] = excludes Spain and Portugal.
[b] = includes Luxembourg.
* = figures not available.

Source: Commission of the European Community (1987) *Developments in Trade with South Africa, Sec 87/1575*, 9 October, Brussels, European Community.

ment and Coordination Conference (SADCC). An extension and more effective deployment of regional funds became the major theme of Community policy in 1987.

Since 1979, Community aid had been used to develop a southern African transport infrastructure, in particular the renovation of the Benguela railway, which sabotage had rendered inoperative since 1975. The Belgian presidency floated a proposal for the neutrality of the Benguela railway. However, the outstanding political difficulties have proved insurmountable to date. In order to succeed, such an agreement would necessitate the recognition of certain groups by the Community, require the consent of the conflicting parties in Angola, and the cooperation of the South African military, as well as involve agreement on international military protection.

The positive and negative measures adopted by the Community in 1986 notwithstanding, a comprehensive long-term policy towards South Africa has yet to be devised. The absence of any such strategy is a serious indictment of EPC. Over the past decade, it has become an outmoded status quo based on the lowest common denominator. The policy revisions adopted by the Community were halfhearted imitations of the more innovative policies of the USA, the Nordic Council and the Commonwealth states. EPC was found incapable of making the radical policy initiatives necessary to achieve the Community's policy objectives. Not only is this to the detriment of EPC, it also leaves the EC with a legacy of prevarication in the future black-ruled South Africa.

NATIONAL ECONOMIC DIFFERENCES

Given the problems of political cooperation, the question remains why EPC has been seen as the appropriate mechanism for structuring relations with South Africa, rather than bilateral interaction. EPC effectively institutionalises the relationship at the EC level, and yet allows the different domestic environments to dictate the content or expression of EPC. The best of both worlds is therefore achieved: collective foreign policy harmony together with virtual national autonomy.

The emphasis on national diversity within the Community is a feature of Wallace's treatment of EPC: he has argued that political cooperation 'serves as an alibi for inaction, a means for deflecting external pressure and a cover for shifts in national policy'.[16] In order to survive as a collective enterprise, EPC must offer individual benefits to states as well as recognise different national priorities that may run counter to collective action. The importance of different domestic environments has been instrumental in shaping the Community's response to South Africa. The smaller states of Belgium, Denmark, Ireland, and the Netherlands, reflecting lower levels of economic interaction with South Africa, have been critical of EC policy. In contrast, the larger and more economically involved Community states have sought to defuse the issue, or, to paraphrase Wallace, used EPC as an alibi for inaction.

Limitations to political cooperation are imposed upon EPC by the different patterns of economic relations with South Africa. While the Community is by far South Africa's most important trading market (in 1985, 41.2 per cent of South Africa's imports and 20.4 per cent of her exports were with the Community) trade is not of equal salience throughout the member countries. The Community's trade is dominated by the United Kingdom, West Germany, and, to a lesser degree, by France, Italy, and the Benelux countries: the remaining member states have limited or no commercial ties. The higher levels of economic interaction of Britain and Germany demand that these two national governments view EPC as a significantly different type of issue than the governments of member states with limited or no economic involvement with the Republic.

Table 3.3 illustrates the distribution of intra-Community trade with South Africa for the period 1977–86. While still significant, the United Kingdom's predominance in the South African market has declined substantially since the 1970s. This diversification in trading relations was not foreseen by Johnson, who argued that 'British consumers had a taste for South African goods which others obstinately refused to develop'.[17] In 1977 the United Kingdom purchased 47.5 per cent of South Africa's exports to the EC; by 1986 this had fallen to 16.9 per cent (reducing Britain to South Africa's fourth most valuable bilateral export market). In contrast, the British percentage of EC exports to South Africa in the contemporary period has been remarkably stable at around 30 per cent, making Britain the Republic's third largest importer. During the 1980s the balance of trade has always been in favour of the United Kingdom, although despite this, the Republic is no longer one of Britain's major trading partners. In 1967 South Africa was Britain's third largest export market; twenty years later it had fallen to nineteenth. In comparison, West Germany has steadily increased trade over the last decade, and by the early 1980s West Germany had replaced the United Kingdom as South Africa's most important European partner. In 1986 Germany provided 42.1 per cent of EC exports to South Africa (outstripping all other competitors) and took 16.1 per cent of South Africa's imports to the Community, ranking Germany as South Africa's sixth largest export market.

In contrast, the economic salience of the South African market to the remaining EC states is limited: in 1984 South Africa was France's twenty-third supplier and its twenty-ninth customer. However, for South Africa, France was the Republic's sixth most important trading partner in 1984, accounting for 4 per cent of imports and 2.4 per cent of exports, though they dropped to eighth position in 1985. Italy and

Table 3.3 Distribution of EC–South African imports and exports, 1977–86

	1977		*1981*		*1983*		*1985*		*1986*	
	ECU[a] (m)	%	ECU[a] (m)	%	ECU[a] (m)	%	ECU[a] (m)	%	ECU[a] (m)	%
EC imports from South Africa										
UK	3154	47.5	1612	22.6	1480	23.0	1792	18.9	1353	16.9
West Germany	930	14.0	1226	17.2	1166	18.2	1359	14.4	1289	16.1
Italy	729	11.0	1549	21.7	1464	22.8	2424	25.6	1951	24.3
Belgium[b]	1244	18.8	1486	20.8	1343	20.9	2226	23.5	2235	27.9
France	431	6.5	886	12.4	645	10.0	825	8.7	480	6.0
Netherlands	107	1.6	193	2.7	116	1.8	237	2.5	220	2.7
Ireland	11	0.2	9	0.1	11	0.2	18	0.2	14	0.2
Denmark	24	0.4	154	2.1	154	2.4	207	2.2	102	1.2
Greece	—	—	19	0.2	44	0.7	57	0.6	54	0.7
Spain	—	—	—	—	—	—	248	2.6	262	3.3
Portugal	—	—	—	—	—	—	62	0.7	61	0.8
TOTAL	6630	100.0	7134	100.0	6423	100.0	9456	100.0	8021	100.0
EC exports to South Africa										
UK	889	31.7	2196	31.7	1901	32.6	1709	30.0	1258	26.9
West Germany	981	34.9	2451	35.4	2194	37.6	2246	39.5	1970	42.1
Italy	229	8.2	656	9.5	534	9.2	434	7.6	357	7.6
Belgium[b]	117	4.2	270	3.9	249	4.3	243	4.3	218	4.7
France	435	15.5	968	14.0	562	9.6	511	8.9	411	8.8
Netherlands	127	4.5	285	4.1	263	4.5	279	4.9	260	5.6
Ireland	9	0.3	31	0.4	45	0.8	41	0.7	41	0.9
Denmark	20	0.7	61	0.9	74	1.3	77	1.4	54	1.1
Greece	—	—	6	0.1	4	0.1*	2	0.1*	2	0.1*
Spain	—	—	—	—	—	—	124	2.1	87	1.9
Portugal	—	—	—	—	—	—	20	0.4	16	0.3
TOTAL	2807	100.0	6924	100.0	5826	100.0	5688	100.0	4674	100.0

[a] = European Currency Unit
[b] = includes figures for Luxembourg
* = less than 0.1%

Source: *Eurostat* (1986–7) Brussels, Commission of the European Communities.

Belgium were the only other EC states ranked among South Africa's top dozen trading partners in 1985.

A similar though less extreme pattern is evident in the levels of EC investment in South Africa. In 1965, 60 per cent of South Africa's foreign liabilities were British-owned; various estimates put the current British share of all foreign investment in South Africa at between 40 and 45 per cent, although their international value has been halved by the depreciation of the Rand. In 1984, the estimate was £11 billion; by the end of 1986 these same investments were worth only £6 billion. As a share of Britain's total overseas direct investment between 1980 and 1983, British direct investment in South Africa varied from 6.2 per cent to 9.5 per cent (£232.3 to £296 million). During this period South Africa was the United Kingdom's second most important area for overseas direct investment, only exceeded by investment in the USA. The value of British investments in South Africa collapsed dramatically in 1984, however, to just 2.2 per cent, with both Canada and Australia moving ahead of the Republic as preferred investment markets.

The decline in British investment was compensated by an increase in German investment activity: since the 1970s the Community has been responsible for more than half of all direct and non-direct investment in South Africa. German direct investment in South Africa was stable during the 1970s. It represented between 1.0 per cent and 1.2 per cent of total direct foreign investment from 1976 to 1979, and approximately 10 per cent of South Africa's total liabilities.[18] Despite this modest commitment, South Africa was the most important African market for German investment. Estimates have valued German direct investment at between DM678–994 million in 1980, with the figures for indirect investment even less precise, ranging from DM4000–8000 million.[19] At the end of 1985 one estimate put German direct investment at DM1.4 billion.

Clearly, the uneven trading and investment ratios between Community members and South Africa have an impact on the policy options available to individual states, and on any collective policy acceptable to both major and minor trading partners. The fact that France was responsible for disrupting the EC's joint approach in 1984 should not be surprising on this basis, and the possibility of any initiative originating from Britain or West Germany was precluded by significant economic considerations. The salience of the South African issue is of greater importance to the United Kingdom and West Germany, and their response is gauged in relation to domestic factors absent from the criteria employed by many of the other EC members. In contrast, France's economic stake was less problematic: the exchange of a minor economic market for the political gain accrued through a demonstrative anti-apartheid stance heightened the domestic rationality of the French initiative for the socialist government of Mitterrand and Fabius. However, since the election of Chirac in March 1986 there has been a transition in French policy. This unequivocal pro-sanctions stance has given way to pragmatism, and a policy of continued economic and diplomatic relations.

Since the mid-1980s, profitability, as the stimulus for closer EC–South African relations, has been declining. The exodus of foreign companies from the Republic was not a simple response to the political costs of involvement with Pretoria, despite the claims of the anti-apartheid lobby. It was also the result of rational calculations of profit margins. From being one of the world's most attractive markets for investment, rising inflation (18.6 per cent by 1986), industrial unrest, civil disturbances, the fall of the rand (from US 93 cents to just 35 cents in July 1985), and the South African government's seven-month moratorium on foreign loan repayments, all served to persuade many foreign companies that more stable and profitable markets existed elsewhere.

The flight of European business has been of minor significance when compared to the disinvestment of numerous American companies since 1986. The most celebrated European withdrawals have been by the British banks Barclay's (November 1986) and Standard Chartered (August 1987). Other notable withdrawals have included the Dutch firm SHV and the French state-owned companies of Peugeot and Renault. In contrast, the Anglo-Dutch Shell oil company remains committed to the South African market, despite being the recent target of an intensified anti-apartheid campaign.

Writing in 1982, Barber, Blumenfeld and Hill warned against over-optimism on the part of the campaigners of disinvestment. They argued:

> It is not always appreciated that physical disinvestment of the existing foreign capital stock is not feasible, and that any attempt to divest on a massive scale could actually benefit South Africa by transferring to it a set of highly productive assets at a substantially reduced price.[20]

The post-1985 trend has been exactly that: foreign companies have sold off their stakes in South African subsidiaries to local managers at suppressed market value. This does not, necessarily, sever the economic link. Through licensing agreements with third-country subsidiaries of the parent company, a continued supply of a product, if under a revised name, can be maintained. The wider implications are that the employment practices of these new operations will now no longer fall under the scrutiny of the government of their former parent companies. Thus the scope of the Code of Conduct for EC firms has been further circumscribed. Given the deepening economic recession in South Africa, there

MAGDALEN COLLEGE LIBRARY

is no guarantee that these new local owners will be able to match the usually generous employment practices of foreign companies.

THE IMPACT OF EC POLICY

In the context of assessing South Africa's ability to survive the imposition of sanctions, it is necessary to explore how successful the Community's 1985–6 measures have been in achieving their objective of abolishing apartheid. In the previous chapter, Braun and Weiland argued for clear and obtainable policy objectives as a prerequisite for the successful application of sanctions. They suggest, firstly, that states wishing to employ sanctions should have 'precise objectives which can be achieved within a set period of time'; and secondly, that sanctions should be applied that 'produce the greatest direct effects quickly in terms of the set objectives'.[21] These two conditions set an appropriate framework for assessing the effect of the Community's policy. Let us examine the first of these prerequisites and apply it to EC–South African relations.

The member states can be roughly divided into two groups: those who regard the restricted measures of 1985–6 as maximums (the United Kingdom, West Germany, and Portugal), and the remaining nine states who view them as minimum standards and independently exceed the measures. Ireland, the Netherlands, and Denmark have taken their individual sanctions to the greatest extent.[22] Although there is a formal requirement on all member states to act in accordance with the collective measures taken since 1986, just one measure has been enacted through a Community Regulation, with a second via a European Coal and Steel Community (ECSC) Decision (see Table 3.4). Only a Regulation is 'binding in its entirety and directly applicable in all member states'.[23] Measures adopted as EPC statements lack any Community-wide legal authority and are implemented at a national rather than EC level. Consequently, an opportunity for differing interpretations by the twelve member states was created, and for the limited sanctions that were agreed to have been implemented neither simultaneously nor comprehensively by all member states, despite a commitment to do so. It remains the case that measures agreed to in principle, remain open to the prerogative of national interpretation and application, the only exception being the Community-wide ban on the import of gold coins originating in South Africa.

In general, the application of national measures by the member

	Application method	Application level	Date of adoption
Economic sanctions			
Trade			
Cessation of oil exports	EPC Statement	National	10.9.85[1]
ban on imports of iron and steel	ECSC Decision (86/459)	ECSC	15.9.86[2]
ban on imports of Krugerrands	Council Regulation (no. 3302/86)	EC	15.9.86[3]
Technology			
prohibition on new collaboration in the nuclear sector	EPC Statement	National	10.9.85
ban on exports of sensitive equipment for security purposes	EPC Statement	National	10.9.85
Financial			
ban on new investments	Council Decision (86/517)	National	15.9.86[2]
Military sanctions			
embargo on import/export of arms and paramilitary equipment	EPC Statement	National	10.9.85
refusal to cooperate militarily	EPC Statement	National	10.9.85
removal of EC military attaches	EPC Statement	National	10.9.85
Cultural sanctions			
Discourage cultural and scientific agreements	EPC Statement	National	10.9.85
Freezing of official contacts and international agreements in sports and security sphere	EPC Statement	National	10.9.85
Diplomatic sanctions			
temporary withdrawal of Ambassadors for consultation	EPC Statement	National	31.7.85

[1] = implemented 31 January 1986
[2] = implemented 27 September 1986
[3] = implemented 27 October 1986

states has appeared to lack coordination, and has been only partially consistent with the intention of Community policy. Consequently, the measures are unlikely to prove effective. In addition, a web of legitimate loopholes through which trade and continued links with South Africa can be maintained has been created by the qualified definitions and exception clauses in EPC declarations, as the Community's oil embargo and prohibition on new investments bear witness.

The September 1986 Community agreement on an oil embargo has so far proved ineffectual. The appropriate national legislation was due to take effect as of 31 January 1986. However, with the exception of Denmark, member states have been lethargic in their response. More significantly, the embargo is not comprehensive. While it banned the sale of crude oil produced in the EC (by the United Kingdom, Denmark and the Netherlands) and of crude oil imported into the Community for re-sale, the substantial volume of crude oil held in bonded storage was excluded from the embargo. According to the Shipping Research Bureau, during 1979–84 twenty-six crude oil cargoes shipped from Rotterdam to South Africa originated from bonded storage. Thus without contravening the terms of the EC's policy, 'in practice it is still possible to load crude oil destined for South Africa in trans-shipment ports in West Europe'.[24]

There are a number of other omissions in the scope of the embargo. Firstly, the measures do not affect the considerable quantities of refined petroleum products exported by six member states to South Africa. Secondly, the refining and marketing of oil in South Africa by British, French and Dutch-owned companies remains unimpaired, as does the transfer of energy technology, offshore equipment, and European bank loans for South Africa's oil industry.[25] Thirdly, EC-registered oil and shipping companies who export oil to South Africa via third countries are not constrained. Lastly, not only is the EC's embargo selective, but few Community mechanisms exist for its application or monitoring, and the available penalties are rarely imposed.

Three factors similarly diluted the strength of the EC's 1986 measures restricting 'new investments': uncertainty over the definition of what constituted new direct investment; the weakness of the Community instrument chosen for its enactment; and the lack of legal compulsion. In October 1986 the member states introduced the measures as a Council Decision rather than as a Regulation. The Decision noted that some member states had already independently suspended investments and that it was important for the Community to take 'harmonised measures'; however, the substance of the agreed action again reflected the lowest common denominator. Article 1 of the Decision states that member states should ensure that new direct investments in South Africa are suspended. However, this requirement 'may be complied with by the issue of guidance' without any legal sanctions for non-compliance.[26] The definition of new investments did not include portfolio investments, or the reinvestment of remittable earnings by South African subsidiaries of EC companies. The measures were further constrained in that the 'execution of contracts' concluded before 27 October, and 'direct investment made with a view to maintaining the level of an existing economic activity' were excluded from the scope of the Decision. Lastly, the Community set no criteria by which the Decision could be revoked or extended.

The issue of investments again illustrated the difficulty of developing a consensus within EPC that could be much more than a reformulation of the status quo. The vast differences in economic involvement with South Africa between the member states necessitated flexibility. The political solution was to implement the measure as a Decision requiring merely 'guidance' rather than as a Community Regulation backed by legal compulsion, despite the costs in terms of the increased probability for non-compliance and prevarication. Of course, by doing so the policy was arguably a success for EPC, if not for the pro-sanctions lobby, maintaining as it did the veneer of collective action.

Closer inspection of the European Coal and Steel Community Decision of 15 September 1986 suspending the import of iron and steel products, and the Community Regulation of 27 October, relating to the ban on Krugerrands, also reveals limitations within these sanctions. Again, contracts signed before these measures came into force were excluded. Given that the Community's intention to ban these items, together with new investments, had been officially signalled at the June 1986 European Council meeting, and informally much earlier, there was an extended period in which ways of circumventing the ban could be devised. There appeared to be no cut-off date when contracts signed before the 15 September and 27 October respectively would be deemed to be subject to the ban. Nor are there any trigger mechanisms by which these embargoes can be automatically revoked or extended, this prerogative lying solely with the consensus within EPC.

The central question that needs to be addressed is whether sanctions have promoted the EC's policy objective. Just as with the Code of Conduct, there was dissonance between ends and means. What the policy was asked to achieve, and what it could realistically be expected to achieve, barely coincided. It still remains to be proved that there is a causal link between the economic consequences of sanctions and a change in political behaviour. Johnson, wisely, avoided the dangers of any such 'predictions'. It is highly questionable that the EC's sanctions, even combined with an internal South African recession, will lead to the end of apartheid. External economic pressure is not, by itself, sufficient, as has been acknowledged by past commentators on South Africa.

> The results of sanctions both economic and political, are inherently uncertain. Consequently, the imposition of sanctions involves an act of faith. This faith may be born of moral conviction or political necessity, but not of economic certainty.[27]

With this rider in mind, how far has the Community met the necessary conditions delineated by Braun and Weiland for the successful application of sanctions?

Within EPC, a lack of consensus on the details of objectives has led to an unsystematic jumble of mainly short-term goals (such as the release of detainees, or ending the state of emergency), with those of a longer term (the abolition of apartheid, and regional development). As Braun and Weiland commented above, 'the inability to reach agreement means that both utopian and pragmatic objectives serve to cement the status quo in South Africa'.[28] Precise objectives that are attainable within a set period of time have not been developed. At no stage has the EC stipulated a specific time-scale, either for the imposition of sanctions, or for the realisation of short- or long-term objectives. Consequently, the EC's policies have become essentially static reactions: they contain no guide to future policy should the South African government, for example, comply with EC demands, or more realistically, continue to ignore them. The mechanisms for a responsive dialogue have not been built into the policy declarations. This omission is compounded by the delay in policy formulation. In the contemporary period, it took the EC almost a decade to move beyond the Code of Conduct as the expression of its foreign policy, and the eventual policy instruments chosen were hardly those which would 'produce the greatest direct effects'; if anything, the converse appeared true.

Various commentators agree upon the range of additional conditions necessary for evaluating the likely success of sanctions. These include the closeness of the economic and political relations between the targeted and sender state; the need for sender states to have realistic assessments of what can be achieved and to incur lower costs when implementing the sanctions; and the requirement that the sanctions be comprehensive in scope, adopted by the maximum number of states and timed to their optimal effectiveness. The process of EPC constrains these facilitating conditions. Firstly, political cooperation has to accommodate the differences in economic and political relations between member states and South Africa and, consequently, the different 'costs' of implementing sanctions. Secondly, there is no common perception of what realistically can be achieved; at the one extreme Denmark advocates comprehensive sanctions as the necessary panacea, while the United Kingdom and West Germany are of the opinion that sanctions *per se* do not work. Thirdly, the characteristically lengthy search for a collective compromise within EPC has been contrary to the optimal timing for enacting sanctions. And lastly, while EPC ensures that Community measures are eventually applied by all member states, allowing the lowest common denominator to determine the process of bargaining and policy-making reduces the scope of the measures taken.

The explanation of why Community policy has not even approximated to the minimum conditions necessary for sanctions to succeed as a foreign policy instrument, is to be found in the structure of the EPC decision-making process. Given that the member states were unable to agree on specific policy objectives, other than the universal one of removing apartheid, it was hardly surprising that the policies adopted reflected confusion and prevarication rather than commitment and singleminded action. The anti-sanctions countries have acted in the traditional manner of all minority groupings within political cooperation. The need to generate a common position from twelve independent national foreign policies offered them the opportunity, or 'alibi' for inaction. However, as was the case for the Code of Conduct, the failure of Community policy in realising its objectives, does not necessarily preclude that same policy from being regarded as a successful example of EPC. Maintaining cooperation, albeit at the lowest of levels, was an important, perhaps dominant, goal for the Community to secure.

POSITIVE MEASURES

Critics who deplore the lack of coordination in the Community's nationally-implemented Decisions have increasingly turned to developing a transitional set of 'positive measures' as an alternative to sanctions. Given the intransigence of the British, West German, and, latterly Portuguese, governments towards further economic sanctions, more modest measures, evoking wider agreement, may be easier to achieve since they do not involve direct conflict with the economic interests of the member states. More importantly, 'positive measures' have the advantage of being active initiatives, as distinct from both the Code and sanctions which were predominantly reactive policies. They also fulfil the general function of advancing cooperation among the member states. The 'positive measures' were set out in a Foreign Ministers' statement on 10 September 1985. The most significant innovation was the special programme of direct aid for the victims of apartheid, organised under the jurisdiction of the EC Commission. Ten million ECUs (European currency units) in aid was provided in the first financial year, increasing to 20 million ECUs in the 1987 budget. Other measures included educational assistance for the non-white population, greater support for the SADCC states, and a wide-ranging intensification of contacts with the non-white community.

One interpretation argues that the emphasis upon 'positive measures' instead of sanctions is indicative of a fundamental shift in the balance between the EC's dual southern African objectives – increasing efforts at the regional level while downplaying direct economic and diplomatic pressure on South Africa. The policies of 1977–86 had been ill-suited to the objective of abolishing apartheid. By redefining aims to emphasise regional economic progress, the Community has set itself a more attainable goal. As expressed by the Community, the abolition of apartheid was a grandly moral, but essentially imprecise and virtually unobtainable policy objective. Concentrating on more modest measures is more realistic and feasible given the constraints of policy-making by consensus. However, an alternative interpretation is less generous in its assessment. It argues that 'positive measures' are designed, just as the Code of Conduct was, to deflect criticism from the EC's continuing ties with South Africa.

At the time of writing it is too early to assess the impact of these positive measures. Certainly, the Community has explicitly signalled its regional concern, something that it perhaps failed to do adequately prior to 1985. The Belgian presidency began to realign EPC towards support for the frontline states, rather than resurrect the divisive issue of further sanctions, and aid to SADCC was increased. There is also the implication that the Community is willing to extend the content of EPC rather than settle for a common facade as in the past. Whether the Community will be more successful in achieving the regional objective of the economic liberation of southern Africa remains to be seen.

However, at least the policies chosen initially appear to be more appropriate for this objective than earlier policies were with the objective of ending apartheid. That is not to say that the Community is unable, ever, to achieve this long-term objective; only that the existing incidental policies cannot achieve it. In principle, any EPC policy can be reversed by consensus, and there are policies that the EC could adopt which make the abolition of apartheid attainable.

CONCLUSION

Yet the central limitation on the EC preventing it from implementing these sorts of policies derives from the contradictions internal to EPC. If the Community wishes to exercise some degree of influence over the unfolding South African crisis, the luxury of reactive foreign policy-making has to be abandoned, so that Community policy becomes dynamic and innovative. And yet the limited scope and authority of EPC makes such a transition extremely difficult. To date, conflicting national interests among the member states have worked against the development of policy by consensus, and the initiatives adopted have not necessarily had a beneficial outcome. It remains the case that effective policies against South Africa are inhibited by the very framework of EPC: structural weaknesses in the decision-making procedures tend to impede initiatives. While political cooperation for its own sake, regardless of content, secures the appearance of collective policy, it is not advantageous to the credibility and efficacy of the EC's South African policy.

The Community's South African policy has displayed all the limitations which characterise EPC: national diversity within a collective response; a reluctance to use binding Community-wide Regulations; a predilection for rhetoric over action; and an alibi for inaction as well as a cover for national shifts in foreign policy. Conversely, EPC does require the maintenance of a collective position where none would probably have existed without it. However, on balance EPC appears to have worked to the benefit of the South African government. From 1977 to 1985, political cooperation kept the Community's more aggressively anti-apartheid members in harness, and thanks to the conservative constraints endemic to consensus-building, the sanctions adopted in 1986 were minimal. Unless the shift of focus to 'positive measures' and regional development proves effective, EPC is in danger of becoming an unwilling, perhaps unknowing, apologist for white political supremacy in South Africa. Despite minor policy revisions since Johnson's analysis, the effect of EC policy has been static rather than promoted change. If left to the process of EPC, South Africa will continue to survive.

Notes

1. The exceptions are C. Hill, *National Foreign Policies and European Political Cooperation*, London, Royal Institute of International Affairs/Allen and Unwin, 1983, which contains four substantial references to EC–South African relations; 'European Political Cooperation and Southern Africa' by Prag N. van, in D. Allen, R. Rummels and W. Wessels (eds), *European Political Co-operation: Towards a Foreign Policy for Western Europe*, London, Butterworth, 1982; and M. Holland, *The European Community and South Africa: European Political Co-operation Under Strain*, London, Frances Pinter, 1988.
2. R. W. Johnson, *How Long Will South Africa Survive?*, London, Macmillan, 1977, pp. 88–90.
3. W. Wallace, 'Co-operation and Convergence in European Foreign Policy', in C. Hill (ed.) *National Foreign Policies and European Political Cooperation*, London, Royal Institute of International Affairs/Allen and Unwin, 1983, p. 10.
4. Ibid., p. 10.
5. C. R. Hill, 'Appendix: French and West German Relations with South Africa', in J. Barber, *The Uneasy Relationship*, London, Royal Institute of International Affairs/Heinemann, 1983, p. 99.
6. J. Barber, *The Uneasy Relationship: Britain and South Africa*, London, Royal Institute of International Affairs/Heinemann, 1983, p. 96.
7. R. W. Johnson, *How Long Will South Africa Survive?*, p. 82.
8. M. Holland, 'Three Approaches for Understanding European Co-operation: a case-study for EC–South African policy', *Journal of Common Market Studies*, 25, 1987, pp. 295–314.
9. Foreign Ministers of the European Community, *Statement on South Africa*, Brussels, European Community, 10 September 1985.
10. J. Lodge, 'The European Community: Compromise Under Domestic and International Pressure', *The World Today*, 42, 1986, p. 194.
11. European Council, *Thirty-Fourth European Council Meeting; statement on South Africa*, The Hague, European Community, 27 June 1986.
12. Foreign Ministers of the European Council, *Statement on South Africa*, Brussels, European Community, 15 September 1986.
13. Council of Ministers, *Decision Concerning the Suspension of New Direct Investment in the Republic of South Africa, 86/517*, Brussels, European Community, 27 October 1986.
14. J. Lodge, 'The European Community', p. 194.
15. H. Wallace, 'The British Presidency of the European Community's Council of Ministers: the Opportunity to Persuade', *International Affairs*, 62, 1986, p. 596.

16. W. Wallace, 'Co-operation and Convergence', p. 10.
17. R. W. Johnson, *How Long Will South Africa Survive?*, p. 89.
18. R. Hermle, 'The Code of Conduct in the Context of the Relations Between the Federal Republic of Germany and South Africa', in A. Akeroyd, F. Ansprenger, R. Hermle, and C. R. Hill (eds), *European Business and South Africa: an Appraisal of the EC Code of Conduct*, Munich, Kaiser-Grunewald, 1981, pp. 45.
19. C. R. Hill, 'Appendix', in J. Barber, *The Uneasy Relationship*, pp. 115.
20. J. Barber, J. Blumenfeld, and C. R. Hill, *The West and South Africa*, Chatham House paper no. 14, London, Royal Institute of International Affairs/Routledge and Kegan Paul, 1982, p. 47.
21. See Chapter 2.
22. For comprehensive details of the application of the EC's restrictive measures by each of the twelve member states, see M. Holland, *The European Community and South Africa*, op. cit.
23. The *Treaty of Rome*, Article 189. ECSC general Decisions are normally interpreted as having the equivalent authority of EC Regulations.
24. Shipping Research Bureau, *West European Loopholes in the Oil Embargo Against South Africa*, Amsterdam, p. 4.
25. Ibid., p. 5.
26. Council of Ministers, *Decision*.
27. J. Barber et al., *The West and South Africa*, p. 70. For an opposite view based on an analysis of the effects of the 1986 economic sanctions adopted by the USA and the OECD countries, see, C. M. Becker, 'Economic Sanctions Against South Africa', *World Politics*, 34, 1987, pp. 147–73.
28. See Chapter 2.

4 The Afrikaner Empire Strikes Back: South Africa's Regional Policy

Gerald Braun

INTRODUCTION: THE WHITE PARIAHS

What comes out of Africa is *déjà vu*. In 1977 R.W. Johnson noted that the difficulties and dilemmas facing the white regime were much the same in each postwar decade: domestic resistance, regional opposition, and global criticism.[1] This remains true towards the close of the 1980s. But each is now graver and threatens to grow more so as the end of the millennium approaches.

Internally, as in the immediate aftermath of Sharpeville, the white minority government temporarily lost control of the course of events. The technocratic dream of the Botha Administration – power-sharing without power loss – mobilised precisely the resistance it was intended to stifle. The modernisation of the apartheid system produced the unexpected renaissance of the ANC – twenty-five years after the organisation had been prohibited. The oldest and least successful liberation movement of the century has successfully established itself as the most serious opposition to the Afrikaner government. The threat of losing face, let alone power, forced Pretoria to choose what in the long term is the worst of all possible options: the proclamation of a state of emergency.[2] Since then a state of emergency has *de facto* been permanently in force at the 'Cape of Black Despair', whether *de jure* or not.

Pretoria's promised Golden Age of peace and prosperity in the region has not materialised. On the contrary, three years after the signing of the Nkomati Accord on non-aggression and good neighbourliness, the undeclared war for control of the subcontinent continues unabated.

Internationally the white minority is more isolated than ever. Domestic political pressure has forced a US administration to impose 'soft economic sanctions' for the first time – ironically during the presidency of the conservative Republican, Ronald Reagan, whose policies up to that point had created the impression of greater concern for the interests of the white minority than for the fate of the black majority. This constructive disengagement by the Western superpower precipitated a run on sanctions among hitherto hesitant allies, accompanied by 'market sanctions' of the international business community. The 'Cape of Good Hope' has become a bad risk.

The following arguments concern the regional aspects of the conflict, looking at the white tribe's struggle for survival, domination, and privilege in southern Africa. I contend that South Africa's regional strategy must be understood in terms of the 'logic' of ethno-struggle, and is one means by which the regime seeks to ensure the survival of 'the *volk*' in South Africa. It is well to first sketch what is meant by ethno-struggle.

BUILDING THE GARRISON STATE

The Swart[3] Gevaar and the politics of survival

The Afrikaners' sense of isolation and discrimination – precursors of their present pariah status – has a lengthy history. For almost two centuries the Afrikaner power elite has lived in a world they have perceived – whether rightly or wrongly – as fundamentally hostile to Afrikanerdom. Although the image of the enemy has changed over the years (British liberalism and its South African variants, international capitalism, communism, and – most recently – radical blacks and Marxist black states) the traumata and obsessions have not. Irrespective of other *'Gevaar'* – *Rooms*, *Engels* or *Rooi* – 'The ultimate threat (now as 150 years ago) is the disappearance of the distinctive Afrikaner volk . . . engulfed by the Black majority.'[4] The *volk* sees itself in a social Darwinistic struggle of apocalyptic dimensions against the 'Black Peril'. In its perception of history only they that rule are not ruled. History is the fight for ascendancy, in the final instance for the existence of Afrikanerdom as a cultural community, as a *volk*.

This narrow vision of the world has incalculable political and theoretical consequences. All social conflicts are traced to ethnic conflicts, and ethnic conflicts are perceived as zero-sum conflicts: no winners without losers. 'Hence, the essential mandate of successive Afrikaner governments has been the will and capacity to guarantee the survival of Afrikanerdom and to maintain its supremacy.'[5]

In an elementary sense survival politics are ethno-politics. Its limits are defined by the interests of the *volk*: its culture, its prosperity, and its political supremacy. This does not exclude alliances of convenience with other communities, that is, enlarging the *laager* in the interests of survival. But this remains 'co-opted dominance'.

From the ethnic point of view, all matters pertaining to inter-ethnic relations are treated as foreign policy, even if within the internationally recognised borders of a sovereign state. This renders the conventional division between domestic and foreign policy on the basis of territorial criteria hopelessly inadequate. The goal of ethno-politics – be they intra- or inter-state – is Afrikanerdom's survival, supremacy and *lebensraum*. In other words: the foreign policy of the Republic of South Africa is Afrikaner foreign policy.[6] Hence, its formulation and implementation has to systematically ignore the interests of the great majority of the population.

National security, both internally and externally, is synonymous with the security of the *volk*. Security, thus understood, no longer serves as a means of realising meta-values, such as liberty, equality, and justice, but has become an end in itself, the supreme value of all survival politics. In the interests of security basic democratic rights can – indeed, under certain circumstances, must – be curtailed. The end justifies the means; whatever helps the *volk* is legitimate.

The modernisation of apartheid and the management of violence

No previous government has practised Afrikaner survival politics as professionally and efficiently as the Botha Administration; nor has any previous government precipitated such catastrophic consequences. Under P. W. Botha – a talented technocrat and former Minister for Defence – controlled societal reform from above, or neo-apartheid, is intended to ensure the long-term ascendancy of Afrikanerdom; neo-apartheid is a consistent concept of counter-revolution. Its success required five crucial, interrelated changes: a new ideology; sophisticated security management; a strategic alliance between the Afrikaner government and the anglophone business community; modernisation of the apartheid system; and a new regional policy.

The new ideology is the doctrine of National Security, a functional equivalent of the outdated Old Testament justification for apartheid. South Africa is ostensibly facing the 'total onslaught' of an alliance of external and internal forces, ranging from Marxist black African states to so-called front organisations. The enemy is everywhere. The logic of National Security requires the security establishment to plan for the worst of all conceivable eventualities. Worst-case thinking inevitably implies the creation of a differentiated arsenal and the militarisation of white society. The armed forces are increasingly referred to the battlefield within South African society.[7] All available means must be deployed to deter the enemy from putative ethnocide – in keeping with the Old Testament dictum of an eye for an eye and a tooth for a tooth. The increasingly destructive potential of black–white, friend–foe images mutually condition each other. Only the totally inhuman enemy justifies total violence and destruction.

The elaborate security system required by such an ideology cannot be entrusted to the arbitrary decisions of 'amateurs'. The responsibility for control and decisions has accordingly been centralised in the National Security Management System (NSMS), run by a new class of civil and uniformed social engineers – Pretoria's Praetorian Guard. The NSMS comprises a complex 'shadow administration' of 500 Security Committees. They are primarily concerned with containing the second, internal front. At the pinnacle of the security management pyramid is the State Security Council (SSC). The SSC is regarded as an 'inner Cabinet' or 'Privy Council'; its membership is drawn largely from the security establishment.[8] It is the centre of Afrikaner power. The expansion of the security apparatus, the new concept of area-defence, an unfolding 'siege-culture', and the advancement of the military in government structures has been likened to a creeping coup, heralding a transition to an authoritarian military-bureaucratic system of ethnic rule. The vanguard of the counter-revolution is essentially a technocratic power elite of Afrikaners with similar socialisation.[9] (Hence the scoffing term, the National Party in uniform.)[10]

A crucial element of neo-apartheid is the attempt to bridge some of the deep tribal and class divisions within the ruling white elite. 'Analysts of the new dispensation of 1983 have made much of the government's effort to "co-opt" coloured and Indian support for White supremacy. That is understandable. But too little attention has been paid to the co-optation of other political outsiders, the English.'[11] The creation of an aligned white society, in which 'Boer' and 'Brit' will bury the hatchet in the face of the common threat, is promoted by a 'New Deal' in economic policy. 'Bothanomics' aims at a transethnic alliance between the political and economic power elites. This is manifest in close collaboration in the field of security,[12] in the promised (but so far halfhearted) privatisation and deregulation of the state sector of the economy, and in the common conviction that defence of the status quo is less costly than any alternative.[13]

Divide and rule has always been elementary to apartheid.[14] Its modernisation involves a strategy of cooptation and repression. The basis of white ascendancy should be expanded by coopting the moderate, non-white middle classes as junior partners in a form of coopted dominance, with carefully regulated economic power as a surrogate satisfaction of political aspirations. At the same time the security apparatus acts ruthlessly against opposition groups in a form of coercive dominance, enforced through draconian emergency laws, mass arrests, and the 'proven' methods of dirty warfare. The loyal ethnic security apparatus ensures that the government's means of repression are far from exhausted.

Finally, the logic of the 'total onslaught' requires a responsible Afrikaner government to guard its open regional flank. As perceived by Pretoria, the regional military threat takes two forms – guerrilla and conventional. The former, partly based in neighbouring states, is epitomised by the ANC in exile. Admittedly, liberation movements represent little immediate threat to the survival of the *volk* , but this is overridden by the conviction that a conventional army that does not win loses, while a guerrilla army that does not lose wins. Pretoria also feels it faces a conventional military threat from abroad, primarily from the 'Marxist' black states of southern Africa, possibly with the support of non-regional powers, such as the USSR and Cuba.[15] Consequently, an efficient security management must be prepared for the worst case, for a *one-and-a-half-war* situation – the combination of conventional attack and revolutionary or civil warfare.

To guard South Africa's regional flank, security planners devised a containment or anti-guerrilla strategy for the regional approaches to the Afrikaner *laager*, comparable to the Israeli security strategy – the Total Regional Strategy. Its goal is the defence of white dominance and white *lebensraum* in the region, its means are the inevitable carrots and sticks – economic cooperation and military-economic destabilisation – which for all practical purposes amounts to the transposition of the concept of internal neo-apartheid to the whole of southern Africa.

PRETORIA'S DEFENSIVE EMPIRE

The policy of the Grand Design

The long-term vision of the security engineers is the erection of a *cordon sanitaire* of black satellite states as a bulwark against the '*Swart Gevaar*'. The first concrete expression was CONSAS, the Constellation of Southern African States. Its promotion rested on the assumption that between seven and ten states south of the Zambezi and Cunene Rivers could be drawn into the South African orbit, united by the common conviction that the 'Marxist threat' can be met only by a region of prosperous moderate states. CONSAS was seen as an attempt to seek 'regional solutions' to regional problems. From the beginning this constellation concept was regarded as a multi-purpose weapon: economic, military, and political. CONSAS was intended, firstly, to entrench South Africa's regional economic domination through close economic cooperation; secondly, to facilitate black African political recognition of the Bantustans and the apartheid system; thirdly, to justify a Botha Doctrine of limiting the sovereignty of the neighbouring black states; and fourthly, to restore, by *de facto* recognition of South Africa's regional hegemony, the international legitimacy of the white minority regime. Finally, on the hidden agenda was the hope that the contrast between the more or less awful reality of black Africa and the stability and strength of South Africa would refurbish the image of organised racism. This would serve to demonstrate unmistakably the alleged inability of black Africa to govern itself. 'In this way, a constellation would have created for the Republic a favourable regional environment compatible with its perceived national interests – political, economic, and military.'[16]

Pretoria's hope in the short- to medium-term has been based on 'exhorting' its black African neighbours to adopt a policy of peaceful coexistence. Its goal is bilateral non-aggression pacts, in effect anti-subversion pacts, in which the regional states bind themselves in international law to refuse to permit liberation movements to operate from their territories. In other words, in agreement with the neighbouring states, the apartheid system should be accorded legitimacy, support for the black population's resistance should not. At the very least, a new *modus vivendi* should include military red-lines, defining the geographical and functional limits to which Pretoria would tolerate black African support for the liberation movements.[17] Further demands, such as no South African refugees in neighbouring states, tacit diplomatic recognition of South Africa, and permission for cross-border incursions by South African troops must be understood in this context. These demands reflect South Africa's desire for recognition of its claim to be the regional policeman. 'At best, the "partnership" South Africa seeks is that which Lord Malvern described as existing in the Federation of the Rhodesias and Nyasaland: a white rider on a black horse.'[18]

Within the framework of the Total Regional Strategy, the separation of political and economic goals and strategies from those more narrowly related to security and power, is somewhat artificial (even at an analytical level). But in reality, it is a doctrine of pre-emptive intervention, based on the arrogance of relative power and conditioned by the *volk*'s interest in survival. Pretoria simply wants to create the external conditions conducive to the maintenance of the status quo within the Afrikaner Republic itself. In other words: 'Afrikaner nationalism is a defensive not an expansionist one.'[19]

The strategy of economic *lebensraum*

The purpose of the strategy of economic *lebensraum* is to effect a regional division of labour on a (neo-) colonial pattern. The white metropolis draws migrant labour and raw materials from the black periphery and supplies black Africa with industrial goods and various services. South Africa has two comparative advantages which ensure its economic dominance. Its range of resources and its level of technological and industrial development differs structurally from those of other states in the region, so the classic centre-periphery relationship between an advanced threshold economy and neighbouring underdeveloped economies already exists. The transport and communications systems of the region are orientated to the needs of South Africa and, thus, manipulable. Paradoxically, these systems align politico-ideologically antagonistic states – for example, South Africa and Mozambique – and separate countries with greater political affinity – for instance, Mozambique and Angola.[20]

Notwithstanding attempts at evolving a 'siege economy', the South African economy is still extremely open, constrained by foreign exchange and its domestic market.[21] Therefore, export expansion is necessary to avoid crippling import capacity – for technology, capital goods, arms, and oil – and to capitalise on economies of scale. This has concrete regional implications for economic strategists and business leaders.[22]

Continuing to expand merchandise exports will both promote South Africa's own regional and sectoral economic growth and maintain its neighbours' dependence.[23] A system of food aid and food exports would be useful. Staple food – maize – can be used as a political weapon.[24] It is necessary to maintain transport dependence in the interests of 'transport diplomacy' (Swaziland–Komatipoort and Botswana–Ellisras rail links), thereby maintaining the most powerful economic leverage while simultaneously sabotaging independent black African transport cooperation. Stimulating transnational investment – both South African and international – would extend South African control over the region and combat socialism. Water and electricity supplies must be secured to weaken two major economic constraints on South Africa. Support for large development projects in neighbouring states will increase asymmetrical dependence.[25] Trans-border migrant labour should not be discouraged, for it is both cheaper than South African black labour and can be used as a pawn against sanctions.[26] 'All of these dependencies could be reduced, but their multiple existence allows South Africa to impose high initial costs in sectors of its choice.'[27]

The regional economic strategy promises not only security advantages. The economic advantages for South Africa of a classical exchange between farms and factories is quite obvious: 'Economic hegemony is important because it pays.'[28] The existing pattern of specialisation assures South Africa of structural balance-of-payments surpluses with its neighbours[29] and a long-term improvement in the regional commodity terms of trade. An indirect transfer of resources from black Africa to South Africa is already in progress – or, if preferred, the black periphery is being exploited by a system of structural imperialism, which includes its functionalisation as a pawn against international sanctions.

The strategy of military-economic destabilisation

Pretoria has adopted its strategy of destabilisation and retaliation to discourage its neighbours from supporting South African liberation movements, namely by systematically raising the costs – in the widest sense – of such support. In practice this means demonstrating to these countries that South Africa is well able to reply in kind to the ANC's strategy of sabotaging strategic installations (hard targets) – only incomparably harder and on the supporting countries' home ground. Moreover, according to Lt-Gen Jan Geldenhuys, Commander-in-Chief of the SADF, the technocratic cost-benefit calculations have shown that 'cross-border operations' are about ten times as cost-effective for the South African forces 'in terms of human lives' as 'playing a waiting game'.[30]

Once again, Pretoria's instruments are economic and military. Economic pressure may be direct or indirect. It ranges from subtle manipulations of economic dependency (for instance within the framework of the Southern African Customs Union with the 'captive' states of Botswana, Lesotho and Swaziland),[31] to the temporary imposition of selective economic sanctions on migrant labour, trade, transport services, and tourism.[32] In brief, Pretoria exploits nearly all the economic dependencies of the regional states in some way or another to achieve its security objectives in the region. At times this is tantamount to economic warfare, something South Africa consistently condemns when it is the target.

Direct military intervention by regular SADF units or special units, ranging from the SADF surrogate, the South West Africa Territory Force (SWATF), to 'special' unconventional units partially recruited from mercenaries.[33] Military operations include the permanent occupation of territory in neighbouring states, either as free-fire zones (Angola) or operational areas (Namibia), as well as temporary cross-border raids or pre-emptive strikes against alleged ANC installations.

An 'elegant' solution to the conflict between the efficacy of intervention and its costs has been the funding, training, and support of resistance and dissident movements so as to destabilise the frontline states.[34] These include UNITA in Angola, Super-ZAPU in Zimbabwe, LLA in Lesotho, and RENAMO in Mozambique. Common to all is anti-communist rhetoric; otherwise their programmes, methods, and, above all, support among the local population differ considerably.[35] As a rule, these movements are more than mere surrogates of the South African security apparatus, but less than independent guerrilla units. The objectives of their 'liberation' or subversion strategies range from attempts at permanent troublemaking through liberating restricted areas, to assuming governmental power, either alone or in coalition with the respective government (for example UNITA in Angola).

Less spectacular, but hardly less efficient, are South Africa's methods of 'dirty' warfare, in terms of publicity and diplomacy a low-key, and hence safer, option, which range from bomb attacks on ANC representatives through subversion by trained task forces to the recent professional death squads in neighbouring countries.[36] All in all – and the same applies to the methods of the regional resistance movements – one can observe a learning process in security management. The methods applied are becoming less visible, more sophisticated, and more selective.

The preconditions for actions of this nature are South Africa's overwhelming economic and military superiority in the region[37] and its determination to use it in contravention of international law, regardless of world opinion. Together, these enable a relatively uninhibited projection of the country's internal problems on to the outside world.

THE RECOLONIALISATION OF A REGION

Pax Pretoriana

P. W. Botha's period in office began with a serious reverse. Zimbabwe achieved independence under a 'Marxist' government. This marked a fundamental change in the constellation of power on the subcontinent. Pretoria lost – apart from Namibia – its last white outpost in southern Africa. The technocratic vision of an extensive constellation of states was shattered. Not only did Zimbabwe refuse to join CONSAS, but to Pretoria's astonishment so did the 'captive' states of Botswana, Lesotho, and Swaziland. The CONSAS concept was reduced to South Africa within the 1910 boundaries of the Union. Pretoria was able neither to prevent the creation of a black African counter-constellation, the Southern African Development Coordination Conference (SADCC), nor to restrict support for South African guerrillas in the frontline states. On the contrary, guerrilla activity in South Africa escalated to unprecedented levels. South Africa was compelled to scale down its plans for regional cooperation; it was a case of reconciling the desirable with the possible. The grandiose scheme for a regional constellation of states gave way to an overriding concern for security. Pretoria felt itself impelled by considerations of security to embark on a large-scale campaign of destabilisation and retaliation.

Phase 1 (1980–82) involved the fairly general and indiscriminate use of destabilisation tactics.[38] These included direct military action, or the threat of such, against a number of regional states – Angola, Botswana, Lesotho, Mozambique, and Zimbabwe. The activities of South African sponsored dissident groups also increased substantially, and economic 'techniques of coercion' were seriously applied for the first time. No carrot, just stick.

In phase 2 (1982–4) destabilisation was intensified, but selectively. Pretoria began to categorise the target states and apply different tactics towards them. 'Moderate' states such as Malawi and Swaziland were treated as potential collaborators. Pretoria offered them a packet of economic, technical, and military incentives to encourage them to cooperate with South Africa (soft loans to and a transport agreement with Malawi; a trade mission and the Ingwavuma land deal with

Swaziland). Angola, Mozambique, and Zimbabwe were classified as the principal adversaries, and accordingly subjected to destabilisation tactics on a much greater scale than previously. In addition to categorisation of antagonistic states, Pretoria's strategists concentrated on two immediate objectives: concluding bilateral anti-subversion treaties and thwarting attempts to reduce economic dependence on South Africa.

To this end Pretoria made use of all its tools of destabilisation. Economic blackmail was applied by withholding customs-union payments, closing the borders with Lesotho, and a trade and locomotive war with Zimbabwe. Military intervention took the form of Operations Protea and Askari in Angola and air raids against Matola, Maseru, and Maputo, and there was support for sabotage actions by dissident groups against transport and infrastructural installations in Matabeleland and Mozambique, and so on.[39]

Initially, this strategy bore fruit on a broad front. The target states were 'softened up'. In some states the already weak basis of power and legitimacy could be further eroded. But the real breakthroughs to coerced peace came in 1984, with Angola and Mozambique.

The Lusaka Accord – the 'Ceasefire and Withdrawal Agreement' between Angola and South Africa – provided, *inter alia*, for the disengagement of both armies in southern Angola, under a joint commission of observers. However, Angola did not bind itself to withhold support from the ANC and SWAPO.[40] Consequently, South African security management regarded this accord as only a partial success or an intermediate step.

With the Nkomati Accord – the 'Agreement on Non-Aggression and Good Neighbourliness' – with Mozambique, for which the US Administration acted as broker, Pretoria realised part of its vision. Despite its official title, the Accord is in effect a mutual anti-subversion pact, in which both sides undertake to deny 'irregular forces or armed bands'[41] any support for violent actions against the neighbouring state, indeed even keep them under strict surveillance. In consequence, the FRELIMO Government requested 800 ANC activists to leave the country, and South Africa sent 1000 RENAMO guerrillas back to Mozambique, apparently fully armed (which was in breach of treaty).

The significance of the Nkomati Accord goes beyond considerations of security and economics. For the first time a frontline state has officially accepted Pretoria's interpretation, not only of the legality of the South African state (which has never been questioned), but also the legitimacy of the current regime, and, hence, that external support for

South African liberation movements is illegal interference in the internal affairs of the Afrikaner republic.[42] The internationally ostracised destabilisation strategy was superseded by agreements binding in international law, whose observance to the letter South Africa can legitimately demand.

Whereas Pretoria saw Nkomati as a breakthrough for its regional policy, Maputo officially interpreted it as a victory for FRELIMO's 'socialist policy of peace' over Pretoria's 'militarism'.[43] In fact, Maputo was hoping for the best in a bad situation. Its freedom of choice is constrained by structural relationships: a distorted colonial economy excessively dependent on South Africa; a set of misguided or poorly implemented economic and state policies; and – above all – Pretoria's destabilisation campaign.[44] It is ironic that Mozambique, a decidedly socialist and anti-racist state, should publicly become the first victim of the South African roll-back. (Only after the signing of the Nkomati Accord did it become known that South Africa and Swaziland had signed a secret treaty on collaboration against 'terrorism and subversion' in 1982.)

In mid-1984 South Africa appeared to be on the verge of success. It was in the process of winning an internal guerrilla war. Simultaneously, southern Africa appeared to be entering the age of the Pax Pretoriana – albeit coerced. The Afrikaner empire stretched from the Cape to the Zambian copper-belt. 'But it is a defensive empire, eschewing innovation, new concepts or new ideas; its sole purpose is to create the external conditions necessary to maintain the status quo within South Africa itself'.[45]

Peaceful coexistence without peace

The hope of a golden age of peace and prosperity in southern Africa proved deceptive. By mid-1984 all parties involved – including the *verligte* Afrikaners – were sobering up. Nkomati was to prove to be not the end but the beginning of Afrikaner neo-colonialism. For, Pretoria's security managers felt South Africa's hegemony would still be at risk unless the following conditions were fulfilled. Firstly, the Nkomati Accord needed to be complemented by a change in power relationships in Mozambique – in the maximal case a government of 'national unity', that is, a FRELIMO/RENAMO coalition. From such a government Pretoria expected recognition of its 'homeland' policy (something Samora Machel had continued to refuse even after Nkomati) and recognition of Pretoria as guarantor of Mozambique's internal stability. Secondly, South Africa needed agreements with the other regional states modelled on the Nkomati Accord. As President Masire put it shortly after the signing of the Nkomati Accord, 'South Africa is bullying us all to signing accords like that'.[46] In plausible cases (Angola) these agreements should also pave the way for satellite governments of national unity. Thirdly, should the first two conditions prove unattainable, the least costly alternative would be strategic buffer-zones or satrapies as in south Lebanon (especially in southern Angola, Matabeleland and southern Mozambique). At the very least the white minority regime wanted to secure a right of veto in the region in all cases in which it felt its – broadly defined – survival endangered. Finally, in the long term a neo-colonial empire was necessary to render the costly destabilisation strategy superfluous: instead of direct military intervention, indirect economic rule. The common denominator of these conditions is a constellation of states in a new guise – a *de facto* Bantustanisation of the black periphery.

The next stage of imperial expansion began with a double breach of treaty. The Lusaka ceasefire agreement of 1984 with Angola was shortlived. By 1985 the South African security establishment no longer made any pretence of observing it. The South African units in Angola had withdrawn after some delay and only temporarily. Cross-border operations were resumed in September 1985; in December 1985 four SADF battalions crossed into Cunene province – as a pre-emptive action against SWAPO's annual campaign as well as to give UNITA support against combined Angolan-Cuban attacks. By May 1986 the military situation in Namibia and Angola was, in the opinion of the South African Commander of the SWATF, Maj-Gen. George Meiring, back to what it had been before Operation Askari in 1983.[47] Furthermore, in late 1987 the SADF had to help UNITA fend off a combined Angolan-Cuban offensive. It was South Africa's most extensive intervention, involving the greatest number of casualties since 1975. 'The South African military won the battle of Mavinga but are not winning the Angolan war.'[48]

The Nkomati Accord with Mozambique was soon not worth the paper it was written on either. 'Far from bringing peace, the Accord brought an escalation in the war.'[49] RENAMO extended its activities to include 'hard and soft targets' throughout the country,[50] in intermittent attempts to invade, or at least isolate, Maputo. In consequence the country's economic and administrative disintegration has accelerated; in certain regions it is difficult to distinguish between guerrilla activity and banditry. Nkomati has also led to an internationalisation of support for RENAMO. Malawi and Swaziland serve increasingly as rear bases, and recently RENAMO has extended its operations into eastern Zimbabwe. After Mozambican and Zimbabwean troops had captured RENAMO's headquarters in Gorongoza, the South African Foreign Minister, Pik Botha, had to concede 'technical violations'[51] of the Nkomati Accord.

Contrary to speculation, these breaches of treaty did not reflect the government's loss of control over the security apparatus. They were necessary if RENAMO was to obstruct the reopening of the Beira corridor. In other words, Pretoria was using all the means at its disposal to keep Zimbabwe within the South African orbit. 'Ironically, the collapse of Nkomati arose from the very forces which brought it about, support for RENAMO.'[52]

The notorious air and commando raids have not ceased: Gaborone was attacked in June 1985, commando raids on ANC targets in Harare, Gaborone, and Lusaka in May 1986, and against Livingstone in April 1987 (probably for South African domestic consumption).[53] In January 1986 Lesotho was again the victim of border blockades and threats of intervention, until power was seized by a military government prepared to expel all resident members of the ANC. As a *quid pro quo* South Africa lifted the blockade.[54]

South Africa's post-Nkomati policy has brought it closer to its goal of neo-colonial hegemony: Mozambique and Swaziland have signed 'peace accords' with South Africa; Namibia is still governed by South Africa; the Mugabe government is faced with two South African supported dissident movements, Super-ZAPU and RENAMO; against their will Zimbabwe, Botswana and Lesotho have agreed to cooperate with South Africa in security matters, though such cooperation does not have the import in international law of the Nkomati Accord.

The result is that all frontline states bordering on South Africa no longer tolerate any operations by South African liberation movements against South Africa from their territory. South African refugees are kept under strict surveillance, and, in security matters, these countries have, for different reasons, taken to cooperating with South African organs.

This coerced rapprochement has had considerable consequences for all parties concerned. The relationship between the ANC and the frontline states worsened immediately after Nkomati, but has normalised since 1985. Apparently, the FRELIMO government had not consulted the ANC prior to signing, 'and the conditions of ANC's future operation (and expulsion) ... proved rather "uncomradely", as one observer described it.'[55] The regional states have promised the ANC moral, political and diplomatic support, but the fact remains: 'No one could possibly pretend that the accord has not adversely affected our freedom to operate ... (*our*) facilities have been seriously restricted, and some spheres totally withdrawn.'[56] ANC Secretary-General Alfred Nzo implicitly compared Mozambique with a bantustan, and the ANC commented: 'Further accords concluded as they are with the regime ... cannot but help to perpetuate the illegitimate rule of the South African white settler minority.'[57]

The frontline states have had to learn two extremely painful lessons. The liberation struggle in South Africa will be far more protracted than they had assumed, and the South African hegemonial policy may result in a roll-back on a broad front, even in the recolonisation of the subcontinent. In consequence, these states have had to redefine their own security policies and formulate a 'new' liberation strategy, which may be tantamount to a gradual withdrawal of frontline support for the liberation movements. The consolidation of their own security and independence has become the keystone of their policies. Although the leaders of the frontline states ritually declare their 'total and unqualified commitment'[58] to the liberation struggle, at the same time they emphasise with increasing urgency their hope of peaceful change – and the fact that the struggle must not only be led by black South Africans but also from 'within their own country'.[59]

Nonetheless, Pretoria has not achieved all its objectives. Despite enormous pressure, the regional states, with the exception of Mozambique and Swaziland, have refused to form non-aggression pacts with South Africa on the Nkomati model. In view of Pretoria's manic desire for international legitimation, its security managers must regard this as a shortcoming, which needs to be overcome by any means possible.

ETHNIC POWER MOBILISED: LIMITATIONS AND CONTRADICTIONS

Afrikanerdom in disarray

An immanent weakness of all approaches to social engineering – including that of the South African security establishment – is the assumption that political realities can be shaped unilaterally and to fit a preconceived grand design. Unfortunately, chronic domestic and regional racial problems do not lend themselves to instant, simplistic solutions. Furthermore, in the long run such 'solutions' are not infrequently counterproductive. South Africa's may well fall into this category. The recolonisation of the region is intended to serve the survival of Afrikanerdom, yet increasingly jeopardises it. The obvious helplessness of black Africa has deprived black South Africans of any hope of being liberated by others. The conviction has grown that they are masters of their own fate. The double triumph of Afrikaner nationalism in 1984 – Nkomati and the new Constitution – mobilised black nationalism to greater resistance than ever before. Even before P. W. Botha had been elected State President the white army had to be deployed to crush an incipient civil war. Pretoria's 'indirect rule' in the black townships collapsed, and P. W. Botha's moderate black middle class helped the ANC to re-emerge as a major political force inside the 'laager'. Pretoria's regional strategy resulted, directly or indirectly, in the re-importation of the liberation movements – that is, in rising costs of privilege maintenance.[60] Even more dangerous for an ethno-policy, the ethnic power mobilisation has led to signs of erosion within the white tribe. Paradoxically, just as the ruling Afrikaner power elite succeeded in rallying growing numbers of the anglophone community behind it,[61] it traumatically split Afrikanerdom. Right-wing dissidents denounced P. W. Botha's 'adapt or die' as 'adapt and die', whereas left-wing dissidents – 'the critical moralists'[62] – demanded not the modernisation but the abolition of apartheid. This second group, comprising PFP politicians, leading clergymen and businessmen, and Afrikaner students, has developed a parallel or alternative foreign policy to Pretoria's 'Total Regional Strategy'. They want to work out together with the prohibited ANC the outlines of post-apartheid society.[63] But for the time being Afrikaner power is gathered around the loyal security apparatus, loyally determined to ensure unbroken Afrikaner dominance. Hence, the significance of the new dissidents should not be exaggerated.[64]

However, their existence alone may be enough to promote an 'aligned' *volks*group, united by growing fears of survival and an extreme need for security. Such group situations are characterised by, to use the apposite psychological term, 'pathological learning'. Regardless of the reality, (inter-) national reality is perceived only as threat. Selective perception can lead to an extreme pattern of autistic[65] communication, in which the environment, as it exists in the group's 'own world', is increasingly divorced from reality. With time the group lapses into a vicious circle, which renders self-correction of its perception and its actions increasingly difficult, if not impossible. The smaller, more self-centred, and isolated a group is, the greater the probability that its distorted perceptions will produce autistic behaviour. Afrikanerdom and the Afrikaner power elite fulfil these conditions. Conflicts in an autistic system generate a degree of violence which is out of all proportion to the actual behaviour of the 'opponent' (who has to be perceived as 'the enemy'). Conflict can then be comprehended only in terms of aggressive self-dynamism which has to be unloaded both inwardly and outwardly.

The results of empirical studies in South Africa indicate that such a development is not pure speculation. In 1986 80 per cent of responding white voters were of the opinion that 'a serious Communist threat against South Africa' exists, 70.9 per cent thought that 'the government of Zimbabwe constitutes a threat to South Africa's safety', and 81.6 per cent felt 'that SA should militarily attack terrorist bases in its neighbouring states'.[66] The conclusion to be drawn is that 'the vast majority of white South Africans seem to share the government's perception of a serious Communist threat . . . [*and*] . . . the overall impression is that of a decidedly militant or "hawkish" white voting public'.[67]

The dialectics of Afrikaner neocolonialism

The outwardly-directed Total Regional Strategy is just as ambivalent (and perhaps counterproductive) as the inwardly-directed Total National Strategy. At times it is argued that Pretoria's regional strategy is merely crisis management without a grand design. By and large, this is an unfair criticism. Certainly, strategic thinkers in the SSC have devoted a great deal of energy to devising a winning strategy for the undeclared war in the region.[68] Both cooperation and destabilisation have a purpose: the dominance of Afrikanerdom.

However, there are serious differences between the military and the politicians within the SSC, between the SSC and the business community, and even within the business community.[69] The reason is obvious: Pretoria's vacillation between the two regional options, between the two poles of stabilisation and destabilisation, is an expression of an insoluble contradiction. The cooperation strategy is based by and large on the presumption of social stability, security, and economic confidence in the region. These conditions are necessary for low-risk, profitable trade and investment. Destabilisation produces the exact opposite: social instability, insecurity and an unfavourable economic climate.

As even the military command assume that the conflicts in southern Africa are primarily political, not military, under most circumstances the security establishment favour the strategy of neo-colonial cooperation (even if 'going soft' is generally unpopular in the white community): 'Direct intervention is always expensive in both economic and political terms, and thus is reserved for extreme situations ...'[70] Methods short of direct intervention are generally preferred. Indirect rule by economic imperialism is quieter, cheaper, and more effective than military intervention. The strategy of destabilisation is at best a 'second-best' option. Its pursuit is a sign of Pretoria's weakness, not strength.

As a rule, grand designs are expensive and Pretoria's art of the impossible is in danger of systematically overestimating its own strength. Economically it is hardly in a position to solve its own problems of (under-) development, let alone those of the entire region. 'In short, serious domestic employment creation and simultaneous external development aid preclude each other.'[71] In military terms, South Africa is restricted to *blitzkrieg* and hit-and-run operations. As Johnson recognised in 1977, on account of its small manpower base, the South African army dare not risk any long-term or wide-ranging intervention, for this could result in overstretched lines, or worse, a Vietnam on the doorstep.[72]

The grand design of a hegemonial constellation is not only impossible, it has produced its own counter-constellation: SADCC. Already in 1980 the regional states had formulated a double strategy. Regional cooperation should help mobilise the economic and military potential of the black subcontinent and gradually reduce dependence on South Africa. In view of the heterogeneity of the member states, it is doubtful whether SADCC could have emerged and survived without the pressure exerted by South Africa. South Africa's destabilisation strategy has imposed high costs on SADCC members.[73] But it has not succeeded in breaking SADCC or in making its own constellation more attractive. On the contrary, at the 1985 Arusha Summit seven member states reiterated their support for sanctions. Two (Malawi and Swaziland) remained silent, but did not dissent. As was to be expected, the decisions could not be implemented. At the 1987 Gaborone summit the group was unable to agree on a binding sanctions package.[74] Notwithstanding this: 'The dream of regional economic liberation, which the regional total strategy was intended to kill, lives on and is pursued by SADCC at least as determinedly as in 1980.'[75] The strenuous, international efforts to repair the regional transport network and the collaboration to protect it are signs of a new quality in the politics of regional cooperation.

Even worse than non-fulfilment of Pretoria's visions would be their fulfilment. Governments of 'national unity' are, by experience, costly to maintain: dissident movements are much cheaper as protégés than as subsequent partners. As regimes they normally lack legitimation and stability; it is doubtful whether their protectors gain many benefits. 'They can promise their patrons heaven and earth, but are rarely capable of delivering the goods. In some places, puppets change their political taste after having been helped to power by the patrons.'[76] The new government in Lesotho is a case in point;[77] and UNITA, given its long anti-apartheid tradition, is possibly another.

Finally, Pretoria's strategy of destabilisation has increasingly isolated it and internationalised the conflict, but not, ironically, provoked greater Cuban–Soviet involvement in the region, contrary to what Pretoria had apparently anticipated.[78] The USSR welcomed – albeit reluctantly – the Nkomati Accord, and under Gorbachev has continued its cautious policy of limited involvement. The Kremlin has perceived that Moscow's role has begun to change substantially. Far from being a revolutionary power, it has become a counter-revolutionary one; but this development has not yet been worked out within the ideological context. Equally unanticipated by Pretoria, its strategy provided the USA and the Western world with grounds for sanctions. In addition, certain former colonial powers (including France, Portugal and the United Kingdom) have realised that frontline black Africa is too poorly armed to meet the South African threat (and is, thus, also a potential market)[79] – a development summed up with foresight years ago by E. Pisani, a member of the EC Commission: 'This game of building-up and blowing-up must be stopped.'[80]

CONCLUSION

The achievements of Pretoria's regional policy over the past decade may be summarised in three points.

Johnson's prognosis that black Africa would not be able to destabilise the white state has proved correct. If anything, the Afrikaner empire has turned the clock back in the 1980s, stepping, as it were, into the shoes of British imperialism. Through a strategy of buying time Pretoria has created a regional constellation which assures the white tribe survival, privilege, and dominance, albeit at growing social and moral cost.

Internally, white ascendancy can be maintained only through a state of emergency and growing militarisation of society. Within the region the white garrison state has won many battles but not yet decided the war. The consequences of South Africa's regional policy in recent years reaffirm two simple but bitter truths: one-sided 'solutions' to conflicts do not solve but aggravate conflict in the longer term; and violent means serve, at best, to control but not to solve social conflicts. The bitterness will remain as long as the South African regime treats only the symptoms and not the cause: the system of legalised racism, apartheid.

Notes

1. Cf. R. W. Johnson, *How Long Will South Africa Survive?*, London, Macmillan, 1977, pp. 287ff.
2. President Botha's justification is revealing: 'There were times in the history of nations when a choice between unpleasant alternatives was inevitable ... The choice was between war and a dishonourable fearful peace ... The decision to announce a State of Emergency represented such a choice.' *Africa Contemporary Record* (ACR), 18, 1985/86, New York 1987, p. B 800.
3. The Afrikaans word for 'black', one of a number of adjectives used in conjunction with 'gevaar' (danger, peril), – 'Swart Gevaar' – to form phrases connoting menace, usually insidious and often conspiratorial, to *traditional values or the survival of the volk*. Other examples in the following paragraph are *Rooms* = Roman (Catholic), *Engels* = English, and *rooi* = Red.
4. Jaster, 'South Africa's Narrowing Security Options', in Robert Jaster (ed.), *Southern Africa: Regional Security Problems and Prospects*, Aldershot, Gower, 1985, p. 72.
5. Ibid.
6. Cf. Deon Geldenhuys, *The Diplomacy of Isolation: South African Foreign Policy Making*, New York, St Martin's Press, 1984.
7. According to Seegers, 'The Defense Amendment Bill of 1984 ... states that the SADF is to be used for defense against external attack, the prevention and suppression of terrorism and internal disorder and, significantly, the preservation of life, health, and property and the maintenance of essential services'. Annette Seegers, 'Apartheid's Military: Its Origins and Development', in Wilmot G. James (ed.), *The State of Apartheid*, Boulder, Colorado, Lynne Rienner, 1987, p. 159.
8. See Chapters 5 and 13 for more detail on the SSC.
9. This applies to the army as a whole. 'It is clear that the UDF (Union Defence Force) by the 1960s and later was an Afrikanerized institution. In

1974, for example, 85 percent of the army PF (Permanent Force) was Afrikaans speaking, compared to 75 percent in the Air Force and 50 per cent in the navy.' Annette Seegers, 'Apartheid's Military', op. cit., p. 148.

10. This group is not, nor ever has been, monolithic. Conflicts between 'doves' and 'hawks' over power and responsibility may well be the rule, not the exception. But these are conflicts over ways and means of maintaining ethnic supremacy, not over the end itself. That the end enjoys unanimous approval is made thoroughly clear in Afrikaans literature. Cf. Stanley Uys, 'Whither the White Oligarchy?', in Jesmond Blumenfeld (ed.), *South Africa in Crisis*, London, Croom Helm, 1987, pp. 59ff.
11. Richard John Neuhaus, *Dispensations. The Future of South Africa as South Africans See It*, Grand Rapids, Michigan, Eerdmans, 1986, p. 69.
12. For instance, in the Defence Advisory Council (DAC) and in the military-industrial complex. In 1980 members of the DAC included top executives from several top companies: among others, Anglo American (G. Relly, later to become Chairman), Barlow (M. Rosholt, Chairman), Sanlam (F. J. du Plessis, later to become Chairman), Old Mutual (J. G. van der Horst, Chairman), SA Breweries (D. Goss, Managing Director), Gencor, Volkskas, Tongaat, Anglovaal, Standard Bank, and Nedbank; cf. Joseph Hanlon, *Beggar Your Neighbours*, London, Catholic Institute for International Relations, 1986, p. 14. At the centre of the military-industrial complex is ARMSCOR. ARMSCOR has an annual turnover of R2.200 millions, employs 23 000, and has 1000 private contractors working for it; cf. *ACR*, 18, op. cit., p. B 804.
13. According to Tony Bloom, Chairman of the Premier group (quoted in Stanley Uys, 'Whither the White Oligarchy?', op. cit., p. 70), most anglophone businessmen voted for the tricameral parliament, most welcomed the imposition of a state of emergency, not many support the call for the release of Nelson Mandela, and even fewer want the ANC unbanned.
14. The government defines what is legitimate political opposition and what is subversion and, therefore, is able to control opposition to both itself and its policies. The situation of the white minority state is the converse of that of the black resistance: the former is strong on organisation and weak on legitimation, the latter strong on legitimation and weak on organisation.
15. 'The Defence Minister, Gen. Magnus Malan, dismissed as "nonsense" any idea of a conventional attack on SA. But highly unlikely as such an attack was in the foreseeable future, he added that if it did eventuate, the SA Defence Force was fully capable of repelling it.' *ACR*, 18, op. cit., p. B 802.
16. Deon Geldenhuys, *The Constellation of Southern African States and the Southern African Development Coordination Council: Towards a New Regional Stalemate?*, Johannesburg, South African Institute for International Affairs, 1981, p. 3.
17. Cf. M. Tamarkin, 'South Africa's Regional Options: Policy Making and Conceptual Environment', *International Affairs Bulletin*, 7, 1983, p. 55.
18. Reginald H. Green and Carol B. Thompson, 'Political Economies in Conflict: SADCC, South Africa and Sanctions', in Phyllis Johnson and

David Martin (eds), *Destructive Engagement*, Harare, Zimbabwe Publishing House, 1986, p. 246.

19. Heribert Adam and Kogila Moodley, 'Interstate Relations under South African Dominance', in Wilmot G. James (ed.), *The State of Apartheid*, op. cit., p. 179.
20. At least 50 to 60 per cent of the trade of Malawi, Zambia, and Zimbabwe and 80 to 100 per cent of that of Botswana, Lesotho, and Swaziland goes through the South African transport system. In 1982 South Africa took approximately 17 per cent of total exports of the nine member states of SADCC and provided nearly 22 per cent of their imports. By comparison, total intra-SADCC trade was only about 5 per cent of total SADCC trade. There are roughly 300 000 (1986) citizens of black neighbouring states employed on contract within South Africa (140 000 workers from Lesotho, 69 000 from Mozambique, 30 000 from Malawi, 28 000 from Botswana, 22 000 from Swaziland, and 7 500 from Zimbabwe). In addition, perhaps as many as 700 000 'illegals' from neighbouring states are believed to be working in South Africa at any given time. Cf. United States Information Service, *South Africa Advisory Committee Report, Special File*, 11 February 1987, pp. 46f. Accordingly, the economic and infrastructural dependence of the individual target states varies considerably, ranging from the 'captivity' of Lesotho, Swaziland, and Botswana through the 'moderate' dependency of Mozambique, Zimbabwe, and Zambia, to the virtual economic independence of Angola and Tanzania. For an analysis of these dependencies cf. Gavin G. Maasdorp, 'Squaring up to Economic Dominance: Regional Patterns', in Robert I. Rotberg *et al* (eds), *South Africa and Its Neighbours*, Lexington, Massachusetts, Lexington Books, 1985, pp. 91ff.
21. Reginald H. Green and Carol B. Thompson, 'Political Economies in Conflict', op. cit., p. 246.
22. For details cf. Joseph Hanlon, *Beggar Your Neighbours*, op. cit., pp. 61f.
23. Almost all of South Africa's merchandise exports go to southern Africa as South Africa is not competitive in the markets of industrialised countries.
24. 'South Africa is the foremost source of imported maize and other foodstuffs, especially for Botswana, Lesotho, Swaziland and SWA/Namibia.' Erich Leistner, 'South Africa's Agricultural Interaction with Africa', *Africa Insight*, 17/2, 1987, p. 97.
25. Cf. *The Economist*, 305, no. 7521, 24 October 1987, pp. 93f.
26. In recent years the number of (contracted) migrant workers from black Africa has been declining, from 441 000 in 1972 to approximately 300 000 in 1986, mainly because of mechanisation, the lengthy recession, and substitution by 'homeland' migrant workers. Cf. Fion de Vletter, 'Recent Trends and Prospects of Black Migration to South Africa', *The Journal of Modern African Studies*, 23, p. 672, and n. 19 above.
27. Reginald H. Green and Carol B. Thompson, 'Political Economies in Conflict', op. cit., p. 247.
28. Ibid., p. 246.
29. In 1985 South Africa's annual $2200–2500 million surplus on trade in goods and non-factor services with SADCC states exceeded South

Africa's total current account surplus for that year. Cf. United States Information Service, *South Africa Advisory Committee Report*, op. cit., p. 247.

30. 'Rural Insurgency and Counter-measures', in Mike Hough (ed.), *Revolutionary Warfare and Counter-Insurgency*, Institute for Strategic Studies, Pretoria 1984, pp. 40ff.
31. 'For BLS the customs union simply means money; for South Africa it means protectionism, markets, and industrial dominance of the region.' Joseph Hanlon, *Beggar Your Neighbours*, op. cit., pp. 87f.
32. For details cf. Phyllis Johnson and David Martin, *South Africa Imposes Sanctions Against Its Neighbours*, United Nations Centre Against Apartheid, Notes and Documents 6/87, May 1987.
33. The SWATF was formed in 1980 (after the United Nations' Resolution 435 had been passed); *Koevoet* (crowbar) is the most notorious of the unconventional units. It has been transferred from the South African Police (SAP) to the 'South West African Police'. Number 32 Battalion is a black mercenary force led by white officers of the South African Permanent Force and white mercenaries. Members have been recruited from UNITA, the FNLA, and among black Mozambicans (*Flechas*). Number 44 Battalion consists chiefly of ex-Rhodesian Light Infantry (RLI). Cf. Peter Manning and Reginald H. Green, 'Namibia: Preparations for Destabilization', in Phyllis Johnson and David Martin (eds), *Destructive Engagement*, op. cit., pp. 126f.
34. Steven Metz, 'The Mozambique National Resistance and South African Foreign Policy', *African Affairs*, 85, October 1986, p. 492.
35. For instance, UNITA draws its support from the Ovimbundu, who make up about one-third of the Angolan population. RENAMO was, for a long time, little more than the extended arm of first the Rhodesian and then the South African secret service, but has taken to exploiting the growing dissatisfaction of the Mozambican population. Cf. Allen Isaacman, 'Mozambique and the Regional Conflict in Southern Africa', *Current History*, May 1987, pp. 213ff.
36. According to *Africa Research Bulletin* (ARB): 'The Swazi killings are the most recent of a series of assassinations, kidnap attempts, bomb explosions, and cross-border raids into neighbouring states such as Botswana and Lesotho and in countries further afield such as Zambia and even Britain in which more than 300 ANC cadres are believed to have lost their lives, according to a recent estimate by Mr Mike Hough, a security analyst at Pretoria University.' *ARB*, Political Series, 15 August 1987, p. 8577.
37. South Africa accounts for about 66 per cent of total military expenditure in the region. Cf. *The Military Balance 1986–7*, London, International Institute for Strategic Studies, 1986, pp. 113ff. This figure is exclusive of security expenditures for the police, secret services, etc.
38. Cf. Robert Davies, *South African Strategy Towards Mozambique in the Post-Nkomati Period*, Uppsala, Scandinavian Institute for African Studies, 1985, pp. 12ff., upon which this section is based.
39. For excellent documentations of the South African strategy of destabilisation see Phyllis Johnson and David Martin (eds), *Destructive Engagement*, op. cit.; Joseph Hanlon, *Beggar Your Neighbours*, op. cit.

40. Angola was able to bargain from a position of relative strength, owing to the presence of Cuban troops and sufficient liquidity from oil and diamonds.
41. For the text of the Accord see: *ARB*, Political Series, 1–31 March, 1984, pp. 7166ff. The accord raises questions with far-reaching consequences for Mozambique, especially with respect to its membership in the Liberation Committee of the OAU. Cf. Winrich Kühne, *Südafrika und seine Nachbarn: Durchbruch zum Frieden?*, Nomos Verlagsgesellschaft, Baden-Baden, 1984.
42. The US Under-Secretary of State for African Affairs, Chester Crocker, who was closely involved in the negotiations, emphasised these consequences when he said: 'Nkomati brings for the first time in Southern Africa the observance of OAU principles.' *Guardian*, 20 July 1984.
43. Quoted in Robert Davies, *South African Strategy*, op. cit., p. 17. The FRELIMO Government went as far as to interpret the Nkomati Accord in the tradition of the Lusaka Peace Agreement of 1974, which sealed the fate of Portuguese colonial rule in Africa, and the Lancaster House Agreement of 1979, which heralded majority rule in Zimbabwe – as though the Nkomati Accord were of comparable import for the white minority government in South Africa.
44. Cf. Allan Isaacman, 'Mozambique and the Regional Conflict', op. cit., p. 213.
45. Theodor Hanf, 'Konflikte im südlichen Afrika', in Hans-Peter Schwarz and Karl Kaiser (eds), *Weltpolitik: Strukturen – Akteure – Perspektiven*, Bonn, Bundeszentrale für politische Bildung, 1985, p. 660.
46. *The Star*, 16 March 1984.
47. *The Star*, 30 May 1986.
48. *Africa Confidential*, 28/23, 18 November 1987.
49. Joseph Hanlon, *Beggar Your Neighbours*, op. cit., p. 145.
50. The climax of its activities so far has been the Homoine massacre in July 1987, which claimed over 400 civilian victims. Cf. *ARB*, Political Series, 15 September 1987, p. 8591. This incident recalls the Wyviamu massacre by Portuguese troops in the final days of colonial rule.
51. These 'technical violations' include South African deliveries of arms and other supplies to RENAMO *after* the signing of the Accord and – as proved by documents found in the Gorongoza base – regular meetings between RENAMO and South African officials, among them three visits to Gorongoza by Minister Botha's deputy, Louis Nel, in Summer 1985. Cf. *ACR*, 18, 1985/86, pp. A 25f.
52. Peter Vale, 'Regional Policy: The Compulsion to Incorporate', in Jesmond Blumenfeld (ed.), *South Africa in Crisis*, op. cit. p. 187.
53. Apparently, fear of the extreme right provoked P. W. Botha into a demonstration of strong-arm tactics in the run-up to the May 1987 elections.
54. Cf. *ACR*, 18, 1985/86, op. cit., p. B 654.
55. Heribert Adam and Kogila Moodley, 'Interstate Relations', op. cit., p. 189.
56. Official comment of the South African Communist Party in 'What the

Nkomati Accord Means for Africa', *The African Communist*, 98, 3rd Quarter 1984, p. 11.

57. The ANC's condemnation of the South African–Mozambique agreement, Radio Freedom, Addis Ababa, *Summary of World Broadcasts, Middle East and Africa*, 7595/B-10-12, 19 March 1984.
58. Final communiqué of the meeting of frontline presidents in April 1984, *Supplement to AIM Information Bulletin no. 94*, April 1984, pp. 22ff.
59. Ibid.
60. A regime's undiminished capability of winning direct confrontations should not delude as to its gradual decline.
61. The traditional ethnic divisions in white politics disappeared in the May 1987 elections. For the first time in South African history a substantial majority of English-speakers voted – together with the Afrikaner middle class – for the ruling National Party; the Conservative Party polled some 35 per cent of the Afrikaner vote, mostly blue-collar workers, lower and middle-level bureaucrats and farmers.
62. Heribert Adam and Kogila Moodley, *South Africa Without Apartheid*, Berkeley, California University Press, 1986, pp. 73ff.
63. Cf. for example the various meetings with ANC representatives in Lusaka, *ACR*, 18, op. cit., p. B 787.
64. 'Afrikaner nationalism ... is still capable of commanding extraordinary loyalty and remains a powerful force, even if its institutional embodiments are divided. In fact, the politics of "ethnic outbidding", which occur in situations of organizational disunity, can make nationalism even more intense.' Stanley Uys, 'Whither the White Oligarchy?', op. cit., p. 59.
65. Autism is the term used in psychiatry and behavioural psychology to describe abnormal self-absorption, characterised by lack of response to people, actions, and surroundings and limited ability to communicate. Although customarily used in reference to individual behaviour, usually of children, I think the concept may be applied with advantage to group behaviour.
66. Deon Geldenhuys, *What Do We Think? A Survey of White Opinion on Foreign Policy Issues*, no. 3, Johannesburg, South African Institute of International Affairs, May 1986, pp. 8, 9, and 14. The responses to each of the three statements have been virtually identical in the three surveys since 1982. The values for English-speakers were significantly below average, those for Afrikaner politicians and state bureaucrats significantly above.
67. Deon Geldenhuys, *What Do We Think? A Survey of White Opinion on Foreign Policy Issues*, no. 2, Johannesburg, South African Institute of International Affairs, 1984, pp. 7 and 10.
68. Cf. Kenneth W. Grundy, *The Militarization of South African Politics*, London, Tauris, 1986, p. 94.
69. Export-oriented business and the outward-looking power elite centred around Pik Botha – the 'doves' – favour regional cooperation, the former in the hope of new markets, the latter because the international community is its arena of reference. By contrast, Afrikaner-orientated small business fears imported competition from regional cooperation, and the military 'hawks' believe in the possibility of military solutions to regional conflicts.

70. Steven Metz, 'The Mozambique National Resistance', op. cit., p. 492.
71. Heribert Adam and Kogila Moodley, 'Interstate Relations', op. cit., p. 187. P. W. Botha stressed after Nkomati that South Africa could not play 'Father Christmas' to Mozambique, that he was depending on private capital. But that was not available due to recession and financial sanctions. ASSOCOM's proclaimed 'business safaris' up to 'the equator' did not materialise. Cf. Joseph Hanlon, *Beggar Your Neighbours*, op. cit., p. 40.
72. Despite ARMSCOR, the United Nations' arms embargo of 1977 has further weakened the SADF. In the event of lengthier conflicts, logistics and spare parts for certain weapons systems which are essential for successful offensive warfare (helicopters, fighter aircraft, electronic systems) are not guaranteed.
73. According to rough estimates of SADCC, more than 100 000 people have been killed, and more than one million displaced. The financial costs exceed $10 000 million (1980–84). Cf. SADCC memorandum in Joseph Hanlon, *Beggar Your Neighbours*, op. cit., pp. 265ff. An even higher figure – $12 940 million – is given in, *Children on the Frontline: A Report for UNICEF*, New York, 1987, p. 32.
74. The strongest proponents of sanctions – within the Commonwealth as well – are Tanzania, Zambia and Zimbabwe. However, in July 1987 the Zimbabwean Cabinet rejected Prime Minister Mugabe's suggestions for trade sanctions: 'There will now be no high-profile government policy of imposing sanctions', *The Economist Intelligence Unit Country Report: Zimbabwe, Malawi*, no. 4, 1987, p. 4.
75. *ACR*, 18, 1985/86, op. cit., p. 114.
76. M. Tamarkin, 'South Africa's Regional Options', op. cit., p. 67.
77. It has refused to conclude a Nkomati-type agreement, remained committed to SADCC, maintained its diplomatic relations with the socialist bloc, and continued to support sanctions.
78. Pretoria needs a communist bloc in the region, to justify the communist threat, to equate neo-apartheid with the defence of Western Christian values, and to obtain Western support as an anti-communist bastion. Cf. Robert Price, 'Pretoria's Southern African Strategy', *African Affairs*, 83, 1984, p. 25.
79. Apart from regional security cooperation – between Zimbabwe, Mozambique, Malawi, and Tanzania – bilateral cooperation agreements exist between Angola and France (helicopter gunships), Angola and Spain (military advisers), Zimbabwe and the United Kingdom (military advisers), and Mozambique and the USA (non-lethal military equipment). The gradual rapprochement between Angola and Mozambique and the West (membership of the Lomé Convention, World Bank, and IMF) must be seen in this context.
80. Quoted in Winrich Kühne, 'Ein Damoklesschwert hängt über dem Staat am Kap', *Das Parlament*, 15 August 1987, p. 9.

5 Afrikaner Politics 1977–87: from Afrikaner Nationalist Rule to Central State Hegemony

Hermann Giliomee

INTRODUCTION

In *How Long Will South Africa Survive?*, R. W. Johnson attaches prime importance to internal political developments in assessing future stability. By implication Johnson argued that white rule could extend well into the twenty-first century, as long as the ruling oligarchy remained unified, was prepared to use severe repression, and avoided risky military adventures across its borders. In his 1977 study Johnson expected that the oligarchy would become more united and hence better able to resist majority rule.

Johnson's perspectives on stability in South Africa accord with observations made on a general or theoretical level about revolutions. Both activists and scholars are virtually unanimous in stressing ruling group cohesion and adaptability as a crucial variable in the maintenance of coercive systems. The two master revolutionaries, Trotsky and Lenin, agreed about this. High up on Trotsky's list of the required elements for a revolution is a ruling class which has lost faith in itself, is torn by conflicts between groups and cliques, is incapable of practical action, and rests its hopes on miracles and miracle workers.[1] First among Lenin's requirements is a nationwide crisis characterised by splits and conflicts within the ruling class and its regime over how to resolve its dilemmas.[2]

The various generations of theories about revolutions have likewise identified ruling-group disintegration as a critical variable. In an early generalisation Crane Brinton identified the alienation of ruling-class intellectuals as a recurring phenomenon in regimes which were overthrown by revolution. According to Brinton, alienation repeatedly manifested itself in a declining sense of destiny and superiority, feelings of guilt over privileges, and a general loss in self-confidence.[3] The next generation of studies on revolution also highlighted the performance of the ruling elite. Eckstein's 1965 work on what he calls internal wars contends that a sufficient explanation of the occurrence of many internal wars might be found in elite characteristics alone. Even a relatively weak popular opposition may overthrow a ruling elite which is torn by conflicts, reluctant to use force, and lacking in political skills. Some theories even maintain that elite characteristics are so decisive that one can practically ignore the quality of the insurgents in accounting for the outbreak of revolutions.[4]

This theme is reiterated in the most recent analyses which constitute the 'third generation' of writings on revolution.[5] The work of Theda Skocpol has been particularly influential. While giving more attention than previous studies to international pressures and changes in the world system, Skocpol singles out as being of critical importance the capacity of the state to respond to challenges. In relatively autonomous states what matters most is, in Skocpol's terms, the support and acquiescence not of the popular majority of society but of particularly powerful and mobilised groups, invariably including the regime's own cadres. Even after a great loss of legitimacy a state can remain quite stable if its coercive organisations (the army, police and civil bureaucracy) remain coherent and effective, and if they are in harmony with the state apparatus as a whole and the dominant class forces.[6]

In the ten years since the Soweto uprising of 1976 activists and observers of the South African scene have paid special attention to the cohesion of the ruling group as the decisive factor in assessing the durability of the state. Samuel Huntington, in a 1981 article on stability on South Africa, articulated this perspective succinctly:

> It seems likely that a minority-dominated hierarchical ethnic system in South Africa will become increasingly difficult to maintain . . . Revolutionary violence does not have to be successful to be effective. It simply has to create sufficient trouble to cause divisions among the dominant group over the ways to deal with it. At this point, one of the three stanchions [white political unity] of the existing system begins to disappear, and the ability of the government ruthlessly to apply its instruments of coercion becomes compromised.[7]

The extent to which ruling-group cohesion occupies the mind of the African National Congress (ANC) leadership became clear to me personally in a July 1987 conference in Dakar, Senegal where a group of internal South Africans met with a delegation of the ANC. The ANC delegates did not expect a military victory in conventional terms. Instead they believed that continued pressure through an ANC-orchestrated 'people's war' would bring about a loss of morale among whites and fatal political splits in the ruling Afrikaner group and in the security forces. In similar terms Stanley Uys, doyen of political journalists, in mid-1986 anticipated a mighty upwelling of black rage that 'will sap and haemorrhage the white power structure until it falls in on itself'.[8]

The same perspective is apparent in the work of some academic observers. Towards the end of 1986 the University of Witwatersrand political scientist Mark Swilling remarked that major white interests had become alienated and that signs of significant disaffection were evident among white business leaders, white students, churches, academics, the press, political parties and even within National Party (NP) circles. It has led Swilling to observe: 'The logical conclusion of the process is a point where the state can no longer govern because the distance between itself and civil society has become unbridgeable.'[9] In his 1987 inaugural address, the historian Colin Bundy calls it 'incontrovertible' that the South African ruling class is experiencing fission and defections. He cites as examples the 1986 decision of the Leader of the Official Opposition to exchange Parliament for extra-parliamentary forums, the meeting of top business elites with the ANC leadership, the defection of pro-regime intellectuals from the National Party, and the continuing emigration of managers and professionals. While noting the loyalty of the security forces despite upheaval and turmoil, Bundy wonders how much of a problem it would be for the state if large sections of the police force identify with forces well to the right of government.[10]

This chapter will investigate the political implications of the divisions which have opened up in the ruling group in the years since Johnson's book appeared, and the extent to which they affect the survival prospects of the South African state.

ROOTS OF WHITE DISUNITY, c. 1970–c. 1987

In 1970 a scholarly analysis could categorically declare:

> The Whites want continued prosperity and continued supremacy, and the government is seeking to secure both of these goals together. The true rationale of apartheid policies is thus to maximise econ-

omic development both for the sake of White prosperity and for the material protection of White supremacy.[11]

The analysis pointed to the fact that income inequality between whites and Africans had grown, real per capita expenditure on African education was less than twenty years before, and African workers were more restricted in movement and organisation than ever before. At the same time, Afrikaner unity, the basis of NP rule, was still intact. No single class within the Afrikaner nationalist movement was clearly seen as sacrificing the other in its own interests, and the government was credibly projecting itself as an even-handed mediator of conflicting Afrikaner, and broader white, interests.

The past fifteen years have seen a steady erosion of undiluted white supremacy and white prosperity. When Johnson's book appeared in 1977, the process was already well advanced, paving the way for both the restructuring of the state and the major black challenge to the state which started in September 1984, and which has not been fully crushed three years later. By such time Afrikaner political unity was lost and the ruling group was much more divided than Johnson had envisaged. The next section will briefly discuss the causes underlying the erosion of white prosperity and supremacy. This will be followed by an analysis of the extent of the divisions and of its implications for political stability.

The declining white demographic base

A main force behind both political reform and growing white disunity is the decline of the white population's demographic base. In South African history from the beginning of the seventeenth to the middle of the twentieth century, the proportion of whites in the overall population was always sufficient to man virtually all the strategic positions in the political, economic, and administrative systems of the country. Whites governed, owned the land, controlled the skilled and most of the semi-skilled jobs, and staffed the top and medium-level positions in the civil service and security apparatus. Between 1910 and 1950 whites constituted just over 20 per cent of the total population. But from then the white proportion started to shrink fairly rapidly. It fell from 20.9 per cent in 1950 to 15 per cent in 1985, and it is projected to decline to 11 per cent by the first decade of the next century. As a result, an acute shortage of white manpower has developed in both the public and private sectors.

By the mid-1970s the apartheid state had come up against its own limits. It had overreached itself in its own spending and administrative capacities, and there were simply not enough whites available to implement the myriad of apartheid laws. The state found itself more and more incapable of stemming the flow of Africans to the cities, and of people of all black groups to some previously all-white residential areas, such as Hillbrow in Johannesburg. Increasingly the government wanted blacks to implement influx control, take over the administration of their own communities, and to supplement the thinly stretched white security forces.

A similar development occurred in the private sector. After the rapid economic growth of the 1960s white workers were unable to satisfy the need for skilled labour. Between 1971 and 1977 white males contributed only a quarter of the increase in skilled employed blue-collar labour (15 600 out of 65 700). Members of the three black groups provided 76 per cent of the increment in artisans and 104 per cent of the increment in semi-skilled blue collar male workers.[12] This skilled-labour shortage, together with spiralling strikes by black workers and overseas pressure, forced the government to embark on a series of labour reforms. It removed the restrictions on the training of blacks and on black participation in collective bargaining, and set up a common industrial relations system. By 1981 a striking change in the racial profile of the labour market had become apparent. The percentage of whites in medium-level manpower had dropped from 82 per cent in 1960 to 65 per cent in 1981. On the other hand, whites still filled 91 per cent of all the top (senior administrative and management) jobs in 1981.[13]

Economic stagnation and redistribution

Another reason for the widening cleavages in white society is the combination of a stagnant economy, state and employer efforts to redistribute wages in favour of blacks, and a growing tax burden. When Johnson's work was published in 1977, South Africa was barely three years into its economic troubles. These troubles, it is now clear, are of a structural nature. Between 1964 and 1974 the Gross Domestic Product grew at approximately 5 per cent per year, but between 1974 and 1984 the rate dropped to below 3 per cent. The causes are complex,[14] as Chapter 6 below makes clear, but among the most important are the declining markets and increasing competition which South African minerals and metals have been experiencing on world markets since the early 1970s (gold and platinum initially were exceptions), the spiralling oil price, rises in black wages which were not accompanied by commensurate increases in productivity, and a restricted market due to apartheid, which kept a large part of the black population outside the formal sector of the economy.

It was from a much expanded economic base (compared to the 1950s), but one which was growing only slowly, that the state and the private sector in the early 1970s embarked on an effort to narrow the large disparities between white and black wages. The disparity had built up over the preceding four or five decades. Wages of African farm workers had stayed static from 1910 to the early 1960s. On the gold mines the cash component of African wages was the same in 1969 as it had been in 1911. In factories the average real wage for an African worker increased by less than 10 per cent between 1948 and 1970, while that of whites rose by 50 per cent in the same period. The efforts to close the racial wage gap were triggered by the 1970 rise in the gold price and the ripple effect of sharp increases in African goldmining wages throughout the labour market. It was given further momentum by strike action by African workers starting in Durban in 1973, and international pressure. In the early 1970s the government also committed itself to narrow, and eventually eliminate, racial discrimination in public sector salaries.

The closing of the wage gap was quite staggering in the goldmining sector. African wages quadrupled between 1971 and 1982 and the ratio of white to African wages fell from 20.9:1 to 5.5:1. On a more modest level the same trend was evident in other sectors – in manufacturing, for instance, the ratio declined from 5.8:1 to 4.1:1 between 1970 and 1980. The white share of total personal income in South Africa fell from 71.7 per cent in 1970 to 61.5 per cent in 1980, while the African share rose from 19.8 per cent in 1970 to 29 per cent in 1980.[15]

For our purposes the important fact is that during this considerable redistribution, white incomes declined. A 1986 Bureau of Market Research survey calculated that between 1972 and 1980 white incomes rose only 0.3 per cent annually, while those of Africans rose 4.7 per cent per year, Coloureds by 1.5 per cent, and Asians by 3 per cent. Between 1975 and 1979 real white wages fell on average by 9.7 per cent, while real African wages rose at roughly the same rate. In the first half of the 1980s the redistribution continued. During the five-year period July 1981 to March 1986, white salary increments lagged behind by 18.9 per cent compared to those of blacks. Another study calculated that between 1980 and 1985 the personal disposable income of whites fell by 17.9 per cent. A combination of declining income, high inflation, and a growing tax burden has caught many whites in a vicious squeeze. In 1985 whites paid on average 15.1 per cent of their incomes in direct tax compared with 8.8 per cent in 1980. Studies showed that in 1986 a person in the middle income category earning R26 000 a year paid three times the level of tax such an income attracted in 1981. The individual taxpayer is increasingly footing the state's bill. In 1981 some 17 per cent of the state's tax revenue came from individuals, but by 1988 this is projected to rise to 34 per cent. Companies appear to be successfully avoiding the tax treadmill. In 1981 company tax represented 41 per cent of the total tax burden, but by 1986 this had dropped to only 22 per cent.[16]

This has set the stage for the sharp white political backlash which has exposed the deep divisions in Afrikaner nationalist ranks. Since the late 1970s the right-wing press and white trade unions have been engaged in a vociferous campaign against redistribution. They gave great prominence to statements by Prime Minister Vorster and other government spokesmen in which this policy was articulated. In 1978 Vorster warned that the abolition of social and economic inequities would demand significant sacrifices in the living standards and material aspirations of whites. In 1981 the Director-General of Finance declared that there would occur a drastic increase of state spending on blacks at the expense of whites. He added that the great claims of blacks on the Treasury with respect to education, housing and public health, would be accompanied by a stagnation of spending on whites until a greater equilibrium was reached. The right-wing press, and in particular *Die Afrikaner*, published expositions of the 'disastrous consequences' of this policy of 'racial equalisation' in the economy. (It was later revealed that the main anonymous contributor was a senior Treasury official.)

These expositions started with the premise that the low wages the private sector paid to black workers compelled the government to pay large housing, transport and food subsidies. The government was prepared to do this since it had forged an alliance with big business, one that was symbolically sealed at the Carlton conference in 1979. The accounts asserted that although whites in 1983 paid 80 per cent of all taxes 'astronomic amounts' were spent on black education, housing, the budgets of the homeland governments, and repairs after riots in black townships. Direct taxes and a 'calculated policy' of inflation, were disastrously eroding the living standards of whites in the middle and lower income categories. The right-wing press also argued that the government was deliberately selling out white civil servants in the low and middle salary categories. It calculated that the average real income of white civil servants had dropped by more than 8 per cent between 1974 and 1983. In 1985 it calculated that, with the government refusing to grant any raises in 1985 and with an anticipated annual inflation rate of between 15 and 20 per cent, the average white civil servant by the beginning of 1986 would be worse off by 20–25 per cent compared to 1974. In contrast, the average real remuneration of black civil servants had increased by more than 59 per cent compared to 1974.[17]

It is obvious that the calculations made by the right-wing press of a drop in income in certain occupations, would vary considerably depending on the periods chosen for comparison. Calculations by academics show that on average the decline in social welfare spending on whites has in fact not been disastrous. The white share dropped from 61 per cent to 56 per cent in 1975/76 and at present is perhaps just above 50 per cent.[18] However, there can be little doubt that whites in the lower half of the income bracket have indeed experienced an erosion in living standards which have strained white unity to an extent that Johnson could not have foreseen in 1977.

The decline of apartheid and white privilege

At the time of his writing, Johnson could not foresee the extent to which apartheid would be watered down. This process had started in the early 1970s when the shortage of white manpower compelled the government to relax some of the restrictions on black labour. At the same time, elements among the Afrikaner nationalist elite began to lose faith in the ability of apartheid to guarantee security and justify white privilege. By eliminating all points of racial friction, apartheid was held, prior to this, as the only policy capable of securing Afrikaner, and larger white, identity and racial peace. As Deborah Posel phrases it: '"Being White" meant being socially and culturally distinct, politically and economically privileged and physically segregated from all those who were not.'[19] But apartheid was more than a variant of white supremacy. It encapsulated the Afrikaners' drive to exert control over their own destiny without, according to Afrikaner nationalist ideological perceptions, denying other nations similar aspirations. Separate homelands were the cornerstone of the ideology. They served three functions: they enabled Africans to enjoy 'separate freedoms', justified discrimination in 'white' South Africa and increased white security by deflecting and splintering black political aspirations.

By the early 1970s it was no longer possible to overlook the deficiency of the homelands as an ideological justification. Nationalist commentators expressed concern. Piet Cillié, editor of *Die Burger*, wrote on 4 July 1970: 'Bantu homelands are the essential cornerstone of our (race) relations policy over the long term. They have fallen by the wayside in our interest and beliefs, which in turn undermine our credibility. We must imbue our policy with idealism and urgency or else our future will become pitch dark.'[20] The removal of the protective belt of white-ruled states on the northern and eastern borders, and the perceived communist-inspired onslaught, gave rise to a search for new ways to underpin white control and security. Phil Weber, an ex-editor of *Die Burger*, declared in a public lecture: 'We cannot fight on the borders and continue to play constable over blacks in our country.'[21]

The restructuring of supremacy based on Afrikaner unity and the new language of domination sprang to an important extent from these security fears. In the course of the 1970s these fears were strongly articulated by the security establishment, and in particular by P. W. Botha as first Minister for Defence and later as Prime Minister and State President. A 'total strategy' against a perceived 'total onslaught' came to be accepted as a more efficient and sophisticated form of securing control for Afrikaner and the larger white group, replacing the homelands policy and an insistence on Afrikaner (and white) exclusivity.[22]

Above all this has meant that state security and development imperatives have taken precedence over narrow ethnic concerns. Coloured, Indian and later also African spokesmen and representatives have been co-opted into common decision-making or consultative structures and given the opportunity to administer their own communities. To justify this, Botha asks rhetorically 'Must I estrange these people, or must I take them with me so that the country's security can be maintained?'[23] Doing away with unilateral white decision-making was only one (but symbolically the most important) aspect of diluting the sense of white superiority and exclusivity. Over the past fifteen years, but particularly in the decade since Johnson's book appeared, the state has backed off in various ways from upholding white privilege and intervening in favour of whites. This period has seen the elimination or narrowing of the racial salary gap in the civil service, the ending of statutory job reservation and a commitment to equalise spending on white and black social services. It has been accompanied by a concerted ideological effort to present the state as natural and impartial, and hence able to mediate conflict, and to persuade the African working class to see the political and economic order as legitimate. A particular theme has been free enterprise rhetoric, which, as Stanley Greenberg phrases it, 'represents an idiom and a bargaining resource that, political leaders hope, will bring closer business–state cooperation and broaden support for the state in society'.[24]

Thus, in the decade since Johnson's book appeared, the NP government has begun to move away from apartheid as the final answer to the political crisis, and has suspended its suspicion of English-speaking big business as a section espousing dangerous liberal tendencies. It has begun to accept forms of racial integration and big business as possible partners in combating the security threats of mass unemployment and acute poverty in the homelands. The deracialisation of the state and the search for new allies have not meant a shift away from domination. While the government has a clear desire to give all groups a say in government (in Afrikaans the untranslateable term *inspraak* is often used), the government equally has no inclination to abandon its power to have the final say. In fact, despite the government's protestations, power has been further centralised in central government's hands and its sense of accountability has even further diminished. In the Constitution of 1983 the Indian and Coloured houses enjoy no effective veto and the government's attempts to restructure the second and third tier of government has seen a further concentration of power in Pretoria's hands.

There is thus a distinct double-edged quality in the constitutional dimension of what can be called 'reform-apartheid'. On the one hand, there is a new willingness among Afrikaner leaders to accept that wealth, opportunities and even decision-making will have to be shared among all the peoples. On the other hand, there is the Afrikaner government's firm conviction that only continued Afrikaner rule can ensure progress along that road. Or to put it differently, the government accepts economic growth, training, job creation and stable food prices as primary goals, but premised on the maintenance of firm control by an Afrikaner leadership.

Despite its continued commitment to Afrikaner rule (but bolstered by co-opted blacks), the NP has lost support to the right-wing parties. This is due both to the decline in white living standards and to the NP sacrificing aspects of Afrikaner nationalist practice and ideology. The Conservative Party (CP) has defined the issue dividing it from the NP in ideological terms: it accuses the NP of betraying the principles of apartheid and the integrity of the *volk*. As *Die Patriot* expressed it in 1982:

> A party once described by Dr Malan as the 'political national front of the Afrikaner' is now visibly associating with the traditional enemy of the Afrikaner, namely Hoggenheimer, to form a relationship against fellow Afrikaners. Such a relationship can destroy the ways of the Afrikaner volk.[25]

RESPONSES TO THE CRISES, 1977–1987

The entry of black workers in the middle levels of the economy, the limited redistribution away from whites and the political and ideological dilution of white supremacy, and black protest action and foreign pressure, have all served to strain white unity. We shall discuss the different white responses briefly below, before analysing the significance of white divisions for the stability of the state.

White worker disaffection

A large section of white workers saw the new system as a direct threat to their traditional privileged position. For the first time since the early 1920s, serious class divisions have opened up within the white group. In the first half of the 1970s the government had given firm assurances to the white workers that they would not be betrayed. In 1972 the Minister for Labour had declared that the NP 'stands between the survival and doom of the white worker, for if the white worker falls, the NP too will fall'.[26] In 1976 Labour Minister Fanie Botha expressed his belief that the white worker had to be protected and that the job reservation clause had to remain on the statute books.[27] In the same year Prime Minister Vorster had stated emphatically that the government would continue to honour its undertakings to the workers.[28]

When the first labour reforms were introduced in 1979 large sections of white labour, spearheaded by the all-white South African Confederation of Labour (SACLA), responded with profound dismay. Not only were white workers feeling the pinch of a loss of real income, but the years of dependence on the state (and on trade unions which had become inefficient bureaucracies) had left many white workers quite unprepared for the new labour dispensation. At present, all-white or predominantly white unions still represent about 500 000 workers who dominate the skilled trades. Two basic postures can be perceived among the white workers. In the one camp, some unions, particularly in the mining and building industries, are seeking to block the deracialisation of industry in every possible way. However, they are confronted with the erosion of their support base. The number of white-only registered unions dropped by a third from 88 in 1972 to 59 in 1984, and their total membership from 240 000 in 1980 to a present figure of below 100 000. This was mainly a result of the defection of unions which, in opposition to the confederation's policy, wished to open their ranks to other races.[29]

The other white labour camp is comprised of the reformists. It includes most of the craft unions and is well reflected in the Confederation of Metal and Building Unions. This camp also faces severe organisational problems. It lacks a national voice following the demise of the Trade Union Council of South Africa (TUCSA), which in 1983 still had 57 affiliates and 508 179 members, but decided to disband in 1986.[30] The new black-dominated unions and federations hold little attraction for white workers. Apart from the traditional racial prejudices there is also a structural reason. The black unions put a premium on democratic worker participation and control of decision-making, while in most white unions sole authority is in the hands of a few officials. As a result few white workers today belong to the high profile trade union federations, which increases their sense of isolation and betrayal. While TUCSA and SACLA had 60 per cent of the economically active labour force as members in 1977, this figure had declined to only 6 per cent in 1987.

Two recent studies show strong white worker resistance to the new order, ranging from resentment over the desegregation of facilities to strong objections to working under blacks. They confirm the impression that widespread fears exist among white workers that, under the new labour order, employers will use cheap labour to undercut white wages, will replace white workers by blacks or will, in response to pressure, practise reverse discrimination by appointing blacks in positions for which they are not qualified.[31] A study conducted in 1985 among a group of forty whites in Pretoria in the artisan and workshop environment, revealed that more than two thirds 'disagreed' or 'definitely disagreed' with the concept of blacks receiving the same training as whites to work in white areas, 62 per cent 'rejected' or 'strongly rejected' accepting blacks as equal in the work situation, 73 per cent 'rejected' or 'strongly rejected' the appointment of a black employee as an equal, one-half felt that white superiors paid too much attention to the demands of blacks, and 53 per cent that blacks were promoted merely to satisfy wider demands with little regard to their ability. Overall, only 20 per cent were 'unconcerned' or 'very unconcerned' with changing labour conditions.[32]

In a 1986 study of employees based on a larger sample of whites, and covering much broader spectra of educational qualifications (Standard 8 to university degrees), job category and salary group, more mixed attitudes were recorded. In general, however, white attitudes to black trade unionism were negative, with 62 per cent having a 'negative' or 'very negative' attitude and only 20 per cent a 'positive' attitude. Many claimed that reverse discrimination was taking place. A negative attitude was 'held' or 'strongly held' by 52 per cent of respondents, with only 25 per cent indicating a 'positive' view of the increasing promotion of blacks up the occupational structure. Consistently those in white collar jobs expressed more liberal views than production workers.[33]

A recent report on a Transvaal industrial shopfloor captures white worker sentiment.

> The present mood of the white working class seems surly and unsettled. White management is rightly introducing racial reform into industry but wrongly imposing it on the white workers who suffer it with silent ill will. The white workers feel that they are being sacrificed on the altar of middle-class morality but there is no one in the establishment they can turn to voice their resentment.[34]

Instead of action on the shop-floor, white workers are increasingly turning to the right-wing political parties and movements. The report speaks of the intensifying class overtones of the campaigns of the right-wing movements, which project the white workers as 'being bled dry' by big business. The writer remarked that even if the majority of the white electorate could be persuaded to accept some form of democracy, it could all come to nought 'if every pit and workshop and turbine hall were controlled by white workers loyal to the AWB (the semi-fascist Afrikaner-Weerstandsbeweging), prepared to resist change with force, and backed by at least the lower ranks of the police and the armed forces'.[35]

The intensifying class conflict within white ranks stands in strong contrast to the mid-1970s, when white labour was one of the strongest pillars of white rule. At the same time the attitudes described above appear to leave little ground for the expectation among some Marxist scholars that tensions produced by capitalist growth will, over the medium to long term, lead to white and black workers joining forces against the capitalist class. At this stage there seems to be no possibility of an alliance of white and black workers aimed at overthrowing the capitalist state.[36] However, one has to be more tentative with respect to another Marxist expectation, that capitalist growth will exacerbate class tensions within the white group, thereby threatening the political cohesion of white supremacy. Instead of action on the shopfloor, white workers are increasingly turning to the right-wing political parties and movements.

White political divisions

The political divisions which manifested themselves in the general elections of 1977, 1981 and 1987 are reflected in Table 5.1.

Table 5.1 Percentage gained of vote at the polls at 1977, 1981 and 1987 general elections

Party and position on spectrum	*1977*	*1981*	*1987*
Right-wing (HNP and CP)	3	14	30
Centre-right (NP)	65	53	57
Centre (NRP and Independents (1987))	12	6	3
Centre-left (PFP)	17	18	14

In the NP the ethnic vote broke down as shown in Table 5.2.

Table 5.2 Ethnic support for NP within the white group (%)

	1977	*1981*	*1987*
Afrikaners	85	63	55
English-speakers	33	28	47

Sources for Tables 5.1 and 5.2: Craig Charney, 'Class Conflict and the National Party Split', *Journal of Southern African Studies*, 10, 2, 1984, pp. 269–82; Lawrence Schlemmer *et al.*, 'The National Party', in Peter Berger and Bobby Godsell, *South Africa Beyond Apartheid* (forthcoming).

The key question is how serious the divisions are at the polls, especially with respect to the ruling group's ability to retain the required cohesion. Do the electoral results of 1987 point to a future political paralysis with an increasingly erratic and schizophrenic NP government frantically trying to ward off an unstoppable CP electoral threat, while at the same time trying to accommodate partially the aspirations of the blacks and demands generated by economic growth?

The CP's rise to the position of Official Opposition in the 1987 election has sparked off conflicting interpretations of electoral trends since 1977. This can largely be attributed to the fact that parties such as the NP and the New Republic Party (NRP) are so difficult to classify. Du Toit has argued that there has been a shift to the right following the declining support of the reformist parties, like the NRP, from 30 per cent in 1977 to 18 per cent in 1987.[37] This, however, presupposes that the NRP was solidly reformist, but the party should rather be seen as pro-English (or pro-Natal) and as ambivalent (or confused) on the issue of reform. Schlemmer, in contrast, argues that the shift has been to the left, with some 70 per cent now in the reform camp against only 30 per cent in 1977. His argument is that the NP has moved from a conservative position in 1977 to that of conservative-*reform* in 1987.[38] While Schlemmer is clearly correct in his categorisation of the party, the question is whether the NP support could be classified *en bloc* as conservative reformists. It can also be argued that not much has changed. In a *Rapport* poll on the eve of the 1977 general election 50.3 per cent of a sample of whites said that the government was proceeding at the right pace with reform.[39] In 1987 the NP attracted 53 per cent of the support of whites, who presumably were all happy with the pace of reform.

This juxtaposition is, of course, disingenuous. Everyone knows that attitudes expressed in surveys and electoral behaviour are not nearly identical, one of the reasons being that party ties fade only slowly, particularly so in South Africa. The relatively strong showing of the NP in 1977 was due to the fact that the party was still a genuine ethnic coalition with an appeal to Afrikaner ethno-nationalism directed at all classes within Afrikanerdom. But 1977 already heralded major Afrikaner divisions. The 65 per cent poll was relatively low and the percentage of voters who went out to vote for the NP fell from 43.8 in 1966 to 41.9 per cent in 1977, declining further to 37 per cent in 1981. These trends, and several attitude surveys, showed that there were large numbers of voters who were unhappy with the NP, but could not be mobilised by an extremist right-wing party, such as the HNP with its lower-class and loser image.

In 1981 roughly a third of Afrikaners did not vote for the NP for right-wing reasons. In 1987 the CP is estimated to have attracted 37 per cent of the Afrikaner vote. It has managed to absorb the large numbers who abstained in 1981 and the great majority of those who voted HNP. But the significant fact is that the CP in 1987 did not substantially increase the proportion of Afrikaners ready to be mobilised on the right of the NP. This was despite the fact that Dr Treurnicht and the CP parliamentary representatives projected a 'respectable' or middle-class image, despite the continuing erosion of white incomes, or the black uprising which broke out in 1984, or the widespread suspicion among sections of the white population in 1985 and 1986 that the government was caving in to foreign pressure. Moreover, the CP did not succeed in attracting strong support among the upper-middle income groups. This is a prerequisite, for a predominantly Afrikaner party needs to construct an effective ethnic alliance to snatch power from the NP. The class composition of the main parties is shown in Table 5.3.

Other factors are also working against the CP. While the white working class is bitterly discontented, the proportion of working-class whites is steadily declining as whites continue to move up on the job market. White attitudes are becoming more open: the attitude surveys since 1977 show that there is an ever-increasing acceptance among whites of some measure of residential integration (over 60 per cent according to the most recent survey), and for a constitutional dispensation in which all groups have a say. The anticipated large influx of Africans to the cities over the next 15 years will make the right wing's plans for partition ever more unrealistic.

Some analysts have calculated that of the 166 seats in Parliament, the CP is within reach of 62 (including the 22 it currently holds).[40] But one

Table 5.3 Household income rating by party support, February 1986 (%)

	PFP	*NP*	*HNP/CP*
Household Income	38	20	10
Upper-middle/middle	43	45	49
Lower-middle/lower	19	35	41

Source: Lawrence Schlemmer, survey for *Market and Opinion Surveys*, 1986.

should not infer from this that the CP is within reach of power. In the 1970 general election, the United Party (UP) drew 37 per cent of the votes, captured eight NP seats and was believed to be within striking distance of power. However, after a reverse in the 1974 election, it started to disintegrate and disbanded in 1977.[41] As then, much now depends on how the government handles the situation. Right-wing support will surge if residential integration occurs chaotically, or if the release of a political prisoner leads to a temporary breakdown of stability, or if the government seems to wilt in the face of foreign pressure. The government knows this and can be expected to cover its right flank on all these scores. While this is the case, the CP may increase, and even double, its seats without expanding its base sufficiently to become a disruptive or destabilising force in the system. Limited CP successes in fact have served to stabilise the system. Before the 1987 election most right-wing organisations were becoming disillusioned with the parliamentary strategy to advance their objectives.[42] Now, however, they are kept in the system by the illusion of being within reach of power.

While the NP is finding itself, for the first time in nearly forty years, with minority Afrikaner support, it has become more a white 'national' party reflecting the 60:40 Afrikaners/English-speakers breakdown in the white population. In the wake of the disintegration of the UP in the mid-1970s, a large section of English-speakers had no regular party loyalty for quite some time. In 1981 this was true of 37 per cent of upper-status English-speakers, and 46 per cent of blue-collar ones.[43] Since then one of the minor 'laws' of white electoral behaviour in South Africa started to assert itself. This posits a strong correlation between growth of right-wing parties or factions and increases of English-speaking support for the NP. When the right wing did well in the 1981 election, large numbers of English-speakers were up for grabs. In 1982, surveys showed that the NP stood to make considerable gains at the expense of the PFP if it projected a clear policy of reform.[44] Although the NP continued to obfuscate the matter, more than 50 per cent of English-speakers voted yes in the constitutional referendum of 1983. From 1984 the security issue accelerated the shift of English-speakers away from the PFP to the NP. Among English-speakers in particular there is a strong tendency to vote for the NP as a political vehicle to secure their interests and negotiate on their behalf, rather than for the NP's policy, ideology or leadership.

At this stage another danger for the NP is an erosion of support on its left, by Afrikaner intellectuals, professionals and businessmen who are significant opinion-formers in their community. Together with their counterparts, they are being drawn to the Independent Movement and the National Democratic Movement. It is still too early to assess the growth prospects of these movements.

The rise of the hegemonic central state

Johnson's study was produced in the years 1975–77, when the ruling group in South Africa for the first time faced an internal mass uprising, concerted foreign pressure and a menacing situation on its borders. This occurred at a time when Vorster's inner cabinet was bogged down by indecision, leadership clashes, feuding between the police and military bureaucracies, and the burgeoning information scandal that sapped Vorster's energies. The incursion of South African forces into Angola in 1975–76 was a near-débâcle, due to the lack of military objectives and vacillation over day-to-day directives. The Soweto uprising of 1976 caught the security police, by their own admission, unawares. The state had no clear conception of how to deal politically with the urban black communities. The Black Consciousness movement was crushed and Chief Gatsha Buthelezi was considered an upstart homeland leader who had to be rebuffed (and even told by the Minister for Justice and the Head of the Police that he could not enlist non-Zulus in his Inkatha movement). The government had alienated even the (Coloured) Labour Party. Together with Inkatha and the (Indian) Reform Party, the Labour Party formed the South African Black Alliance in 1977, and it came out in favour of an economic boycott and sanctions on investment.

It was in these circumstances that Johnson foresaw the possibility of the downfall of white rule somewhere around the turn of the century. The scenario which he sketched saw Mozambique becoming a guerrilla sanctuary, supplied with a substantial defensive capability by Russia. He also anticipated an increasing number of guerrilla attacks in South Africa and a rising tempo of unrest among urban blacks inside the country. In such circumstances the 'Pretoria regime will find itself threatened on all sides at once and in desperate need of help'. Johnson believed that at this point the United States would gain the same leverage over Pretoria that Pretoria held over Smith in 1976 and would press for majority rule.[45] Four years later, in 1981, Samuel Huntington presented roughly the same scenario: 'At some point in the next decade or two, some combination of black mobilization, economic trouble, and external threat are likely to create a crisis within the South African political system that will only be resolved by fundamental change of the system'.[44]

In 1977, the year in which Johnson's book appeared, a White Paper on Defence was published which encapsulated the belief of the security establishment that the country faced an onslaught in various fields. It advocated a total national strategy which would aim at coordinated action between government departments and other authorities 'to counter the multi-dimensional onslaught against the Republic of South Africa in the ideological, military, economic, social, psychological, cultural, political and diplomatic fields'.[47]

The anxieties about an onslaught went back to the early 1970s. They were partly related to the efforts of the security establishment, in particular the army, to enhance its power and resources. However, there were also tangible reasons for concern. In the 1960s much of the overt Western support was withdrawn as a result of South Africa's illegal occupation of Namibia, its involvement in the Rhodesian civil war, and its racial policies. The security elite greatly dramatised South Africa's security troubles by presenting the struggle between white and black as part of the conflict between the West and the East, and between free enterprise and communism.[48] A 1971 commission report on state security referred to the perception that the Republic's numerous enemies were intent on overthrowing the existing order and were trying to attack in numerous fields, including '(i) military, (ii) political, (iii) economic, (iv) social, (v) educational, (vi) psychological, (vii) subversion, (viii) terrorism, (ix) sabotage and (x) espionage. . . .'[49] This sense of threat was greatly intensified by the Durban strikes of 1973, the fall of the colonial regimes in Angola and Mozambique, and the introduction of Cuban and other Russian auxiliaries on the subcontinent.

These security concerns have been a main source of the changes in the system of rule that South Africa has undergone over the past decade. By 1977 the NP was still a party that was ethnically exclusive, populist and ideologically committed to apartheid. It was generally accepted as the custodian of the Afrikaners' group interests and cultural aspirations. While the party's leadership had always assumed a vanguard role there was still a strong sense in 1977 among NP rank-and-file that policy was shaped in interaction with them and that the party was responsive to grass-roots pressures. Moreover, the ethos of the original Afrikaner *volksbeweging* (national movement) was still alive. The *volksbeweging* was based upon the conviction that the NP and other nationalist organisations supported the party and each other in a spirit of 'independence-in-commitment'. This meant that the NP, the Afrikaans press, organised (Afrikaner) business, the church and the Afrikaner Broederbond, were all joined together in a movement in which each pursued the same nationalist goals, but with each protecting its own space in which it could debate policy according to its own professional or organisational commitments. 'Independence-in-commitment' was bolstered by Vorster's leadership style, which emphasised the slow building up of consensus on all levels of the party and support organisations. While not denying the oligarchic thrust of the party, it was possible to see NP policy in 1977 as the outcome of several battles fought on different sites within the nationalist movement.

Rampant 'departmentalism' within the state bureaucracy formed yet another site of struggle. Ministers imposed their own political will upon policy execution. Civil servants were able to sabotage reform initiatives. They were aided and abetted by a government that was predominantly reactive and without any clear objectives, except that of 'holding the fort', as Vorster once phrased it. The chief impression of the state in 1977 was that of an uncoordinated, poorly managed (Afrikaner) family firm. It maintained its coherence by virtue of the extraordinary Afrikaner ethnic support for the NP and the overwhelming resources the state enjoyed compared to the weak and divided opposition.[50]

By 1987 the political system had come to look quite different. Instead of being predominantly based on the Afrikaner group (as represented by the NP) the state now rests on a dual base. Alongside the party there has developed a centralised state structure which is increasingly absorbing co-opted elements from outside the ranks of the NP. The NP itself has changed in character. The 'vanguardist' role of the party leadership is now much more pronounced and unambiguous. Policy-shaping interaction with its primary constituency (Afrikaner nationalists) occurs on much more unequal terms. The NP provincial congresses, once the scene of charged debates over ideological deviations, have become low-key discussion forums routinely rubberstamping government decisions. A symbolic watershed occurred in 1979 when Botha distinguished between party principles, which could not be changed without congress approval, and the routine execution of policy, which falls outside the scope of congresses. The NP's parliamentary caucus can still restrain the cabinet in the case of ideological issues (Group Areas and state schools are particularly sensitive), but frequently finds itself ignored on security issues. The second state of emergency was announced on radio before caucus was informed, although Parliament was in session at the time.[51] Nevertheless, the party remains of crucial importance. It is virtually the only avenue for the recruitment to political office, and the all-important party leader (and by extension the State President) is chosen by the parliamentary caucus. The fact that neither big business nor the military can influence this choice signifies the continuing importance of the party as a base upon which the state rests.

The other base is the central state structure. This is comprised of three power-centres: the office of the State President, the security bureaucracy and the financial and technical bureaucracy. As a result of an 'organisational revolution' carried out by P. W. Botha, there now exists much better coordination of the bureaucracies and a centralisation of political power in the executive branch. This impetus behind the thoroughgoing reorganisation was not only the administrative inefficiency of the Vorster years, but also the economic crisis and shortage of resources, and, more importantly, both the perceived total onslaught from without and the rising black resistance from within. Botha for the first time created a genuine office of the Prime Minister (later State President), a cabinet secretariat and five standing cabinet committees. This enabled him to oversee effectively policy coordination and the proper execution of policy.

The security bureaucracy revolves around the State Security Council (SSC), the most important of the cabinet committees entrusted with formulating security strategy. It also eliminates much of the feuding between the intelligence and security services characteristic of the Vorster years. The financial and technical bureaucracies consist of a loose assembly of the Finance, Manpower, Education and, occasionally also, the Constitutional Development bureaucracies. They are drawn together in standing cabinet committees and also in the State President's Committee on National Priorities, which serves to coordinate the financial priorities of the various levels of government in line with a set of national guidelines.

The centralised state structure is increasingly assuming a position of hegemony. As head of both the party and the state, Botha would ideally base himself and his government equally on both. However, in practice there has been a continuing strengthening of the state at the expense of the party and other white institutions. The government is not responding to demands flowing up from representative institutions but has imposed structures in a top-down fashion to provide the necessary machinery for addressing the needs of people in areas such as housing, health and education. In a sense it resembles an Eastern

European 'dictatorship over needs', which justifies political repression by claiming for the oligarchy an indispensable role in meeting social needs.[52]

At this stage, the state is engaged in restructuring the local level and regional levels of government. At the same time as removing the (white) provincial councils it has introduced mixed Regional Services Councils (RSCs), drawing their representation from segregated local authorities. They are designed to serve the central state's aim of redistributing resources on the local level in order to upgrade black townships. The state has also established an elaborate National Security Management System. In 1987 there were 12 Joint Management Centres (JMCs) countrywide, each consisting of about 60 civil servants and security officers. Beneath these there were 60 sub-JMCs, roughly coinciding with the metropolitan regions due to be administered by the JMCs, and consisting of civic officials, and local military and police chiefs. At the lowest level were 448 mini JMCs corresponding to the areas covered by municipal councils, and including civil defence officers, fire-chiefs, postmasters, and municipal officials. Reporting to the State Security Council, these structures are used by the central state in a dual capacity. On the one hand they serve as an early-warning system spotting potential areas of friction, and coordinating its strategy for improving material conditions in black areas. On the other hand, they are used to counteract popular organisations working outside government structures for radical change. In general, these structures reflect the central government's managerial approach which assumes that it can modernise society without involving 'politics' (that is elected officials), and that blacks are primarily interested in having their needs met rather than expressing their democratic rights.[53]

Through these new structures, from the reorganised cabinet and the bureaucratic centres of power at the top, to the RSCs and JMCs at the regional and local level, the centralised state expresses the will of the white nation to allow only a slow and controlled redistribution of wealth and a very gradual phasing in of blacks into government structures. This hegemonic central state has much less need for the NP as a mediating organisation, since in times of crisis or during election campaigns it speaks directly to the electorate through the state media and through advertisements in newspapers. The clout of the Afrikaner electorate has been reduced, because on issues such as security (and, to a lesser extent, financial and technical matters) the state controls much of the information released to the public. It is because this state is much less of an Afrikaner state and much less racially exclusive, that English-speakers can begin to identify with it and express support through voting for the NP. And it is because it is much less populistic than the NP of old that the CP is able to draw support from Afrikaners who resent the idea of a state which is technocratic, impersonal and divorced from direct electoral pressures.

In 1977 it was almost unthinkable that the NP would react with a relative degree of equanimity to the 1987 general election result in which it was reduced to attracting minority support from the Afrikaners. While the CP has eaten into the base on which the government rests, this has effectively been neutralised by substantially increased English-speaking support. Moreover, the centralised state, as a virtually autonomous base of government, has grown enormously over the past decade.

The form of rule which the NP government now fully represents, is what LaPalombara and Weiner in a general context have called a 'hegemonic system', which describes situations 'in which over an extended period of time the same party . . . hold governmental power',[54] and in which the distinctions between ruling party, government and the state have become blurred. It is difficult to see any alternative white party challenging the position of hegemony of the government resting both on the NP and the central state structure. Political disunity among Afrikaners has not weakened the overall commitment of the ruling white group to defend the hegemonic system which the government has constructed.

CONCLUSION

This chapter has looked first at the degree to which the white right wing threatens the cohesion of white South Africa. Evidence has been cited of discontent among white workers and the rise of the CP to the position of Official Opposition has been analysed. Since the white unions have become ineffective, it is the CP and the semi-fascist movements close to it which pose the greatest threat to the effective functioning of the government. It will constrain its ability to modernise the regime through reform. A CP electoral victory would probably have a disastrous impact on white–black relations. However, there is no evidence at this stage to project a major increase of seats for the CP over the next three to five years, provided there is not a negative turn of events which could be laid at the door of government. This could include ruinous inflation, chaotic residential desegregation or the temporary collapse of public order. It is also doubtful that right-wing whites would engage in vigilante actions which would destabilise the regime. Whites are, after all, the regime's major beneficiaries, in the form of substantially superior social services and opportunities for employment in the middle level and top ranks of the public and private sectors. But what if the CP, contrary to our expectations, grows to a point where it stands ready to capture power? There is little doubt that the civil politicians and the military leadership would suspend elections and rule through referenda and by decree.

Among elites on the Afrikaner left there is clearly waning enthusiasm for the NP under its current leadership. However, these elites have no intention of withdrawing their support from the central state structure or the white-controlled regime at large. The Afrikaner business leaders, for instance, moved much closer to their English counterparts in the ten years since 1977 in advocating the removal of apartheid controls over blacks. In the escalating unrest of 1984–86, Afrikaner business organisations and spokesmen joined a common business front in advocating faster reforms. In September 1985 the Afrikaanse Handelsinstituut (AHI) joined other major business organisations in presenting a comprehensive statement to United Nations hearings. The statement stressed the need for a South African business charter which would outline the objectives and principles for power-sharing and the advancement of Africans. In the same month the chief executives of the AHI and other business organisations called on Western multinational companies to join them in a reformist alliance to prepare the climate for a national convention.[55]

Yet when it came to the crunch, the Afrikaner business leaders drew back from giving concrete effect to these ringing calls, and from doing anything which could weaken the regime. Two of the most prominent Afrikaner business leaders (Anton Rupert and Fred du Plessis) turned down an invitation to join a delegation of English-speaking South African businessmen who had talks with ANC officials in September 1985. This was not only due to pressure by President Botha but also because these men did not want to assist the ANC in its declared strategy of using talks with business leaders to isolate the government politically. The limited measure of activism waned even further after the state of emergency was declared and more comprehensive economic sanctions were implemented by Western governments. The immediate effect of sanctions was to draw business across the language divide closer to the state in the efforts to overcome sanctions. The brief flirtation of Afrikaner business leaders with a common business front against government seems something of the past. A similar phenomenon occurred in 1960 in the aftermath of Sharpeville.

The degree of political discontent of Afrikaner professionals, academics and students should also not be overestimated. These elites are now more prepared to support a party to the left of the NP (provided its leadership and ethos is sufficiently Afrikaans), but there are virtually no signs of serious regime disaffection. The number of Afrikaner emigrants is still so low that news of someone leaving the country is received with a mixture of surprise and shock. In a recent poll more than half of English-speakers between the ages 18 to 23 (the period when white men are liable to be called up for military service) indicated that they considered leaving the country against only 6 per cent of Afrikaners.

There is little active opposition to the draft. The University of Stellenbosch is the most liberal of Afrikaner campuses, but a 1987 study established that only 2.1 per cent of a representative sample had joined the End Conscription Campaign (ECC). Very few of this proportion have as yet publicly announced that they will refuse to do military service.[56] A study undertaken by Stellenbosch political scientist, Jannie Gagiano, tried to discover the degree of political disaffection of Stellenbosch students by tapping attitudes towards state coercion, the behaviour of the regime's opponents and forms of protest. He found that while 32.3 per cent no longer supported the NP, only 3.3 per cent could be considered as fundamentally alienated from the regime.[57]

Compared to ten years ago the white ruling group is undoubtedly in more disarray politically, but one cannot really speak of a significant weakening of regime support. There is still very little indication of pressures by the resistance movement causing large numbers of whites to suffer a loss of morale and to contemplate surrender. The decisive moment in many uprisings occurred when part of the security forces sided with the revolutionaries, became dispirited or were recalled to a remote metropole. Such a moment still seems distant in the course of South African political development. The loyalty of the armed forces, even of its black complement, is undisputed. For all these reasons one must conclude that the degree of political dissent within Afrikaners (and broader white ranks) is not yet of a degree which threatens white solidarity, and with that, white rule.

Notes

1. Leon Trotsky, *The History of the Russian Revolution*, Ann Arbor, 1957, p. 311, cited by Harry Eckstein in Bruce Mazlish et al., *Revolution: A Reader*, New York, Macmillan, 1971, p. 311.
2. V. I. Lenin, '"Left-Wing" Communism – an infantile disorder', in *Collected Works*, Vol. 31, Moscow, 1974, pp. 84–5, cited by Colin Bundy, 'History, Revolution and South Africa', *Transformation*, 4, 1987, p. 69.
3. Crane Brinton, *The Anatomy of Revolution*, New York, Vintage, 1965, p. 65.
4. Eckstein, 'On the Etiology of Internal Wars', *Revolution*, p. 29.
5. J. A. Gladstone, 'Theories of Revolution: The Third Generation', *World Politics*, 32, 1980, 425–53.
6. Theda Skocpol, *States and Social Revolutions*, Cambridge, Cambridge University Press, 1979, pp. 29–32.
7. The other two are superior white coercive power and black political fragmentation. Samuel P. Huntington, 'Reform and Stability in a Modernizing, Multi-Ethnic Society', *Politikon*, 8, 1981, p. 11.
8. Stanley Uys, 'Blacks know that they are going to win', *Guardian*, 1 June 1986, p. 7.
9. Mark Swilling, 'Living in the Interregnum', *Third World Quarterly*, 9, 2, 1987, p. 426.
10. Bundy, 'History, Revolution and South Africa', pp. 70–72.
11. Frederick Johnstone, 'White Prosperity and White Supremacy in South Africa Today', originally published in 1970 and reprinted in A. Paul Hare et al. (eds), *South Africa: Sociological Analyses*, Cape Town, Oxford University Press, 1979, p. 358.
12. J. L. Sadie, 'Contemporary White Population Growth and its Labour Force Implications', *Journal of Labour Relations*, Vol. 4, nos 3 and 4, 1980, p. 49.
13. S. S. Terblanche and J. J. Jacobs, *Struktuurverandering in die middelvlakmannekrag*, Pretoria, HSRC, 1983, pp. 17–22.
14. One of the most illuminating reports on the economy is a confidential study by the Economics and Planning Division of the Standard Bank, dated January 1985.
15. Francis Wilson, *Labour on the South African Gold Mines, 1911–1969*, Cambridge, Cambridge University Press, 1972, p. 46; Merle Lipton, 'White Farming', *Journal of Commonwealth and Comparative Politics*, 1974, pp. 43–61; Stephen Devereaux, *South African Income Distribution, 1900–1980*, Cape Town, SALDRU, 1983.
16. *Business Day*, 10 July 1986; *The Star*, 12 December 1985, p. 21; *Financial Mail*, 2 October 1987, p. 39.
17. For some of the articles see *Die Afrikaner*, 26 September, 3 October and 28 November 1984, 23 January and 20 March 1985.
18. M. McGrath, *Trends in the Distribution of Personal Income in SA*, Durban, University of Natal, 1984, Table 18; S. J. Terreblanche, *Politieke Ekonomie en Sosiale Welvaart*, Pretoria, Academica, 1986, pp. 268–69.
19. Deborah Posel, 'The Language of Domination, 1978–1983', in Shula Marks and Stanley Trapido (eds), *The Politics of Race, Class and*

Nationalism in Twentieth-Century South Africa, London, Longman, 1987, p. 439.
20. *Die Burger*, 4 July 1970, editorial.
21. Phil Weber, *Republiek an Nasionale Eenheid*, Stellenbosch, 1973, p. 13.
22. Philip H. Frankel, *Pretoria's Praetorians: Civil–Military Relations in South Africa*, Cambridge, Cambridge University Press, 1984, pp. 62–3.
23. Cited by Posel, 'The Language of Domination', p. 430.
24. Stanley Greenberg, 'Ideological Struggles within the South African State', in Marks and Trapido, *The Politics of Race, Class and Nationalism*, p. 412.
25. Cited by Posel, 'The Language of Domination', p. 435.
26. Verbatim copy of speech released to the press by Marais Viljoen, 3 November 1972, quoted by Willem Kleynhans, 'Die Rol van die Blanke Vakbonde in die Ekonomiese en Staatkundige Lewe van Suid-Afrika', unpublished paper, 1980.
27. *(Hansard) House of Assembly Debates*, 1976, cols 9250–69.
28. *Die Burger*, 9 October 1976.
29. This and the following paragraph is mainly based on Bobby Godsell, 'Engaging Labour', *Leadership South Africa*, Vol. 6, no. 4, 1987, p. 28; *Survey of Race Relations*, Johannesburg, SAIR, 1981, p. 184; 1983, p. 177; 1984, p. 308; 1985, p. 185.
30. Mark Bennett, 'Maligned and Unaligned: Labour's Oldguard after Tucsa', *Indicator South Africa*, 4, 3, Summer 1987, p. 82.
31. H. R. Griffiths and R. A. Jones, *South African Labour Economics*, Johannesburg, McGraw-Hill, 1980, pp. 199–200, 240–43.
32. Linda Human and Nicholas Icely, 'Trends in the Attitudes of White Workers to the Upward Occupational Mobility of Blacks: Findings from Two Companies', *South African Journal of Labour Relations*, 11, 2, 1987, pp. 4–23.
33. Linda Human and Huntly Pringle, 'The Attitude of White Workers to the Vertical Occupational Mobility of Blacks: An Introductory Survey', *South African Journal of Labour Relations*, 10, 3–4, 1986, pp. 21–34.
34. Andrew Kenny, 'White Revolution', *Frontline*, June 1987, p. 33.
35. Ibid., p. 35.
36. Frank Parkin, *Marxism and Class Theory: A Bourgeois Critique*, London, Tavistock, 1979, pp. 38–9.
37. Andre du Toit, 'The Elections for the South African House of Assembly on May 6, 1987, *Electoral Studies* (forthcoming).
38. Lawrence Schlemmer, 'After Soweto and Sebokeng', *Indicator SA*, 4, 4, 1987, p. 10.
39. *Rapport*, 9 October 1977. See also K. A. Heard, 'Change, Challenge and Response – A view of the 1977 SA General Election', unpublished paper, Dalhousie University, 1978.
40. On the HNP and CP see Simon Bekker and Janis Grobbelaar, 'The White Rightwing Movement in South Africa: Before and After the May 1987 White General Election', to appear as a chapter in *The South African Election of 1987: An Analysis*, Pinetown, Owen-Burgess, 1988. For a more comprehensive survey of the entire right-wing movement, see Helen Zille's chapter in Peter Berger and Bobby Godsell (eds), *South Africa Beyond Apartheid* (forthcoming).

41. B. M. Schoeman, *Parlementere Verkiesings in Suid-Afrika, 1910–1974*, Pretoria, Aktuele Publikasies, 1977, p. 476.
42. Zille, in Berger and Godsell, *South Africa Beyond Apartheid*, op. cit.
43. Craig Charney, 'Towards Rupture or Stasis? An Analysis of the 1981 SA General Election', unpublished paper, presented to the African Studies Institute, University of Witwatersrand, 1982. See also Craig Charney, 'Class Conflict and the National Party Split', *Journal of Southern African Studies*, 10.2, 1984, pp. 269–82, which contains much of the material of the paper.
44. *Survey of Race Relations in South Africa*, 1981, p. 1; *Survey*, 1982, p. 7.
45. R. W. Johnson, *How Long Will South Africa Survive?*, London, Macmillan, 1977, p. 326; see also p. 314.
46. Huntington, 'Reform and Stability', op. cit.
47. *Republic of South Africa, White Paper on Defence*, 1977, p. 8.
48. Annette Seegers, 'Extending the Security Network to the Local Level', unpublished paper, 1987.
49. *Republic of South Africa, Report on the Commission of Inquiry into Matters Relating to the Security of the State*, Pretoria, Government Printer, 1971, p. 34.
50. A good account of decision-making within the 1977 NP is Robert Schrire, 'The Formulation of Public Policy', in Anthony de Crespigny and Robert Schrire (eds), *The Government and Politics of South Africa*, Cape Town, Juta, 1978. I discuss the workings of the political system by 1977 in Heribert Adam and Hermann Giliomee, *Ethnic Power Mobilized: Can South Africa Change?*, New Haven, Yale University Press, 1979, pp. 196–257.
51. At present the only analysis of decision-making under the 1983 Constitution is an unpublished paper by Robert Schrire.
52. I elaborate on this in 'Apartheid, Verligtheid and Liberalism', in Jeffrey Butler *et al.*, *Democratic Liberalism in South Africa*, Middletown, Wesleyan University Press, 1987, pp. 382–3.
53. For an illuminating discussion see Seegers, 'Extending the Security Network to the Local Level'. See also Chris Heymans, 'Local Government Restructuring in South Africa: A Bottom-up View of a Top-down Strategy', paper presented at the Political Science Association of South Africa, Stellenbosch, 1–3 October 1987; *Cape Times*, 9 July 1987, 'Complex Network of Security'.
54. Joseph LaPalombara and Myron Weiner, 'The Origin and Development of Political Parties', in LaPalombara and Weiner, *Political Parties and Political Developments*, Princeton, Princeton University Press, 1966, p. 35.
55. *Race Relations Survey 1985*, Johannesburg, South African Institute of Race Relations, 1986, pp. 562–4.
56. One of the very first is Andre Zaaiman, 'Ek hoef nooit so ver te gereis het nie', *Die Suid-Afrikaan*, December 1987, pp. 35–7.
57. For this study and for other references see Jannie Gagiano and Hermann Giliomee, 'Ruling Group Cohesion in Contemporary South Africa', unpublished paper.

6 'Probably the Best Laager in the World': the Record and Prospects of the South African Economy

T. C. Moll

INTRODUCTION

South Africa is an intriguing anomaly within the world economic system. Internal and external forces are increasingly pressurising the repressive laager of white political domination and economic privilege. Yet while government officials claim the economy is fundamentally sound and recovering from a temporary slump over the last few years, some critics argue it is in a state of 'crisis' resolvable only via fundamental political and economic restructuring of society.

This was one of the issues examined by R. W. Johnson in his 1977 book, *How Long Will South Africa Survive?*[1] His answer: for a long time yet. Unlike many observers in the early post-1976 period, he argued that while South Africa's sociopolitical structure was under severe stress, the combination of white political power and economic resilience would enable the white power bloc to thwart the short-run political threat with which it was faced. A novelty of this analysis was its historical and economic focus. He drew close parallels with the post-Sharpeville crisis, which was the first significant political threat faced by the apartheid state. The 1950s was a decade of steady economic growth, and the progressive implementation of apartheid policies in South Africa. The emergence of widespread but weak black resistance culminated in 67 Africans being shot dead by young white police constables during an anti-pass demonstration on 21 March 1960. For once, Western investors in South Africa sat up and took notice. As Johnson observed, the Sharpeville killings:

> occasioned a deep crisis of confidence in the White establishment. ... Foreign investors, the local business community, and indeed

White society as a whole suffered a tremendous blow in confidence and morale.[2]

The immediate economic effect was a balance of payments crisis. The South African economy in the 1950s was reliant on foreign capital inflows to provide investment funds and strengthen the balance of payments, largely to pay for imported capital goods and machinery. When nervous foreign investors began taking capital out of the country, the balance of payments went into the red, consumer confidence, investment and aggregate demand fell, and the economy slowed down for a period.[3] The state was quick to respond. Strict import controls and policies to reduce capital outflows were complemented by vigorous repression of African political movements. Immigration of skilled workers to South Africa rose again, the Johannesburg Stock Exchange recovered and investors regained strong interest in South Africa. Given the context of rapid economic growth in Western economies, this helped lead to an era of unparalleled growth and diversification in the South African economy, lasting roughly from 1962 to 1974. This was a period in which the state was also able to enforce its homelands policy, raise defence spending, and undermine mass resistance without great difficulty.

The economy had weakened by 1976 due to a slump in the world economy and a slight fall in the dollar price of gold, rising oil import costs, a post-Angola decline in the stock market, and a slowdown in foreign investment.[4] Recession led to retrenchment, cuts in government spending, and falling African employment, while inflation reduced real wages. Given this background, Johnson suggested, conditions were ripe for an outbreak of black resistance.[5] He showed that the economic effects of the 1976 unrest were similar to those of 16 years before. Once again, capital fled the country, talk of sanctions and disinvestment flourished internationally, white immigration slowed, and the country suffered a prolonged balance of payments crisis. When combined with high inflation and high levels of government debt, this led to the application of deflationary macroeconomic policies. However, this slump was to last far longer than the earlier one, and was far more severe; in fact, real Gross Domestic Product rose by only 0.1 per cent in 1977, the lowest growth rate on record since 1932.

Johnson argued, however, that the state would ultimately suppress black resistance, and that investor confidence, the gold price, and economic growth would ultimately recover. He proved correct. Newly-established trade unions and political organisations in the late 1970s were weak, unemployment was increasing, and rural Africans were isolated and helpless. Vigorous repression and selective concessions enabled the state to take charge of the political arena, and combined with the soaring gold price and renewed economic growth in the West, facilitated the economic boom of 1979–81. By the beginning of the 1980s, investor confidence was again high and the gloomy talk of a few years previous had passed:[6] only to resume in the post-1982 slump – again accompanied by a surge in black political resistance.

There are two levels of analysis that can be adopted of a conflict-ridden economy like that of South Africa, both of which were implicit in Johnson's book. The first is the long-run growth and welfare position of the economy. This can be seen as an ever-changing function of patterns of natural resources, capital accumulation, technology, international linkages, labour control, and skills over long periods; and temporary economic fluctuations and political events do not greatly affect it. The second is a short-run level at which variables like inflation, the exchange rate and balance of payments, and investment become far more important. These variables fluctuate considerably and can be directly influenced by short-run political developments. There are two crucial links between these levels. Firstly, investment (and hence future growth rates) can be affected by short-run factors if they act strongly enough, such as severe balance of payments crises induced by a politically-inspired flight of capital. Secondly, rising costs of apartheid and repression compel the state to raise current unproductive expenditure in these areas, and hence taxes, which lowers real investment and incomes. An extended political crisis, then, has the potential to reduce investment, and capital accumulation in the economy.

A typical scenario of the *economic* effects of political resistance in South Africa might thus run as follows: an upsurge in black resistance leads to uncertainty and trepidation among capitalists. Foreign investors take money out of the country and investment slows down, weakening short-run economic indicators and the balance of payments, leading to the state applying deflationary macroeconomic policies. Profitability falls, local and foreign investors become edgier still, and some make reformist noises about the need for political accommodation with black resistance movements. Mesmerised by apocalyptic press accounts of the magnitude of black resistance, some capitalists may even anticipate national economic collapse, revolutionary take-over and loss of their South African investments. However, in reality the state's political offensive regained the initiative in 1960 and 1976 soon enough for capitalists to regain confidence in the economic prospects of South Africa. Investment and profits recovered, the balance of payments stabilised and talk of reform subsided. As a result, long-run economic trends were affected surprisingly little.[7]

Even Johnson overestimated the economic effects of political resistance in South Africa. The 1960 and 1976–77 unrest phases occurred during economic slumps, partly linked to downswings in the world economy, and many economic effects thereof have incorrectly been ascribed to political events. In the first case, the nadir of the slump was in 1958, and recovery, while temporarily reversed in 1960–61, proceeded rapidly thereafter.[8] In fact, while Johnson claimed economic growth in South Africa 'came to a halt' during 1960–61 as a result of Sharpeville,[9] the evidence suggests otherwise: according to official sources South Africa grew at around 3.5 per cent in real terms in both 1960 and 1961.[10] It thus seems the extent of the *economic* crisis of 1960–61 has been exaggerated. In the second case, the economy peaked in 1974 and was in a severe slump from 1975 to 1977, with recovery beginning in 1978.[11] In both, then, long-term South African economic developments appear to be more a function of internal economic dynamics, international economic linkages, and the gold price, than of political factors.

The questions which thus arise, and which are addressed here, are: how has the South African economy performed since Johnson's arguments were presented in 1977, and what are its prospects for the near future? How long can the South African economy survive in present form as the ultimate laager of white power and privilege?

THE SOUTH AFRICAN ECONOMY IN THE LONG TERM

To understand the economic prospects of South Africa, it is useful to follow Johnson's historical approach and begin by examining its overall record since the mid-1950s – a timespan which excludes the rather special years after the Second World War. This will help decide whether the current poor performance of the economy is a temporary phenomenon, or whether it is part of some persistent downward trend. Until the 1970s, the overall story of South Africa's development was fairly typical for a medium-sized open economy with plentiful natural resources, closely integrated into the international capitalist system. The central factor determining economic growth in South Africa has always been her links with the advanced Western economies, most importantly, trade and capital flows. If these economies boom, international raw materials prices (and hence South African export earnings and investment) rise and sometimes capital inflows also increase, especially in manufacturing, leading to an economic upswing in South Africa a couple of years later. If they enter a slump, these processes are reversed, and South Africa follows suit. This pattern is depicted in Figure 6.1.

From the 1950s until the early 1970s, an increasingly open and buoyant world economy, with high demand for South African raw materials, allowed the real Gross Domestic Product to grow steadily (see Table 6.1) and to use foreign exchange earned to import capital equipment, and build up local manufacturing and technology behind tariff barriers.[12] This was reinforced by vigorous state policies designed to disorganise African workers and keep African wage levels low.[13] While all sectors of the South African economy grew over this period, three overall tendencies are particularly significant.

Firstly, the primary foreign exchange-earning sectors of agriculture and mining, grew relatively slowly. Their shares of real output fell gently, and of employment more quickly (with an absolute fall in

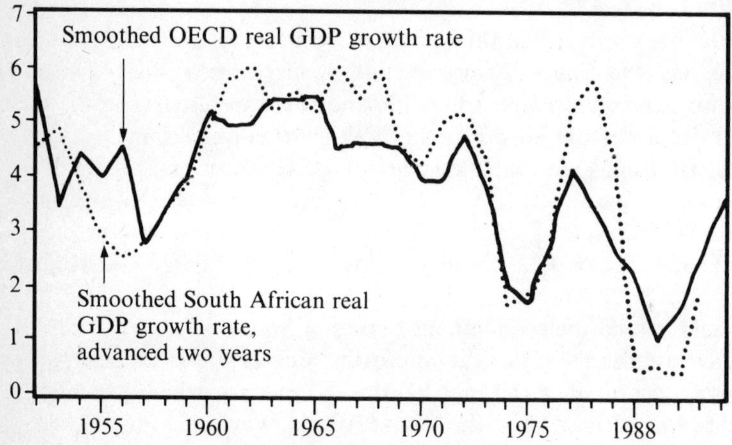

Figure 6.1 Growth in South Africa and in the advanced capitalist countries
Note: Graphs are smoothed using three-year moving averages.
Sources: South Africa: South African Reserve Bank, *A Statistical Presentation of South Africa's National Accounts for the Period 1946 to 1980*, Pretoria, 1981; South African Reserve Bank, *Quarterly Bulletin*, June 1987; data modified as described in the Appendix to this chapter. Organisation for Economic Cooperation and Development countries: OECD *Economic Outlook* (Paris), various issues 1982–87 for the post-1961 period; Angus Maddison, *Phases of Capitalist Development*, Oxford, Oxford University Press, 1984, p. 86, for the 1950s.

Table 6.1 Economy-wide growth rates

	Average real growth rates of GDP at 1975 prices
1957–64	4.1
1964–69	5.4
1969–74	5.2
1974–80	3.4
1980–84	1.5

Note: Exponential growth rates are calculated between business cycle peaks to allow long-term comparisons (see the Appendix to this chapter).
Sources: Basic data from South African Reserve Bank, *A Statistical Presentation of South Africa's National Accounts for the Period 1946 to 1980*, Pretoria, 1981; South African Reserve Bank, *Quarterly Bulletin*, various issues, 1982–85; Chamber of Mines of South Africa, *Ninety-Sixth Annual Report*, Johannesburg, 1986; recalculated as described in the Appendix to this chapter.

agricultural employment). Secondly, other goods-producing sectors (manufacturing, electricity, and construction) grew more rapidly than the economy as a whole, and their shares of employment also grew steadily. These sectors enjoyed cheap imports due to a strong exchange rate, and tariff and other protection in the case of manufacturing. Finally, output and employment in tertiary sectors (especially government) grew steadily, with employment probably contracting only in the personal services sector (most importantly, domestic service). These trends are broadly depicted in output terms in Table 6.2.

Overall in this period, South Africa followed a typical pattern of structural change for developing countries with rising incomes, with a shift in productive structure and employment from agriculture to manufacturing and, increasingly, the services.[14] The major exceptions from this pattern were: (i) an exceptionally large and important mining sector, due to South Africa's mineral resources and colonial heritage; (ii) an especially large share of employment in services and government,[15] due to widespread domestic service and state stimulation of these sectors to absorb white workers.

Since the early 1970s the situation has changed dramatically. Whereas in the 1960s South African Gross Domestic Product grew faster than that of the average middle-income developing country, since then her performance has been decidedly poorer.[16] There has been a steady slowdown in economic growth since 1974, with real GDP growth rates falling to 1.5 per cent in the 1980s (Table 6.1). This slower growth has occurred unevenly through the economy. Due to rising and erratic world gold prices, mining earnings have boomed, while agriculture and

Table 6.2 The structure of output in South Africa – constant 1975 prices

Factor incomes, measured at constant 1975 prices (millions of rands)	*1955*	*1970*	*1985*
Agriculture	1 374	1 753	2 291
(percentage)	(13.2)	(8.5)	(7.1)
Mining	2 247	3 196	4 632
(percentage)	(21.5)	(15.6)	(14.3)
Secondary industry	2 099	5 878	9 473
(percentage)	(20.1)	(28.7)	(29.2)
Services and government	4 707	9 679	16 062
(percentage)	(45.1)	(47.2)	(49.5)
TOTAL	10 485	20 411	32 458

Note: The base year for prices is 1975. The internationally-determined gold price has soared and varied wildly since 1971; 1975 was a not-atypical year for the period since. Trends tend to be valid regardless of the base-year used. 'Real' gold output is determined as described in the Appendix to this chapter.
Sources: South African Reserve Bank, *A Statistical Presentation of South Africa's National Accounts for the Period 1946 to 1980*, Pretoria, 1981; South African Reserve Bank, *Quarterly Bulletin*, various issues, 1982–87.

manufacturing have struggled; since 1982, real manufacturing output and employment have been growing more slowly than the economy as a whole. The tertiary sector has continued growing, chiefly led by government. Growth rates of employment over the business cycle peaked in the 1960s and have been falling since (see below).

ECONOMIC DEVELOPMENT IN SOUTH AFRICA: THREE CONSTRAINTS

Three central aspects of South Africa's economic record can be identified: the balance of payments, the manufacturing sector, and the employment situation. Developments in these areas are having important economic and political effects in South Africa, and will help determine whether the economy will continue surviving as Johnson suggested.

Firstly, the balance of payments has always been a potential constraint on growth in South Africa. Compared to most developing countries, however, South Africa has an unusually strong balance-of-payments situation. Her valuable mineral exports have been a continual and fairly steady source of foreign exchange, providing her with a relatively high and consistent level of imported goods, given her low level of manufacturing exports. The usual pattern is of a trade surplus produced by raw materials (agriculture and mining), exports, much of which is 'consumed' by industrial sectors being net users of foreign exchange,[17] and large invisible deficits (interest payments, royalties, and so on). Capital inflows attracted by high profit rates have also been an intermittent source of savings and foreign exchange.

On the exports side, South Africa's position has not changed much in the period under consideration. South Africa has always exported largely raw materials, a small number of which come to a high share of total exports. The mining share in merchandise exports has averaged over 60 per cent, while the manufactures share has been consistently low. Excluding 'Unclassifiables' (see Note to Table 6.3 below), however, the manufacturing share of non-gold merchandise exports has been slowly rising, reaching 42 per cent in 1985, indicating an increasing degree of international competitiveness.

In import terms, again excluding 'Unclassifiables', the share of consumer goods has steadily dropped and that of capital goods has risen since 1945 (supplies were reduced during the Second World War), with machinery and transport equipment, for example, reaching 49 per cent of the total in 1985. South Africa has been largely self-sufficient in consumer goods since the 1950s, aided by significant levels of effective protection, but these have been much lower on intermediate inputs and capital goods.[18] Hence, although South Africa has built up a capital-goods industry, imported machinery forms a high proportion of capital goods used. The share of merchandise imports in GDP of around 22 per cent has remained roughly constant since the mid-1950s, with the economy becoming increasingly reliant on imports of sophisticated machinery and technology,[19] aided by variable but overall relaxation of forms of import control since the late 1960s. As a result, balance-of-payments deficits have always tended to bite during boom periods in South Africa, with imports rising sharply, necessitating eventual economic clampdown and monetary contraction.

After 1971, the international gold price (which had been nominally constant in US dollars and falling in real terms since 1949), began rising, albeit erratically. This boosted mining profits and government tax revenues, allowed the first significant real rise in black mining wages since the early 1900s,[20] and eased South Africa's balance-of-payments constraint. It implied potentially higher domestic output growth rates if the extra income were to be used productively. The state economic

Table 6.3 South African exports and imports. Proportions of total imports and exports by various categories (figures are in percentages unless otherwise indicated and refer to the Standard International Trade Classification).

MERCHANDISE EXPORTS			
	1955	*1970*	*1985*
Non-gold merchandise exports:			
Food & beverages (0 & 1)	22.0	22.2	9.9
Crude materials & products (2 & 4)	44.2	25.7	37.7
Mineral fuels (3)	1.5	5.6	
Chemicals (5)	4.4	4.4	5.8
Manufactures (6 & 8)	23.6	34.3	41.6
Machinery & transport equipment (7)	4.2	7.7	5.1
TOTAL (%)	100.0	100.0	100.0
Total (Rm, SITC 1-8)	660	1 422	17 644
Unclassifiables (9, Rm)	3	112	3 201
GRAND TOTAL (Rm)	663	1 534	20 845
Gold exports (Rm)	365	837	15 467
MERCHANDISE IMPORTS			
	1955	*1970*	*1985*
Food & beverages (0 & 1)	5.5	5.2	5.9
Crude materials and products (2 & 4)	8.2	5.3	7.4
Mineral fuels (3)	7.7	5.1	
Chemicals (5)	7.0	8.0	14.8
Manufactures (6 & 8)	39.4	28.9	21.0
Machinery & transport equipment (7)	32.2	47.6	49.3
TOTAL (%)	100.0	100.0	100.0
TOTAL (Rm, SITC 1-8)	949	2 492	18 628
Unclassifiables (Rm, 9)	13	48	4 063
TOTAL (Rm)	962	2 540	22 691

Note: South African trade statistics are complicated by a very large and suspicious 'Unclassifiables' section (Standard International Trade Classification 9) which suddenly appeared in 1974. This apparently includes oil imports, military trade etc., but no details are provided.

Source: *South African Statistics*, Government Printer, Pretoria, various issues; Central Statistical Services, *Quarterly Bulletin of Statistics*, June 1987.

strategy in the 1970s, however, was poor – typical of many countries which received such bonanzas, though usually from oil. When the gold price was high, government spending, consumption levels and luxury imports soared, the exchange rate was strengthened, foreign loans were taken out under the expectation of high future gold incomes,[21] but little effort was made to move the additional resources into real investment. So money incomes rose but the economy failed to benefit much (as in the 1980–81 boom), with goods output rising little and inflation accelerating. When the gold price fell, the economy was suddenly weakened, the exchange rate was pressurised, and the state was left with large projects on its hands, which instead it paid for with foreign loans – a fatal long-run move, for they eventually had to be repaid at high real interest rates, particularly in the early 1980s.[22]

Overall, South Africa has been able to run a steady non-gold trade deficit, saved by large gold mining surpluses. Why, then, is South Africa's current balance of payments position often seen as weak and vulnerable?

1. South Africa's nominal exchange rate (pound and rand) was fixed to the British pound after the Second World War, though is now on a managed float. The rand was valued high, so that it was unprofitable to try to export manufactures, and supported by gold exports; this cheapened imports, especially of capital goods. As a result, South African industry has both failed to achieve economies of scale and international competitiveness via exporting, and has remained over-dependent on capital goods imports, without being able to reap the full learning effects of producing them locally and for export (note the small proportion of machinery and transport equipment exports shown in Table 6.3 above). This was only disturbed by the sudden weakening of the rand in 1984, but short-term effects on industry have been negative as the current scope for exports is limited by sanctions, and import prices – and hence costs – have escalated.

2. South Africa is reliant on raw material exports and imports of manufactures. Non-gold net barter terms of trade[23] remain stable during international booms but deteriorate during slumps. Further, her export earnings tend to be erratic, dependent on variable international raw material prices and agricultural fluctuations. Gold was a stabilising factor until the early 1970s (with the world market absorbing all South Africa's output at a given price), but real gold earnings have fluctuated wildly since – though on a strongly upward long-run trend.

3. South Africa has opened up the trade and capital accounts of her

balance of payments since the later 1970s, with moves towards a 'market-oriented monetary strategy',[24] including financial deregulation, more variable and erratic interest rates,[25] a more open balance of payments designed to encourage international trade and capital flows, and a floating and fluctuating exchange rate.[26] This had two important effects: South African banks and the state raised foreign loans at (then) low real interest rates, which are now being repaid at much higher real rates; and allowed an important role for destabilising short-term capital flows. These have rendered the South African economy, balance of payments and foreign exchange situation far more vulnerable to vicissitudes in the international economy in the 1980s, and also make it an easier target for sanctions.

The *second* important determinant of the long-run prosperity of the South African economy is the vitality of her manufacturing sector. This sector is central in growing economies. Its products enjoy a high real income-elasticity of demand, it is subject to substantial economies of scale, with productivity-gains transferable to other sectors via providing them with cheaper and more efficient machinery, it tends to have much scope for raising employment at earlier stages of development, and rapid manufacturing growth has a boosting effect on output and employment in other sectors, especially services.[27]

The South African manufacturing sector grew rapidly in the 1950s and 1960s, at over 7 per cent per annum in real terms (see Table 6.4). This was for several reasons: buoyant international demand and stable terms of trade, an active state import-substitution policy, and intervention in strategic economic sectors, cheap raw material and electricity inputs, capital controls compelling higher levels of local investment, and low black wages.[28]

The record has negative aspects, however. The import-substitution programme was weakened by the lack of export strategy, and the

Table 6.4 Manufacturing output growth rates

	Average real growth rates of manufacturing value added at 1975 prices
1957–64	7.3
1964–69	7.4
1969–74	6.3
1974–80	5.1
1980–84	−0.1

Notes and sources are as for Table 6.1.

reliance of industry on protection and ever-more-advanced machinery imports, hence entrenching the international non-competitiveness of local production,[29] the typical pattern for developing countries with natural resources which have attempted import substitution behind tariff walls.[30] Real manufacturing import levels as percentage of GDP failed to fall, as South Africa moved 'up' the imports scale, requiring increased inputs of imported machinery, transport equipment and technology to keep industry going.[31] The 'easy' stage of import substitution in local consumer goods, some durables and simpler machinery was basically complete by the early 1970s, with further scope for import-replacement limited to capital and intermediate goods and high-technology sectors.[32] A better strategy might have been a more open export-orientated phase in the 1960s, to continue manufacturing growth, allow further scale economies to be reached, and open the economy to some international competitive pressures, but this option was opposed by vested (and highly monopolised) industrial interests which were quite satisfied with their protected position and comfortable profits, and by politicians fearing rises in costs of living of white consumers.

In the 1970s, manufacturing growth began to slow, and rather halfhearted government efforts at stimulating exports and the processing of primary products have not been effective.[33] The recent record has been particularly poor; manufacturing volume of production in 1986 was 10.3 per cent below its 1981 peak.[34] The manufacturing sector has entered a phase of 'deindustrialisation' in which it contracts relative to other sectors (its share of real GDP has fallen from a high of 25.5 per cent in 1981 to 22.3 per cent in 1985), with inefficiencies and a limited internal market restricting local sales, and a strong exchange rate of the rand (until 1984) and trade sanctions limiting export growth. This is particularly unfortunate for an economy at South Africa's stage of development, as it implies slower future growth rates for the economy as a whole. In fact, there is evidence from developed countries that where manufacturing output growth slows and the ratio of manufacturing output to GDP perhaps falls, it rarely recovers, a tendency reflected even more strongly in employment terms.[35]

Thirdly, perhaps the most important economic factor directly influencing political change in South Africa is levels of black employment. To understand long-term trends here, it is useful to consider economy-wide inter-sectoral differences in labour productivity and labour absorption capacity. The South African economy includes a spectrum of forms of economic activity, ranging from those which are

MAGDALEN COLLEGE LIBRARY

highly productive and capital-intensive and pay high wages (manufacturing, finance) to those which are unproductive and pay very little (African agriculture, the urban informal sector). This pattern developed for various reasons. The most important is the colonial origins of the South African economy, with white-owned capitalist production (particularly in mining and agriculture) coming into being and gradually subordinating and undermining African economic activities. The former used advanced Western technology, creating significant productivity differentials. These were exacerbated by state policies assisting capitalist production and undermining African economic activities in the twentieth century (for example regarding the labour supply, state assistance and intervention in manufacturing, support for white agriculture, and so on). Over the years these have widened intersectoral productivity differentials. Finally, deliberate work and education policies have served to lower African skills, earnings and education, and raise those of whites;[36] racial earnings differentials only began slowly falling in the 1970s.[37]

One effect of these processes is that South Africa has the most unequal distribution of income and wealth in the world, with a high proportion of the population (largely black and rurally-based) living in dire poverty and lacking access to jobs, land, education and health facilities, and social welfare.[38] Another is that they have affected the employment-creation prospects of the economy. A major indicator of the health of an economy is the extent to which it can provide employment and incomes to its labour force. In these terms, South Africa's performance was impressive until the early 1970s. Employment in most of the formal, high-productivity sectors of the economy grew steadily, with employment growth rates of 3.3 per cent per annum between 1964 and 1974 in those sectors for which more reliable official data is available (see Figure 6.2). Open African unemployment rates seem not to have risen in the 1960s.[39] Since then, the position has drastically deteriorated. Employment growth rates have fallen sharply in the past ten years, averaging only about 1 per cent per annum over the 1980–84 cycle, but African population and labour force growth rates have remained high, leading to a large and continually expanding pool of labour which is 'surplus' to the needs of the modern sector of the economy.[40]

To understand this problem, it is illuminating to examine productivity trends in South Africa. In manufacturing, for example, two phases are very clear. The first, until about 1974, had high rates of employment growth of 4.3 per cent per annum accompanying rapid increases in output of 7 per cent per annum. The second, since 1974, is characterised by rather more capital-intensive production and mechanisation,[41] with slow output growth and stagnating employment, growth rates averaging 2.9 per cent per annum and 0.8 per cent per annum respectively over the 1974–84 period. If this trend continues, it implies that for employment in manufacturing to grow as fast as the labour force until the year 2000 (around 2.8 per cent per annum),[42] real output will have to grow at around 5.3 per cent per annum – a most unlikely proposition.[43] Even this is based on an optimistic assumption, for it is clear that manufacturing is becoming steadily more capital-intensive, with tendencies towards raising labour productivity further, rather than employment.

Outside manufacturing, long-run employment possibilities are little better. Commercial agriculture has been mechanising and shedding labour since the 1960s,[44] the mining sector cannot be relied on to greatly expand employment,[45] and construction employment seems unlikely to grow very quickly. That leaves trade and services; but commerce and private services not driven by a dynamic goods sector of the economy are unlikely to grow rapidly and raise worker incomes much,[46] while rising government employment is often of entirely unproductive bureaucrats, and constrained by a weak state fiscal position. In short, the employment outlook is very bleak indeed, and government efforts at stimulating the informal sector and labour-intensive employment[47] are not likely to reverse employment trends. Increasing numbers of people are likely to end up in such 'casual work' activities, if only out of desperation, usually in services, and self-employed or in tiny informal enterprises, but labour productivity and incomes are likely to remain very low for most of them.[48]

Together, these trends have important implications. Unemployment and underemployment are likely to rise rapidly in the foreseeable future, as a rapidly-growing labour force encounters a stagnant employment position in the economy. Increasing economic and social differentiation may emerge within the labour force, between people in high-productivity higher-income jobs and the unemployed or underemployed. The services will be the main source of employment growth, and the share in total employment of self-employment, part-time and other insecure jobs, and women, will probably rise further.[49] This employment situation is likely to have contradictory effects on worker organisation and politics in South Africa. Soaring unemployment and falling real wages can strengthen worker dissatisfaction and political protest; rising labour productivity and skills trends in traditionally low-wage, anti-union sectors like mining and commercial agriculture are

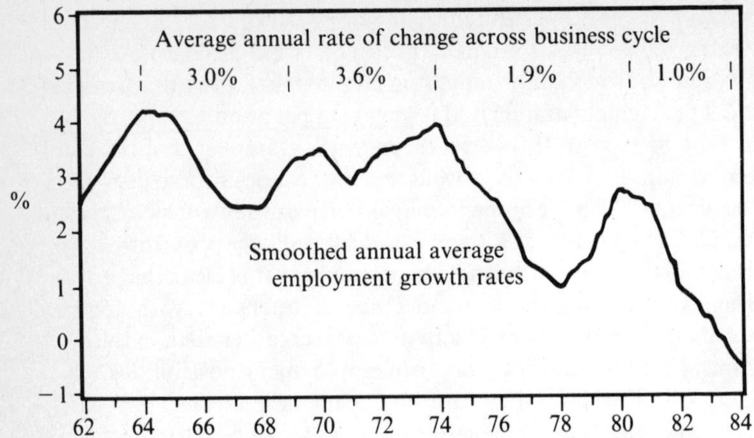

Figure 6.2 Employment growth rates across most economic sectors
Notes:

1. Employment data in South Africa are poor, especially for the 1950s and 1960s, see C. E. W. Simkins, 'Measuring and Predicting Unemployment in South Africa 1960–1977', in C. E. W. Simkins and D. Clarke, *Structural Unemployment in South Africa*, Pietermaritzburg, University of Natal Press, 1977. Some important sectors for which reasonably reliable data are available are included above: mining, manufacturing, electricity, gas and steam, commerce, catering and accommodation, South African Transport Services and the Post Office, and government services. According to Simkins, they total around 70 per cent of formal non-agricultural employment over the period (ibid., p. 31). The most important omissions are agriculture, construction, and most business and private services.
2. Exponential growth rates are smoothed using three-year moving averages.

Sources: *South African Statistics 1982*, Pretoria, Government Printer, 1982; Central Statistical Services, *Quarterly Bulletin of Statistics*, various issues, 1982–87; South African Reserve Bank, *Quarterly Bulletin*, June 1987. Small changes in sectoral coverage (particularly for manufacturing) have been allowed for by assuming employment growth rates in subsectors affected were equal to those in the rest of the sector. Simkins' interpolations for some missing data in the early 1960s are used ('Measuring and Predicting Unemployment', pp. 23ff).

likely to strengthen workers' bargaining power in them; while increasing urbanisation of the labour force will lessen some barriers to political and trade union organisation. On the other hand, the fear of unemployment and lack of alternative income sources may dampen political activities, especially amongst marginal, less skilled, and rural workers, and rising numbers of people in low-income 'casual work' activities will be difficult to organise; such workers have often adopted conservative political stances elsewhere in Africa.[50] These factors may increase difficulties in organising any worker-based challenge to the South African regime.[51]

FUTURE IMPLICATIONS

The South African economy enjoyed an all-time growth boom in the 1960s, and its macroeconomic performance since has steadily deteriorated. Is it best seen as enduring a particularly severe cyclical downswing, from which it can recover in due course, or is it in a phase of protracted long-term decline? This is of course a strongly ideologically-loaded question, since the former position tends to be associated with the South African government,[52] and the latter with its left-wing opponents who foresee national economic recovery only when significant economic and political restructuring of society has taken place, as part of a transition to majority rule.[53]

Neither position seems correct. Most of the short-run weaknesses of the economy are being brought under control, and no signs of economic collapse are present. As of mid-1987, inflation rates were falling, the exchange rate of the rand had recovered somewhat from its 1984–85 slump, foreign debts were steadily being paid off (using large current-account surpluses of the balance of payments induced by economic recession), and in some sectors, signs of recovery could be perceived.[54]

Such recovery may not last for very long, however, due to low recent investment levels in the economy. Table 6.5 shows growth rates of capital stock (land, buildings, machinery and equipment) for the economy as a whole, and for the manufacturing sector, since the 1950s. Real economy-wide growth rates of around 6.8 per cent in the early 1970s, have slowed down to 4.6 per cent in the early 1980s – a period in which the capital:output ratio rose by around 2 per cent per annum and is likely to increase in the future.[55] This pattern is even more noticeable in manufacturing. Hence, while the economy has endured such a severe slump recently that any increase in demand is likely to raise output and employment, this expansion may soon be cut short as productive capacity has been growing relatively slowly in recent years. Simply extrapolating recent economic trends in South Africa, it seems unlikely that total output will grow faster than perhaps 2 per cent per

Table 6.5 Growth rates of fixed capital stock

	Average real percentage growth rates at 1975 prices over periods indicated:	
	Economy-wide fixed capital stock	*Manufacturing fixed capital stock*
1957–64	4.5	7.0
1964–69	5.9	8.0
1969–74	6.8	8.3
1974–80	5.0	5.9
1980–84	4.6	4.0

Notes and sources are as for Table 6.1.

annum over the next decade, and given persistently high population growth rates, real incomes per capita are likely to fall steadily. Growth projections for the 1986–90 period of 3.2 or 3.3 per cent per annum[56] thus seem quite unrealistically high.

The long-term prospects of the South African economy under the present regime are also unpromising. For a developing country, the structure of the economy is not healthy – most noticeably in the weak position of manufacturing, and in South Africa's appalling recent job-creation record. It is also reflected in a weak state finance position (affecting investment in infrastructure and parastatals), and in the relatively poor performance of employment-creating small-scale manufacturing and services over the past few years, despite state efforts to encourage them. More importantly, perhaps, the world economy seems unlikely to grow as rapidly again as in the 1960s, and has begun moving away from some of South Africa's raw material exports. South Africa will attempt to export manufactures, but faces stiff competition from other newly industrialising countries, and may be hamstrung by looming trade sanctions. Further, foreign capital and finance is increasingly suspicious of the South African situation, and South Africa will be forced to survive largely without new inflows of foreign capital to relieve the balance of payments constraint and raise savings. In the long run this is likely to reduce the growth rate by at least 2 per cent per annum, especially if accompanied by diminished access to foreign technology and skills.[57] Gold, uranium and coal exports, however, will continue to provide valuable foreign exchange, and better state balance of payments and exchange-rate policy could enable the economy to benefit more from it than in the recent past. This would especially be the case when foreign debt is paid off and high balance of payments surpluses are no longer necessary,[58] and inflation is seen as being under control.

There are indications, however, that the current political situation is having a *particularly* negative effect on the South African economy, on a scale not hitherto experienced. Consider again the two political-economic connections hypothesised above. Firstly, political 'unrest' tends to lower investment levels and induce capital flight and balance of payments crises, leading to deflationary macroeconomic policies, and slower economic growth.[59] The logic seems simple: investors fear profits will be undermined by continual political struggle, with the added danger of possible expropriation or nationalisation of their investment.[60] To this can be added pressures on foreign firms operating in South Africa, due to increasing anti-apartheid feeling in the West. These patterns have been very noticeable in South Africa over the past few years, especially during the 1984–85 stage of black resistance. As usual, the balance of payments suffered first, but more importantly, real gross domestic fixed investment has been falling steadily since a peak in 1981 (halving in manufacturing by 1986), and real net domestic investment by private firms in 1985 and 1986 was negative, for the first time in South Africa's postwar history![61] Complementary to this has been a switch from long-run investments (yielding returns over perhaps 20 years) to short-run investments or to financial speculation, often with funds locked up inside South Africa by capital controls. Hence the Johannesburg Stock Exchange has been booming while the goods-producing sectors of the economy have experienced continued economic decline. Finally, South African firms are themselves divesting from South Africa, and moving funds and operations elsewhere on an increasing scale.[62]

Secondly, the economic effects of the apartheid system are mixed. Until the late 1960s the apartheid system probably aided economic growth in South Africa. Its fiscal costs were low and it encouraged rapid capital accumulation via ensuring a cheap labour supply for white firms (via influx control, migrant labour, and so on) – a factor which was particularly important to goldmining and commercial farming.[63] By the late 1960s, this position had begun to change. The production pattern in the economy as a whole was moving increasingly towards higher-wage skill- and capital-intensive sectors, most importantly in manufacturing and commerce, but also to an extent in agriculture and non-gold mining.[64] These sectors were less dependent for survival on cheap unskilled black labour, and the labour controls they suffered prevented the dissemination of skills and hampered productivity growth.

As corollary to this, the recent fiscal costs of apartheid have soared. The real defence budget rose at around 5.7 per cent per annum between 1970/71 and 1986/87[65] (substantially faster than GDP), complemented by expensive efforts to make *political* apartheid work (homelands, bureaucracies, local authorities, for example), and politically necessary attempts to lower the costs of apartheid to some black workers via fast-rising subsidies on housing, transport and education.[66] The net effect of all this is that the total financial costs of apartheid are rising steadily in a period when the state can ill afford them, thus compelling it to raise taxes or loans to cover spending.

The current political impasse is having an increasing and long-term negative effect on the economy. Black political resistance is surviving a major state assault; to the trepidation of investors, trade and investment sanctions are looming, and if effectively applied, would reduce capital goods imports and hence investment, output and employment quite quickly,[67] while the harmful economic effects of apartheid are steadily rising. It has been estimated that the system of grand apartheid (via inefficiencies and wastage, sanctions, lost opportunities, and so on) reduced local economic growth rates over the past few years by around 2.5 per cent per annum.[68] This perhaps irreversible combination of falling benefits and rising costs of apartheid over an extended period of time is unique to the current phase of South African history.

CONCLUSION

Johnson's 1977 analysis of the South African political economy still seems applicable today. The social fabric of South Africa is under greater threat than ever before but shows no immediate sign of crumbling. The economic basis of white rule, while undergoing long-term decline, will certainly be able to provide comfortable incomes for most whites, and support a huge military-apartheid apparatus for a long time yet. The economy has certain strengths[69] – a strong food-producing sector, valuable mineral resources, a limited dependence on oil, a fairly developed manufacturing sector, some local technological knowhow, and fair levels of local savings – which will enable it to certainly *survive*, and perhaps grow slowly, as long as large-scale trade sanctions are not applied.

It is worth drawing out some of the political consequences of this situation. Firstly, as Johnson suggested after Soweto:

> The economy may well appear to tremble on the brink of the apocalypse but it is too fundamentally strong not to pull through by the simple expedient of off-loading most of the costs of recession on to the blacks.[70]

Blacks still bear heavy and rising costs of recession and unemployment in South Africa. The political effects of this, however, are indeterminate. Worker grievances are increasing, but the disciplining effects of unemployment and various forms of labour-force differentiation may make it difficult to organise them effectively. The record since 1980 suggests that these difficulties are being overcome, with progressive trade unions growing rapidly and stabilising their organisation despite unemployment and retrenchments, while migrants, services workers and women are steadily being incorporated.[71] Their ultimate economic and political impact has yet to be seen, however, and increasing numbers of marginalised rural and casual urban workers remain unreached.

Crucially, the South African state's capacity to spend its way out of trouble in order to stabilise itself is increasingly constrained by the poor overall economic climate, and its weak fiscal position. This has encouraged some recent 'free enterprise'-inspired moves towards lower state spending, privatisation of government functions, self-funding government services, and so on.[72] These have generally not been carried out. In some cases where they have been attempted, however, the political effects have been destabilising. For example, the raising of rents and transport costs (via lower state subsidies) for Transvaal townships in late 1984 helped to spark off the widespread protest which led to a phase of black resistance.[73] As a result there could be widespread community and township politicisation over the next few years.

As a political strategy to strengthen itself, the state will be compelled to raise welfare, educational, developmental, and job-creation spending on blacks to help redress past inequalities and pacify resistance. Rather ironically, this may reinforce the conservative white backlash in South Africa, which draws to a large extent on those whites who suffer the most from economic recession, and from black competition – formerly protected white workers, drought-stricken farmers, lower-level state employees, and the like. The effects of the revitalisation of the white right-wing on the stability of the system of white political supremacy has already been addressed in Chapter 5.

On the other hand, the pro-sanctions argument sometimes encountered, that a 'weaker' and more isolated economy will undermine the government's fiscal position and lead to lower military spending, is questionable as it stands. Compared to countries like Israel, South Korea, Peru, and Zimbabwe, there is a relatively low proportion of government spending in South Africa on the police and army.[74] In times of real crisis, the state response to declining revenues would more likely be to lower spending on education, health, and welfare, followed by reducing infrastructural and homelands spending, while *raising* expenditure on the military and police – suicidal in the long run, perhaps, but a strategy quite capable of overcoming any short-run military and civil threat.

Such a possibility is reinforced by an ominous move amongst South African economic policy-makers towards a 'laager economy' option: reducing economic links with the outside world and attempting to become more economically self-sufficient – and hence freer from outside political pressures.[75] This makes a virtue of necessity, for South Africa can no longer rely on foreign capital inflows, and some trade links are threatened. Instead, the local manufacturing sector will be relied on to provide the necessary machinery, capital goods and technology to keep the economy and military establishment functioning. It has been suggested that if carried out cunningly, such a strategy might induce a shift towards labour-intensive production methods, which will raise both employment and output growth rates, in line, apparently, with South Africa's 'comparative advantage'.[76] However this argument is based on a number of quite false assumptions.[77] It is more likely that the laager-economy outcome would be the exact reverse – perpetuating inefficiency and clumsy government intervention in the economy, raising production costs and lowering output growth rates further, perhaps the entrenchment of capital-intensive methods of production,[78] and increased dependence on erratic mining revenues. As the Governor of the South African Reserve Bank put it,

> If we have to go into a siege economy we will have to make the best of a bad situation, but it is still a bad situation.[79]

This 'backs-to-the-wall' option has ominous implications. If a 'revolutionary transition' is not forthcoming in South Africa, it implies a lengthy period of economic decline, with white morale bolstered by nationalism, anti-communist feeling, and state propaganda, and with per capita incomes falling and white unemployment rising. Within the white establishment, this might strengthen conservative groups and weaken the position of those who want to see an end to the system of white political supremacy. And the longer, more tortuous and economically destructive the path towards black majority rule, the weaker the economy will be at its end, and the greater the economic constraints on any post-apartheid government which would like to attempt policies of income and wealth redistribution.[80] The manufacturing sector will likely be diversified but inefficient and heavily subsidised, export markets will have been permanently lost, South Africa's position in the world economy will have drastically deteriorated, and savings and investment levels will be low. Perhaps most importantly, South Africa will have a huge number of poor and unemployed people, with little hope of providing them with reasonably paid work for many years. Any post-apartheid efforts at socialism may be subsumed beneath the urgent immediate need to reconstruct the economy and create jobs.

Admittedly, the rest of the world would rejoice to see apartheid ended and aid might be made available, lower levels of unproductive state spending might free funds for investment and redistribution, and the ending of trade and investment restrictions would allow a more aggressive South African export strategy, and lower costs of capital imports.[81] The Zimbabwean experience, however, indicates that outside assistance is not to be relied upon.[82] In short, precisely because of its current resilience, policies to undermine the South African economy could have multiplied negative effects on the political system that replaces apartheid, which poses a difficult tactical dilemma for those who seek an end to white political supremacy.

Appendix

The above analysis differs in two major respects from conventional accounts of South Africa's postwar macroeconomic performance. Firstly, exponential growth rates are calculated between successive peak years of business cycles to allow comparisons not biased by temporary economic fluctuations.[83] The major business cycle indicators used are real GDP, real industrial growth, and industrial employment. The post-1980 depression shows little sign of ending; the brief surge of 1984 is the closest available to a peak.

Secondly, official South African estimates of 'real' output use Laspeyres quantity indexes of volume and output, valued at base-year prices. In the case of gold, the world price is given and South African mines mine poorer ore, and hence reduce their total output of fine gold, as the price rises.[84] The measure used in this chapter recalculates real gold output on the basis of an index of tons of gold ore milled drawn from the Annual Reports of the Chamber of Mines of South Africa; this gives a better picture of how the real *productive capacity* of the economy has changed over time.[85] Compared to conventional measures, it slightly lowers measured growth rates in the 1950s and early 1960s, and raises them in the 1970s and 1980s. It also raises the share of mining in real GDP in the pre-1972 period.

Notes

1. R. W. Johnson, *How Long Will South Africa Survive?*, London, Macmillan, 1977.
2. Ibid., p. 26.
3. J. L. Sadie, 'Principal Events in South Africa's Economic Development 1961–1966', *Statistical Year Book 1966*, Pretoria, Government Printer, 1966, p. 31; South African Reserve Bank, *Annual Economic Report 1961*, Pretoria, 1961, pp. 1–4. Business responses are discussed by Heinz Hartman, 'Enterprise and Politics in South Africa', Department of Economics, Princeton University, Research Report Series No. 2, 1962, pp. 18–38.
4. D. J. Smit and B. E. van der Walt, 'Growth Trends and Business Cycles in the South African Economy, 1972 to 1981', South African Reserve Bank, *Quarterly Bulletin*, June 1982, pp. 45–7.
5. Johnson, *How Long Will South Africa Survive?*, pp. 201ff.
6. Cf. Gerhard de Kock, 'The New South African Business Cycle and its Implications for Monetary Policy', *South African Journal of Economics*, 48.4, 1980.
7. In both cases, real goods-sector investment stagnated during and shortly after the 'crisis', falling briefly but significantly in the manufacturing sector. This did not greatly impede subsequent recovery. See South African Reserve Bank, *A Statistical Presentation of South Africa's National Accounts for the Period 1946 to 1980*, Pretoria, 1981, Table 15.
8. Cf. D. J. Smit and B. E. van der Walt, 'Business Cycles in South Africa during the post-war period, 1946–1968', South African Reserve Bank, *Quarterly Bulletin*, September 1970, pp. 34–40.
9. Johnson, *How Long Will South Africa Survive?*, p. 27.
10. This is based on two estimates using constant 1963 prices: Central Statistical Services, 'Gross Domestic Product at Constant Prices by Kind of Economic Activity', *South African Statistics 1972*, Pretoria, Government Printer, 1972, p. 30, measuring GDP at factor incomes, output-based; and South African Reserve Bank, *A Statistical Presentation of South Africa's National Accounts for the Period 1946 to 1970*, Supplement to South African Reserve Bank, *Quarterly Bulletin of Statistics*, June 1971, measuring GDP at market prices, expenditure-based.
11. Smit and Van der Walt, 'Growth Trends, 1972 to 1981', pp. 53–5.

12. J. J. Stadler, 'Some Aspects of the Changing Structure of the South African Economy since World War II', *South African Statistics 1968*, Pretoria, Government Printer, 1968, pp. 7–9.
13. See Martin Legassick and Duncan Innes, 'Capital Restructuring and Apartheid: A Critique of Constructive Engagement', *African Affairs*, 76, 1977; and the reply by Merle Lipton, 'The Debate about South Africa: Neo-Marxists and Neo-Liberals', *African Affairs*, 78, 1979.
14. Such patterns are described in detail in Hollis Chenery, *Structural Change and Development Policy*, Oxford, Oxford University Press, 1979, Ch. 1. 'Large' countries (population greater than 10 million) classified as comparable to South Africa include Thailand, Peru, and Spain, and among the import-substituting group, Argentina, Brazil, and Mexico (pp. 30–33).
15. C. E. W. Simkins, 'South African Development in International Perspective, 1950–1975', Development Studies Research Group, Working Paper No. 8, Pietermaritzburg, 1979, pp. 6–7.
16. See World Bank, *World Development Report 1982*, Oxford, 1982, p. 112.
17. J. C. du Plessis, 'Investment and the Balance of Payments of South Africa', *South African Journal of Economics*, 33.4, 1965.
18. Martin Fransman, 'The South African Manufacturing Sector and Economic Sanctions', Geneva, International University Exchange Fund, 1980, pp. 23–30.
19. Martin Fransman, 'Capital Accumulation in South Africa', in Martin Fransman (ed.), *Industry and Accumulation in Africa*, London, Heinemann, 1982, pp. 249–53.
20. F. A. H. Wilson, *Migrant Labour in the South African Gold Mines*, Cambridge, Cambridge University Press, 1972, pp. 46–7.
21. For example, the South African Economic Development Plan of 1981 assumed on the basis of the 1980 gold price (over $600 per ounce) that the 1987 price would be around $1000 per ounce. (Republic of South Africa, *Ninth Economic Development Programme for the Republic of South Africa 1978–1987. Revised Edition for 1981–1987*, Pretoria, Government Printer, p. 33.) Given the actual price fall to around $400 per ounce in 1987, it is probable that government trade and tax plans were severely disrupted.
22. The problem is ultimately that natural resource 'windfalls' tend to be wasted, and when they dwindle, the economy is revealed to have been irrevocably weakened, particularly the manufacturing sector. See Stephen R. Lewis Jr., 'Development Problems of the Mineral-Rich Countries', in Moshe Syrquin, Lance Taylor and Larry E. Westphal (eds), *Economic Structure and Performance*, Orlando, Academic Press, 1984; Michael Roemer, 'Dutch Disease in Developing Countries: Swallowing Bitter Medicine', in Mats Lundahl (ed.), *The Primary Sector in Economic Development*, London and Sydney, Croom Helm, 1985, pp. 247–50.
23. The ratio of export prices to import prices. This measure is particularly important since South Africa has tended to take export earnings for granted since the 1940s and has never had a vigorous manufactures export programme. Adjustment to deteriorating terms of trade under such circumstances is difficult.
24. *The Monetary System and Monetary Policy in South Africa. Final Report of the Commission of Inquiry into the Monetary System and Monetary*

Policy in South Africa (Commission headed by G. de Kock), RP70/1984, Pretoria, Government Printer, 1984, p. A19.

25. T. C. Moll, 'Monetary Policy, Small Firms and Welfare in South Africa', Post-Carnegie Working Paper No. 17, Cape Town, University of Cape Town, 1986, pp. 5–7.
26. M. G. Holden and Paul Holden, 'Alternative Measures of Exchange Rates and Exchange Rate Policy in South Africa', *South African Journal of Economics*, 53.4, 1985.
27. John Cornwall, *Modern Capitalism*, London, Martin Robertson, 1977, Ch. 7; C. H. Kirkpatrick and F. I. Nixson, 'Introduction. The Industrialisation of the Less Developed Countries', in Kirkpatrick and Nixson (eds), *The Industrialization of the Less Developed Countries*, Manchester, Manchester University Press, 1983; Ajit Singh, 'Third World Industrialization and the Structure of the World Economy', in D. Currie, D. Peel and W. Peters (eds), *Microeconomic Analysis*, London, Croom Helm, 1981.
28. The overall picture is succinctly described by Fransman, 'Capital Accumulation', pp. 243–59.
29. Ibid., pp. 251–2.
30. Kirkpatrick and Nixson, 'The Industrialization of the Less Developed Countries', pp. 14ff; H. Zarenda, 'Tariff Policy: Export Promotion versus Import Replacement', *South African Journal of Economics*, 43.1, 1975.
31. Fransman, 'The South African Manufacturing Sector', pp. 14–19; also *Report of the Study Group on Industrial Development Strategy* (Study Group headed by S. J. Kleu), Pretoria, Government Printer, 1984, pp. 71–5.
32. Anthony Black and John Stanwix, 'Crisis and Restructuring in the South African Manufacturing Sector', delivered at a Workshop on Macroeconomic Policy and Poverty in South Africa, Department of Economics, University of Cape Town, Cape Town, 29–30 August 1986.
33. Anne E. Ratcliffe, 'Industrial Development Policy: Changes during the 1970s', *South African Journal of Economics*, 47.4, 1979, pp. 406–8.
34. South African Reserve Bank, *Quarterly Bulletin*, June 1987.
35. Pascal Petit, *Slow Growth and the Service Economy*, London, Frances Pinter, 1986, Ch. 3; Joachim Singelmann, 'The Sectoral Transformation of the Labour Force in Seven Industrialized Countries', *American Journal of Sociology*, 83.5, March 1978.
36. These issues are widely discussed in the South African literature. A recent presentation is Alf Stadler, *The Political Economy of Modern South Africa*, Cape Town, David Philip, 1987, especially Ch. 3.
37. See the estimates compiled by Stephen Devereux, 'South African Income Distribution 1900–1980', Southern African Labour and Development Research Unit Working Paper No. 51, Cape Town, 1983, Ch. 2.
38. On income inequality, see Michael McGrath, 'Inequality in the size distribution of incomes in South Africa', Staff Paper No. 2, Development Studies Unit, University of Natal, Durban, 1984. His data can be compared to those for other countries in Jacques Lecaillon, Felix Paukert, Christian Morisson and Dimitri Germidis, *Income Distribution and Economic Development*, Geneva, International Labour Organisation, Ch. 2. The Second Carnegie Inquiry into Poverty and Development in Southern

Africa collected a vast array of material on the causes and effects of poverty, presented in 300 published papers at a Conference at the University of Cape Town on 13–19 April 1984, and to be summarised in several forthcoming books.

39. Trevor Bell, 'Issues in South African Unemployment', *South African Journal of Economics*, 53.1, 1985, pp. 24–6.
40. See Trevor Bell and Vishnu Padayachee, 'Unemployment in South Africa: Trends, Causes and Cures', *Development Southern Africa*, 1.3/4, 1984; A. Roukens de Lange and P. H. van Eeghen, 'Employment in South Africa: Evaluation and Trend Analysis', unpublished report, Institute for Futures Research, University of Stellenbosch, 1984.
41. Black and Stanwix, 'South African Manufacturing', pp. 23–31.
42. Calculated from labour force data in J. A. Grobbelaar, 'The Economically Active Population in South Africa 1980–2015', Bulletin, Institute for Futures Research, University of Stellenbosch, 1984.
43. This is estimated by regressing annual rates of manufacturing productivity growth (Pmf) on output growth (Qmf) over the 1974–84 period, under the assumption that they are related via increasing returns to scale in manufacturing. The simplest equation (t-values shown in parentheses) is:

$$\underset{}{Pmf} = \underset{(0.31)}{0.23} + \underset{(4.09)}{0.51}*Qmf \qquad R^2 = 0.65 \quad DW = 0.83$$

This method is suggestive at best, due to mild first-order autocorrelation (when allowed for, it hardly affects parameter values), the small sample, and its weak theoretical basis; see A. P. Thirlwall, 'A Plain Man's Guide to Kaldor's Growth Laws', *Journal of Post-Keynesian Economics*, 5.3, 1983.

44. This is evident even from the rather poor data in agricultural censuses; for an in-depth study of forces at work, see Michael de Klerk, 'Mechanising Farming: Implications for Employment, Incomes and Population Distribution', paper no. 27 delivered at the Second Carnegie Inquiry into Poverty and Development in Southern Africa Conference, University of Cape Town, 13–19 April 1984.
45. Arnt Spandau, 'Mechanisation and Labour Policies on South African Mines', *South African Journal of Economics*, 48.2, 1980; Norman Bromberger, 'Mining Employment in South Africa, 1946–2000', Southern African Labour and Development Research Unit, Working Paper No. 15, Cape Town, 1978, pp. 94–8.
46. United Nations Industrial Development Organisation Secretariat, 'Industrialization and Employment Generation in the Service Sector of Developing Countries: An Appraisal', *Industry and Development*, 15, 1985.
47. See for example, Republic of South Africa, *White Paper on a Strategy for the Creation of Employment Opportunities in the Republic of South Africa*, WPC-1984, Pretoria, Government Printer, 1984.
48. Roukens de Lange and Van Eeghen, 'Employment in South Africa'; C. M. Rogerson, '"Late Apartheid" and the Urban Informal Sector', in John Suckling and Landeg White (eds), *After Apartheid: Renewing the South African Economy*, London, James Currey, forthcoming.

49. This is the trend from other countries, see Thomas M. Stanback, Jr., *Understanding the Service Economy*, Baltimore and London, Johns Hopkins, 1979, Ch. 4; Norman Gemmell, *Structural Change and Economic Development*, London, Macmillan, 1986, Ch. 6. Similar trends are suggested for South Africa by Georgina Jaffee and Collette Caine, 'The Incorporation of African Women into the Industrial Workforce: Its Implications for the Women's Question in South Africa', and Christian Rogerson, 'Late Apartheid', in Suckling and White, *After Apartheid.*
50. Richard Sandbrook, *The Politics of Basic Needs. Urban Aspects of Assaulting poverty in Africa*, London, Heinemann, 1982, Chs 5–6.
51. This is anticipated by Martin Legassick, 'South Africa in Crisis: What Route to Democracy?', *African Affairs*, 84, 1985.
52. It is implicit in 'Quarterly Economic Review', South African Reserve Bank, *Quarterly Bulletin*, June 1987; and Pamela Freer, *South Africa to 1990. Growing to Survive*, London, The Economist Intelligence Unit Special Report 239, 1986.
53. John Saul and Stephen Gelb, *The Crisis in South Africa*, London, Zed Press, 1986; and Vella Pillay, 'Rising Cost of Apartheid: The Economic Crisis', in Southern African Research and Documentation Centre (ed.), *Destructive Engagement. Southern Africa at War*, Harare, Zimbabwe Publishing House, 1986.
54. The post-1981 economic record of South Africa is analysed by Jesmond Blumenfeld, 'Economy Under Siege', in Blumenfeld (ed.), *South Africa in Crisis*, London, Croom Helm, 1987, pp. 30–32. According to South African economists and government officials, recovery was well under way by mid-1987, and some were hoping for 3 per cent growth in 1987. See Magnus Heystek, 'Optimism for Economic Turnaround is growing', *The Star* (Johannesburg), 30 May 1987; Barend du Plessis, Budget Speech in Parliament, 3 June 1987, quoted in *South African Digest*, 12 June 1987, p. 3.
55. *Study Group on Industrial Development Strategy*, p. 139; Jesmond Blumenfeld, 'Investment, Savings and the Capital Market in South Africa', in Suckling and White, *After Apartheid.*
56. Freer, *South Africa to 1990*, update, p. 93; N. J. Barnardt and J. du Toit, *Macroeconomic Forecast for South Africa 1986–1991*, Stellenbosch, Bureau for Economic Research, 1986, p. 28.
57. See T. Malan, 'Economic Sanctions as Policy Instrument to Effect Change – the Case of South Africa', *Finance and Trade Review*, Volkskas, Pretoria, 14.3, 1981, pp. 95–8.
58. Gerhard de Kock, 'The Capital Outflow – Present Situation and Prospects', South African Reserve Bank, *Quarterly Bulletin*, September 1986.
59. In the case of foreign firms selling their South African operations, local firms are boosted via acquiring capital stock cheaply, but long-run implications of this are negative.
60. It can be inferred that foreign investors in South Africa are exceptionally shortsighted, or subject to a Keynesian 'bandwagon mentality', as they seem to respond largely to *publicity* about black resistance. Hence, for example, capital flows and foreign investment in South Africa recovered

somewhat after the news blackout and state of emergency in the second half of 1986.

61. South African Reserve Bank, *Quarterly Bulletin*, June 1987. Real fixed capital stock growth rates comparable to those in Table 5 for 1984–86 were 1.8 per cent per annum for the whole economy, and −2.1 per cent per annum for manufacturing.
62. David Kaplan, 'The Internationalization of South African Capital: South African Direct Foreign Investment in the Contemporary Period', *African Affairs*, 83, No. 329, 1983; 'Fright at the Flight', *Financial Mail*, 13 June 1986, p. 42.
63. Classic arguments along these lines include F. A. Johnstone, 'White Prosperity and White Supremacy in South Africa Today', *African Affairs*, 69, 1970; Harold Wolpe, 'Capitalism and Cheap Labour-power in South Africa: From Segregation to Apartheid', *Economy and Society*, 5.4, 1976. See also Merle Lipton, *Capitalism and Apartheid*, Aldershot, Wildwood House, 1986, Chs 4–5.
64. Lipton, *Capitalism and Apartheid*, pp. 251–2.
65. See *Statistical/Economic Reviews in Connection with Budget Speeches*, various years, Government Printer, Pretoria. 'Defence' spending has been deflated by the Producer Price Index, collected from South African Reserve Bank, *Quarterly Bulletin of Statistics*, various issues, 1975–87.
66. Michael Sutcliffe, 'The Crisis in South Africa. Material Conditions and the Reformist Response', *Geoforum*, 17.2, 1986, p. 3.
67. See studies quoted in Malan, 'Economic Sanctions'; Roger Omond, 'Why Sanctions?', in Roger Omond and Joseph Hanlon, *The Sanctions Handbook*, Harmondsworth, Penguin, 1987, Chs 8–9.
68. The figure is quoted in Michael Savage, 'The Cost of Apartheid', Inaugural Lecture (Sociology), University of Cape Town, 1986. Such estimates should of course be treated with considerable scepticism.
69. Some are discussed by L. H. Gann and Peter Duignan, *Why South Africa will Survive*, London, Croom Helm, 1981, pp. 175–184.
70. Johnson, *How Long Will South Africa Survive?*, p. 323.
71. Jon Lewis and Estelle Randall, 'Survey: The State of the Unions', *South African Labour Bulletin*, 11.2, 1985; Dave Lewis, 'Trade Union Organisation and Economic Recession', *South African Labour Bulletin*, 8.5, 1983; Roger Southall, 'Migrants and Trade Unions in South Africa Today', *Canadian Journal of African Studies*, 20.2, 1986; Jaffee and Caine, 'The Incorporation of African Women'.
72. Wolfgang Thomas, 'Macroeconomic Policy-Making in a Divided Society: The Fiscal-Monetary Mix and Poverty', presented at a Workshop on Macroeconomic Policy and Poverty in South Africa, Department of Economics, University of Cape Town, 29–30 August 1986.
73. See Martin Murray, *South Africa: Time of Agony, Time of Destiny*, London, Verso, 1987, pp. 242ff.
74. See broad comparisons in World Bank, *World Development Report 1986*, pp. 222–3. In South Africa this proportion reached a peak of 20.6 per cent in 1977/78 and fell thereafter, but has begun rising again (references as for note 65). Much military-type spending occurs under other guises – see

Horace Campbell, 'The Dismantling of the Apartheid War Machine', *Third World Quarterly*, 9.2, 1987, pp. 480.

75. Pieter le Roux, 'The State as Economic Actor: A Review of the Divergent Perceptions of Economic Issues', presented at The Southern African Economy After Apartheid Conference, University of York, Centre for Southern African Studies, 29 September–2 October 1986. See also Blumenfeld, 'Economy Under Siege', pp. 30–32.
76. See, for example, J. A. Lombard (ed.), *Industrialization and Growth*, Mercabank, Focus on Key Economic Issues No. 36, Johannesburg, May 1985.
77. For a critique, see T. C. Moll, 'Macroeconomic Policy and Poverty in South Africa: The Crucial Issues', Post-Carnegie Working Paper, University of Cape Town, Cape Town, forthcoming, pp. 50–54.
78. Cf. Michael McGrath and Gavin Maasdorp, 'Some Limits to Redistribution', presented at The Southern African Economy After Apartheid Conference, Centre for Southern African Studies, University of York, 28 September–2 October 1986, pp. 11–12.
79. Gerhard de Kock, quoted in *Financial Mail* (Johannesburg), 4 October 1985, p. 37.
80. This factor is underestimated by many authors writing on the topic. See, for example, Roger Southall, 'South Africa: Constraints on Socialism', presented to The Southern African Economy After Apartheid Conference, Centre for Southern African Studies, University of York, 29 September–2 October 1986; Robert Davies, 'Nationalization, Socialization and the Freedom Charter', *South African Labour Bulletin*, 12.2, 1987.
81. Savage, 'The Cost of Apartheid'; Robert Browne, 'South Africa: Assistance and Aid Programmes', *Third World Quarterly*, 99.2, 1987.
82. Despite many bland promises from the West, Zimbabwe has received little foreign assistance and support since Independence. See Xavier M. Kadhani, 'The Economy: Issues, Problems and Prospects', and Theresa Chinambe, 'Foreign Capital', in Ibbo Mandaza (ed.), *Zimbabwe. The Political Economy of Transition 1980–1986*, Dakar, Codesria, 1986.
83. This method was used by T. F. Cripps and R. J. Tarling, 'Growth in Advanced Capitalist Economies 1950–1970', Department of Applied Economics, University of Cambridge, Occasional Paper No. 40, pp. 38–9.
84. J. A. Lombard and J. J. Stadler, *The Role of Mining in the South African Economy*, Pretoria, Bureau for Economic Analysis, University of Pretoria, 1980, pp. 6, 63.
85. Ibid., p. 7.

7 The KwaNatal Indaba and the Politics of Promising Too Much[1]

Nicoli Nattrass

This chapter investigates certain political and economic questions raised by an evaluation of the KwaZulu–Natal Indaba.[2] Briefly, the Indaba refers to a series of negotiations towards the construction of a regional alternative to apartheid, taking place between governing bodies and interest groups in the geographical region (nicknamed 'KwaNatal') comprising the white province of Natal and the black 'homeland' of KwaZulu. The most important participants in the discussions are Inkatha, the KwaZulu Cabinet (dominated by Inkatha), the Natal Provincial Council Executive, and various business lobbies, such as the South African Sugar Association, the Natal Chamber of Industries, and the Durban Metropolitan Chamber of Commerce. At the time of writing, the talks were still in progress and only broad principles had been accepted by the participants.

One may well ask what a chapter on the KwaNatal Indaba is doing in a book whose central theme is the evaluation of the 'Johnson thesis' ten years on. To castigate Johnson for not being clairvoyant enough to predict that a process of discussion and negotiation would occur in the KwaZulu/Natal region between black and white politicians, sugar farmers, business organisations and various 'experts' and academics is somewhat harsh, especially when the wideranging and speculative nature of his book militated against any specific regional focus.

There are, however, four justifications for the incorporation of a discussion of the Indaba in a volume such as this. Firstly, constitutional exercises, like the government's current dispensation, and the Indaba, are new ingredients since 1977, and therefore need to be addressed in any reassessment of Johnson. To assess the likely effects the Indaba will have, is also an interesting corollary to examining the consequences of the government's constitutional structures for Johnson's arguments, which Chapter 11 does in this book. Secondly, the importance of regionalism in South African politics has become dramatically more pronounced since Johnson wrote in 1977. Because KwaNatal regionalism has had the most coherent expression, both as regards the high level of economic integration within the region, and concerning political pressure for devolution, the Indaba provides a useful way of introducing this development. Thirdly, paralleling Johnson's prophetic tendencies, many observers of and participants in the Indaba see the 'regional experiment' as a testing ground for a future post-apartheid national administrative and constitutional set-up.[3] While this is a highly suspect but interesting and debatable proposition, this chapter will address the idea only tangentially by pointing out that the fiscal constraints facing the Indaba are a good illustration of those to be faced by a post-apartheid national government. Such a focus is consistent with that of Johnson who continually emphasised the economic consequences of, and constraints upon, political policies and events. Fourthly, and with more direct relevance to Johnson, the fact of the Indaba's existence casts aspersions on the methodology underlying his analysis in 1977. It will be argued that it highlights a theoretical weakness in his work which could have been reasonably remedied at the time and thus constitutes a fair criticism of his approach.

In accordance with the above observations, the chapter is divided into two main sections. The first deals with the nature and origin of the Indaba, providing both a brief account of what the Indaba is, and a forum for discussing the weakness in Johnson's methodology. The second section deals very specifically with the fiscal constraints facing any non-racial KwaNatal government which is serious about providing more than mere rhetorical content to the concepts of equality or equal access to social services enshrined in the Indaba's Bill of Rights. Both political and economic lessons will be drawn from this for any post-apartheid national government attempting a similar exercise (as, for example, demanded in the Freedom Charter). In this sense, the chapter further develops the theme with which Chapter 6 in this volume ends; namely, the economic limits to redistribution.

THE NATURE AND ORIGINS OF THE INDABA

Although the concept of a 'KwaNatal Indaba' was first publicly coined in May 1985 by the then leader of the Progressive Federal Party (PFP) Van Zyl Slabbert, its roots are older. Without the Lombard Report of 1980 into 'Alternatives to the Consolidation of KwaZulu', and the work of the Buthelezi Commission into the level and potential of Natal and KwaZulu regional integration, Slabbert's call for an Indaba to devise a political solution for the region would have had little resonance. Likewise, if the Lombard and Buthelezi investigations had not been initiated and backed by powerful regional interest groups, they would never have materialised.

The Lombard investigation was commissioned by the South African Sugar Association, which was concerned by the possible loss of valuable sugar lands through the political consolidation of KwaZulu. As Natal's capital-intensive sugar mills have a breakeven point of about 70–75 per cent of planned mill capacity, they require a large continuous supply of cane.[4] Consequently, it is not surprising that Bantustan consolidation and 'development' which threatens available supplies and possibly implies competition (from developing KwaZulu milling capacity) is an anathema to the South African Sugar Association. Apart from recommending 'co-ordination and co-operation across the entirety of Natal' as an alternative to the regional consolidation of KwaZulu, Lombard advocated a constitutional dispensation for Natal involving separate but equal representation for KwaZulu, rural Natal, and the Durban metropolitan area within a consociational framework, including, *inter alia*, a Bill of Rights, an independent judiciary and guaranteed protection of private property.

The Buthelezi Commission, initiated by Inkatha and chaired by Professor Schreiner of Natal University, took the initiative further. Specialist committees into education, economic development and the like, recommended 'basic needs' development within the context of a mixed economy, where various joint planning bodies would ensure a measure of economic redistribution from Natal to KwaZulu. On the constitutional front, consociational devices were advocated to encourage inter-group accommodation.[5] These proposals were the most concrete of those adopted by the Indaba at the time of writing. Given the nature of the proposals and the image projected by the Commission as representing the voice of moderation, it is not surprising that the project has been described as 'essentially Buthelezi's blueprint for a Lancaster House solution in South Africa'.[6]

What is more interesting than the nature of the 'blueprint' *per se*, is the impetus which led to the move from mere argument and investigation to actual negotiation between interest groups in the KwaNatal region, culminating in the Indaba. On one very important level it was the failure of the tricameral dispensation on the national level to even remotely respond to the demands for national African participation in government, which breathed new life into the KwaNatal devolutionist lobby. The increasing level of unrest imparted a new urgency on the part of the two main interest groups, Inkatha and the Natal business community, to find a solution for the KwaNatal region. The business community obviously has an interest in the maintenance of a capitalist economy and in social stability, while Inkatha has an interest in asserting itself over rival groupings such as the United Democratic Front (UDF) and the Congress of South African Trade Unions (COSATU).

Essentially, Inkatha is offering Natal's whites a liaison with a conservative pro-capitalist tribalistic movement as a buffer against black (often pro-socialist) radicalism, in return for the extension of its power base beyond that of a Bantustan, thus strengthening its arm in the national struggle for power in the post-apartheid era.

While the price to be paid by white Natal involves the loss of white political supremacy, the rewards include the relative stability expected to be engendered by the settlement, the economic benefits to be reaped from an unrestricted regional labour market,[7] and the implied fiscal savings of an integrated economic and social infrastructure. However, the implications of the Indaba extend beyond the fate of regional interest groups. As Glaser points out, 'in contrast to other post-1976 business "reform" initiatives, (like the Urban Foundation) KwaNatal actually entails an explicit attempt by businessmen (amongst others) to present a reformist but hamstrung central state with alternative political models'.[8] Furthermore, the concept of a devolved region replacing a Bantustan and province, has an echo in government thinking and policy, and thus could act as a catalyst for the adoption of an alternative political model.

Government policy of import here concerns the regional development and administrative changes in the 1980s. Since the unveiling of the 1981–82 'Good Hope Development Plan', the government has accepted the economic and spatial interconnectedness between the Bantustans and white South Africa. While retaining the political independence of the Bantustans, the government committed itself to planning on a regional level in accordance with nine 'development regions'. This particular shift in policy was a response to the substantial changes that have occurred in South Africa's spatial economy since the 1960s. From a spatially 'dualistic' configuration (Bantustan vs white urban areas), the spatial economy is now characterised by 'metropolitan centered urban regions radiating outward from metropolitan cores in white areas and enmeshing a substantial part of the neighbouring Bantustans'.[9]

The KwaNatal region is a classic example of such development.

Apart from manifesting close functional economic independence,[10] the spatial economy is increasingly becoming dominated by the Durban Metropolitan Area, which incorporates KwaZulu townships like Umlazi and KwaMashu, 'unincorporated' townships, such as Lamontville and Chesterville, white areas extending from Durban to Pinetown and Hammarsdale, and informal settlements like Inanda.

Coupled with this move towards regional development, the government has also pursued policies of regionalising local government (via the Regional Service Councils) and the regionalisation of second-tier administration (where the Provincial Councils have been replaced by 'Executive Committees'). Although such moves centralise authority rather than devolve it, as the Indaba wishes, the principle of 'functional consolidation' of neighbouring racially-segregated municipalities is one close to the heart of the Indaba initiatives, albeit not in the form of Regional Service Councils, which Buthelezi has rejected outright.

Thus although the central state has largely rejected the Indaba experiment, the proposed devolution does not fly entirely in the face of government thinking. Nevertheless it does not seem likely that any present or forthcoming proposals of the Indaba will materialise in the near future given the defeat of the Natal 'pro-Indaba' candidates in the May 1987 election and the growing right-wing drag on the government's 'reform' initiatives. Not even this 'counter-revolutionary'[11] development is likely to see the light of day given the present intransigent nature of the central state.

IMPLICATIONS OF THE INDABA FOR JOHNSON'S METHODOLOGY

Given the involvement of business in the Indaba initiatives and the central state's response to it, we have here a good example of a clear break between the interests and actions of various allied capitalists and that of the central state. Johnson's theoretical approach hangs on the notion that white supremacy is the central tenet of both the South African state and all white reformers, who at best will concede ground only in the sphere of social apartheid.[12] Pitting himself against the liberal tradition in South African historiography (which sees apartheid as a deadweight on the development of capitalism and by implication casts capitalists in a reformist light),[13] Johnson posits a far closer alliance between business and the state. He asserts that while 'tensions between the business and political leaderships of the White establish ment'[14] may exist, the whites realise that they 'cannot afford to disregard the National motto "unity is strength"' and thus 'tendencies towards conflict within the White establishment will remain mere tendencies it is safe to predict'.[15] This prediction has, of course, turned out to be far from safe in the current context of businessmen visiting the ANC in Lusaka and lobbying the government to reform the system in order to defuse the political crisis. The example of business in Natal negotiating with Buthelezi to create a devolved alternative to apartheid is another nail in the coffin of Johnson's prediction.

However, as indicated earlier, this coffin was entirely of Johnson's own making and not constructed by the carpenter of historical accident. By tying the interests of capital so closely to white supremacy, he was blind to the contradictory relationship between the white state and capitalism. While being closer to the radical than liberal tradition, Johnson's theoretical approach lacks the flexibility inherent in a Marxist approach which allows for the undermining of political institutions by economic developments.[16] Johnson's postulate about the sacrosanctity of white unity, on the other hand, forces him by the unyielding logic of his own analysis to disbelieve in the possibility of capitalists breaking with the racist state and opting for new alignments with black interest groups such as Inkatha. A more flexible approach emphasising how, under certain political conditions and stages of accumulation, capitalists' interests are furthered by white supremacy, would have been more useful to Johnson both as regards his overall analysis and the predictions he bravely makes in his concluding chapter.

THE POLITICS OF CONSTITUTION BUILDING

The Indaba's political proposals clash with those of the broad democratic movement in radical politics over both the nature of participation in the Indaba and the underlying form of democracy envisaged for the devolved region. Concerning participation, Dhlomo (Inkatha General Secretary) and Martin (Natal Provincial Council Executive Committee), members of the Indaba's 'Strategic Planning Group', declared, when announcing the April 1986 launch of the Indaba, that 'everybody' would be invited and that those who did not participate, 'effectively excluded themselves' from the path of moderation and peaceful change. In total, forty-six organisations were invited ranging from the Herstigtige Nasionale Party (HNP) (which declined the invitation on the grounds that such negotiation threatened white supremacy) to the Pan-Africanist Congress (PAC); thirty-eight accepted.

Each group was offered equal representation irrespective of size and invited to participate in meetings conducted behind closed doors. It is not surprising that the democratic organisations on the left, declined the offer. Apart from rejecting the secrecy and lack of accountability inherent in such a structure, their constituencies would have fundamentally objected to the negotiation with a Bantustan government and to the fragmentation of South Africa into regional authorities serving local interests. Finally, as the ANC and PAC would have been unable to attend the Indaba because they are banned in South Africa, the invitation extended to them was a cynical one.

Perhaps the most fundamental clash of ideology between the democratic groups on the left and the Indaba concerns the form of democracy applicable to South Africa. The principle of universal franchise in a unitary state, favoured by all radical non-racial organisations, is at complete loggerheads with the idea of a 'consociational democracy' within a 'plural society' which finds expression in the Indaba's proposals. At present, the Indaba envisages a system of two legislative chambers through which all legislation must pass.[17] The first chamber, consisting of one hundred members, is elected on a one-man-one-vote basis, where 1 per cent of the vote elects one seat. The second chamber, consists of fifty seats, which are allocated to five 'background groups'[18] on the basis of ten seats each. These 'background groups' are 'Africans', 'Afrikaners', 'English', 'Asiatics' and 'South Africans'. Voters may choose whether they are registered as 'South Africans' or as one of the former four categories. When political power is distributed according to culturally defined entities, whose legislative strength is not proportional to size, it becomes easier to protect capitalist interests, as class-based mobilisation is superseded and diffused by ethnically-based organisation. It is not surprising that the Indaba business lobby sees its interests best served under such a system, rather than for example, by a Freedom Charter-flavoured majoritarian democracy. What is also disturbing about the second chamber, is that as more non-racially orientated people elect to become 'South Africans', power will become increasingly maldistributed, as the diminishing racial constituencies become over-represented. This will certainly put a break on liberalising reform. Furthermore, this tendency will be exacerbated by the proposed 'Cultural Councils', which can be set up by any groups that can demonstrate support, which have the right to see any proposed legislation and then apply to the supreme court for an injunction if they feel their rights, identity, and so on, are severely affected by it.

Many observers, however, take solace in the much-publicised Bill of Rights of the Indaba, which promises 'equal rights before the law', 'equal access to social services' and other democratic, welfarist ideals. Surely if these rights are guaranteed, the argument goes, constitutional inadequacies and weaknesses become of secondary importance. This argument however, has justification only in circumstance in which these promises can be fulfilled and when the government supports them in a way more substantial than mere political rhetoric. It will be the contention of the following section that the promise of equal access to social services cannot be fulfilled, since it envisages public expenditure levels that are a fiscal impossibility given current levels of spending in the region. There are real economic constraints on the extent to which constitutional exercises can be used to strengthen the position of the various political groupings in South Africa, irrespective of whether this is to maintain white political supremacy, to create a consociational variant thereof, or even the creation of universal franchise in a unitary state. Leaving aside the problem this constraint creates for the government tricameral constitutional structure, it should be noted that the Indaba is generating, among many black South Africans, politically significant expectations about life in a post-apartheid Natal which are bound to be disappointed. That the left-opposition to the Indaba is silent on this point is illuminating. One suspects that such criticism might hazard a boomerang effect, because to point to the fiscal constraints on the Indaba's Bill of Rights, is to invite similar observations concerning the Freedom Charter, which promises even wider-ranging social reforms and equality. In this sense, the analysis in the following section carries implications relevant to all the future constitutional dispensations promised by the various protagonists in the national political struggle.

THE COSTS OF ADVOCATING EQUALITY

If we assume that current levels of public spending in Natal and KwaZulu are fair approximations of the resources which would be available to an Indaba government in the region, then an analysis of 1983–84 spending in the Natal–KwaZulu area will serve to illustrate the scale of the problem to be faced.[19]

In the 1983–84 financial year, which gives the latest available KwaZulu spending figures, money was disbursed in the region through three main channels: the KwaZulu government (for spending in KwaZulu); the Natal Provincial Council (NPC) (mostly for spending on whites in Natal); and the central state spending on 'coloureds', blacks and Asians in Natal, and on various services in KwaZulu. Nowadays spending in Natal on all races is almost totally controlled by the central state, and the NPC is defunct. However, the 1983-84 pattern of spending is useful in so far as racial disparities in state spending are more easily highlighted.

Let us first take the case of public spending in KwaZulu. As can be seen from Table 7.1, total spending by the KwaZulu government in 1983–84 was R569 398 525. Of this, the Health and Welfare spending accounted for 38 per cent, with Education and Culture, and Works, following with 23.4 and 23 per cent of the total respectively.

In addition a further R503 598 295 was spent by the central state on grants and services in KwaZulu. A breakdown of this is given in Table 7.2. It is certainly a sign of the times and the relative priorities of the South African state that spending on police and prisons in KwaZulu is 84 times that on community development!

As the 'Cooperation and Development' allocation includes a statutory grant to the KwaZulu government[20] of R416 529 901 (which comprises 73 per cent of KwaZulu's budget), we need to subtract this amount in order to avoid double-counting when it comes to determining total public spending in KwaZulu. Total public spending is thus

Table 7.1 KwaZulu expenditure 1983–84

Department	*Expenditure (in rands)*	*Expenditure as % of total*
Chief Minister	15 578 182	2.8
Interior	5 338 881	1.0
Works	131 227 558	23.0
Education and Culture	133 216 809	23.4
Agriculture and Forestry	28 258 081	5.0
Justice	5 193 556	1.0
Health and Welfare	217 678 266	38.0
Police	5 712 155	1.0
Finance and Economic Affairs	26 126 068	4.6
Salaries of members	1 068 969	0.2
Grand total	569 398 525	100.0

Source: KwaZulu Government Auditor-General's Report 1983–84

Table 7.2 Central state expenditure in KwaZulu 1983–84

Department	*Expenditure (in rands)*
Community development	289 933
Prisons	3 793 963
Justice	43 982
National education	319
Audit	198 558
Police	20 618 162
Cooperation and development	438 568 708
South African Development Trust	40 084 138
Education and training	532
Grand total	503 598 295

Source: South African State Auditor-General's Report 1983–84.

R503 598 295 (central state), plus R569 398 525 (KwaZulu), minus R416 529 901 (statutory grant), giving a total of R656 466 919 for the KwaZulu region.

Looking now at Natal, as shown in Table 7.3, R702 969 837 was spent by the NPC in the same financial year. It is interesting to note that the proportions spent on education and health by the NPC and the KwaZulu government are very similar. However, while spending on education in Natal is on white children only, the health expenditure in the region includes spending on black hospitals and clinics.

In addition to NPC expenditure, the central state spends a certain amount directly on blacks, Asians and 'coloureds' in the province. However, because the government publishes only total spending on

Table 7.3 Natal provincial council spending 1983–84

Heads of expenditure	*Expenditure* (R)	% *of Total*
General administration	29 147 568	4.1
Education	171 078 216	24.3
Medical and health services	257 028 005	36.6
Roads and bridges	144 299 435	20.6
Provincial building services	64 881 687	9.2
Miscellaneous services	36 534 926	5.2
Total	702 969 837	100.0

Source: NPC Auditor-General's Report 1983–84.

'non-whites' outside homeland areas for the whole of South Africa, spending on these racial groups in Natal needs to be estimated. If one assumes that each province receives the relevant funding in proportion to its share of each population group living within its boundaries, the following magnitudes can be calculated: R155 859 690 for blacks, R243 694 819 for Asians, and R27 004 450 for 'coloureds'.[21] If we add the above estimates to NPC spending, we get the grand total of R1 129 528 796 for public spending in Natal in 1983–84. There is, of course, a further component of indirect spending by the central state, such as an attributed share of Natal's gains from non-provincial specific spending on categories such as 'roads', 'commerce tourism and industry', 'defence', etc. However, as this is difficult to estimate in any meaningful sense,[22] and because a devolved government would not have access to it anyway, we shall ignore it for the purposes of this exercise.

Taking the public spending magnitudes as outlined, and using the 1980 census estimates of the population in Natal and KwaZulu, the following per capita magnitudes can be calculated. Natal Provincial Council spending per white head in Natal comes to R1251. Of course not all this money is spent directly on whites, as categories such as 'road maintenance' indirectly benefit blacks and the health service financed by the NPC includes black patients. Per capita spending on whites only, is thus hard to disentangle. If we arbitrarily assume that only a third of the NPC health budget goes on whites, then the per capita expenditure figure drops to R946. As this is probably a fairer estimate of spending on whites, we shall use it in subsequent calculations.

Central state spending per black head in Natal comes to R115. If we include two-thirds of the NPC health budget here, per capita expenditure rises to R241. As regards central state spending on 'coloureds' and Asians in Natal, the per capita expenditure amounts to R358. KwaZulu government and central state spending per black head in KwaZulu is of course much lower and amounts to only R193 per head: about a fifth of what is spent on whites in Natal from public finances.

If the total population in Natal and KwaZulu were to enjoy the same level of per capita expenditure as that currently enjoyed by whites, R5 769 162 080 would need to be spent. This represents an additional R3 983 166 365 over and above current total spending in the region. Furthermore, this financial requirement takes no account of the need to upgrade existing inferior black facilities and services – it is simply a current expenditure calculation. If instead of using spending on whites as a yardstick, we approach the problem another way and ask how much we could spend per head of population given existing budget constraints, a different picture emerges. Dividing total expenditure by total population in the region, one arrives with a figure of R293 available to be spent per capita. This involves a 77 per cent drop in white per capita expenditure and an 18 per cent drop in expenditure on coloureds and Asians. The corresponding increase in per capita spending on blacks in Natal and KwaZulu would be 255 and 152 per cent respectively.

In absolute terms, this means that whites must forgo R653 per head in order that spending on blacks in Natal and KwaZulu can go up by R53 and R100 respectively. Given the size of the absolute loss to be borne by whites, this constitutes an important political problem, to put it mildly. One is reminded of the story of the rabbi's answer to the question of whether a peaceful road to socialism is possible: 'There are two such roads,' he said, 'one natural and one supernatural. The natural one is this; the Archangel Michael could descend from heaven with a fiery sword and transform the capitalists (in this case read also whites) into pillars of salt. The supernatural way is that the capitalists would give up their power without a fight.' Likewise, given the dire need on the part of blacks for additional finance to make up for the years of state neglect, this measly addition to their present allocation is also likely to be a political problem. One is reminded of a slogan popular during the Soweto uprising of June 1976: 'We don't want more bread. We want the whole bloody bakery.'

The above exercise, however, is conducted morc as an illustration of the limits to a strictly egalitarian concept of equality, irrespective of whom adopts it, than as a critique of the Indaba as such. While leaving the content of their concept of equality ambiguous (probably in order to win support from as broad a constituency as possible) one can surmise that the Indaba views redistribution only as far as the provision of 'basic needs' is concerned. Even so, there are severe fiscal constraints to this constitutional exercise. The region does not have nearly enough finance to provide even education (which is a 'basic need' and a politically explosive issue) of a standard remotely consistent with popular expectations. This contention is explored in the next section.

EDUCATION IN NATAL AND KWAZULU

Because the 1980 population census gives the latest available breakdown of the population into schoolgoing and other age categories, we shall use expenditure figures from 1980–81 in this section. For the financial year 1980–81, the NPC-funded Natal Education Department (NED) spent R106 724 630 on white education in Natal.[23] If we estimate Natal's share of central state spending on blacks, 'coloureds' and Asians in white areas (on the basis of population shares) we arrive at spending figures of R34 249 146, R377 895 and R25 877 672 respectively. If we include the similarly-estimated share for Natal of 'National Education' (which funds non-school, non-university educational institutions in South Africa) we arrive at a total for educational spending in Natal of R215 083 237. As regards KwaZulu, R66 410 097 was spent on education in 1980-81 by the KwaZulu government and a mere R361 by the central state on 'National Education' in KwaZulu. If we add total spending on education in KwaZulu to that of Natal we arrive at a total of R281 493 695 for the region.

Taking the total number of pupils in non-university education in Natal and KwaZulu (see Table 7.4) the following per capita spending magnitudes for 1980–81 can be calculated. Per (pupil) capita spending on education in Natal for whites is R192; for Asians in Natal this comes to R134; and for blacks in KwaZulu the figure amounts to R75. 'Coloured' education is ignored here because so few 'coloureds' live in Natal that per capita calculations become relatively meaningless. Appalling though they are, the above discrepancies become even more pronounced when we consider that many fewer black and Asian children of schoolgoing ages are in school than their white counter-

Table 7.4 Pupils and teachers in Natal and KwaZulu

	School		*Total pupils*[a]
	Pupils	*Teacher/pupils*	*in Non-univ. education*
Blacks (KwaZulu)	878 226	1:51	883 197
Blacks (Natal)	169 332	1:44	169 816
Whites (Natal & KwaZulu)	108 735	1:16	117 085
Asians (Natal)	181 778	1:26	192 685
'Coloureds' (Natal)	27 905	1:26	29 187
Total	1 365 976	1:38	1 394 970

[a]School pupils plus those in special education, vocational education, teacher training, etc.
Source: Buthelezi Commission Report on Education 1982.

parts. For instance, if we divide spending on black education in Natal and KwaZulu by schoolgoing-age child rather than by enrolled pupil, per capita spending drops to R75 and R49 respectively.

Working mainly with the discrepancy between pupil enrolment and the numbers of children in the schoolgoing-age groups, and using white enrolment in the Natal Education Department (NED) as the standard, the Buthelezi Commission estimated the 'backlog' of children who ought to be in school. The numbers are shown in Table 7.5. If current public spending levels are divided by the number of pupils plus the backlog, the following per capita magnitudes are obtained: white children in Natal remain the same at R912, black children in Natal fall to R77, Asian children to R111, and black children in KwaZulu to R39.

Let us now turn to an examination of the implications of equalising spending with the NED. To do this, the KwaZulu government would have to increase educational expenditure to R805 475 665 if enrolment figures are considered, and to R1 572 135 696 if the backlog is added. This is respectively 12 and 24 times the 1980–81 spending on education in KwaZulu and even exceeds the *total expenditure* of the KwaZulu government in 1983–84. To bring educational spending per head on blacks in Natal to the level enjoyed by the NED, the central state would have to increase its spending to R154 872 192 if only actual enrolment figures are considered, and to R403 276 368 if the backlog is taken into account. This is respectively 4.5 and 11.8 times the 1980–81 spending on black education in Natal. Similarly, to bring educational spending on Asians to the level of NED spending, expenditure would need to rise

Table 7.5 Backlog of pupils in Natal and KwaZulu

Backlog of pupils	*KwaZulu*	*Natal (blacks)*	*Natal (Asians)*
Primary school	183 658	74 970	5 016
Secondary school	502 600	157 302	27 227
SCHOOL TOTAL	686 258	232 272	32 243
Special education	45 522	11 604	4 423
Teacher training	28 438	7 820	1 639
Advanced tech. ed.	80 418	20 677	2 671
Vocational ed.	—	—	—
Total (non-univ.)	840 636	272 373	40 976

Source: Buthelezi Commission Report on Education 1982.

to R175 728 720 if enrolment only is considered, and to R213 098 832 if the backlog is taken into account. This is respectively 6.8 and 8.2 times the 1980–81 level of spending on Asians in Natal.

In other words, just to equalise 1980 enrolled per capita expenditure figures to the Natal Education Department level, an additional R1 009 539 662 needs to be found, representing 57 per cent of the *combined total state expenditure at all levels in Natal and KwaZulu in 1983–84*. If the backlog of pupils is brought into play, an additional R2 188 510 896 is needed, which amounts to 123 per cent of total spending in Natal and KwaZulu in 1983–84.

Unfortunately, even if this impossible demand on KwaNatal's resources was met as regards current expenditure, we would not have proceeded very far down the path of equal educational provision. Leaving aside the vast problem of providing books, equipment, and so on, let us simply examine the financial implications of building enough classrooms to accommodate the backlog of pupils in Natal and KwaZulu. According to the Buthelezi Commission, if we take a teacher-pupil ratio of 1:20 (which is higher than the NED ratio of 1:16) there is a backlog of 24 373 primary and 4549 secondary classrooms in KwaZulu, and 4563 primary and 595 secondary classrooms in Natal. If we cost the construction of classrooms at a very basic and conservative level of R20 000 each, this implies an additional transfer of R681 640 000. If we intended catering for the backlog of students, a further 45 926 classrooms will be needed, which implies an additional R918 530 000. In short, just to build enough classrooms to cater for the needs of black schools in Natal and KwaZulu on a teacher-pupil ratio of 1:20, R1 600 170 000 is needed. Then to give each school enough finance so that per capita education spending levels are equal to those currently enjoyed by white students, R2 188 510 896 is needed. This amounts to R3 788 680 896, which is over twice as great as the total public spending in Natal and KwaZulu in 1983–84.

If we were to downgrade our hopes for attempted equalisation of education with the NED and to settle instead for the provision of very basic education (for example to operate with a teacher–pupil ratio of 1:40 and to spend only half the amount per head currently being spent on white children), then an additional R800 085 000 will be needed for classrooms, and spending would have to rise to R987 706 032: still about two million rand more than total public spending in the Natal-KwaZulu region for 1983–84. Furthermore, these figures do not include the cost of financing Asian or 'coloured' classrooms, nor the huge costs of getting the schools anywhere nearly as adequately equipped as their white counterparts. They also ignore issues like getting electricity to rural schools, developing school transport networks, sporting facilities, and so on. Finally, whether the above downgraded proposals would be politically acceptable, is a moot point. Because resistance by black pupils to Bantu Education was very much formulated in the context of an implicit comparison with white schools, expectations concerning an acceptable education system in the future will be shaped by this.

One suggested alternative to upgrading education to NED levels is to leave education largely in the hands of the private sector and to issue parents with 'vouchers' towards the costs of their children's education. Parents would send their children to the schools of their choice using the vouchers in total or partial payment of the fees which would in turn 'vary from school to school along with the quality and cost of the education that each school provides'.[24] The balance would be made up by parental contributions, scholarships, and the like.

This fairly bizarre interpretation of 'equal access to education' unsurprisingly has a following in the ranks of the Indaba. While removing distasteful racial overtones, this system is tailor-made to widen inequality along class lines – which in South Africa closely correspond to racial divisions. The richer, better schools would attract the richer (white) families who would in turn contribute proportionately more in the form of grants and donations than poorer (black) families at inferior schools. Also, if any of the poorer schools actually give a refund on the voucher (because their quality of education is so low), there will be an incentive on the part of destitute families to send their children to such schools in order to supplement their incomes. To describe such a system as 'equal access to education' makes a mockery of the very principle. This point is lost, however, on those who see the problem of apartheid as solely construed in racial terms. Nevertheless, one can assume that the tradition amongst blacks, of community solidarity and resistance to class-based issues (like rent and bus fare increases) in conjunction with school boycotts, will result in immense pressure being put on such a system should it ever see the light of day.

CONCLUSION

There are perhaps three general lessons which can be drawn from the preceding analysis. There is first the issue of the economic constraint on constitution making and geopolitical change. This constrains both the government, as it attempts to strengthen its position via constitutional tinkering, and its opponents, whether represented by the Indaba or advocates of the Freedom Charter. More specifically, negotiations over abstract principles like equality, and even weaker demands such as 'basic needs provision', which have not been concretised or costed in any meaningful way in relation to available resources and conflicting priorities, are at best a waste of time and at worst dangerous. Glossing over substantial competing claims for scarce resources with slippery political promises, simply propels the problem into the future where it will come home to roost with a vengeance. A fledgling government in a post-apartheid Natal or South Africa generally, could suddenly find itself torn apart by internal divisions, facing a disillusioned and disgruntled electorate bent on blaming the form or composition of the government for the lack of progress rather than financial constraints which should have been made clear at the outset.

This has consequences for the democratic opposition movements dedicated to the eradication of apartheid. As a strategy, pains should be taken to stress that things will be difficult, and that resources will be as strained, if not more so, after apartheid has fallen. The gaping chasm between equality with whites (and even the provision of very basic needs) and the resources available to provide this, is too large for this to be otherwise, whether for a national government or a devolved Natal. While this may arguably reduce the effectiveness of opposition mobilisation, and in the short term possibly even strengthen the position of the government, it seems grossly unlikely that oppressed people in South Africa need to be bribed by sweeping promises in order to oppose the regime. Moreover, stressing the difficulties on the path ahead, will probably lessen the likelihood of unrest, and especially counter-revolutionary unrest, under a future non-racial democratic government. As Amilcar Cabral used to warn his socialist revolutionaries: 'Tell no lies. Claim no easy victories.' The opponents of apartheid therefore face as crucial a Rubicon as the government, and the choices they both now make affect more than the survival prospects of the apartheid system, for they determine the stability and peace of the very thing that replaces it.

Notes

1. I would like to thank Jill Nattrass, John Brewer and Bill Johnson for helpful comments on earlier drafts. The mistakes, as ever, remain my own.
2. 'Indaba' is a Zulu word for a conference or talks.

3. See Buthelezi Commission Report Vol. 5, 1982, p. 31 and F. Martin, 'The Administration – Rationalisation, Integration, Modernisation', in L. Boulle and L. Baxter (eds), *Natal and KwaZulu: Constitutional and Political Options*, Cape Town, Juta, 1981, p. 153.
4. D. Glaser, 'Behind the Indaba: The making of the KwaNatal Indaba', *Transformations*, 2, 1986, p. 16.
5. See Buthelezi Commission Report, Vol. 5, 1982, pp. 106–16.
6. G. Mare, 'Regional Rule for Inkatha?', *Work in Progress*, 46, 1987, p. 7. As Buthelezi himself articulates, 'I have more than any other leader produced some formula for power-sharing for people of all races in South Africa through the Buthelezi Commission in 1982. The KwaZulu–Natal Indaba proposals are also the fruits of my politics of negotiation'. Quoted in the *Guardian*, 25 July, 1987, p.14.
7. See Buthelezi Commission Report, Vol. 2, 1982, pp. 181–9.
8. D. Glaser, 'Behind the Indaba', p. 17.
9. Ibid, p. 9. See also W. Cobbett *et al.*, 'South Africa's Regional Political Economy: A Critical Analysis of Reform Strategy in the 1980's', in SARS (ed.) *South African Review*, Johannesburg, Raven, 1986.
10. See J. Nattrass, 'Natal and KwaZulu: An Economic Profile – its Relevance for a new Dispensation' in L. Boulle and L. Baxter (eds), *Natal and KwaZulu*, 1981, and J. Du Pisanie, 'The Economic Realities of Natal and KwaZulu' in *ibid.*
11. G. Mare, 'Regional Rule for Inkatha?', 1987, p. 1.
12. R. W. Johnson, *How Long Will South Africa Survive?*, London, Macmillan, 1977, p. 289.
13. See W. Hutt, *The Economics of the Colour Bar*, London, André Deutsch, 1964; M. O'Dowd, 'South Africa in the Light of the Stages of Economic Growth', mimeo, Cape Town, 1964; R. Lewis et al., *Apartheid: Capitalism or Socialism?*, Hobart Paperback number 22, London, Institute of Economic Affairs, 1986; and M. Lipton, *Capitalism and Apartheid: South Africa 1910–1986*, Aldershot, Wildwood House, 1986.
14. R. W. Johnson, *How Long Will South Africa Survive?*, p. 292.
15. Ibid, p. 293.
16. See for example, H. Wolpe, 'Capitalism and Cheap Labour Power in South Africa: From Segregation to Apartheid', *Economy and Society*, 1, 4, 1972; and more recently J. Saul and S. Gelb, *The Crisis in South Africa*, London, Zed Press, 1981, 1986.
17. O. Dhlomo, 'The KwaZulu–Natal Indaba', *Speech*, Oxford Union Debating Society, Oxford, May 1987.
18. Ibid, loc. cit.
19. Alternatively, we could project the rate of growth of GDP (on the basis of previous growth rates) in Natal and derive a 'tax base' for an independent Natal. However, such projections are highly dubious given the current nationwide recession which appears set-in for some time (see Chapter 6). Furthermore, the determination of actual tax revenue from the tax base is very difficult without detailed information about income distribution and the nature of the tax regime to be implemented.
20. KwaZulu's statutory grant from the central state is determined by section 6 2(c) and (d) of Act 21 of 1971.

21. See N. Nattrass, 'The High Cost of Equality: The Case of the KwaZulu/Natal Indaba', Paper presented at the *ECPR* workshop on change in South Africa, Amsterdam, April, 1987, Appendix A.
22. Ibid.
23. Because we have been focusing on public spending we shall ignore the twenty-four private schools in Natal which house approximately 800 pupils and receive R30 000 000 in fees.
24. J. Du Pisanie and J. Meintjies, *Implications of Fiscal Parity in KwaZulu and Natal by 1995 and 2000 respectively*, Joint Senbank and Bepa Report, Pretoria, 1986, p. 4.

8 Internal Black Protest

John D. Brewer

INTRODUCTION

The widespread political unrest which erupted in South Africa during 1976 was probably the single most important occurrence prompting Johnson's analysis of South Africa's prospects of survival. He predicted with great perception that the unrest would lead to a 'new assertiveness', and a growth in political consciousness amongst black South Africans.[1] However, history, as he put it, was not on their side, but on that of their opponents. The reasons for this mostly had nothing to do with the dynamics of black protest but lay in forces outside. Yet Johnson did write a little on the nature of black protest as he foresaw it in the post-1976 period, identifying some inhibiting factors in the process.[2] He implied that there would be two vital limitations. It was unlikely that black protest movements would develop organisational capacity and skill, and mass collective action was likely to be ineffective. Thus, while he thought that guerrilla warfare would intensify, he did not think it would be coordinated with political action or linked to wider political mobilisation. Connected to this was the belief that the African National Congress (ANC) would not reassert itself politically within the country again, while Black Consciousness movements would find it difficult to recover from the heavy blows dealt them by the state. Collective protest would be hampered, he thought, by the absence of trade union organisation, and by divisions of interest between migrants and relatively secure and privileged 'urban insiders'. The likely effects of increased black unemployment would only be to make sufferers apathetic and cowed, and collective protest was not expected to break out in rural areas, therefore restricting it to the smaller and more heavily-policed population of urban workers.

In the period since Johnson's analysis there have been significant changes in the level of mobilisation, political consciousness and organisational skill of black South Africans. Most of these changes were not foreseen by Johnson, while some of the eventualities which he thought unlikely have arisen. This chapter will identify these changes and reconsider Johnson's arguments in the light of them.

BLACK PROTEST SINCE 1977

While the problems black South Africans now face may be old and familiar, the circumstances within which they confront these problems are new; so too are the alliances and strategies employed to solve them, changing the nature of the 'revolutionary terrain' in South Africa.[3] Two factors have primarily been responsible for this shift. First, a series of deracialisation measures have been implemented by the state which have had implications far beyond those the government intended. Although there were concessions granted to black South Africans before, deracialisation has quickened since Johnson's analysis, changing the circumstances within which black opposition to apartheid operates. Secondly, there has been a vociferous period of protest and resistance. Forty, or even thirty years ago, many of the reforms would have been heralded as very significant indeed, but the fact that they are now abused as inadequate by most black South Africans is testimony to how radicalised they have become. As a result of these two factors black opposition has been changed in such a way as to strengthen it.

The hesitant deracialisation process which characterises modern South Africa has had an effect on black protest in many ways. On the one hand the reform process demonstrates black opposition to be legitimate by proving it can change government policy. Conversely, the deracialisation measures have in two ways provided new and more effective platforms from which to engage in protest. First, the state-sponsored platforms, such as community councils and independent homeland legislatures, can be used as platforms of protest, although they tend not to be. But secondly, and most important, the reform process has strengthened black protest outside state-sponsored platforms. One can illustrate this by citing examples. There has been a tremendous increase in expenditure on black education, but education is a means of militant mobilisation and all the state has done is create a more highly educated and politicised subject population. It has created people who are acutely aware that along with their greater access to education, there has not been a similar opening-up of those political, civil and economic privileges normally associated with an educated society. The expansion of educational provision for blacks has therefore led to an expansion of political aims. This is one of the reasons why there have been education boycotts continually since 1976, and why students play a pivotal role in township unrest. To give another example, the government's constitutional reform in 1983 was one of the factors behind the reinvigoration of black protest from that date, with widespread collective protest against the constitution, and new organisations and alliances created to oppose it. The proposals united the various forces within the black communities who opposed constitutional reform, leading to the formation of the United Democratic Front (UDF), which has now emerged as the majority element in internal black opposition.

Another example of how these deracialisation measures are altering the revolutionary terrain is that they are reinforcing those economic and demographic changes which are granting black South Africans enormous economic power. The end result has been a change in the occupational structure of black employment and the growth of a black skilled, technical and managerial class. Accompanying this there has been a closing of the wage gap and an increase in the consumer power of black South Africans, making economic growth partly dependent on the growth of the black market. Hence black South Africans have economic power as consumers and they have been prepared to use consumer boycotts as weapons in the political struggle. But above all, blacks now have enormous power as producers and black trade unions are providing a source of power in the absence of direct access to political power.[4] As emphasised below, and in Chapter 10, not all unions are in favour of politicising the workplace, but political unionism, as it is called, is increasingly deployed by black trade unions, some of whom are affiliated to the leading political organisations. It is comparatively easy to crush a street demonstration, but it is more difficult to break a sustained offensive by black workers and consumers, which is why such spheres have been politicised as opposition is pursued through consumer and transport boycotts, and industrial and community strikes. The rural areas have become involved in these boycotts, as shown by the transport boycotts in the Ciskei and KwaZulu. These boycotts have successfully drawn into the political struggle many of the varied people who dwell in rural areas, such as frontier commuters and those who live in the resettlement camps, although it is still the case that most rural unrest occurs in the peri-urban areas which border on the homelands.

There is a third way in which the reform process has affected black protest in such a way as to strengthen it. As Johnson predicted, the state uses reform as an attempt to coopt middle class and economically privileged blacks in order to give them a stake in maintaining the status quo. But on the whole the reforms have been rejected by the very groups they were designed to placate, so that deracialisation itself has become a source of critique because it lacks substance or no longer goes far enough. There is some evidence here to support what is known as the rising expectations theory of revolution, for clearly those groups who are the object of the cooption policy are at the forefront of black unrest, such as trade unionists, and many middle-class and 'insider' groups like students, churchmen, community workers, teachers, and journalists.

These are some of the factors lying behind the intensification of opposition since Johnson's analysis. Black political activity before the 1976 disturbances fell to a very low ebb. Survey results showed that in the late 1960s blacks generally were politically apathetic because they regarded the power structure as impermeable. But the more or less spontaneous outburst of protest in 1976 and its aftermath changed this. Political self-effacement and quiescence have given way to a willingness to confront the regime: the apartheid system is no longer regarded as invincible. Thus, one of the most simple and obvious distinguishing features of current black opposition to apartheid is its intensity. This is nowhere better demonstrated than in the diffusion of protest throughout the whole of everyday life. Black opposition to apartheid is expressed in the rich indigenous poetry emerging from literary groups in the townships, in sport, in the newly-formed religious groups, in dance and song, in schoolchildren boycotting classes, in press copy, street daubings, worker activism and consumer boycotts. This diffusion is another of the new characteristics of resistance, making it more difficult to suppress. In 1960 the defiance campaign came to an end when it resulted in the Sharpeville massacre and the banning of the leading political organisations. This historical lesson shows how easy it is to neutralise protest by banning the organisational thrust behind it. By contrast, the state of emergency twenty-five years later did not neutralise the protest precisely because it had become so diffused throughout the whole of black life. This will also nullify the restrictions placed on the UDF in 1988.

This diffusion is not as amorphous as it seems. At one level mass collective action has the value of uniting communities in action and can be effective in the short term in registering collective anger and protest. But in the long term collective action should be judged by whether it raises the consciousness of participants and leads to organisational forms of opposition. Despite the brutality of the state's repression, collective action has been successful when measured in this way. The initial demonstration in Soweto in 1976 and many of the subsequent incidents elsewhere, were organised independently by students, but student-based action has been effective in expanding the constituency for change, in winning people over to direct action, and in facilitating the expansion of the immediate concerns into a more generalised and diffuse challenge to apartheid. But it is also characteristic of black protest now that it shows increasing tactical and organisational sophistication. A variety of organisations have been formed to harness the power of diffuse collective action and to pursue the demands of participants more effectively. These organisations have channelled the protest and made it more concrete. Tactical agility is also apparent. The various committees which have sprung up around collective protests have occasionally called temporary halts to the protest in order to provide time for their short-term demands to be met and for a breathing-space in which to consolidate their gains. Moreover, students have realised the limits of working alone and now link up with workers, trade unions and adult-led organisations, in whose campaigns students become increasingly involved. Therefore, there is a high level of organisational capacity, reminiscent of the defiance campaign in the 1950s, but distinguished from earlier periods by the new organisations, alliances and strategies employed.

NEW STRATEGIES AND ALLIANCES

Because greater functions than ever before have been devolved to sponsored political machinery, pragmatists have some justification in arguing that using sponsored platforms is an effective strategy. This is why sponsored platforms have attracted a more astute type of politician. The Urban Bantu Councils were discredited institutions which attracted a set of dubious political characters, and at first the community councils attracted a similar sort – in some cases the membership of the two bodies was almost identical. With the devolution of greater functions to local councils they have been able to attract less peripheral politicians, as Inkatha's support shows. A similar process has benefited Inkatha, for a number of exiled radicals have returned to South Africa and joined the organisation. In this way, the deracialisation process has lent greater credence to the strategy of collaboration, giving black politicians certain short-term advantages by being able to make decisions affecting the immediate lives of black people, distribute scarce resources, and satisfy some socioeconomic needs in a way that was never possible before. But collaborators suffer under a society whose problems become their responsibility, while they are helpless to deal with the root causes behind them. Hence two types of collaboration need to be distinguished, the second of which more actively attempts to address the basic issues.

'Open collaboration', in what Adam and Moodley call patronage–client alliances between the state and a variety of sponsored platforms,[5] is a strategy which openly and voluntarily accepts the opportunities provided by the state. This contrasts with what has been called 'collaborative opposition' and 'pragmatic institutional opposition',[6] which uses the protective umbrella of state-sponsored machinery to educate and politicise a constituency which is intended eventually to overthrow the system they now operate. This is how Inkatha, and the coloured and Indian politicians who participate in the constitution see their role. It also describes those black trade unions which have opted to register with the state's industrial relations machinery in order for their role in collective bargaining to be officially recognised. Some of these unions tend to eschew direct affiliation to political organisations to concentrate on building an effective plant-based organisation which can later be used as a means of opposition. This strategy tends towards political moderation as a result of the bureaucratic pressures the state has enmeshed around the platforms, and the lack of credibility it entails. In the case of most of the registered unions, political moderation is an unintended consequence of concentrating on plant-based issues, while for most other collaborators it is an intentional choice. For example, Buthelezi describes himself as a responsible conservative, offering Inkatha to the state as a cooptable ally, albeit on his own terms. This conservatism is not a feature of those unions which eschew politics in favour of patient plant-based organisation, for while they reject political unionism to the extent of opposing affiliation to the main political organisations, they have taken a radical stance on many political issues. For this reason they have not lost credibility, unlike Inkatha.

For a long time after the banning of the main political organisations in 1960, non-collaboration was forced into clandestine activity, separating it from overt political mobilisation. The ANC was originally a movement based on overt mass mobilisation and as a result its transformation into a guerrilla organisation was hampered. Leaflet bombs acted as an occasional compromise but the dilemma of the ANC was clear: it was cut off from mass mobilisation but could not renounce it, which in turn weakened the ruthlessness of its sabotage. In the end it did neither effectively, although its support in the black community remained high. For this reason, the strategy of non-collaboration pursued by Black Consciousness organisations was for a long while unique. They refused to participate in government-sponsored platforms but retained a commitment to pursue opposition through peaceful and overt political mobilisation.

However, considerable changes have occurred in the strategy of non-collaboration, resulting in new alliances. Black Consciousness organisations encountered problems in reaping the legitimacy of non-collaboration. They engaged in mass mobilisation while enunciating a philosophy which hampered their effectiveness, cutting them off from a constituency in the black working class, and from white liberals working in the trade unions or in opposition parties who were pushing for change. Additionally, the politics of exile isolated the ANC from the mass political mobilisation it aspired to. The rapidly developing struggle between the community councils and their opponents over leadership in the urban townships convinced the ANC that it needed to be a part of this struggle and directly influence its outcome. It first courted Inkatha, which was understandable for Inkatha's membership figures imply that it is effective in mass mobilisation. Black Consciousness groups were not mass organisations in that sense, only having a stable constituency among the black middle class, and a support base restricted to the urban areas. Conversely, Inkatha only effectively mobilises among Zulu and its policies after 1978 involved a compromise which the ANC rejected. The first signal that some Black Consciousness organisations were prepared to cooperate with the ANC came in 1979 with the opening up of the Committee of Ten to mass membership and its reorganisation into the Soweto Civic Association, and a new emphasis on class and worker issues. Black Consciousness was left in a state of disarray by this shift in strategy. The Azanian People's Organisation (AZAPO) has not thought through the logic of its class approach, for it rejects the contact with whites that has been championed by the ANC since its banning, while Dr Motlana and Allan Boesak remain in favour of free enterprise but are currently among those who are leading the move to re-establish the ANC inside the country. Their supporters in this include such former Black Consciousness stalwarts as the Congress of South African Students (COSAS), and the Azanian Students Organisation (AZASO), who equally espouse AZAPO's class analysis but who also favour the non-racialism which AZAPO rejects. During 1981 COSAS and AZASO changed their position on negotiation and cooperation with whites, supporting the idea of non-racialism alongside those whose vision of Azania is very much a capitalist one. Before it was banned, COSAS opened itself up to membership from whites. Some independent unions formerly within the Black Consciousness tradition also moved toward non-racialism, most notably the South African Allied Workers' Union and the General and Allied Workers' Union. Thus, as many people predicted, including Johnson, some Black Consciousness groups have become radicalised and now associate themselves directly with the ANC.[7] But Johnson was incorrect in believing that it would be the 'vulgar Marxism' of the communist faction of the ANC which would attract Black Consciousness. While AZAPO advances a socialist manifesto, it does so in order to oppose the ANC, and the radicalised Black Consciousness organisations which are associated with the ANC in the UDF, are linked to the charterist faction within the ANC.

The association between the ANC and radicalised Black Consciousness groups intensified with the formation of the UDF in 1983, whose policy statements, support base and political activities reflect the themes and aspirations of the ANC's Freedom Charter. Its affiliated organisations include such former ANC supporters as the Transvaal and Natal Indian congresses, who are now linked with such radicalised Black Consciousness organisations as COSAS, AZASO, the Committee of Ten, the Port Elizabeth Civic Organisation, and the Media Workers' Association of South Africa, as well as a variety of registered and unregistered unions. Alliances like this bring their own problems and conflicts, which pose a threat to any future cooperation between the parties involved. As a result of these changes the squabbles within Black Consciousness have been vituperative, and similar debates must be occurring within the ANC. The state also poses a threat, for the link exposes the UDF and the radicalised Black Consciousness organisations to the same suppression reserved for the ANC. None the less a new alliance has emerged within the umbrella of the UDF, encouraging some analysts to suggest the formation of a new party, the United African National Party, symbolising the association between the ANC, UDF and radicalised Black Consciousness organisations.[8] This is what is significant about the period after the 1976 disturbances, for it presented black opposition to apartheid with different circumstances, and with the new problems came new solutions. A situation has arisen where the various groups employing non-collaboration have united around two broad factions, centred on the larger and more popular UDF, and the smaller and less popular National Forum, the latter representing the more orthodox Black Consciousness tradition of AZAPO. The ANC's current strategy therefore seeks to coordinate guerrilla tactics with specific political struggles, as occurred during campaigns against township rent and service charge increases, the constitutional referendum, the opening of parliament under the new constitution, and various elections, and to accompany military activities with overt political mobilisation via the UDF and its affiliates.

THE RE-EMERGENCE OF NON-RACIALISM

Not all changes in internal black opposition to apartheid are new, for the historic idea of non-racialism has re-emerged as the basis of a new alliance. As Johnson stated, Black Consciousness dominated black student and community politics in the 1970s, and the revolutionaries in exile had little connection with internal politics. But Black Consciousness has been replaced as the dominant element in black politics by the ANC's traditional theme of non-racialism, which is espoused by the UDF and its affiliates. These organisations have successfully reintroduced the ANC into internal politics, where it is becoming as active as it was before it was banned. An index of its growing importance to internal politics is provided by the various groups who have met with ANC officials in exile; another is the widespread recognition of the symbolic importance of Nelson Mandela, whose release became a strong domestic and international issue in this period.

Survey research confirms the popularity of the theme of non-racialism and the associated revival of the ANC. Schlemmer and Welsh provide figures showing that 40 per cent of respondents on the Witwatersrand were prepared openly to admit their support for the ANC.[9] In another study by Schlemmer in 1984 amongst African industrial workers in the Witwatersrand and Port Elizabeth areas, 39 per cent expressed support for the ANC, UDF and affiliates, with 5 per cent supporting AZAPO, and 14 per cent Inkatha. Only in the Durban area did Inkatha's support exceed that of the ANC, UDF and affiliates; but the latter's support there only dropped by 4 per cent.[10] This illustrates how geographically widespread the support for the ANC, UDF and affiliates is, compared to the narrow geographical base of Inkatha.[11] Indeed, in this poll collaborationist parties like Inkatha and Sofasonke did better than AZAPO in both areas where the survey was conducted. When respondents were asked to choose between leaders rather than political organisations, the same trend continued. Southall quotes surveys which show that in May 1985 Mandela was rated 'best leader' by 48 per cent of respondents in Durban's Black townships, compared to 19 per cent for Buthelezi, suggesting that Inkatha's support had declined even in its main constituency. By September of that year Mandela's support had risen in metropolitan Durban to 53 per cent while Buthelezi's declined to 5 per cent. A similar gulf in support existed in a survey on the Witwatersrand.[12]

There are a variety of reasons which explain why the ANC and the theme of non-racialism have re-emerged to become so popular in internal politics. Despite its isolation from the internal political struggle after its banning, there was always a residue of support for the organisation but the prominence of the ANC's military activities since 1979 have given it a prestige which in internal politics legitimated the non-racialist stance of the UDF and its affiliates, some of whom were connected with the ANC in an earlier period. There was also a recognition of the ANC's historic role, with black political activists becoming aware that the political struggle did not begin with Black Consciousness in the 1970s, but has a long tradition beginning with the ANC. The maturity of the ANC's leadership reinforces this continuity. Terror Lekota was once a leading figure in Black Consciousness and was imprisoned on Robben Island in 1976. Fellow defendants in his trial emerged from prison to join AZAPO and eventually to found the National Forum, but Lekota became a leading figure in the UDF. He explained this transformation as the result of Mandela's influence upon him while on Robben Island, whereupon Lekota realised the broader context of the struggle: 'Those of us who participate in the UDF do so fully aware that the struggle of our people does not begin today. An increasing number of young people in the townships are now saying openly that the ANC was formed over seventy years ago, as the first liberation organization of our people, and by that fact alone the ANC is our natural political home.'[13] There is also a reawareness among radical blacks of the contribution some whites have made to the liberation struggle. In late 1981 many white trade unionists, students and community leaders were detained in an extensive police swoop, one of whom was Neil Aggett, who eventually died while in detention. Other whites have subsequently been imprisoned for treason as a result of their political activities, and the 'End Conscription Campaign' further symbolises the contribution whites are making. Moreover, with the ANC's lifelong commitment to non-racialism and its multi-racial organisational and leadership structure, some black South Africans are beginning to see the ANC itself as a microcosm of South Africa's own non-racial future, allowing the UDF to benefit in the same way.

There are additional factors which explain why the UDF and organisations within the radicalised faction of Black Consciousness were prepared to advance non-racialism in order to identify themselves with the ANC rather than orthodox Black Consciousness. Some Black Consciousness students came under the protection of the ANC when they fled into exile and have since returned as ANC activists. The leading Black Consciousness organisations active in the late 1970s were led by ex-ANC figures, and their ineffectiveness in contesting the leadership struggle in the urban townships made Black Consciousness leaders realise that a broader power base was needed, especially contact with workers. The adoption of a class analysis was also facilitated by structural changes in the economy which increased black economic power. The emphasis on class culminated for some Black Consciousness organisations in support for the theme of non-racialism, for many Black Consciousness organisations thought through the logic of a class analysis and linked themselves with whites working for change in the trade unions, and in extra-parliamentary politics. Non-racialism is a necessary corollary of the emphasis upon class, which gives AZAPO's ideology an inherent contradiction. Moreover, in their conflict with the community councillors for leadership of the townships, it became obvious to Black Consciousness spokesmen that they were prolific articulators of grievances but they had not constructed the viable grass-roots structure and organisation around their high reputation. The ANC had the viable structure and itself used cooperation with radicalised Black Consciousness groups within the umbrella of the UDF to reinstate itself in the country. The growing intensity of the political struggle inside South Africa convinced the ANC of the limitations of an exile-based strategy built primarily around sabotage. Some activists within the ANC argued that sabotage alone would not bring an end to apartheid,[14] and the idea of non-racialism became a unifying theme which allowed the ANC to cooperate with organisations who were playing an active role in internal politics, many of whom were led by ex-ANC figures anyway.

Supporters of orthodox Black Consciousness thus accuse the ANC of having hijacked them, and of exploiting a wave of protest for which Black Consciousness organisations were originally responsible. Saths Cooper said: 'Look, the ANC was banned in 1960. What presence did they maintain in this country until Black Consciousness came up? Nothing. They had abrogated responsibility for leadership. Then Black Consciousness arose and took the people to a cataclysmic type of reawakening that you saw happening in 1976. Now this wasn't attributable at all to the ANC, but purely to [a] Black Consciousness orientation. This is a fact: these organizations which were haemorrhaging got new blood transfusions from the exodus of post-76. The ANC's frontline slaughter sheep are products of Black Consciousness. They are the product of Soweto, of Black Consciousness, who have been reoriented into a vicious anti-Black Consciousness line'.[15] Cooper's analysis is entirely correct, although the inference he draws is not. Indeed, the ANC's advocacy of the theme of non-racialism makes them better able to exploit this situation because the idea is consistent with trends in black public opinion, allowing political organisations advancing this theme to tap these sentiments.

A number of surveys by the same analysts over a number of years show that there is considerable sympathy amongst black South Africans for political consultation and negotiation, and despite their high level of dissatisfaction and anger, the minimum demands of a wide cross-section of blacks are moderate and amount to a substantial compromise with white interests.[16] The historic Freedom Charter, which epitomises the ideal of non-racialism, has come to represent this compromise and is widely supported again. Accepting some form of negotiation and consultation with whites is linked to this compromise, so long as it is negotiation over fundamental issues. Kane-Berman quotes an opinion survey which revealed that two-thirds of a sample of Soweto residents would support the local council if those elected to it were to change the body into one which 'really represented Africans' and 'gained improvements'.[17] This confirmed the research of Schlemmer and Welsh that an 'exceedingly high' proportion of Africans were prepared to accept a second-best political solution if it meant an improvement in the provision of basic services.[18] Clearly blacks want material advancement, and non-collaborators are presented with a problem when they shun involvement with those opportunities which could genuinely provide material gain. The moves within some Black Consciousness organisations and the UDF towards some form of consultation with whites come from their awareness of this problem. Yet this 'second-best political solution' does not extend to support for separate development institutions. What precisely the term 'second-best' means is difficult to judge, but there is evidence of what it is not. Schlemmer and Welsh make it clear that economic advancement should not be at the expense of political equality with whites. Their respondents were envisaging a second-best political solution which still involved equality, for when presented with a choice between higher material gain coupled with continued inequality and lower material gain but equality with whites, 8 out of 10 respondents chose lower material gain.[19] Blacks want material gain but not at the expense of full political liberation. This is a trend in public opinion which, for example, the black trade union movement has begun to incorporate in its demands.

There are implications for other opposition forces. Some form of negotiation seems to be legitimated so long as it does not compromise longstanding hopes for an end to apartheid, political equality and a redistribution of wealth. This is the position which the ANC adopted in a letter from Oliver Tambo which circulated in the underground in 1979 and which stated that some form of consultation with whites was legitimate so long as it was done for the right reasons. More recently Adam and Moodley describe Tambo as willing to engage in dialogue with the government so long as it is about 'how to extend democracy'.[20] These are the conditions which the UDF and the radicalised Black Consciousness organisations formally set out as necessary to persuade them to negotiate. The fact that Inkatha has compromised them and is prepared to accept considerably less, distinguishes its stand on the issue of negotiation. This trend in black public opinion towards supporting some limited negotiation but only over certain central issues, was another factor which forced some Black Consciousness organisations and supporters to move away from their original stand against contact with whites, and against consultation on any terms. This change culminated in their rejection of the philosophy of orthodox Black Consciousness to support the UDF, ANC and the theme of non-racialism.

CONFLICT AND DIVISION WITHIN BLACK OPPOSITION

With the changing strategies and alliances have come new conflicts, but since some alliances coalesce around earlier themes, old conflicts have also resurfaced. However, the depth of the divisions and the violence which has accompanied them are new, constituting another distinguishing mark of current internal black opposition. Whereas the pattern of earlier periods of resistance was that of a rather one-dimensional conflict against apartheid, currently there are widening cleavages within black protest.[21] The cleavages are complex and are not adequately captured by contrasting Inkatha and the ANC, or non-racialism and orthodox Black Consciousness.[22] There are obvious conflicts between the respective supporters of the strategies of collaboration and non-collaboration, but divisions also exist within each. Amongst those who support the strategy of collaboration, for example, there are differences over what degree of collaboration is legitimate and what reforms are necessary to win further participation in state-sponsored political machinery. An instance of this is the conflict between Inkatha and the coloured and Indian parties which decided to participate in the new constitution, eventually leading to the break up of the Inkatha-dominated South African Black Alliance. Another is the divisions between the various parties who offer themselves for election to local councils in the African townships. For example, the Sofasonke party fought the 1983 election in Soweto on a far more radical manifesto than hitherto, which led to bitter in-fighting among councillors over whether the council should be destroyed from within, and to the assassination of Edward Manyosi just hours before he was due to take his office as mayor. The registered unions, as more reluctant collaborators, often find themselves opposed to those who more willingly adopt the strategy of collaboration, but they are also divided amongst themselves over such issues as the optimal organisational scale, union democracy, whether mobilisation should be plant-based or community-wide, and related differences over the utility of politicising the workplace. Some of these conflicts are an obstacle to unity among the trade unions.

Within the strategy of non-collaboration, the theme of non-racialism is a major source of division, but there are equally important differences of opinion over whether it is legitimate to consult with the state, and what reforms are necessary to begin the process of negotiation. The vexed question of how legitimate it is for a trade union to register is a variant of this dilemma. Unregistered unions also have to confront the same internal organisational and administrative problems as their registered counterparts, as well as whether or not to affiliate to the main political organisations.[23] Tactical questions are very important within this strategy because of state harassment, and they provide another source of division, especially the question of how closely to become associated with the ANC, leading to related conflicts over the role of armed struggle. But there are also divisions over fundamental principles, such as whether the liberation struggle should be one to achieve a socialist Azania or for the introduction of more liberal-democratic civil rights. There are disagreements over the character of the post-apartheid economy and polity, and whether the rights of the white minority should be guaranteed. Thus AZAPO focuses upon what it calls 'racial capitalism', which they argue can only be overthrown by a socialist revolution in which, rather orthodoxly, the working class alone can participate. Ignoring advances in the conceptualisation of class, they relegate the importance of other social groups, especially the rural outsiders and the radicalised middle class, the latter of which constitute what Habermas calls 'educated labour', and are normally key agents in social change.[24] Conversely the UDF advocates what Adam calls 'capitalist non-racialism',[25] which endorses a mixed economy with liberal democratic civil rights. Hence AZAPO abuses the UDF, and the Freedom Charter, as bourgeois, although, ironically, they are simultaneously accused by the South African state of fronting the South African Communist Party.[26]

These cleavages manifest themselves in an array of issues, on which different stances are taken by the various protagonists within black opposition, making them important to black politics. The issues include the establishment of a Bill of Rights, support for the Freedom Charter compared to the Azanian People's Manifesto, the question of universal franchise, support for a unitary state over consociational and confederal political solutions, the issues of sanctions and disinvestment, the utility of boycotts, the priority of worker, community or political action, the issue of peaceful change versus violence, the question of whether a National Convention should be established, the issue of sporting contacts, public ownership versus a mixed economy, economic decentralisation, policies of cultural revivalism, and many more. The cleavages within black protest are complicated by the fact that the stances taken on issues such as these transcend any simple contrast between collaboration and non-collaboration, or non-racialism and racial exclusivity. Supporters of a particular strategy or alliance are often divided amongst themselves on a concrete issue, with some adopting a position similar to their opponents. Hendrickse's challenge to segregated facilities, Sofasonke's demand for an economic and industrial base in Soweto, or Inkatha's support for aligning worker, trade union, and political mobilisation are examples of this from within the collaborationist strategy. Conversely, the ANC's support for a Bill of Rights parallels that of Inkatha's. The ambivalence of some radical trade unions towards disinvestment blunts a sharp contrast between their position and Inkatha's, while the UDF's desire for peaceful change mirrors that of Buthelezi. And despite obvious differences, there are many issues on which the UDF and AZAPO agree.

Therefore, certain issues provide a basis of consensus, which adds force to the arguments of those political leaders who urge unity. The UDF has said that it is prepared to discuss with AZAPO the possibility of joint action on specific issues, which has occurred several times, and it met with Inkatha during December 1986 to discuss differences between the organisations. The ANC's call in December 1985 for a grand coalition of anti-government organisations was premised on the awareness that short-term tactical alliances can be forged around key issues. The formation of the Congress of South African Trade Unions (COSATU) in the same year, after protracted unity talks among registered and unregistered unions, is an example of how pragmatic alliances can come from agreement upon a few central issues. COSATU has subsequently identified itself with the ANC, thus extending the alliances within black politics.

Yet the intra-black violence which has accompanied these cleavages makes the use of violence itself an important source of division, working against any superficial unity. For many analysts, intra-black political violence is the major distinguishing feature of current opposition, for this is the period in which physical attacks upon opponents became commonplace, when some Inkatha officials arm themselves with guns in order to lead the attacks on UDF supporters, and when the 'necklace' became a method of protest for UDF supporters against those employing the strategy of collaboration.[27] This violence is not characteristic of earlier phases of resistance and it is necessary to consider why it has become so in this period. The South African government considers intra-black violence as unmotivated murder devoid of any political content. The fury of excited youngsters has proved difficult for leaders to control, but this is not because of mindlessness, or, as Adam and Moodley argue, an absence of political organisation in the townships.[28] On the whole it reflects the reverse.

The struggle against apartheid has intensified to such an extent that increased political consciousness has led to the formation of a variety of new protest organisations, which has increased the competition for political support in the townships. As a result of this heightened consciousness, political activists are increasingly refusing to flee into exile, as they did in 1976, deciding now to remain inside South Africa to work at grass-roots level organising around township and national issues. The political violence has to be fitted into this background. But this heightening of consciousness and proclivity for dissension and debate, which in other circumstances would be taken as a sign of vitality, is not in itself sufficient to explain the violence. Heightened consciousness and political competition have turned violent only in a situation where the state's escalation in violence has created a political struggle in which violence of all sorts in the townships is a daily occurrence. Moreover, the reform process itself engenders violence. For example, township violence has to be linked to the failure of black wages to keep pace with inflation in a context where increases in township rent and service charges are now being imposed by African local councillors themselves, compounding their lack of legitimacy. The deracialisation measures have also divided blacks because of the differential incorporation and inducements they entail. But above all, government policies have enshrined political apartheid by seeming to exclude Africans from parliament forever. In a situation in which political consciousness has intensified, and in which state violence is a daily occurrence, anger at the apartheid system easily gets misdirected against those symbols of the system who are more readily identifiable and accessible to township residents: that is, township policemen, local councillors and fellow residents who support different strategies for the overthrow of apartheid.

CONCLUSION

Internal black opposition to apartheid since 1976 has intensified (even to the extent of turning violent), become diffused throughout everyday life, but also solidified around a number of organisations which support the strategy of non-collaboration. However, collaborationist organisations are relatively powerful. Inkatha is the most notable example, especially since it was exempted from the restrictions placed on black political organisations in February 1988. But the government did Buthelezi no favours by this special treatment, for it further reinforced Inkatha's ostracism from radical blacks. As a result Buthelezi is too weak to rule the post-apartheid South Africa by himself, but he is presently too powerful for it to be ruled without him. As Massing correctly notes, the ANC is going to have to do a deal with Inkatha.[29] Yet it is also clear that the non-collaboration which is so legitimate for most black South Africans, is of a particular kind. The new political environment has produced a situation in which the black majority expect opposition forces to negotiate when it is beneficial, and when it is over fundamental issues. For the ANC, this facilitates discussion with Buthelezi as much as it does with P. W. Botha. However, there is also an obverse to Massing's point. What is significant about black protest is that the ANC has re-emerged as a strong internal force to an extent that Buthelezi and Botha cannot ignore. The formation of the UDF, and the association within it between the ANC and radicalised Black Consciousness organisations, bears directly on Johnson's argument in 1977 that black protest would be incapable of weakening the system of white political supremacy.

Many changes have occurred in internal black opposition which have strengthened it since Johnson made this claim, and the alliance represented by the UDF is the most significant. Even if the conflicts between the UDF, Inkatha and AZAPO remain to divide black protest, as seems likely in the short term, and despite restrictions on UDF political activity, the realignment represented by the UDF portends a new era for internal black opposition to apartheid. The alliances to which the UDF gives organisational expression are fragile, but if they continue (which also appears likely), they link the black professional middle-class support of radicalised Black Consciousness with the working-class support of the ANC. They provide the ANC with an internal wing so that a strategy based on armed struggle and mass political mobilisation can be forged. They also marginalise still further the collaborationist forces by isolating them from the radicalised black communities, forcing them to rely on the diminishing constituency of moderates. Finally, these alliances make class and labour issues more important to internal black politics, making black workers a powerful force pushing for political change. These conditions define the beginnings of a new phase to internal black opposition to apartheid, giving black protest unprecedented strength.

This strength is divorced from the particular organisation which gives institutional expression to it. Banning the UDF or preventing it from engaging in political activity, as occurred in February 1988, only touches the organisational expression of a much broader structural change and realignment in black politics. For example, the South African government does not just confront escalating but essentially sporadic civil unrest and guerrilla warfare, as Johnson thought. It is not the extent or the spontaneity of the violence which chiefly distinguishes current black protest, but the organisational skill of black political movements, and the level of mobilisation they are able to achieve amongst black South Africans. Therefore, new organisations which give expression to the new alignments will emerge to replace those banned or proscribed. Further, black activists are now better able than ever before to coordinate strike action by workers and boycotts by consumers, with mass political action in the townships against local and national issues, and well-timed military actions by formal guerrilla elements and informal people's militias, drawing into the struggle the urban working and middle classes, trade unionists and many rural dwellers. There has been a parallel expansion in political aims. The goals to emerge ten years after the 1976 disturbances are symbolised by the now ubiquitous slogans 'Make Apartheid Ungovernable', and 'A People's War'. And a decade later the means to realise these aims involve a range of insurrectionary tactics beyond undirected violence, including the establishment of local neighbourhood committees and people's education classes as organs of self-rule. This sort of coordination has its roots in the alliances that comprise the UDF (or whatever new organisation emerges to replace it), and makes internal black opposition better able today to challenge the system of white political supremacy.

Moreover, one of the warnings Johnson cautioned has diminished in importance. The repressive power of the South African state is immense, and if anything has grown since Johnson's analysis, but the changed form and character of black protest described above makes it more capable of resisting suppression. Because of these changes, the restrictions the state placed on the political activity of the UDF and several other organisations in February 1988 will only have a superficial effect on black opposition. For example, black South Africans have been radicalised in both aims and conduct, and while it is possible for the state to suppress some of the means by which this radicalism is manifested, it is difficult to see blacks becoming quiescent again. Part of the reason for this lies in the sharp rise in the expectations of most black South Africans, and the success which black protest has had, as they see it, in winning policy changes from the government, whether it be the abolition of instruction in Afrikaans in Soweto schools in 1976, or the whole deracialisation process since. Nor is the state able to suppress all expressions of radicalism. Black protest has become diffused throughout the whole of everyday life and is more difficult to crush. Banning a major organisation or detaining its leaders has little effect on dampening the mood of resistance at the local level because opposition is so dispersed. The government discovered this in the states of emergency imposed in 1985 and 1986, for banning COSAS or detaining UDF leaders did contain the violence but did not reduce the mood of opposition. The UDF's amorphous, popular front type of organisational structure adds further protection against moribundity upon the detention of particular leaders, and with the restrictions imposed on its political activities, its affiliates are likely to regroup themselves and form other organisations on which there are no proscriptions, as occurred after the banning of political organisations in 1977. Moreover, there are few means available to the state to overcome a consumer boycott, or rent and service charge boycotts in the townships, which explains why many businesses and township authorities have gone bankrupt. It has tried to counter them by crude repression, but suppressive police and army tactics are counterproductive and actually promote black opposition. The conduct of the security forces in quelling unrest is treated by blacks as a litmus test of the state's commitment to change, and the inference they draw from police action is that the state is not serious about reform, serving as a further stimulus to a mood of opposition.[30]

Yet perhaps Johnson's most important point still holds. What was special about his argument in 1977 was its demonstration of how complex and interwoven were the internal and international forces that threatened South Africa, with each particular element of the matrix being relatively ineffective by itself. Despite the strengthening of internal black protest, this remains true ten years on, for although they are significant, the effects of the changes in black protest on their own lead to only a marginal weakening of the system of white political supremacy, especially since few legal forms of political activity, by which this heightened mood of opposition can be expressed, survived the clampdown of February 1988. Even if new organisations replace the UDF, black protest alone will never bring the apartheid state to breaking point, but crucial tactical breakthroughs have been made within black opposition which make it more capable of doing this when combined with other elements of the matrix. The balance of forces is shifting, if only crescively, in favour of black South Africans.

Notes

1. R. W. Johnson, *How Long Will South Africa Survive?*, London, Macmillan, 1977, p. 295.
2. Ibid., pp. 296–7.
3. For a selection of works which discuss this shift see: H. Adam and K. Moodley, *South Africa Without Apartheid*, Berkeley, University of California Press, 1986; J. Brewer, *After Soweto: An Unfinished Journey*, Oxford, Clarendon Press, 1987; A. Callinicos and J. Rogers, *Southern Africa After Soweto*, London, Pluto Press, 1977; R. Cohen, *Endgame in South Africa*, London, James Currey, 1986; J. Frederikse, *A Different Kind of War*, London, James Currey, 1986; H. Giliomee, *The Parting of the Ways*, Cape Town, David Philip, 1983; B. Hirson, *Year of Fire, Year of Ash*, London, Zed Press, 1979; J. Kane Berman, *Method in the Madness*, London, Pluto Press, 1978; T. Karis, 'Revolution in the Making: Black Politics in South Africa', *Foreign Affairs*, 62, 1983; T. Lodge, *Black Politics in South Africa Since 1945*, London, Longman, 1983; S. Nolutshungu, *Changing South Africa*, Manchester, Manchester

University Press, 1982; R. Price and G. Rosberg, *The Apartheid Regime*, Berkeley, Institute of International Studies, 1980; J. Saul and S. Gelb, *The Crisis in South Africa*, New York, Monthly Review Press, 1981.

4. See J. Blumenfeld, 'Economic Relations and Political Leverage', in J. Barber, J. Blumenfeld, and C. Hill, *The West and South Africa*, London, Routledge and Kegan Paul, 1982, pp. 86–7.
5. Adam and Moodley, *South Africa Without Apartheid*, op. cit., p. 78.
6. A. du Toit, 'Economic Strategies for Political Control', in Price and Rosberg, *The Apartheid Regime*, op. cit.
7. See R. First, 'After Soweto: A Response', *Review of African Political Economy*, 11, 1978; R. W. Johnson, *How Long Will South Africa Survive?*, op. cit., p. 295; T. Lodge, *Black Politics in South Africa Since 1945*, op. cit.; F. Molteno, 'The Uprising of 16 June', *Social Dynamics*, 5, 1979; S. Nolutshungu, *Changing South Africa*, op. cit.; J. Saul and S. Gelb, *The Crisis in South Africa*, op. cit.
8. R. Cohen, *Endgame in South Africa*, op. cit., p. 89.
9. L. Schlemmer and D. Welsh, 'South Africa's Constitutional and Political Prospects', *Optima*, 30, 1982, p. 225.
10. L. Schlemmer, *Black Workers' Attitudes*, Durban, Centre of Applied Social Sciences, 1984.
11. On Inkatha's membership, see J. Brewer, 'Inkatha's Membership in KwaMashu, *African Affairs*, 84, 1985; id., 'Inkatha's Membership in KwaMashu: A Rejoinder to Southall', ibid., 85, 1986; R. Southall, 'A Note on Inkatha Membership', ibid.
12 Southall, 'A Note on Inkatha Membership', op. cit., p. 582.
13. Quoted by J. Frederikse, *A Different Kind of War*, op. cit., pp. 157–8.
14. See Adam and Moodley, *South Africa Without Apartheid*, op. cit., p. 125; J. Brewer, *After Soweto*, op. cit., pp. 135–7.
15. Quoted in J. Frederikse, *A Different Kind of War*, op. cit., p. 38. This view is disputed by those who argue that the ANC did take a leadership role in the 1976 events, such as B. Hirson, *Year of Fire, Year of Ash*, op. cit. However, those who claim so are very much in a minority.
16. See J. Brewer, *After Soweto*, op. cit., pp. 141–3; L. Schlemmer, 'Build up to Revolution or Impasse?', in H. Adam, *South Africa: The Limits of Reform Politics*, Leiden, E. J. Brill, 1983.
17. J. Kane Berman, 'Inkatha: The Paradox of South African Politics', *Optima*, 30, 1982, p. 160.
18. Op. cit., p. 226.
19. Ibid., p. 225.
20. Adam and Moodley, *South Africa Without Apartheid*, 20, op. cit., pp. 98, 117–28.
21. Analysts note this polarisation with regret, with some describing it as disarray, while others refer to it as civil war. See respectively, T. Karis, 'Revolution in the Making', op cit., p. 392: Adam and Moodley, *South Africa Without Apartheid*, op. cit., p. 85.
22. On the former see M. Massing, 'The Chief', *New York Review of Books*, 34, 1987; R. Southall, 'A Note on Inkatha Membership', op. cit., p. 573. On the latter see H. Adam, 'Racial Capitalism Versus Capitalist Non-

Racialism', *Ethnic and Racial Studies*, 7, 1984; D. Welsh, 'Constitutional Change in South Africa', *African Affairs*, 83, 1984, p. 160.

23. On this see P. Bonner, 'Independent Trade Unionism Since Wiehahn', *South African Labour Bulletin*, 8, 1982: D Innes and R. Fine, 'Trade Unions and the Challenge to State Power', ibid., 9, 1983; I. Silver and A. Sfarnas, 'Debates: The UDF', *South African Labour Bulletin*, 8, 1982.
24. For an application of this notion to black protest in South Africa see J. Brewer, 'Black Protest in South Africa's Crisis', *African Affairs*, 85, 1986.
25. H. Adam, 'Racial Capitalism Versus Capitalist Non-Racialism', op. cit.
26. For an account of the varying responses to the Freedom Charter see J. Brewer, *After Soweto*, op. cit., pp. 257, 271–3.
27. One distinguishing feature is that Inkatha's position on violence is ambiguous, whereas violence is unsanctioned in the UDF. I argue elsewhere that this systematic ambiguity is vital to Inkatha's own contradictory role in black politics. See John D. Brewer, 'From Ancient Rome to KwaZulu: Inkatha in South African Politics', in S. Johnson (ed.), *South Africa: No Turning Back*, London, Macmillan, 1988.
28. Adam and Moodley, *South Africa Without Apartheid*, op. cit., p. 116.
29. M. Massing, 'The Chief', op. cit.
30. See the chapter on the South African police in J. Brewer, A. Guelke, Ian Hume, E. Moxon Browne and R. Wilford, *The Police, Public Order and the State*, London, Macmillan, 1988; also, J. Brewer, 'The South African Police', in S. Johnson (ed.), *South Africa*, op. cit.

9 The United Democratic Front: Leadership and Ideology

Tom Lodge

INTRODUCTION

The United Democratic Front (UDF) is essentially a federation linking a large and heterodox collection of organisations varying in function, size, and popular impact. It is strongest in the Eastern Cape, traditionally the stronghold of the ANC, with which many local UDF leaders are historically associated. Class and communal cleavages as well as the presence of rivals with a popular following, make the UDF comparatively weaker in Cape Town and Durban. In the industrial heartland of the Transvaal, the UDF is undoubtedly paramount, but the sheer size of the urban centres, their social complexity, and the uncertainties of the UDF's relationship with a well-established trade union movement, make its own capacity for marshalling disciplined support questionable. In the Transvaal, to a greater extent than in its other four main regions, the UDF has come to depend upon a tacit alliance with an increasingly politicised yet politically independent trade union movement. Any analysis of the UDF, though, should not be limited to the bureaucratic boundaries of its often patchy organisation, for the UDF functions more in the fashion of a social movement than a deliberately contrived political machine. With this consideration in mind, two questions need examining. Which social constituencies does the UDF represent? Is it possible to perceive in the UDF's ideological discourse the interests or concerns of particular social classes?

LEADERSHIP

In one essential sense, the UDF is a working-class movement. In a social context in which a black bourgeoisie scarcely exists, in which members of petty bourgeois or middle-class groups at best constitute a thin layer, and in which the rural population is largely proletarianised or at least dependent on wage labour, any popular organisation has to have a working-class base. This is as true for a conservative movement such as Inkatha, as for a radical one like the UDF. To understand the social character of a political body it is more helpful to look at leadership, or rather different layers of leadership, and the relationship which leaders have with particular constituencies.

Taking the national executive, together with the five most developed regions, the most recently elected UDF leadership comprises sixty-six people.[1] The majority of these are men – only eight are women. They are mainly young; of fifty whose ages can be specified, seventeen are in their thirties, eleven in their early forties, and six in their twenties. Four are in their fifties and ten are over sixty. Fifteen are ANC veterans; most of these are in the over-sixties group but it includes younger men who were involved in clandestine ANC activities in the 1960s and 1970s. Of the ANC group, five were also members of Umkhonto we Sizwe, seven were involved in SACTU (in some cases the same people), and seven have served long prison sentences for political offences in Robben Island or Pretoria Fort. Another four UDF leaders received prison terms after the 1976 Soweto uprising. Apart from the Congress group (augmented by another four people associated with the NIC and TIC revivals), UDF executives include former adherents of the Liberal Party (2), the Coloured Labour Party (2), the Black Consciousness Movement (6), and the Unity Movement (1). Socially, UDF leadership is heavily middle-class - eleven from highly-paid professional backgrounds – legal, medical or academic, and three priests, eight teachers, a nurse, a legal clerk, a social worker, a researcher, and two technicians. Amongst the other leaders whose occupations can be identified, 17 are workers, three of them skilled artisans and the rest labourers or industrial workers. At least four of the workers are full-time trade-union officials. The working-class group also includes the SACTU veterans, some of whom are no longer working. Finally, there are six executive members who are professional activists, mainly youth or student congress organisers. Notably absent from the UDF leadership are people from middle-level management, modern commercial occupations, township business, and petty trading. There are traders, though, in one of the regional executives, not covered in this survey, the Northern Transvaal. UDF leadership, finally, is predominantly African, though the five executives also include six Indians, eight coloureds, and five whites.[2]

Regionally, the two largest executives, Natal and Transvaal, are socially the most heterodox. The Western Cape's fourteen members are almost evenly balanced between workers and professionals, with three of the seven professionals from working-class backgrounds. The Eastern Cape's executive comprises two old SACTU/Umkhonto stalwarts, two teachers, a factory worker, and a technician with some experience as a trade union organiser. Too little data is available on the Border executive to make useful generalisations.

The Transvaal executive provides the most representative social profile of the movement as a whole: it is the most youthful and has an unusually high proportion of people (ten) with some experience of working in youth organisations during the 1970s and 1980s. Detailed data exists for Natal's executive[3] (see Table 9.1).

What is demonstrable from this biographical profile is true also for other executives. Though the Natal leadership falls largely into the professional/middle-class categories, sociological classifications are not by themselves very helpful. For these are people who have often become prominent in the organisation of popular movements around the preoccupations of the poor: rents, housing conditions, transport, and the cost of services. They belong to an intellectual middle class rather than an entrepreneurial one. Mobilised youth is well represented on the executive, both generationally, and with youth organisation office-bearers. Organised labour is under-represented considering its strength in Natal; its limited presence in the two 1950s trade unionists and the President of the National Federation of Workers indicate the distance between the Natal UDF and contemporary mainstream black trade unionism.

For the UDF, though it is very largely a movement of the poor, is not one which normally mobilises its following through direct appeals to class identity. Its preferred social constituencies are usually socially amorphous: 'youth', 'community', or 'progressive' whites. This is partly a reflection of the historical experiences of the last decade: educational breakdown, school-leaver unemployment, demographic explosion, the fiscal disarray of local government, the rising cost of living, and the state's efforts to create for itself a widened popular legitimacy. The conflicts produced by such developments do not lend themselves to precise social configurations. Then there is the ideological legacy of the Congress tradition which stresses social unity rather than class confrontation. Finally, there is the disproportionate share in leadership of a radicalised intelligentsia whose members, even if they are philosophically influenced by Marxism, speak a language very

GUMEDE, A.	Age: 72; profession: lawyer; residence: Clermont, Durban; organisational affiliation: ANC, Liberal Party, Joint Commuters' Committee, Release Mandela Committee (RMC).
XUNDU, M.	Age: 52; profession: priest ; residence: Lamontville, Durban; organisational affiliation: ANC, vice-chairman – JORAC.
NAIR, B.	Age: c. 60; profession: trade unionist; residence: Durban; organisational affiliation: NIC, Natal secretary – SACTU, Umkhonto we Sizwe (1963–83, Robben Island).
MOHAMED, Y.	Age: c. 30; profession: attorney; residence: Durban; organisational affiliation: NIC.
TSENOLI, S.	Age: 31; profession: teacher/translator; residence: Lamontville, Durban; organisational affiliation: JORAC, Lamontville Youth Organisation.
MXENGE, V.	Age: 43; profession: midwife/lawyer; residence: Umlazi, Durban; organisational affiliation: treasurer – RMC, Umlazi Water Committee, Natal Organisation of Women.
COOVADIA, J.	Age: 46; profession: doctor/academic: residence: Durban; organisational affiliation: NIC.
AFRICA, S.	Age: 30; profession: researcher; residence: Sydenham, Durban; organisational affiliation: Durban Housing Action Committee.
MPANGA, R.	Age: c. 50; profession: labourer; residence: Umlazi, Durban; organisational affiliation: ANC (Robben Island), RMC, Umlazi Residents' Association.
NDABA	Age: 35; profession: teacher: residence: Clarewater, Durban; organisational affiliation: coordinator – NECC.
KOZA, R.	age: c. 25; profession: technician; organisational affiliation: AZASO, NAYO, NECC.
BONHOMME, V.	Age: 42: profession: upholsterer; residence: Durban; organisational affiliation: Labour Party (1969–79), Furniture and Allied Workers' Union, DHAC.
NOSIZWE, M.	Age: 35; profession: medical technician; organisational affiliation: Natal Organisation of Women.
KEARNEY, P.	Age: c. 45; profession: teacher/Director – Diakonia (Ecumenical organisation); residence: Durban; organisational affiliation: Diakonia.
NXUMALO, T.	Profession: teacher/trade unionist; organisational affiliation: National Federation of Workers.
NDLOVU, C.	Age: c. 60; profession: activist; residence: Durban; organisational affiliation: GWU (Garment Workers' Union), ANC, SACTU, Kwa Mashu Residents' Association (1960), South African Railway and Harbour Workers' Union, Umkhonto we Sizwe (Robben Island, 1964–84).

removed from the experience and culture of working-class people. As a correspondent in *Grassroots* observed after the UDF launch:

> Most of these workers are not educated. That is why there are no workers in the UDF. To open your mind, if you can look at the meeting that was held at Mitchell's Plain. The workers were there. But the workers didn't understand what that meeting was for. Because the language that was used, is the language that is not known by the workers.[4]

When UDF leaders do speak a popular language, it is usually (though not always, as we shall see) a populist one. This is not surprising, for their most deeply-felt area of common experience with their working-class constituency is not the struggle between capital and labour, but rather the conflict between people and state.

IDEOLOGY

What the UDF stands for ideologically is complicated. First, it is a social coalition embracing different groups which have different social, political and economic agendas. Such differences, though, are not always easily apparent from formal statements and authorised comments. Secondly, the UDF's character is to a degree shared by the conscious views and perceptions of its ideologues, but it is also influenced, perhaps more profoundly, by the behaviour and culture of its popular following. The organisation's ideological impetus may derive as much from the unselfconscious perceptions and actions of ordinary people as the intellectual constructs of sophisticated leaders.

The UDF was conceived of as a transitional front, not a political party, nor a rival to already established liberation organisations. Consequently, initial programmatic statements were usually limited to a few key principles intended to unite the broadest of social spectrums: 'from workers to students, from priests to businessmen, Nyanga to Chatsworth, to Soweto to Elsies River'.[5] The UDF stood for nonracial 'unity of all people', for a 'government based on the will of the people', for 'a willingness to work together' despite 'different approaches to the problems that confront us'.[6] Notwithstanding the 'Charterist' allegiance of some of the major organisations which affiliated to the Front, at its inception leaders insisted that 'it was incorrect to link the UDF directly to the Charter',[7] that the UDF was 'not Charterist'.[8] In fact, though, from the beginning, adherence to the Charter was viewed by most UDF leaders as signifying an advanced stage of ideological progress. Albertina Sisulu, opening the SOYCO launch in July 1983, held that the guidance supplied by the Freedom Charter 'would prevent reactionary agents from hijacking the struggle'.[9] Samson Ndou informed a commemorative meeting on 23 June 1983: 'We want to place on record that we subscribe to the Freedom Charter. Therefore we are members of the UDF'.[10] Two years later, Western Cape Secretary Trevor Manuel argued that different opinions and perspectives '[are] emerging ... [it] is necessary to do battle at the ideological level to define a clearer ideological stance'.[11] Accordingly, UDF's *Update* suggested:

> Although the UDF has not adopted the Freedom Charter, 'We believe that the Freedom Charter is the most democratic document expressing the wishes and aspirations of our people.'[12]

In June 1985, UDF affiliates distributed half a million copies of the Charter on house-to-house visits and rallies to celebrate the thirtieth anniversary of the Congress of the People.[13] By April 1986, Stone Sizane of the East Cape UDF executive was telling a local newspaper that the UDF 'subscribed to the Freedom Charter'.[14]

In reality acceptance of the Freedom Charter was understood as the logical accompaniment to the perception of the 'National Democratic nature of our struggle'.[15] Such a struggle was one for the 'broadest possible alliance'.[16] It was a struggle of 'the people's camp', 'the overwhelming majority of South Africans – the black working class, the rural masses, the black petty bourgeoisie (traders), and black middle strata (clerks, teachers, nurses, intellectuals)' as well as 'several thousand whites who stand shoulder to shoulder in struggle with the majority'.[17] The national democratic struggle had three objectives: 'the struggle to remove all racial oppression; the struggle to remove the grip of the monopoly companies over our country; and the struggle to build democratic majority rule in a unified South Africa'. In this struggle 'the UDF has identified the working class as the leading class'.[18] Why not, then, a struggle for socialism? Largely because 'we must not forget there are different interests among the oppressed. While they are united around the immediate task of destroying national oppression, their long-term interests are not identical'.[19] Does the UDF, then, leave entirely open the question as to which long-term interest in the end should predominate? That depends on how attentively one reads the

UDF's theoretical publications. In *Isizwe*, an article on unemployment suggests that 'the struggle against unemployment is also struggle against capitalism and national oppression'.[20] Despite such contentions, though, the anonymous writers in *Isizwe* are very critical of those who view national democracy as a tactical concept rather than one of long-term principle:

> We are thinking here of those who pay lip service to our broad struggle of national democratic struggle. That is, those who say: 'Yes, the popular struggle, NDS is important.' But they do not really believe these words in their hearts. For these watered down workerists the national democratic struggle is simply a tactic of the moment. For them the broad front of the UDF is an unfortunate and temporary structure. Our talk about national democratic struggle is 'merely a concession to the traditions and culture of the masses in South Africa'.[21]

For mainstream UDF thinkers, 'weeding out' the petty bourgeoisie would be a strategic mistake; for it would risk increasing the prospects of the state security obtaining more 'collaborators and more legitimacy'.[22] In other words, despite the antipathy to workerists, the virtues of social alliances for democrats may have little to do with long-term ideological principles.

Here some UDF leaders are quite unambiguous. Billy Nair, when asked whether he thought 'that capitalism would not survive the implementation of the Charter' replied:

> Of course! The implementation of the Charter is the first step towards the establishment of socialism. The demands of the Charter cannot be met within the present social, political and economic order. The Charter serves as the basis from which workers can build a free, equal and just society. The Charter is so far the only guarantee towards the realisation of that peaceful society, it is not an end in itself.[23]

Not all UDF ideologues would go as far as this; the preferred formulation is usually less specific:

> At this point when these decisions are being made, the balance of forces in the country would determine the shape of things to come. It

> would determine how quickly the demands in the Charter could be implemented. The level of mass consciousness would determine that too . . .[24]

Nair himself, in a later interview, conceded that 'we are going to have to carry over some of what exists in our present society into the new one' and that it would be necessary 'to cater for small traders and small farmers, and to even protect them as long as they do not threaten to become big capitalists'. Opposition to big capital could provide an essential unity of interests for all oppressed classes – 'the working class, in particular, the small peasant, the small business people, even the small manufacturer' – for all were enmeshed in 'the vice-grip of the massive monopolies which have developed and which are encouraged to develop by the Nationalist government'.[25]

Opposition to monopoly capital, then, can be the principled basis for unity between the working class, the petty bourgeoisie, and 'the middle strata'. Even assuming that the nuances of UDF theoretical expositions are widely understood within UDF leadership, which is unlikely, there is clearly, within the framework provided by the notion of national democratic struggle, room for the expression of different positions. At leadership levels these can be placed in three groups. For the sake of convenience, these can be labelled nationalist, national democratic and socialist. These categories are, of course, idealised; elements of all three positions may influence to a greater or lesser degree the outlooks of individual leaders.

The nationalist position was more conspicuous in the early days of the UDF. Its strands usually include an emphasis on a heroic tradition of nationalist resistance, the celebration of an iconography of martyrs and, as a subsidiary element, a populist conception of economic nationalism. Nationalist ideology is usually to the fore when leaders wish to express the UDF's intention to 'bring together all classes'. But it is also given prominence by particular sections of leadership. The Release Mandela Campaign, for example, often provides a platform for nationalist sentiment. Its Transvaal Chairman and former UDF NEC member, Aubrey Mokoena, is one of the foremost exponents of a nationalist position with his promotion of a cult of charismatic leadership around Nelson Mandela. For Mokoena, Mandela 'is the pivotal factor in struggle for liberation. He has the stature and charisma which derives from his contribution to the struggle'.[26] Mokoena's language is not atypical. Mewa Ramgobin told his audience at a Soweto RMC meeting in July 1984 that:

> I want to make bold and say in clear language that the human race must remain grateful, that the human race must go down on its knees and say thankyou for the gifts it has been endowed with the lives of the Nelson Mandelas of this country.[27]

Associated with the tendency to accord reverence to brave leaders is the depiction of the Freedom Charter as a sacred symbol of patriotism. 'Betray the Freedom Charter and you betray the people', argued Zinzi Mandela at a 1983 TIC meeting. 'We consider it treason to turn against the people's demands as set out in the Freedom Charter.'[28] This is not a view which encourages discussion or debates as to how the Charter should be interpreted or which even allows for the possibility of different interpretations of the Charter being possible; for here the Charter is understood as emanating from an organically unified general will. On economic issues, the language of UDF nationalism is often strongly anti-capitalist, but it is communalist, not socialist, in its prescriptions. Allan Boesak, in his evidence to the Carnegie Commission on poverty, described poverty as primarily a 'moral challenge' and delivered a scathing critique of 'white greed' and 'free market' economics. Nevertheless, despite his condemnation of 'the inequitable system which capitalism is', his 'call for clear political action' was firmly within a well-entrenched South African populist tradition:

> To 'get up and walk' means for us no less than what it meant for the Afrikaner to whom D. P. Malan spoke, and that is to work for the day political, social and economic change shall become a reality, so that all South Africa's people, including the poor, shall be able to live as God had intended for them to live.[29]

Advocates of individual entrepreneurship are unusual in the UDF, for while not wholly absent they are not strongly represented in leadership. Nthato Motlana, Chairman of the Soweto Civic Association, and a frequent spokesman on UDF platforms, is one of the very few popular political figures who can be associated with a capitalist ideal. He is currently, for example, one of four Soweto notables who have formed a company, Black Equity Participation, with the aim of taking over the assets of departing American corporations.[30] Businessmen, though, are quite rare even within the leaderships of local affiliates. It is the case that some township traders were involved in the consumer boycott committees – in Pretoria, for example[31] – and it is true that the boycott organisers appeared to envisage a progressive political role for business urging it to become 'more aware of its political responsibilities'.[32] But businessmen seem to have shied away from substantial involvement in civic structures. For example, in Tumahole, in the Orange Free State, though the ad hoc committee set up in July 1984 to lay the groundwork for a civic association included three shopkeepers and two priests, these people found they were too busy to join the leadership of the Tumahole Civic when it was launched in October. They had apparently been frightened off, partly by the radical language of the core group of student activists and trade unionists around which the Civic started, and also by the risk of losing their trading licences.[33]

A capitalist perspective is unlikely to emerge in UDF nationalism from the influence of the very small group of black entrepreneurs who have so courageously participated in UDF-led structures. What is possible is that the UDF leadership may tone down some of its economic rhetoric to win more favour within the white community. If the UDF succeeds in any future efforts directed towards winning a substantial white constituency, it is likely that there may emerge a rather stronger liberal democratic theme than exists in UDF discourse at the moment. Significantly, Billy Nair, in a pamphlet issued during the 'Call to Whites' campaign, referred to Lincoln's Gettysburg address as the essence of the UDF's conception of democracy.[34]

The national democratic position is dominant within UDF leadership. As we have seen, its advocates understand the ultimate foe to be monopoly capitalism but believe that opposition to capitalist imperialism in South Africa can, because of the existence of national oppression, be most effectively mobilised through a 'strategy of broad popular alliance'. The working class is the leading class in such a strategy, but the social objectives of the 'people's camp' would be both more and less than the class interests of an industrial proletariat. The Freedom Charter accommodates the aspirations of a broad range of groups; small businessmen, professionals, peasants, and of course, workers. In fact, though 'national democracy' is rarely spelt out at public meetings as carefully as it is in polemical and academic journals. 'Capitalism, not Whites, was what Black people had to regard as the enemy', proclaimed Curtis Nkondo, a member of the first UDF NEC at the inauguration of the Port Elizabeth Youth Congress (PEYCO).[35] Significantly he spoke in the Eastern Cape, where anti-capitalist sentiment appears to have a genuine popular resonance. Here is Wonga Nkala, president of the Uitenhage Youth Congress addressing 30 000 people the day after the Langa massacre:

> The Western imperialists do not see or hear the cries of the black majority. Their eyes are covered by gold-dust, and their ears by diamonds. They are only concerned about the wealth they are raping out of our country. So their response to the massacre, led by Reagan, was hypocrisy of the worst kind. They too are responsible for killing unarmed and defenceless people, by supporting reactionary governments here and in other parts of the world. Local capitalists called for all parties to meet. They want to be heard protesting because they fear the massacre will fuel the disinvestment lobby. But not out of concern for us.[36]

Nkala's speech was not unusual. According to *State of the Nation* in October 1985, common themes at funerals have included 'the nature of imperialist interests and their role in attempting to misdirect the struggle; and the interests of the ruling class'. Elsewhere, though, there has been evidently less unanimity on the nature and identity of imperialism. Allan Boesak in early 1985 invited Senator Kennedy to South Africa. Kennedy spoke to enthusiastic meetings but not all UDF supporters were happy. Through his visit, contended 'Doubtful' of Athlone, a letter writer in *Grassroots*, 'the broad aim of bringing working issues, especially economic demands of the UDF took a step backwards', thus preventing 'the development of the UDF into a stronger, militant and tighter body'.[37]

For its interpreters, 'national democracy' is not liberal democracy. In the view of a contributor to *New Era*, a Cape Town UDF-affiliated publication:

> Democracy means, in the first instance, the ability of the broad working masses to participate in and to control all dimensions of their lives. This, for us, is the essence of democracy, not some liberal, pluralistic debating society notion of a 'thousand schools contending'.[38]

For national democrats, democracy is created through the organisational structures which emerge in the course of struggle; it is these rather than precisely elaborated social programmes which ensure that the ultimate society will be one in which the needs of popular classes will be met. A constant refrain in UDF speeches and statements is the notion that leaders are at most bearers of a popular mandate, that as delegates they are directly accountable, that democracy should be the politics of popular participation. Hence, for example, the antipathy amongst many UDF affiliates to the concept of a leaders' constitutional convention or a Lancaster House type of transfer of political power.[39] Of course, in reality the UDF does not constantly function according to such prescriptions. Strategic decisions have not in every instance emanated from or been sanctioned by mass meetings or street committees. But much has depended upon grass-roots initiatives. The stronger civic and youth affiliates have often been organised and led by trade unionists who have taken as their inspiration democratic trade union organisations. For example, the Tumahole Youth Congress (TOYCO) took as its model the structure of the Chemical Workers' Union at nearby Secunda.[40] Such literal imitation is exceptional, but more widely the adoption by civics during 1982–83 of fee-paying membership and elected branch officials grew out of recent trade union experience in many centres. In particular, the notion of a mandated leadership with very limited decision-making authority is ascribable to the influence of trade unionism.

National democracy, then, allows for the construction of a radically egalitarian social order. Such an order should be based on 'the will of the people'. 'Our structures must become organs of peoples' power'. 'Ordinary people [must] increasingly take part in all the decisions. . . . Few people making all the decisions must end.'[41] This romantic conception of the popular will pervading social and political organisation, is often linked with a spontaneous and voluntaristic understanding of political struggle. During the Soweto consumer boycott, trade unionists on the Committee objected to the youth stoning wholesalers' trucks which were replenishing township shops. UDF leaders were reluctant to discipline the youth: 'It is not our duty to tell them not to stone or burn the trucks. We can only tell them why.'[42] The people determine their own forms of political assertion; leaders may inspire or advise but not prescribe. Despite the disclaimers of its advocates, national democracy is in essence populist, and it accommodates at best awkwardly the more disciplined and vanguardist notions of class mobilisation.

Nevertheless, as should be clear by this point, socialists have found room beneath the UDF's umbrella. Certain trade unionists urge that workers have no alternative but to participate in the UDF if their class objectives are to be realised. 'By actively participating in these [broader] struggles, we can influence their direction and goals. Worker leaders, emerging from the training ground of unions, can take their places amongst the leadership of the political struggle.'[43] In a leaflet circulated in 1984 by the Transvaal Anti-President's Council, socialism is perceived as intrinsic to the process of national liberation:

> We believe that the struggle in SA has two aspects (NOT phases or stages). We believe that it is not enough just to have 'one person–one vote'. For the majority of South Africans (namely the working people) 'liberation' will be meaningless and empty unless the economy is restructured because that is the only way to guarantee significant and lasting improvements in the quality of life of our working people. Hence the CLASS STRUGGLE is a vital component of our fight for change. Here the working class and its allies confront the owning class and its allies. Because of the increasing development and industrialisation of the SA economy and the increasing organisation of the working class into independent trade unions, we perceive AN INTENSIFICATION OF CLASS STRUGGLE IN SOUTH AFRICA.[44] (emphases in the original)

Nor do all UDF socialists share the sanguine expectation that because 'it is impossible to separate off Apartheid from the capitalist system . . . truly committed opposition to Apartheid . . . will lay the foundations for a fundamental change'.[45] Hence the concern expressed by Port Elizabeth UDF executive member, Derek Swartz, about the:

> criticisms of the 'popular' nature of our strategies and campaigns which did not emphasise the class nature of our struggle . . . students and youth tend to dominate organisations. . . . Although many of them come from the working class, they have a natural populist tendency. Workers have the experience which youth do not have.[46]

In fairness to students, their organisations have often been the first to recognise that workers 'produce the wealth of our country and are the crucial class in bringing about change'.[47] Yet it is the case that youthful activists have often been insensitive to the material considerations which sometimes inhibit workers from supporting militant political actions. In the context of white left student politics in which the UDF finds its principal white constituency, there has developed a 'left opposition' with the UDF. This finds expression in an arcane critical discussion of the internal colonialism thesis. Internal colonialism is an analytical approach to South African politics which originated with the South African Communist Party. It is today influential within UDF intellectual circles in supplying the underpinning rationalisation for the concept of national democracy.[48] The critics of internal colonialism stress the potential for the 'development of a co-opted middle class and for the emergence of reactionary nationalism' *within* the movement for democracy. Fighting racial oppression challenges 'capitalism in its present form' not in substance; 'it does not guarantee its fundamental transformation'.[49] The debate seems to be most vigorous at the predominantly white universities. It may, though, have had a wider impact, for in November 1986, *Isizwe* contained a strong attack on the 'watered-down workerists . . . within our own ranks' with their 'defeatist, passive attitude towards the oppressed, black petty bourgeoisie and middle strata in our country'.[50]

Probably, the finer points of the argument within leadership echelons between national democrats and socialists have not evoked much popular interest. For amongst rank-and-file activists, working-class identity and a socialist understanding of exploitation are two themes which are constantly recurrent in their public rhetoric and private perceptions. Here is an extract from a leaflet distributed in Alexandra during the rent boycott:

> We won't pay to live in these Gettos [*sic*]. We are treated like donkeys, kept in these yards at night, but working for Baas in the day. This Alexandra is like a donkey yard. They let us out to work in Baas se Plek . . . We produce the goods, but we get low wages. And when we want to buy, things are very expensive. Because the bosses have added big profit. We even are the ones who build houses, but they are expensive. Our little money is taken away by *rent* and *inflation*, which are the other names for *profit*. Who gets the profit? Goldstein, Schacat, the Landlord Steve Burger.[51]

Similarly in Soweto an anti-eviction leaflet addressed its readers as 'workers and residents' and called for, in the event of evictions 'an industrial standstill'.[52] One of the most striking indications of the existence of a rank-and-file socialist consciousness is the testimony of twenty-year old Comrade Bongani, a member of the Tumahole Youth Congress. Asked what he understood by capitalism he replied,

> It is a system of private ownership by certain individuals who own the means of production. My parents, from Monday to Friday can make a production of R1000, but he or she is going to get, say, R50. So our parents are being exploited so that individuals can get rich. That's why I prefer socialism, because the working class will control production.[53]

There is evidence, then, to suggest that, regardless of the delicate qualifications to be found in the more cerebral definitions of national democracy, a substantial proportion of the UDF's committed following are motivated through their class identity and inspired by a socialist vision. Whatever the ideological predilections of the largely middle-class leaders of the movement (and many, in any case, are committed to social transformation), such a constituency would be very difficult to demobilise in the event of a retreat from radicalism after liberation. Popular initiatives have played too important a role in the UDF's own development for its ordinary participants to be reduced to the role of a passive chorus. In the long term this may be the most important legacy of the embryonic institutions of popular participatory government which were created in the course of 1985–86. No understanding of the UDF's ideological character can therefore be complete without a consideration of the efforts to build and consolidate 'people's power'.

PEOPLE'S POWER AND PEOPLE'S COURTS

UDF leaders use the phrase 'people's power' to refer to the process in which, after the collapse or abdication of local state authorities, civics and youth organisations assumed administrative, judicial, welfare, and cultural functions within their respective communities. People's power was often represented in modest and pragmatic projects. For example, residents' groups would, in the event of a breakdown in municipal services, organise street cleaning. Children would create 'people's parks' on waste ground, naming them after liberation heroes, and decorating them with gaily-painted scrap-metal sculptures. The National Education Crisis Committee (NECC) subcommittees began devising syllabuses for democratic and non-elitist history and English courses. But of all the manifestations of people's power, the efforts of local organisations to administer popularly acceptable forms of civil and criminal justice were the most challenging to the state's moral authority. More than any other feature of the insurrectionary movement which the UDF's structures straddle, people's justice testifies to the UDF's social and ideological complexity, as well as the extent to which it has been shaped from below by popular culture.

Political activists claim that people began to bring complaints or disputes to community organisations almost from their inception. This reflected a widespread lack of confidence in the police which was accentuated with the outbreak of conflict in 1984. Police were reputed to be inaccessible and unhelpful. The official Commissioner's Courts were believed to be corrupt and arbitrary.[54] The construction of an alternative source of justice and civil order seems to have taken a similar course in most centres. In Pretoria's Atteridgeville, with the effective extension of community organisation at the beginning of the consumer boycott in August 1985, Atteridgeville–Sauskville Residents' Organisation (ASRO) leaders were asked to referee disputes between neighbours or to resolve family arguments. In response, the residents' organisation opened an advice office. ASRO developed a decentralised structure with eleven area committees. These committees began in late 1985 to function as 'people's courts' (though ASRO leaders disliked using this phrase). The Advice Office became the ultimate authority to which people could appeal. Only a minority of Atteridgeville streets had their own committees by the second emergency, but where these did exist they handled family disagreements.[55] Before this system was elaborated, youth groups held 'kangaroo courts'; apparently these characteristically were harsh and unfair.[56] Brutal kangaroo courts run by the Amabuthu emerged in Port Elizabeth between July and September 1985 when the Port Elizabeth Black Civic Organisation and PEYCO leaders were in detention.[57] To curtail their spread, street and area committees started to operate as courts. PEBCO's executive took on the function of final arbiter. PEBCO officials claimed that their courts, in contrast to the Amabuthu tribunals, never inflicted physical punishment. Both in Port Elizabeth and in Uitenhage the activists recognised limits to their judicial competence; murder cases, for example, were referred to the police.[58] In Alexandra a more formalised structure developed. Though the yard, block and street committees were empowered to settle quarrels, for intractable issues and for theft and assault cases, in February 1986 five members of the Action Committee were nominated to sit in judgement. The court was held at regular intervals in a room specially reserved for the purpose. During its operation public complaints at the nearby police station declined by 60 per cent.[59] Comparable systems of people's justice emerged in many of the other centres where strongly-structured local organisations existed. In the Transvaal this included Krugersdorp's Kagiso and Munsieville, Duduza outside Nigel, Mamelodi (Pretoria), Letsilele (Tzaneen), and Soweto. In the Eastern Cape, people's courts functioned in most towns through late 1985 and early 1986.

'The People's Court is not simply a bourgeois court taking place in a back room in a ghetto', insisted a pamphlet circulated in Atteridgeville:

> Unlike the present legal system, it should not be biased in favour of

> the powerful and must not simply be a means whereby the interests of the powerful are ensured at the expense of the oppressed and the exploited.[60]

The solution to each crime 'must conclude with a political thing.'[61] Advocates of people's justice emphasise its conciliatory nature: the ultimate aim is the social reintegration of the offender. Thieves are enjoined to return property or compensate owners. In one well-publicised Alexandra case, the thief, a habitual offender, was placed under the supervision of a committee comprising Alexandra Action Committee members, the man from whom he stole, and his nephews. This would ensure that he stopped drinking and squandering his savings.[62] In Uitenhage, courts 'are not trying to imitate the white courts or trying to beat people. They are trying to create peace among the people'.[63] With those miscreants who resist the injunction 'to become one of us' the ultimate sanction, Atteridgeville organisers claimed, was ostracism.[64] Youthful comrades in Port Elizabeth who persisted in beating people up 'would be suspended' and not allowed to wear PEYCO T-Shirts.[65]

Apart from trying criminals, courts in several centres imposed curfews to lower the incidence of street brawling and alcohol-related violence. Officials ordered shebeens to close early. Comrades searched shebeen customers for weapons. Amabuthu or Comrades authorised as 'marshals' by the civics would police the curfews. In Atteridgeville people complained that marshals stole during the searches. Area committees took on the duty of weapon searches. Civic activists claim that such measures were effective in reducing the number of violent crimes. The organisations were sufficiently effective in their judicial role that the police themselves referred cases to them.[66]

This is the picture of people's justice provided by leading township activists quoted in UDF literature and other sympathetic accounts.[67] It may be rather idealised. For example, in Mamelodi, the Youth Organisations established disciplinary committees in each street. In the event of a crime these could convene a court from any street residents who wished to participate. At least one disciplinary committee sanctioned physical punishment. Its constitution: 25 lashes with a sjambok for 'robbery in the name of the struggle', 15 for rape, and 5 for disrespect to teachers. In Mamelodi, as elsewhere, court officials denied that they executed the guilty.[68] Courts which sanctioned such methods as the 'necklace', they said, were kangaroo courts.[69] They were not connected with their organisations. In Soweto township in Port Elizabeth, named after Johannesburg's main black township, a people's court was administered by the Committee of Ten. The Committee claimed allegiance to PEBCO but this was disputed both by PEBCO and young militants in Soweto. The courts in Soweto were notorious for necklacing. On 9 February 'hundreds of UDF supporters, mostly youths, gathered in the streets of Soweto to seek out the dissidents', as they termed the members of the Committee of Ten. Next day, five charred bodies were discovered.[70] In Kleiskool, outside Port Elizabeth, a 15-year-old rapist was stoned and then stabbed to death after being 'pointed out to Comrades' by the family of a 12-year-old rape and murder victim.[71] Civic leaders opposed necklacing but not everybody shared their conciliatory vision of justice. In Port Elizabeth there was a 'tendency, if people were dissatisfied with the decision (of the area committees), to go to the Amabutho to charge them to sort it out'.[72] A recent court case found the Amabutho guarding PEBCO's president, Edgar Ngoyi, guilty of burning to death one of Ngoyi's visitors, a young AZAPO member who had come to the PEBCO chief to beg forgiveness for his role in a petrol-bomb attack.[73] Pascal Damoyi, a resident of Alexandra and a member of the workerist Residents' Association, contributes a disillusioned account of people's justice in Alexandra. Action Committee and Civic Association comrades arrived to sort out a quarrel in his yard. A family had built a wall which had encroached upon the space of other households. Both sets of comrades were 'aggressive, and in a bloody mood'. They took the sides of their respective complainants, willing to appear accountable only to their 'clients' rather than all the yard's inhabitants. They threatened to sjambok those who objected to their ruling (which upheld the rights of the wall-builders). This may have been an atypical incident – it occurred in an area in which no organised committees existed.[74]

In Mamelodi, the Mamelodi Youth Organisation saw the system as exemplifying entrenched popular custom: 'You have to understand this from a traditional point of view. People in the community must judge others. You cannot look at it from a white point of view.' Consequently in the case of offenders being burnt, such 'acts are not criminal, they are punishments and judgements by the people'.[75] In Alexandra tradition was also summoned to defend the courts by a resident interviewed in *The Star*:

> A popular belief, deeply rooted in society, is that some problems in our townships are beyond the white man's law. Only the people's courts, guided by senior citizens, are competent to sit in trials. We do

not understand why some white man's laws should be applied in what are purely domestic affairs.[76]

It is possible that at least in some centres the justice dispensed through UDF affiliates represented not so much an innovation as an adaptation or reformulation of existing communal mechanisms of social control. In Mamelodi, for example, several systems of 'subterranean' justice operated in the late 1970s and early 1980s. In one ward a crime prevention unit of householders, called the 'volunteers', met regularly to administer floggings to 'recalcitrant youths over whom parents of the ward had lost control'. The volunteers policed the ward with teams of whistle-blowing vigilantes until an end was put to their punitive actions by the Community Council. The volunteers also helped resolve family and neighbourly squabbles. Notwithstanding the floggings, 'the central aim of the Ward Four court proceedings' was 'to prevent the breaking of relationships and to make it possible for partners to live together amicably'. The volunteers were rivalled and eventually eclipsed by a political organisation, the Vukani Vulimehlo People's Party (VVPP). The VVPP later contested and won the community council elections, but before this it built up a predominantly youthful following governed by a military-style hierarchy. It ran a secretive and extremely brutal 'Lekgotla' to enforce its territorial claims, to maintain organisational discipline, and uphold law and order. The VVPP also offered protection to shebeen-owners. The VVPP enjoyed some political popularity; its opposition to shack removals and high rents explained its victory after a relatively high 28 per cent participation in the 1983 Council election. Nevertheless, essentially the VVPP functioned through a patronage system, geared to the supremacy of its 'president for life', Bennet Ndlazi.[77]

Clearly the people's justice activated by MAYO had little in common with the coercive cabal of Ndlazi's Makgotla. The VVPP courts conflicted with other folk conceptions of justice which emphasise judgement by one's peers, informal open procedures, and popular accessibility. The volunteer's courts also differed from MAYO's disciplinary committees because they were run exclusively by householders (rent-payers) and were largely directed at youth. But the three all sprang from a common perception of the inadequacy of official law. And, as with the earlier institutions, MAYO activists would claim for their disciplinary committees the sanction of communal tradition.

Mamelodi may have been a special case but it is unlikely; various forms of Makgotla have existed in other centres.[78] It is probable, therefore, that people's justice expressed an ideological synthesis; externally-derived concepts such as, for example, a socialist critique of bourgeois courts, overlaying but not obliterating more widely-held folk notions of justice and discipline. These could have been especially influential when community organisations successfully incorporated older people into their structures. In Graaff Reinet, for example, the Lutheran church supplied a ready-made grassroots network: 'most of the street representatives are elders and evangelists'.[79] Not that the invocation of tradition was the monopoly of older people. This was tragically evident in March 1985 in Sekhukhuniland, Lebowa, when 32 people were burnt to death after accusations of witchcraft. Witchburnings are not a frequent feature of social life in this region but they have been historically evident during periods of socioeconomic tension or political strife. Witches are blamed for thunderbolts which happen especially often at times of drought. The 1985 witchburnings introduced two departures from custom. They were carried out by youths without the normal affirmation of guilt by nyangas, and the executions were through the necklace method.[80] In towns the victims of necklacing are often suspected informers or collaborators 'with the system' (a category which from a partisan perspective can range across a broad spectrum – community councillors to members of AZAPO). In August 1986, a Soweto journalist recorded in her diary witnessing the distraught mother of a necklaced child 'in a state of shock . . . mumbling that her child is not a witch, but is sick'.[81]

The conception of people's justice described in UDF literature is an essentially humane one. There is no firm evidence to suggest that UDF affiliates have sanctioned or condoned necklacing or similarly brutal forms of killing. But outside the ranks of disciplined cadres there exists a much wider movement which the UDF can claim as a constituency. Even among the activists there is not the same emphasis on the rehabilitative purpose of justice which one finds in the perceptions of leaders. In Mamelodi, MAYO members talk about the necessity to 'get the lumps out of the community . . . the unwanted elements'.[82] As mentioned, justice-seekers in Port Elizabeth, if they were dissatisfied with the decisions of the people's courts, turned to the amabutho for more severe retribution against suspected criminals. The people's courts instituted by UDF affiliates were different from earlier forms of unofficial justice because they were motivated by a deliberate effort to replace the organs of the state and in so doing transform social relationships. But people's justice did not evolve in a cultural vacuum; it was shaped as much by popular beliefs and folk morality as the

MAGDALEN COLLEGE LIBRARY

programmatic concerns of activists. As such it could be ideologically ambivalent, drawing alternately on visions of a classless future and utopian nostalgia for a harmonious past.

CONCLUSION

The popular mobilisation summoned by the United Democratic Front reached a peak in early 1986. As Zwelakhe Sisulu put it in his address to the second conference of the NECC, the movement appeared to be 'poised to enter a phase which could lead to the transfer of power'.[83] Today such an assessment appears very euphoric. The second state of emergency, which began in June 1986, has left few of the organisational structures which developed in the main centres undamaged. The UDF has been unable to successfully mount a major campaigning offensive. In certain local centres a rent strike obstinately persists, with, in Soweto at least, an underpinning network of semi-clandestine activists reinforcing the strikers. But it is a far cry from the day when the UDF's acting national secretary could claim: 'It is our people and the extra-parliamentary movement which today dictates the nature and pace of events in our country.'[84] This view is even more inappropriate following the restrictions placed on UDF political activity in February 1988.

To a much greater extent than was perceived at the time, the UDF's effectiveness was conditioned by the state's toleration of open mass opposition. This was itself a corollary of the government's efforts to create legitimising institutions within black communities. With their failure, an increasingly militarised polity has reverted to more coercive forms of rule. The emphasis in future 'reform' is likely to be on socioeconomic 'upgrading' rather than major attempts to broaden the base of political participation.

Does the state's success in curtailing the UDF's rebellion bring the resistance movement back to square one with no significant gains other than the lessons which may have been absorbed? Or has there been a shift in what Sisulu termed 'the balance of forces' as a result of the events of the last four years? The latter is more likely. First, the township insurrection has internationalised the South African conflict to an unprecedented degree. It is very unlikely that the Republic will ever again, under its present rulers, restore its former outward facade of political confidence and economic vigour. Order has been restored, but with the probable deployment of one-third to one-half of the standing army in the townships, it is likely that the fiscal strain of sustaining white supremacy is to be much greater than in the past. What this chapter has demonstrated is that the movement which the UDF headed was a profoundly popular one, rooted in ordinary people's emotions and infused 'from below' by their beliefs. In this sense it was a much more radical movement than any which had preceded it. In contrast to earlier phases of black opposition, a class-conscious ideology of social levelling was the essential motive force among a large number of rank-and-file activists.[85]

This is not surprising for the political mobilisation represented by the UDF had one set of foundations in the construction of the most powerful trade union movement in South African history. The trade unions provided models and sources of inspiration, but the movement's cadres more often than not came from the growing ranks of unemployed school-leavers. This group seems to have confounded the normal assumptions about the political effects of unemployment. R. W. Johnson, for example, suggested that 'the long-term unemployed tend to be a cowed, weak, helpless and resigned group, not a militant one'.[86] That may be more true of those groups who go through the experience of losing work but may not be applicable to the young men and women who have never experienced formal employment. For them, the millennial alternative held out by the ANC/SACP's 'vulgar marxism' (Johnson's phrase) may be all the more compelling, removed as they are from the compromises and limited rewards of conducting their everyday existence within the labour process of a capitalist firm.

The formal organisational structures built by the UDF are unlikely to survive intact the onslaught of government coercion – though the street-level committees which often developed independently of central direction may be better adapted to a highly repressive climate. The political culture which grew out of the UDF's development may well be more resilient. In itself it is unlikely to stimulate movements which will win victories; insurrectionist explosions by the urban and rural unemployed do not present serious military challenges. But governing South Africa through repression will impose heavy fiscal costs. The revolt in the townships has left South Africa more externally vulnerable than ever before.

Notes

1. United Democratic Front, *National General Council*, Report, April 1985. pp. 3–5.
2. Sources for biographical material on UDF personalities: individual

profiles in *New Nation*, *Weekly Mail* (especially the 'prisoner of conscience' series), *SASPU National*, various UDF and TIC and NIC publications, and Shelagh Gastrow, *Who's Who in South African Politics*, Ravan, Johannesburg, 1985.

3. Source: interview with Paddy Kearney, January 1987.
4. *Grassroots*, 4, 8, October 1983, p. 6.
5. Quotation by Virgil Bonhomme of DHAC on flyleaf of United Democratic Front, *National Launch*, booklet distributed at Rocklands, August 1983.
6. Ibid, p. 8.
7. Trevor Manuel quoted in *The Star*, 2 August 1983.
8. Albertina Sisulu in *SASPU National*, 4, 3, September 1983, p. 3.
9. *Rand Daily Mail*, 1 August 1983.
10. *City Press*, 26 June 1983.
11. Karen Jochelson and Susan Brown, 'UDF and AZPO', *Work in Progress*, 35, February 1985.
12. *UDF Update*, 1, 1, July 1985, p. 3.
13. Ibid.
14. *Evening Post*, 7 April 1986, p. 11.
15. Zac Yacoob in *SASPU National*, 4, 3, September 1983, p. 5.
16. 'Errors of Populism', *Isizwe*, 1, 2, March 1986, p. 16.
17. Ibid., p. 17.
18. Ibid.
19. 'National Democratic Struggle', *Isizwe*, 2, 1, March 1986, p. 32.
20. *Isizwe*, 1, 1, November 1985, p. 39.
21. 'Errors of Workerism', *Isizwe*, 1, 3, November 1986, p. 26.
22. Jeremy Cronin, 'Some Comments on the Labour Monitoring Group Paper', unpublished ms.
23. *SASPU National*, May 1984, p. 17.
24. *State of the Nation*, October 1985, p. 13.
25. Raymond Suttner and Jeremy Cronin, *30 Years of the Freedom Charter*, Ravan, Johannesburg, 1986, pp. 179–80.
26. 'Heed Free Mandela Movement, Government Urged', press cutting used as Exhibit D 30 in *State vs Mewa Ramgobin*.
27. Speech at Release Mandela Committee meeting, Soweto, 8 July 1984, Schedule A, Indictment, p. 19, *State vs Mewa Ramgobin*.
28. *SASPU Focus*, 2, 2, June 1983, p. 26.
29. *Social Review* (Cape Town), issue 24/25, April 1984, p. 38.
30. *Weekly Mail*, 16 January 1987, pp. 1–2.
31. *The Star*, 18 December 1985. Three detained organisers owned one pharmacy and two supermarkets.
32. Jeremy Seekings and Matthew Chaskalson, 'Politics in Tumahole, 1984–85', Association of Sociologists of South Africa conference, Durban, 30 June 1986, paper No. 59, p. 15.
33. *Work in Progress*, 39, October 1985, p. 9.
34. United Democratic Front, *Call to Whites, Join Us!*, pamphlet issued in early 1986.
35. *Rand Daily Mail*, 21 June 1983.
36. *State of the Nation*, May 1985. p. 12.

37. *Grassroots*, 6, 1, February 1985, p. 4.
38. 'Sowing confusion', *New Era* (Cape Town), 1, 1, March 1986, p. 38.
39. *Weekly Mail*, 30 August 1985, p. 13; 30 May 1986, p. 10.
40. Seekings and Chaskalson, op. cit., p. 22. See also the structure and workings of the Alexandra Action Committee as reported in the *Financial Mail*, 16 May 1986.
41. 'UDF Message', *Grassroots*, February 1986, 7, 1.
42. *Work in Progress*, 39 October 1985, p. 23.
43. 'MGWUSA on the UDF', *South African Labour Bulletin*, p. 72.
44. 'Why we cannot participate in the election referendum; the viewpoint of the Transvaal Anti-President's Council Committee', Exhibit D 36, *State vs Mewa Ramgobin.*
45. 'MGWUSA on the UDF', pp. 74–75.
46. *Work in Progress*, 39, p. 10.
47. *State of the Nation*, August 1983, p. 11; see also *AZASO Newsletter*, March 1984, p. 6.
48. For recent discussion inside South Africa of the internal colonialism thesis see Anon., 'Colonialism of a special kind and the South African State', *Africa Perspective* (Braamfontein), 23, 1983; Anon., 'National Liberation', *Spiked* (University of Cape Town, Students for Social Democracy), 3, 1, 1984; Jeremy Cronin, 'The NDS and the question of transformation', *Transformation*, 2, 1986, pp. 73–78.
49. *Update* (University of the Witwatersrand Student Representative Council), 'Working Class politics and popular democratic struggle', 2, 1, July 1984, pp. 8–11.
50. 'Errors of Workerism', *Isizwe*, 1, 3, November 1986, pp. 26–27.
51. 'The Rent Boycott is still on', pamphlet issued in Alexandra, in 1986.
52. 'Asinamali, Asibadali', pamphlet issued Soweto, June 1986.
53. 'Talking to a comrade', *Financial Mail*, 31 October 1986.
54. Raymond Suttner, 'Popular Justice in South Africa', paper delivered at Sociology Departmental seminar, University of Witwatersrand, 5 May 1986, p. 7. John Hund and Malebo Kotu-Rammago, 'Justice in a South African Township: The Sociology of Makgotla', *Comparative and International Law Journal of Southern Africa*, 16, 1983, pp. 182–83.
55. Suttner, op. cit. Also text of Raymond Suttner's interview with Titus Mofolo of ASRO.
56. Cedric Kekana, 'People's Courts in charge', *New Nation*, 13 February 1986, p. 10.
57. 'Ya, the Community is the main source of power', interviews, *Isizwe*, 1, 2, March 1986, pp. 40–41.
58. Ibid., p. 37 and 40.
59. On Alexandra: *The Star*, 25 April 1986, 24 April 1986; Sipho Ngcobo, 'Justice inside a People's Court', *Business Day*, February 1986; *The Star*, 16 March 1987; *Financial Mail*, 16 May 1986.
60. Quoted in Suttner, op. cit., p. 12.
61. Atteridgeville youth spokesman quoted in Suttner, op. cit., p. 18.
62. Ngoobo, op. cit.
63. *Isizwe*, 1, 2, March 1986, p. 36.
64. Suttner, op. cit., p. 20.

65. Ibid., p. 17.
66. Ibid., pp. 10–11; *New Nation*, 13 February 1986.
67. See also: 'Forward to People's Power', *UDF Update*, 2, 1, April 1986, p. 16; 'Red Terror or system of justice', *Upfront* (UDF Area Committee, Observatory), 4 June 1986, pp. 15–16, Kin Bentley, 'Street Committees', *Evening Post*, 7 April 1986, p. 11.
68. Georgina Jaffee, 'Beyond the cannon of Mamelodi', *Work in Progress*, 41, April 1986, p. 8; see also 'Street credibility', *Upfront*, No. 5, October 1986.
69. Peter Honey, 'Street Committees, People's Power or Kangaroo Courts', *Weekly Mail*, 9 May 1986, p. 9.
70. *Weekly Mail*, 14 February 1986; *The Star*, 29 October 1986; *New Nation*, 27 February 1986.
71. *The Star*, 1 June 1986. For report on the excesses committed by an East London people's court see *Weekly Mail*, 7 March 1986, p. 8.
72. *Isizwe*, 1, 2, March 1986, p. 41.
73. *The Weekly Mail*.
74. Pascal Damoyi, 'We must ensure homes for all', *Work in Progress*, 44 September 1986, pp. 12–14.
75. Jaffee, op. cit., p. 7.
76. Rich Mkhondo, 'People's Court not to blame for deaths', *The Star*, 25 April 1986.
77. Hund and Kotu-Rammapo, op. cit.
78. For example, in Crossroads between 1975 and 1978 a network of 'homeguards' and 'wardsmen' dealt with neighbourhood disputes and petty crimes. Josette Cole, 'Crossroads – the destruction of a symbol', *Work in Progress*, 43, August 1986, p. 3.
79. Chris Nissan, 'Bringing down the mountain', *Upfront*, 4 June 1986, pp. 14–15.
80. For Lebowa witchburnings: *Business Day*, 15 April 1986; *The Citizen*, 15 April 1986; *The Star*, 15 April 1986, 16 April 1986, and 17 April 1986; *The Star*, 10 February 1986, 12 February 1986; *State of the Nation*, February 1985; *Weekly Mail*, 25 April 1986, p. 3; *Sunday Star*, 20 April 1986; *Sowetan*, 18 April 1986.
81. Nomavenda Mathiane, 'Diary of troubled times', *Frontline*, November 1986, 6, 6, p. 23.
82. Jaffee, op. cit., p. 7.
83. Zwelakhe Sisulu, 'People's Education for People's Power', *Transformation* (Durban), 1, 1986, p. 98.
84. *UDF Update*, 2, 1, April 1986, p. 11.
85. For comparison with ANC during the 1950s see Tom Lodge,'Political Mobilisation During the 1950s: An East London Case Study', in Shula Marks and Stanley Trapido (eds), *The Politics of Race, Class and Nationalism in Twentieth Century South Africa*, London, Longman, 1987, pp. 310–35.
86. R. W. Johnson, *How Long Will South Africa Survive?*, London, Macmillan, 1977, p. 298.

10 Black Unions and Political Change in South Africa

Mark Mitchell and Dave Russell

INTRODUCTION

One of the most significant changes that has taken place in South Africa since the publication of Johnson's book, has been the development of an extensive network of independent black trade unions that has articulated in an increasingly militant way the frustrations and deprivations of the black African working class.[1] The growth of these unions has created a significant problem for the government and has undoubtedly contributed to the escalating crisis in the Republic. Yet there are important disagreements over the nature and extent of the challenge posed by black unions. Some writers have claimed that this 'new wave' of black unionisation has presented the state with its most serious and profound threat for many years. For example, Adam has argued that it 'would seem to be on the labour front . . . that the South African state faces its most serious challenge and where ultimately the politicization of ethnicity shows its most severe effects'.[2] Friedman, while generally more cautious in assessing the long-term political implications of black unionisation, nevertheless claims that the black trade unions are organisations through which 'hundreds and thousands of working people have gained a sense of their own power which is already changing the factories and may well help to change the country too'.[3] Others, however, have suggested that the combined effects of internal division and structural weakness, together with the debilitating consequences of continued political repression, must inevitably serve to limit the political effectiveness of black unions for the foreseeable future. The fact that during the present state of emergency, trade union activists have been detained in large numbers may be seen as confirmation of the more pessimistic prognosis advanced by Johnson himself when, in attempting to account for the apparent collapse of the upsurge of union activity in the early 1970s, he concluded that 'the efficacy of repression suggested strongly that industrial action held limited possibilities for the frustrated urban blacks'.[4] Paradoxically, Johnson's conclusions are mirrored in the ambivalent attitude towards the new black unions adopted by the South African Communist Party, and, to a lesser extent, by the African National Congress. For, as Plaut has argued, the strategy and tactics of both organisations are premised upon the assumption that 'because of the "fascist" nature of the South African state, the unions were bound either to be crushed or become collaborators'.[5] It is this debate over the political strengths and weaknesses of the black trade union movement that provides the major focus of interest in this chapter.

THE RE-EMERGENCE OF BLACK TRADE UNIONS IN THE 1970s

Black trade unionism has a long and checkered history in South Africa stretching back to the early decades of the twentieth century. However, the upsurge of black unionisation in the 1970s marked a new phase in the evolution of union organisation amongst the black working class, since it was qualitatively different from anything that had existed previously. Most obviously, the growth of these new unions was accompanied by an increase in the level of union militancy. This was in complete contrast to the relative industrial quiescence of the 1960s when the post-Sharpeville repression effectively destroyed the African trade union movement. The virtual elimination of independent black unions created a vacuum which was temporarily filled by a number of conservative-minded 'parallel' unions, each under the paternalistic tutelage of an all-white union affiliated to the Trade Union Council of South Africa (TUCSA).[6] As a result, according to the figures published by the National Manpower Commission, the number of black workers involved in strike action during the 1960s never exceeded 2000 per year. In contrast, the explosion of industrial militancy in 1973 – the year that is conventionally taken to mark the birth of the new unionism – saw around 100 000 workers take part in strike activity; and although the level of militancy later declined, the numbers involved in strike action have never since fallen below 14 000 in any one year. Indeed, the 1980s have seen strike activity at an unprecedentedly high level.[7]

However, the eruption of mass industrial action amongst African workers over the past fifteen years does not in itself provide sufficient grounds for understanding the specific character of the new black trade unions. Similar outbursts of strike activity have previously taken place amongst sections of the black African working class during the 1940s and 1950s. What distinguishes the new unions from their predecessors is their mode of operation and their organisational character, since they are grounded in a vibrant system of factory committees that provide for the democratic involvement of the rank-and-file membership in day-to-day union affairs at the place of work. In contrast, most of the previous attempts to unionise the African work force had paid scant attention to shopfloor organisation. Rather, union activists had typically concentrated their efforts on signing up as large a membership as possible in the pursuit of general, as opposed to factory-specific, objectives. In the South African context, such 'top-down' unions have always been highly vulnerable to state repression since the state can effectively immobilise the whole union organisation simply by detaining a relatively small number of key activists. Consequently, the history of black trade unionism in South Africa is littered with examples illustrating the rapid rise and fall of this type of union organisation. For a time it appeared that the new unions might suffer a similar fate. The Durban strikes of 1973, and especially the 1976 Soweto uprising, were followed by a predictable catalogue of arrests and banning orders which for a time threatened to engulf the black unions.[8] However their survival and subsequent growth is a clear indication of the resilience of this new 'bottom-up' type of union organisation that has its roots in a network of shop stewards who are in turn accountable to the rank-and-file union members at their places of work.

At the same time, it is important to recognise that this catalogue of harassment and persecution represents only one side of the South African state's response to this 'new wave' of black unions. Throughout the 1970s and early 1980s, the government was searching for an apparently elusive combination of reformist and repressive measures that would allow it to come to terms with the reality of black unionisation whilst keeping the unions under the firm control of the state. The 1970s saw two distinct phases in this control-through-reform strategy. The first, dating from 1973, saw the government trying to outflank the independent black unions through a policy of 'parallelism', encouraging TUCSA to resuscitate its system of black 'parallel' unions as rivals to the independents. The second, commencing with the phased introduction of the post-Wiehahn reforms in 1979, involved the state in a more direct attempt to co-opt and incorporate the black trade unions into the established system of industrial conciliation.

BLACK TRADE UNIONISM AND STATE REFORM: FROM PARALLELISM TO INCORPORATION

Having yielded to government pressure and expelled its black affiliates in 1969, TUCSA – in what can only be described as an about-turn – passed a resolution at its 1973 conference urging its constituent unions to organise separate but parallel unions for black workers. Subsequently, a number of such unions were established that were entirely under the administrative control of the sponsoring white union. In most cases, African workers were not even consulted over whether or not they wished to join. Typically, the union representing the skilled white workers at a particular factory would sign an agreement with the employer on behalf of the black parallel union, enrolling all African workers as new members at a stroke. The employer would then agree to deduct union dues from the black workforce on behalf of their union. Further, all bargaining rights were effectively ceded to the parent union which negotiated on behalf of its 'immature' African parallel, not at a factory level but via the national system of Industrial Councils. There was virtually no role for elected shop stewards, nor for any systematic consultation with the rank-and-file members, under this system. Indeed, evidence suggests that many African workers were only nominal members of these parallel unions, having little or no knowledge even of the existence of the union let alone of its policies or of how these might be changed.[9]

Despite its formal policy favouring parallelism, TUCSA's initiative was only partially successful in persuading its affiliated white unions to form parallel black organisations. The sharp decline in levels of industrial militancy after 1974 seemed to induce a sense of complacency within TUCSA and only five black parallels were set up following the 1973 resolution. Undoubtedly, there was a legacy of hostility to the whole idea of black unionism – no matter how carefully controlled – in certain sections of TUSCA. In addition, the cosy, privileged relationship enjoyed by the Council's leaders with both employers and the government, appeared to insulate TUCSA from the changes that were taking place on the factory floor. As a result, there was little evidence of any concerted attempt to 'roll back' the independent unions by TUCSA, since these unions were not perceived by Council affiliates as a serious threat to the established system of industrial relations. If the state was to meet the challenge posed by the independent black unions, which in spite of repression were managing to win a limited number of recognition agreements with employers, it was clear that it could not rely upon TUCSA.

In 1977, concerned that it had so far been unable to contain and control the 'new wave' of black unionisation, the government set up the Wiehahn Commission to examine ways of reforming the existing legislation in the field of labour relations and to make it more effective.[10] The post-Wiehahn reforms that were introduced by the government in stages between 1979 and 1980, and which were themselves only one part of the government's more general 'total strategy for survival', have to be understood as an attempt to secure two interrelated aims. In the first place, the labour reforms were designed to co-opt the emerging leadership of the new unions, binding them more tightly to the established system of industrial relations and thus neutralising their potential for change. Secondly, the reforms must be seen as an attempt to sow the seeds of division and discord amongst the various fractions of the African working class through a deliberate attempt to benefit the strong at the expense of the weak, thereby enabling the South African state to 'divide and rule' its subjugated peoples more effectively.

The first and most blatant of the government's aims was to promote and encourage the incorporation of the black trade unions into the state-controlled system of industrial conciliation. It proposed to achieve this goal through a 'carrot and stick' approach towards the new unions. In return for registration with the state, unions were to be allowed to enjoy new privileges, including the right to organise openly within the law; the right to participate in the industry-wide system of collective bargaining through the Industrial Councils; the right to engage in strike activity if all other avenues of conciliation had been exhausted; the right to utilise the services of the Industrial Court in cases of alleged unfair employment practices; and the right to seek the automatic deduction of union subscriptions by employers. However, these privileges were to be offered at a price. In return for the promise of a limited and subordinate degree of participation within the existing industrial relations system, unions had to submit their constitutions for approval by a new National Manpower Commission and had to be able to demonstrate that they were non-political organisations in the broadest sense. Further, since bargaining rights could only be exercised through the system of industry-wide Industrial Councils, the factory-based committees of shop stewards – the most distinctive feature of the independent black unions – were effectively to be prevented from negotiating directly with management.

Secondly the reform proposals have to be understood as one manifestation of the government's more general attempt to 'divide and rule'. Registration was to be confined to certain sections of black workers who stood to benefit from marginally improved rates of pay, better access to training opportunities and the like. Major sectors of the black population were excluded altogether from these benefits, including important categories within the black working class. Thus black workers employed in the agricultural sector were to be prevented from enjoying the limited benefits of registration, as were those employed in domestic service, the sector that provides the largest number of paid employment opportunities for black women in South Africa. Those employed within the so-called independent Bantustans, already subjected to different labour laws that were often more draconian than those operating in the Republic, were deemed to fall outside the jurisdiction of the proposed reforms. Even migrant workers were to be excluded from the framework of the new legislation since, in contrast to the recommendation of the Wiehahn Commission, the government proposed to deny registration to any union that recruited members from amongst the migrant or commuter work forces.[11] In reality, the proposed reforms were designed to confer limited privileges on particular categories of black male employees in the main those drawn from the ranks of the already advantaged 'urban insiders' who had permanent rights of residence in white urban areas.

THE FAILURE OF STATE REFORM: FROM INCORPORATION TO DECAPITATION

Whatever the government's intentions may have been, there is little doubt that the 'control-through-reform' strategy proved to be an unmitigated disaster for them. As argued in a later chapter, one of the specific characteristics of the South African state is that it lacks the necessary organisational capacities and resources that are an essential prerequisite for any successful strategy of reform. Consequently, the government was hampered throughout the reformist interlude of the late 1970s and early 1980s by the lack of a network of mediating structures that would have facilitated processes of bargaining and negotiation with the black unions. In the absence of such mediating structures, the attempt to engineer 'reform from above' served in effect to render the situation more complex and intractable. This is illustrated by two particular and unintended consequences that resulted from the attempt to implement the labour reforms.

Firstly, the government's decision to exclude migrant workers and commuters from the terms of the legislation provoked near-universal hostility from the trade unions. At a stroke, the state succeeded in uniting the entire independent black trade union movement in opposition to this proposal and the individual unions refused to apply for registration as legally recognised organisations under the new dispensation. The extent to which the South African state was out of touch with even conservative opinion was shown by the fact that several of the officially sanctioned black TUCSA unions rejected registration on these terms. This embarrassing level of non-cooperation forced a hasty and ignominious climbdown by the Minister of Manpower some weeks after the new regulations had come into effect, when he extended union rights to South African migrant workers and commuters by proclamation.

Secondly, even when the obstacle of the ban on migrants and commuters was removed, the strict conditions attaching to registration provoked a wide variety of different responses from the independent black unions. This had the effect of making an already intricate and difficult situation even more complex and unpredictable.[12] Some unions, including the strategically significant National Union of Mineworkers (NUM) and other 'Black Consciousness' unions, who were shortly to come together to form the Council of Unions of South Africa (CUSA), decided to collaborate in the registration process. They saw the reforms as offering real gains to black workers and believed that participation would provide an opportunity to win further concessions in the future. Other unions, including the Metal and Allied Workers Union (MAWU) and others affiliated to the Federation of South African Trade Unions (FOSATU), made registration itself conditional on the state granting additional concessions. In particular, they demanded – and eventually won – the right of a trade union to be formally constituted as a non-racial organisation with a racially mixed membership. Finally, a third group of independent black unions, including the South African Allied Workers Union (SAAWU) and the General Workers Union (GWU), followed a strategy of non-registration, refusing to countenance any degree of cooperation or compromise, however minimal, with the apartheid state.[13] Thus, the net effect of this attempt to impose reforms was to create a set of divergent and contradictory responses from the unions. As a result, worried that the situation was getting out of hand, the government decided in 1981 to extend many aspects of the post-Wiehahn reforms to all unions, whether registered or unregistered.

In practice, largely as a result of the organisational and structural deficiencies of the South African state, the labour reforms completely failed to stem the rising tide of militant black trade unionism. Total union membership rose from under one million in 1980 to over one-and-a-half million in 1983, with the growth in African membership accounting for virtually all of this increase.[14] Although the TUCSA unions increased their levels of membership during this period – prior to the rapid fall after 1983 – the most significant growth occurred amongst the independent black unions, whose membership increased from 70 000 in 1979 to 400 000 by the end of 1983. By 1985 one estimate was that the independents probably had a total paid-up membership of around 520 000.[15] This growth in size was accompanied by a strengthening of the unions' factory base, with perhaps a threefold increase in the number of shop stewards and a near fivefold increase in the number of workplaces organised in the three-year period up to 1985.[16] Not surprisingly, the level of strike activity rose dramatically from 1980, when 52 286 workers went on strike, to 1985, when the corresponding figure was 239 816.[17] More generally, the attempt by the state to depoliticise the union movement was a complete failure as more and more unions were drawn into the escalating tide of protest and violence within the black townships. Of course, it was always totally unrealistic to imagine that the black unions would ever abstain from politics when the South African state itself interferes and intrudes into every aspect of the working lives of black workers. In effect, all that the post-Wiehahn reforms achieved was to create a degree of political space where black South Africans could engage in legal forms of association and organisation effectively denied them elsewhere. Under these conditions, trade union activism became a form of 'politics by other means' and the trade unions themselves became, as Erwin has noted, 'schools for democracy' – if not yet 'schools for revolution'.[18]

The growing politicisation of labour conflicts and the blurring of the distinction between industrial and community struggles has served to amplify the latent contradictions at the heart of the 'total strategy for survival'. Despite the reformist rhetoric adopted by the government in the late 1970s and early 1980s, the principal aim of the total strategy was always the creation of a more militarised society, better able to defend 'white civilisation' from 'the total onslaught'.[19] This growing militarisation of the South African state has had the effect of accelerating the scale of conflict between the state and the black trade unions, with the predictable consequence that cooption and incorporation have now been abandoned in favour of decapitation. Since the declaration of the state of emergency in June 1986, hundreds of union activists have been detained without trial together with thousands of striking workers.[20] In addition, other forms of harassment, such as physical attacks on the national offices of trade unions, including the dynamiting of COSATU's headquarters, have hampered the effectiveness of many unions and disrupted their lines of communication. Yet this decapitation strategy has not entirely paralysed the independent unions. The contrast with 1974, when the banning of a handful of union activists led to the virtual collapse of the unions in the Durban area, could not be greater.[21] Although state repression is bound to hinder their future development, the strong grass-roots organisation of the black unions has proved to be highly resilient to decapitation. The introduction early in 1988 of a further set of repressive measures designed to clip the political wings of the independent unions is clear evidence of the fact that, despite the detention of hundreds of union activists and organisers, decapitation alone has failed to neutralise the challenge of the black unions.

BLACK UNIONS AND THE STRUGGLE FOR LIBERATION

Although the government's bid to coopt and depoliticise the black trade unions has failed, the political challenge of the independent union movement has been blunted by the existence of a significant degree of disunity within the movement itself. In part, this lack of unity reflects the impact of more fundamental structural divisions within the African working class itself. In particular, there are divisions between those in employment and the increasing numbers of black Africans without work, between those employed in different sectors of the economy, and between those affected in diverse ways by the impact of the unique 'spatial relations' that operate in South Africa.[22] But it also has to be recognised that the rapid growth of black unions has brought to the surface deep-seated ideological differences that have their roots in wider political conflicts and disagreements amongst the African population. So, while all the independent black trade unions are formally committed to a policy of opposition to apartheid, there are significant political differences between sections of the black union movement over the precise role that unions should play in the struggle for liberation.

The first of these differences centres on the issue of whether the independent unions should be exclusively black, both in terms of their membership and their leadership, or be formally constituted as non-racial organisations. Currently, this dispute finds institutional expression in the rivalry between the Congress of South African Trade Unions (COSATU) and the Council of Unions of South African-Azanian Confederation of Trade Unions (CUSA-AZACTU).[23]

Thus although CUSA-AZACTU supports a broad policy of 'worker control based on anti-racism/non-racism', it is further committed to 'black working class leadership' and to the view that 'the entire country . . . belongs to the indigenous people of our country'.[24] In reality, this has meant that leadership posts within the federation have been reserved exclusively for blacks, though some of the individual affiliated unions have adopted a more flexible attitude to the issue of non-black members. In contrast, COSATU has non-racialism as one of its central principles and is committed to 'strive for the building of a united working-class movement regardless of "race", colour, creed or sex'.[25] In practice, with whites occupying minor positions within several of its affiliated unions, COSATU has argued that it is up to the union members to select their own leaders, black or white. CUSA-AZACTU has insisted on the principle of black leadership since the membership of the independent unions is almost exclusively black. Despite the fact that these differences are in part a product of longstanding interpersonal rivalries and that the leadership of COSATU itself is now exclusively black, this disagreement nevertheless represents the most recent manifestation of the 'class versus race' debate that divided the liberation movement in the 1950s and 1960s.

Another major source of division within the black trade union movement has arisen because of disagreements over the role that unions should play in wider community struggles. Two major tendencies can be identified, as the independents have tended to adopt either a 'workerist' or 'populist' standpoint. On the one hand, the workerist unions have argued that priority must be given to expanding and strengthening the grass-roots union organisation on the factory floor. Though they recognise the necessity for political change, and indeed are willing to participate in wider community struggles if these are firmly under the direction of the unions, they argue that the working class must play a leading role in the struggle for liberation. Since the organised working class is still relatively weak in South Africa, the primary task must be to consolidate and expand the influence of the black trade unions amongst the African working class. This was the position originally adopted by the FOSATU affiliates and by unions like the GWU.

On the other hand, those unions supporting a strategy of community populism have argued that workerism will only serve to consolidate the relatively privileged position of certain fractions of the black working class. The emphasis given to shopfloor organisation inevitably downgrades the struggles of most black women workers, agricultural workers and, above all, the growing mass of blacks without paid employment who increasingly make up a surplus population destined to remain permanently peripheral to the needs of South African capitalism. Black unions like SAAWU, for example, argue that they have no alternative but to adopt a populist strategy since the Mdantsane township, which is their principal recruitment base, lies within the borders of the 'independent' Ciskei homeland where SAAWU is a banned organisation. The original CUSA affiliates also argued that industrial and political struggles were inseparable and sought to combine an expansion of their factory-based organisation with an involvement in the escalating levels of protest in the townships.

The formation of the UDF in 1983 highlighted these differences very clearly.[26] In all, some thirteen independent unions – including SAAWU and the CUSA unions – affiliated to the UDF. The workerist unions, however, decided not to join, though many issued statements supporting the aims of the UDF and urging their numbers to participate in its campaigns on an individual basis. The FOSATU unions, with their principal membership base in Natal, felt unable to affiliate because of the open hostility that existed between Inkatha and the UDF.[27] Others were concerned at the lack of accountability within the UDF and claimed that organisations like trade unions who were accountable to their members, could well be swamped by a plethora of small and unrepresentative community groups who were often accountable to no one.[28]

For a while, it appeared that these differences might be submerged, as the level of protest intensified throughout 1985 and 1986. The harassment and persecution of union activists had an inevitable 'politicisation effect' on the whole of the movement as the shadow of state repression fell on the best-organised and most successful unions, whether workerist or populist in orientation.[29] The government's attempt to increase township rents and public transport fares propelled several of the workerist unions into the planning and organising of community-based rent strikes and bus boycotts, since these were issues that directly affected the standard of living of their members.[30] Most significantly, the formation of COSATU itself brought together under one umbrella a range of unions that had previously been divided on the issue of unions and politics, and the commitment of the Congress to broad political objectives was as explicit as it was uncompromising. By 1986 it appeared that many of the earlier divisions between workerist and populist unions had been rendered irrelevant by the escalating crisis in the black townships.[31]

However, more recently there are signs that the earlier divisions are re-emerging within COSATU itself. There is growing evidence of dissatisfaction amongst some affiliates and their grass-roots activists with the overtly populist political stance taken by the COSATU leadership. The issue is not over whether the federation should be involved in politics, since there is a broad consensus within COSATU over the inevitability of this in the South African context. Rather, there is dissatisfaction with the style of leadership in the Congress, which has tended to commit the federation to political policies and campaigns which have not been fully debated and approved by workers in the constituent unions. The populist rhetoric of COSATU has already led to a serious split in the National Union of Textile Workers.[32] There are also reports of growing unease amongst the more traditional workerist affiliates to COSATU, such as the GWU and the former FOSATU unions.[33] Given the current political situation in the Republic, the workerist unions are understandably reluctant to voice these criticisms openly. Yet it appears that the union movement may have been swept along by the rapid pace of political events over the past three years in a way that has done little to enhance the prospects of attaining longer-term economic and political objectives. The scattered signs of dissatisfaction amongst some affiliates may mark the beginning of a swing against populism within COSATU; and the government decree introduced early in 1988 banning various forms of political activity by unions, is likely to strengthen the hands of the workerist elements within the federation.

A more recent source of serious division within the black trade union movement has been the issue of economic sanctions against the Republic, involving disinvestment by Western companies. Both COSATU and CUSA-AZACTU made support for sanctions a central feature of their inaugural policy statements. However, this policy proved to be controversial since it appears to offer blacks the prospect of fewer job opportunities and higher levels of unemployment. In particular, COSATU's unequivocal support for disinvestment was a major factor contributing to the decision by Inkatha to launch the United Workers Union of South Africa (UWUSA) as a pro-capitalist, anti-sanctions union in May 1986.[34]

UWUSA cannot seriously claim to be a genuinely independent organisation representing the interests of African workers. Its general secretary is a former businessman who was until recently a director of KwaZulu Transport and of the Inkatha investment holding company, Khulani Holdings.[35] Despite constant denials by both Inkatha and UWUSA, there is evidence to suggest that its commitment to a free enterprise economy has helped to endear UWUSA to some employers and, as a result, 'a key factor in the success of UWUSA so far has been the willingness (often eagerness) of employers to have dealings with the union'.[36] In addition, there is strong circumstantial evidence that state repression has been selectively used to weaken COSATU and its affiliates in the industrial growth area of northern Natal, thus enabling UWUSA to recruit more easily.[37] Yet in spite of this, and in the face of much scepticism over its prospects at the time of the launch, UWUSA has made some inroads in the region where COSATU, and in particular the former FOSATU unions, had traditionally been strong.

In the early 1980s, FOSATU and Inkatha had coexisted uneasily together, which had allowed Inkatha supporters to be drawn into the ranks of the black unions in increasing numbers. COSATU's attempt to forge a link with the wider liberation struggle, through its endorsement of the Freedom Charter and the visit of its leaders to Lusaka to talk with the ANC, disrupted the fragile understanding that had developed between the unions and Inkatha. The launch of a rival union organisation by Inkatha was always likely to undermine the effectiveness of COSATU in the Natal region, since union members belonging to Inkatha found themselves subjected to contradictory demands for their allegiance. UWUSA probably does not have the capacity to displace the COSATU unions from their base on the factory floor. Neither does it have the strength to win more than a handful of recognition agreements. In its organisation and mode of operation, it is much more like a traditional 'top-down' African trade union than one of the black independents. But by exploiting Inkatha's 'culturalist' appeal, UWUSA can wean key activists away from COSATU and can mobilise reactionary sentiments for the purpose of intimidation and violence.[38]

The rise of UWUSA has highlighted fundamental areas of political and ideological disagreement within the union movement and the African population generally over the issue of sanctions. More recently, there is evidence to suggest that COSATU itself has begun to rethink its pro-sanctions policy. In 1986 a COSATU affiliate, the National Auto and Allied Workers Union, called a strike at General Motors' South African car plant to protest at plans by the US parent company to sell off its South African subsidiary to a local management consortium. General Motors, along with other US companies, had been under pressure to disinvest and the union demanded the right to negotiate the terms of withdrawal with the disinvestor. However, this demand was successfully resisted, the sale went ahead and the new South African owners called in the police to break up the strike.[39] Largely as a consequence of this débâcle, COSATU itself commissioned a major report to review the whole question of disinvestment. Among other things, this report suggested that selective sanctions may be a more effective weapon than blanket sanctions.[40] Irrespective of how this issue is finally resolved within COSATU, it seems certain that sanctions and disinvestment will continue to be a major source of tension and division, both within the black trade union movement and more generally in black politics.

STRENGTHS AND WEAKNESSES OF THE BLACK TRADE UNIONS

Despite having had to operate in an increasingly hostile environment, the new black trade unions have displayed more strength and resilience than was envisaged by Johnson in 1977. The black trade union movement today is far stronger and better organised than appeared likely then. Although Johnson was correct to stress the repressive capabilities of the South African state in dealing with the unions, he was unable to foresee the way in which the 'new wave' unionism would develop organisationally. Unlike the old-style 'mass movement' unionism, the new unions are founded upon a solid factory base. Many of the new unions have built up a network of shop stewards accountable to members at their places of work, and, besides enhancing workplace democracy, this form of organisation has proved to be more resistant to the kind of state repression predicted by Johnson. It was these deeper organisational roots that enabled unions to survive in 1986 the state's adoption of an aggressive policy of decapitation against the unions which saw the arrest and detention of many key leaders.

The relative organisational strength of the unions has also been a factor in their effectiveness in securing important gains for tens of thousands of black workers. Considerable success in struggles over wages and conditions, workplace grievances, recognition and dismissals, has won the new unions the kind of 'legitimacy by results' quite unexpected by sceptics like Johnson. Even with the onset of recession, the unions have managed to sustain a high degree of militancy and pressure over wages. Advances have also been made in other directions such as the achievement of the Commercial, Catering and Allied Workers Union of South Africa in negotiating maternity rights for its predominantly female membership.[41] In addition, the unions have played important roles in a variety of community-based struggles, such as the successful bus boycotts and the rent campaigns which took place in the 1983–85 period.

Such activity offers some indication of how the unions have become centrally involved in political action and extra-workplace struggles. As the line between 'industrial' and 'political' issues has become more blurred, so the dynamic towards 'political unionism' has accelerated. In this process the black trade unions have effectively exploited the limited concessions granted by the state to extend their control and influence outside as well as inside the workplace. There is no doubt that, in the continued absence of 'normal' channels for political representation, the unions have become increasingly important avenues for the pursuit of politics by an alternative means. Both in the workplace and the community, therefore, the unions have provided a major focus for political activity in a way quite unforeseen by Johnson.

However, the strengths of the new unionism must be set against a number of serious weaknesses which have served to reduce both its industrial muscle and its capacity to challenge fundamentally the apartheid state. Firstly, it should be stressed that the level of unionisation in South Africa is relatively low by international standards. At around 15 per cent, South African union density is considerably lower than in many other industrial capitalist countries, even those like the USA and Japan, whose labour movements are commonly thought to be weak.[42] Despite a dramatic growth since 1977, the overall size of the movement is still modest, with a large majority of black workers still outside the unions.[43] Furthermore, a great many of these workers, especially those in the agricultural sector and women workers in domestic service, are likely to remain virtually unorganisable. Many individual unions are quite small and in certain regions like the Western Cape the new unions are particularly low on numbers.[44] As the largest single trade union federation, COSATU can only claim around 500 000 members which is at best no more than 5 per cent of the economically active population. It is also the case that, despite the upsurge in industrial militancy, the level of strike activity in South Africa is still comparatively low.[45]

Although the number of strikes per year has greatly increased since 1979, many disputes have been limited to single factories for a short duration. In general, the unions do not possess the financial resources to sustain industrial action for longer periods. The preponderance of small regionalised trade unions, together with the underdevelopment of large national trade unions, has been a real disadvantage to the union movement in a situation where it is confronted by an extremely high concentration of economic power.[46]

Secondly, the strength and bargaining power of black unions has been diluted by the rising level of black unemployment which, in contradiction to the official statistics, is estimated in real terms to be running at anything between one-quarter and almost one-half of the economically active black population.[47] An acute problem of structural unemployment – a permanent feature of the South African economy since the mid-1970s – has been caused by a combination of factors. On the one hand, capital intensification and innovation in production methods, especially in the mining and manufacturing sectors of the economy, has resulted in the disappearance of many jobs.[48] On the other hand, there has been a steady increase in the supply of black labour. For some considerable time therefore, the economy has been unable to provide enough jobs for the expanding black population. A more immediate cause of worsening black unemployment has been the economic recession that has plagued the country since 1982. Additionally, the 'monetarist' policy innovations in this period have inevitably served to speed up the retrenchment of black workers, whilst in a different vein disinvestment has also cost some workers their jobs.

The retrenchment process has had a crucial impact on the emergent union movement. In specific instances union members and activists have been victimised and deliberately made redundant. More generally, the unions have been forced more and more on to the defensive by cutbacks in black employment and, significantly, they have had little choice but to resort to the legal machinery of the Industrial Court in order to protect workers against arbitrary dismissal. Whilst this kind of defensive tactic has produced some notable victories, it also illustrates how unions have been obliged to concentrate largely on the interests of unionised workers at the expense of the growing mass of unemployed black people. The divisive effects of the retrenchment process and the relative inability of the unions to resist this, have also been demonstrated by the growth of sectoral differentiation, with some regionally-based industries being far more affected by retrenchment than others. For instance, workers in the motor industry and more widely in the steel and engineering sectors have been hard-hit by the recession, especially in certain areas like the depressed Eastern Cape region.[49] In the face of plant closures and soaring unemployment, the unions have been unable to prevent a fall in the overall standard of living of the black population. Wage-earners in recent years have found their pay-rises eroded by inflation and state-imposed increases in rents and transport costs. In addition, the swelling ranks of the unemployed have had to be supported by those workers in employment. In general the situation of blacks in terms of poverty and income has actually deteriorated since 1977.[50] The unions have been completely unable to prevent poverty, inequality and unemployment increasing in South Africa during this period.

Thirdly, the power of the unions has also been undermined by the state's unfolding regional strategy.[51] Throughout the reform era the Bantustans have presented difficulties for unions. In some, unions have been illegal, while in others labour laws and minimum-wage legislation have not applied. Consequently, some companies have relocated plants to the Bantustans to take advantage of the plentiful supply of cheap labour and favourable terms of employment. Policy initiatives arising from the government's new regional strategy have attempted to take this an important stage further by creating in the metropolitan peripheries 'deconcentration areas', which can straddle white and Bantustan territories. Firms are being offered incentives to locate plants in these 'enterprise zones' by promising them exemption from minimum-wage legislation, health and safety standards and the jurisdiction of the Industrial Court. Clearly this development threatens to impair the position of the unions in urban white areas as well as the Bantustans.

Fourthly, the strength of the black trade union movement has also been significantly affected by the organisational divisions and rivalries discussed earlier. Division not unity still remains an outstanding characteristic of the black labour movement. Indeed, there appears to have been some consolidation of organisational divisions since the historic formation of COSATU in 1985. However, it has been political divisions rather than shopfloor rivalry which have in the main prevented the unions from uniting under one banner. The launch of COSATU signalled only a partial resolution of the tension between workerist and populist tendencies. The inevitability of some degree of 'political unionism' has now been widely accepted by all COSATU affiliates but what form union politics should take is still a matter of dispute. Whilst COSATU's national leadership has often tended to operate in a populist fashion, many individual unions have stuck to their pre-COSATU style of democratic grass-roots organisation. Furthermore, the limited progress made in restructuring the federation towards single-industry 'industrial unions' owes much to the continuing conflict between rival COSATU unions over this very issue. Much therefore remains to be achieved if COSATU is to become a strong, centralised peak association at the head of a streamlined union structure.

The formation in 1986 of a sizable rival federation, CUSA-AZACTU, offers further evidence of the movement's relative lack of unity and coherence. The ideological appeal of CUSA-AZACTU's unbending commitment to Black Consciousness is likely to prove an enduring obstacle to greater union solidarity. However, it is Inkatha's pro-capitalist, anti-sanctions organisation (UWUSA) that is most at odds with rest of the black union movement. Although, with its limited ethnic appeal, there is little prospect of UWUSA becoming a national union, it appears seriously to have weakened COSATU's domination in Natal within a year of its inception.[52] UWUSA's impact on the shopfloor has so far been limited. Its capacity to organise workers has been enhanced by the alacrity with which some employers have agreed to negotiate with its representatives and by what appears to have been a deliberate attempt by the state to harass rival COSATU unions in regions like northern Natal.[53] The launch and better-than-expected regional success of UWUSA has been a further blow to the unity of a movement beset by political divisions and shifting alliances.

CONCLUSION

It is clear that Johnson did not fully appreciate the significance of the rise of the 'new wave' black unions in the early 1970s. Contrary to his pessimistic predictions, the rapid expansion of the independent union movement in the 1980s has been accompanied by the adoption of a more overt political stance by the unions. Not only have the unions come to play a leading role outside the workplace, but strikes and other forms of industrial action have in turn become politicised and linked to the community struggles in the townships. Thus the government's attempts to restrict black trade unions to a narrow economistic role have completely failed. In reality, although the regime is likely to continue its efforts to limit the role of the unions, there is little prospect that they can now be depoliticised. In spite of the repression unleashed against them, the unions have survived, battered but unbroken, and in better shape than many of the community-based groups who have also felt the full force of the apartheid state's iron fist. Today, it is the black trade unions who present apartheid with its most serious political challenge, and the well-publicised contacts between COSATU and the ANC underline the fact that the government has little alternative but to strive to contain and neutralise the independent unions.

In view of this, the package of measures announced in February 1988, designed to prevent black unions from engaging in a variety of forms of political activity, is an entirely predictable development. The effect of these new restrictions is uncertain. It may be that the ban on sympathy strikes, the redefinition of unfair labour practices, and above all the attempt to make unions legally accountable for the consequences of 'illegal' strikes, will have the effect of lowering levels of industrial militancy. Nevertheless, we believe that the black unions are equipped to survive this new and intensified state offensive. Above all, their resilience is due to the strength and vitality of their shopfloor organisation. But significantly some employers, fearful of the chaos that may follow any attempt to outlaw the unions, have spoken out against the banning of union activists and may be unwilling to enforce the letter of the new legal restrictions against political unionism. The government too, though it would dearly love to neutralise the independent unions politically, is unlikely to seek to eradicate them completely, since this would require the regime to dismantle one of the central planks of its self-proclaimed reform programme. In short, black trade unions are in South Africa to stay! For the foreseeable future, they will continue to be a thorn in the side of a government unable either to destroy or coopt them.

Nevertheless, the black unions on their own lack the capacity to mount a sustained challenge to the militarised might of the South African state. Even in the industrial sphere, they possess a limited capacity for large-scale industrial action and have often failed to win concessions in major confrontations. Recently, the independent union movement has suffered a number of demoralising industrial defeats, as in the case of the NUM which called tens of thousands of miners out on strike in August 1987. With no strike fund and faced with the prospect of mass dismissals amongst its membership, NUM leaders decided to back down and abandon a struggle, the scale and intensity of which had clearly shocked both employers and the government. Some months earlier, the strike by black railway workers in the state-controlled South African Transport Services met with similar intransigence and also ended in defeat. In general, strikes invariably prove difficult and costly for black unions and their members, as the industrial dice are heavily loaded against them. This has been compounded by the inability of the independent union movement to transcend the ideological and organisational divisions that it has inherited from the past. As a result, the unions are ill-equipped to confront in any fundamental way the power of the apartheid state. Rather, they remain an obstacle to the attempts by the South African state to streamline its system of racial domination, and a stumbling block to its political ambitions.

Notes

1. The term 'black trade unions' is used throughout this chapter to refer to those independent unions that recruit the vast majority of their membership from amongst the black African population and which have been established over the last fifteen years in opposition to other officially sponsored and approved unions of black workers.
2. H. Adam, 'South Africa's Search for Legitimacy', *Telos*, 59, 1980, p. 60.
3. S. Friedman, *Building Tomorrow Today*, Johannesburg, Raven Press, 1987, p. 4.
4. R. Johnson, *How Long Will South Africa Survive?*, London, Macmillan, 1977, p. 87.
5. M. Plaut, 'The Political Significance of COSATU', *Transformation*, 2, 1986, p. 62. See also M. Plaut, 'Changing Perspectives on South African Trade Unions', *Review of African Political Economy*, 30, 1985, pp. 116–23.
6. In 1969 TUCSA itself, under pressure from both the government and from its own all-white skilled workers' unions, agreed to expel black unions from the organisation. A number of the unions who were forced out of TUCSA at this time later became important in the early stages of the development of the new unionism.
7. Figures on the levels of strike activity from year to year are given in: S. Friedman, *Building Tomorrow Today*, op. cit., p. 125 ff; M. Plaut, 'The Political Significance of COSATU', op. cit., p. 63; R. and L. Lambert, 'State Reform and Working Class Resistance, 1982', in *South Africa Review One: Same Foundations, New Facades*, Johannesburg, Ravan Press, 1983, p. 220.
8. In November 1976, twenty-eight activists from the new union movement were banned. See M. Murphy, *Trade Unions in South Africa*, London, Workers' Educational Association, 1984, p. 14. Much lower levels of union militancy were recorded during 1977 and 1978 following the post-Soweto repression. See R. and L. Lambert, 'State Reform', op. cit., p. 220.
9. For a discussion of TUCSA, see S. Friedman, *Building Tomorrow Today*, op. cit., pp. 69–84; C. Cooper, 'The Established Trade Union Movement', in *South Africa Review One*, op. cit., pp. 204–17. TUCSA, which for many

years was the largest of the trade union federations in the Republic, began to decline in size in the early 1980s, losing over 200 000 members through disaffiliation between 1983 and 1985. See *Annual Report of Labour Relations in South Africa 1985–86*, Johannesburg, Andrew Levy and Associates, p. 8. In late 1986 the Executive Committee of TUCSA recommended that the federation be dissolved. See the interview with R. Botha, President of TUCSA at the time of its demise, in *South African Labour Bulletin*, 12, 1986, pp. 60–66. The gap created by TUCSA's demise has since been filled by the National Federation of Trade Unions, founded in April 1987.

10. For a summary of the major recommendations of the Wiehahn Commission, see W. Vose, 'Wiehahn and Riekert Revisited: A Review of the Prevailing Black Labour Conditions in South Africa', *International Labour Review*, 124, 1985, pp. 449 ff.
11. Commuters are African workers who reside in a so-called black homeland but who travel to work on a daily basis to a designated white area in the Republic.
12. For a more detailed discussion of these different responses to registration amongst the black trade unions, see M. Mitchell and D. Russell, 'South Africa in Crisis: The Role of the Black Trade Unions', in W. Brierley, *Trade Unions and the Economic Crisis of the 1980s*, Aldershot, Gower, 1987, pp. 195 ff.
13. This rejectionist stance coincided with the call to boycott the registration process issued by the exiled South African Congress of Trade Unions (SACTU).
14. These figures and others in this section are taken from J. Lewis and E. Randall, 'The State of the Unions', *Review of African Political Economy*, 35, 1986, pp. 68–77. This is an abridged version of a longer article first published in *South African Labour Bulletin*, 11, 1985.
15. Ibid., p. 72. It is customary to quote two figures for union membership in South Africa, as the number of paid-up members is always smaller than the number of signed-up members. Lewis and Randall estimate that in 1985, the latter figure stood at nearly 800 000 for the non-TUCSA black trade unions.
16. These figures are based on a survey of twenty-three independent black unions conducted by Lewis and Randall, ibid., pp. 72–3. The degrees of change are derived on the basis of a comparison with the survey reported in E. Webster, 'New Force on the Shop Floor', in *South Africa Review Two*, Johannesburg, Ravan Press, 1984, pp. 79–89.
17. Strike figures are quoted in M. Plaut, 'The Political Significance of COSATU', op. cit., p. 63.
18. A. Erwin, 'On Unions and Politics', paper presented to the ASSA Conference, University of Cape Town, July 1985. Erwin is the white education officer of the Congress of South African Trade Unions.
19. For a detailed discussion of this drive towards militarisation, see M. Mitchell and D. Russell, 'Militarisation and the South African State', in C. Creighton and M. Shaw, *The Sociology of War and Peace*, London, Macmillan, 1987, pp. 99–120.
20. One authoritative survey reports that: 'By the end of the second week of

the state of emergency, a total of 171 trade unionists and 821 striking workers were known to have been detained. By the end of the sixth week, this figure had grown to 321 elected office bearers and union officials, and to over 2,000 workers.' See 'Trade Unions and the State of Emergency', *South African Labour Bulletin*, 11, 1986, p. 77. This survey also shows very clearly that it is the unions affiliated to COSATU that have borne the brunt of state repression.

21. See S. Friedman, *Building Tomorrow Today*, op. cit., p. 60, for a discussion of this rapid decline in union membership.
22. The impact of these structural divisions on the independent unions will be discussed in the final section of this chapter.
23. COSATU was formed in November 1985 and probably has around 565 000 paid-up members. CUSA-AZACTU was established in October 1986 through a merger of the two organisations that had previously cooperated closely together. It has a paid-up membership of around 220 000. For membership figures, see J. Lewis and E. Randall, 'The State of the Unions', op. cit., p. 72.
24. The policy statement issued to coincide with the launch of CUSA-AZACTU is reprinted in *South African Labour Bulletin*, 12, 1986, pp. 49–52.
25. Taken from the opening speech by Cyril Ramaphosa at the Congress called to launch COSATU. This is reprinted in *Review of African Political Economy*, 35, 1986, pp. 77–83.
26. For a clear statement of the workerist misgivings over affiliation to the UDF, see the interview with David Lewis, a former general secretary of the GWU, 'General Workers' Union and the UDF', *Work in Progress*, 29, 1983, pp. 11–18. For a statement of the opposing populist standpoint by one of the leaders of SAAWU, see S. Njikelana, 'The Unions and the Front: A Response to David Lewis', in *South African Labour Bulletin*, 9, 1984, pp. 76–83.
27. Joe Foster, former general secretary of FOSATU, stated quite openly that, in the interests of unity, the FOSATU unions were unable to affiliate since a section of their membership was openly hostile to the politics of the UDF. See H. Barrell, 'The United Democratic Front and the National Forum: Their Emergence, Composition and Trends', in *South African Review Two*, op. cit., p. 14.
28. This is one of the major arguments advanced by David Lewis. See 'General Workers' Union and the UDF', op. cit., p. 11.
29. The survey by the *South African Labour Bulletin* showed that the two unions most affected by the detention of union officials were MAWU and the Commercial, Catering and Allied Workers Union of South African (CCAWUSA). MAWU, one of the original FOSATU affiliates, was traditionally located firmly in the workerist camp. CCAWUSA, though it has never completely neglected shopfloor organisation, has always adopted a more populist stance. See 'Trade Unions and the State of Emergency', op. cit., p. 80.
30. For a brief discussion of the successful 1985 Empangeni bus boycott and the role of the unions in this, see P. Green, 'Northern Natal: Meeting UWUSA's Challenge', *South African Labour Bulletin*, 12, 1986, pp. 76–7.

A short account of the attempt to replicate the Empangeni campaign in Pietermaritzberg, is given in 'How Fares the Struggle', *Industrial Relations Data 5*, Johannesburg, Andrew Levy and Associates, May 1986, p. 11.

31. This was our conclusion in an earlier paper. See M. Mitchell and D. Russell, 'South Africa in Crisis', op. cit., p. 202.
32. For details, see 'Fabric Rent Asunder', *Industrial Relations Data 6*, op. cit., September 1986, pp. 4–7.
33. See for example 'COSATU: The MKHE Factor', in *Industrial Relations Data 5*, op. cit., pp. 8–11.
34. A clear indication of UWUSA's policy on sanctions is given in an interview with Simon Conco who was to become general secretary of the organisation. See *South African Labour Bulletin*, 11, 1986, pp. 51–61.
35. For further details see P. Green, 'Northern Natal: Meeting UWUSA's Challenge', *South African Labour Bulletin*, 12, 1986, pp. 75–6.
36. 'UWUSA – One Year Old and Where To Go?', *Industrial Relations Data 6*, op. cit., March/April 1987, p. 15.
37. For a summary of this evidence, which became the basis of a COSATU application to the Natal Supreme Court for the release of union activists detained in Northern Natal, see P. Green, 'Northern Natal', op. cit., pp. 78–9. It would appear that to date, no UWUSA official has been detained under the state of emergency.
38. For some examples of this violence, see 'UWUSA – One Year Old', op. cit., p. 15.
39. For details see 'Sanctions In Action: The Trade Union Dilemma', *Front File: Southern Africa Brief*, 2, May 1987.
40. Ibid.
41. M. Murray, *South Africa: Time of Agony, Time of Destiny*, London, Verso, 1987, p. 164.
42. In 1983, Webster compared the figures for union density in South Africa, which he claimed was 'the lowest percentage of workers unionised in the developed capitalist world', with the figures for Sweden (83 per cent), the United Kingdom (50 per cent), West Germany (38 per cent), Japan (33 per cent), and the USA (20 per cent). Our figure of 15 per cent union density is an estimate and compares with Webster's 1983 figure of 12 per cent. E. Webster, 'New Force', op. cit., p. 80. Adam and Moodley have also recently quoted a figure of 15 per cent. See H. Adam and K. Moodley, *South Africa Without Apartheid*, Berkeley, University of California Press, 1986, p. 183.
43. See J,Lewis and E. Randall, 'The State of the Unions', op. cit.
44. M. Murray, *South Africa: Time of Agony, Time of Destiny*, op. cit.
45. According to Webster, in 1981–82 Sweden had the highest number of days lost per annum per 1000 workers, with 105 days lost. The corresponding figures for the UK, USA and South Africa were 45, 32 and 26 respectively.
46. M. Murray, *South Africa*, op. cit., pp. 130–1.
47. Vose in 1985 estimated the long-term rate of black unemployment to be 25 per cent. More recently, Sarakinsky and Keenan have suggested on the basis of several rural and urban micro-surveys that unemployment runs at about 25 per cent of the black population, or 48 per cent of the

economically active population. This gives a massive figure of about 6.5 million blacks without work. On an alternative method of estimating black unemployment, Sarakinsky and Keenan offer upper and lower totals of approximately 5.3 million and 4.2 million respectively. This compares with the official unemployment rate that has been variously estimated in the last five years at between 10 and 20 per cent, with the official figure for black unemployment at 519 000 in June 1986. See: W. Vose, 'Wiehahn and Riekert Revisited', op. cit., p. 459; and M. Sarakinsky and J. Keenan, 'Unemployment in South Africa', *South African Labour Bulletin*, 12, 1986, pp. 20ff.

48. R. Davies, D. O'Meara and S. Dlamini, *The Struggle for South Africa, Vol. 2*, London, Zed Books, 1984, p. 55; J. Keenan, 'The Recession and the African Working Class', in *South Africa Review Two*, op. cit., p. 138.
49. G. Jaffe, 'The Retrenchment Process', in *South Africa Review Two*, op. cit., p. 125; J. Lewis and E. Randall, 'The State of the Unions', op. cit., p. 72.
50. J. Keenan, 'The Recession', op. cit., pp. 133–4.
51. W. Cobbett, D. Glaser, D. Hindson and M. Swilling, 'South Africa's Regional Political Economy: A Critical Analysis of Reform Strategy in the 1980s', in *South Africa Review Three*, Ravan Press, Johannesburg, 1986, pp. 137–68.
52. *Industrial Relations Data 6*, op. cit., March/April 1987, pp. 14–16.
53. 'Trade Unions and the State of Emergency', op. cit., p. 79; P. Green, 'Northern Natal', op. cit., pp. 78–80.

11 Constitutional Change and International Norms

Adrian Guelke

INTRODUCTION

While Johnson alluded in passing to the possibility of constitutional reform, the main thrust of his comments in this area suggests that he expected little change to be made to the structure of white political supremacy. However, it is worth noting that the likely shape of constitutional change, in particular that there would be an attempt to coopt coloureds and Indians into the political system, was already apparent in the first half of 1977 when Johnson completed *How Long Will South Africa Survive?* One reason why Johnson may have neglected the area of constitutional reform was the assumption he made that in the last resort the United States, and, by implication, the West generally, would accept nothing less than majority rule.[1] Consequently, there was little reason to suppose at that time that reform in this area could transform the Republic's relations with the West, an obviously important consideration for the South African government.

However, Johnson did address the question of the likely consequences of reform as a more general process and in this context showed considerable prescience. He argued that there were lessons to be learnt from the transition to majority rule in other African countries where white settlers had been a dominant political force. None had managed the transition peacefully and typically there was a cycle in the process of reform so that while initially support could be secured for reform, 'the onset of actual change – not just the prospect of it – quickly led to a White reaction' and that 'by the end of the cycle reform was more distant than ever'.[2] While there is overstatement in Johnson's thesis that 'history [is] on the side of the verkramptes',[3] he was clearly right to see both violence and a white backlash as probable consequences of reform. An important aspect of Johnson's approach which will be followed in this chapter was the emphasis he placed on the influence of the international order on the prospects for change in South Africa.

In August 1977 proposals for establishing a tricameral parliament with separate chambers representing whites, coloureds, and Indians were presented to the parliamentary caucus of the National Party, and reported in the South African press. Under this dispensation it was proposed that a council representing the three chambers would mediate disputes in relation to matters of mutual concern, with ultimate power being exercised by the State President, which was no longer a merely ceremonial position. The origin of these proposals went back to the deliberations of the Theron Commission, which had been appointed in March 1973 to examine the position of the coloured community. Its report in June 1976 recommended that 'provision should be made for satisfactory forms of direct Coloured representation and decision-making at the various levels of authority and of government'.[4] The government responded to this recommendation by setting up a cabinet committee to examine the place of coloureds and Indians within the political system. The result was the proposals put before the caucus in August 1977.

In broad outline there was relatively little difference between these proposals and the constitutional reforms enacted in the Republic of South Africa Constitution Act of 1983. However, in fleshing out the original proposals, particularly the invoking of power-sharing, the government prompted fierce controversy within the National Party. This resulted in a number of defections from the ruling party and the formation of the more right-wing Conservative Party in 1982. The main provisions of the 1983 Act were as follows: the creation of an executive Presidency; the establishment of a tricameral parliament with each chamber being serviced by its own ministerial council and having jurisdiction over its respective community's 'own affairs'; provision for the referral of disputes among the chambers over matters of common concern or 'general affairs' to the President's Council, a body broadly representative of the three chambers; representation within this structure of whites, coloureds, and Indians on a proportional basis of 4:2:1 according to population and ensuring an overall white majority within the system.

The new constitution provided for the election of the State President, who was to be both head of state and head of the government. He or she was to be elected by an electoral college consisting of 50 members of the white House of Assembly, 25 members of the coloured House of Representatives, and 13 members of the Indian House of Delegates. The members of the electoral college were themselves elected by a simple majority in each House. Consequently, the majority party in the white House of Assembly was in a position to elect the State President without support from the white opposition parties or from any of the parties in the other Houses. The constitution laid down that the President's Council would consist of 60 members, 20 elected by majority vote in the white Assembly, ten by the coloured Representatives, and five by the Indian Delegates. In addition, the State President was empowered to nominate 25 members. It was a requirement that ten of the nominated members should be opposition MPs from the three Houses. The arrangements were specifically designed to prevent an alliance between the coloured and Indian Houses and the liberal white opposition (however large it became) from overturning any decision of the majority party in the House of Assembly. Furthermore, this effective white veto was not counterbalanced by a coloured or Indian veto. The appearance of power-sharing under the constitution was therefore thoroughly deceptive. Inadvertently, the opposition from liberals and blacks to the new constitution, which quite naturally focused on the issue of the exclusion of Africans from the system, contributed to the deception, since the emphasis on African exclusion implied that coloureds and Indians had gained a real say in the government of the country. This was emphatically not the case. Opposition to the new constitution from the right also made much of the issue of power-sharing, despite its tenuous basis. However, what in substantive terms was of concern to the right was the powers the new constitution gave to the State President. The fear of the right was that once elected, a State President would be able to use the position to push through reforms that an exclusively white parliament subject to pressure from the white electorate might be persuaded to reject.

The changes were endorsed by a large majority of white voters in a referendum in November 1983, and, following the election on low turnouts of a coloured House of Representatives and an Indian House of Delegates in August 1984, the new constitution formally came into effect on 3 September 1984. The inauguration of the new constitution witnessed the outbreak of serious unrest which was to result in successive states of emergency and a sharp deterioration in South Africa's relations with the rest of the world, including the major Western powers. Paradoxically, whereas the South African government's initial commitment to reform, especially after P. W. Botha became Prime Minister in September 1978, had helped to improve the Republic's relations with the West, the actual implementation of constitutional reform, through its unleashing of violent protest, triggered the growth of demands within a number of Western countries for sanctions against South Africa. In particular, just a few months prior to his elevation to the position of State President, P. W. Botha had been well received by a number of governments during a very successful tour of Europe that appeared to herald an easing of the Republic's isolation in the wake of the white referendum on the constitution and the signing of the Nkomati Accord with Mozambique.[5] Indeed, in the middle of 1984 the extent of South African domination of neighbouring states appeared a more salient issue than whether white supremacy would survive within the Republic.

Part of the reason for this change in South Africa's prospects was the election of conservative governments in the leading Western powers: Thatcher in Britain in 1979, Reagan in the United States in 1980, and Kohl in West Germany in 1982. These governments strongly favoured evolutionary change and were ready to applaud Botha's constitutional reforms as steps in the right direction. This represented a considerable shift from the hostility towards the Republic and the championing of majority rule by the Carter Administration in its first year, the period when Johnson concluded his analysis. However, by the end of 1984 it was already clear that the question of whether and in what form South Africa would survive as a political entity was once more at issue, notwithstanding the strength of conservative forces within the West. It was also apparent that the South African government was threatened not simply by domestic unrest but by the interaction of internal turmoil with foreign reaction. Indeed, the adverse impact that the new constitution has had on the prospects for the survival of White supremacy in the Republic can most easily be understood in the first instance from an examination of the South African political system in an international perspective.

INTERNATIONAL NORMS AND SOUTH AFRICA

Within the broad area of South Africa's relations with the rest of the world, two very different approaches have tended to be followed. One is foreign policy analysis in the realist tradition, with its emphasis on interstate relations and power politics. The other takes as its starting point the fact that there is almost universal hostility towards South Africa's racial policies and examines what the international community can and should do to bring the practice of apartheid to an end. While many studies naturally combine both perspectives, until relatively recently the different time frames within which they operated made it difficult to reconcile the two approaches fully and, just as importantly, reduced the need to do so. From the perspective of strategic studies the immediate situation has been the focus of attention, with the result that greater emphasis is given to the durability of white rule in South Africa than is the case in the more future-orientated work concerned, from a normative perspective, with the transition to majority rule. As a slightly crude generalisation the strategic perspective has tended, whether approvingly or not, to portray Western policy in less liberal terms than the normative approach which has been readier to accept Western protestations of a desire to see an end to white rule in South Africa at face value.[6] The strategic approach has appeared most persuasive in periods of relative internal peace in South Africa, while violence and instability in South Africa has naturally tended to underline the relevance of Western efforts to promote change within the country.

In practice, Western policy towards South Africa has been guided by both perspectives with the mix varying according to the situation and the political philosophies of the governments in power. However, the shortening of the time scale for political change in South Africa has made it more difficult for Western governments to construct policies that can credibly incorporate both approaches, and has exposed more starkly the contradictions between them. For example, there is an obvious contradiction between the imposition of American sanctions and the efforts of the Reagan Administration to incorporate South Africa in its global strategy of selective deterrence against the Soviet Union, that is to say, the policy of supporting insurgencies directed at what the Administration sees as the weakest links in the Soviet chain of influence – radical governments in the Third World. The Reagan doctrine has involved not just a readiness to channel support for UNITA through the Republic, but also apparently enlisting South African aid in supplying the Contras in Central America.[7]

That the contradiction involves more than simply a difference in approach between Congress and the Administration is shown by the opening of a dialogue with the African National Congress by the Administration, on the one hand, and, on the other, by Congress's repeal of the Clark Amendment blocking aid to UNITA in Angola. So we have the ironical spectacle of members of the Reagan Administration playing down the ANC's links with the South African Communist Party and of Congress aiding South Africa's policy of destabilisation in southern Africa, reinforcing 'Apartheid's Second Front'.[8] The contradiction is also reflected in the ambivalence towards the ANC that runs like a thread through the Anti-Apartheid Act passed by Congress over President Reagan's veto in October 1986. On the one hand, the Act calls for the release of political prisoners, the unbanning of political organisations such as the ANC, and the initiation of a dialogue between the American Administration and representatives of black opinion in South Africa. On the other, the Act requires the President to report to Congress on communist infiltration of the opposition to the South African government and postulates that the ANC is engaged in 'terrorism', while calling on the South African government to initiate 'power-sharing with the Black majority'.[9] This formulation suggests that Congress sees the possibility of the West's difficulties being resolved through evolutionary change initiated by the South African government. This raises a further question. What is the impact of the contradictory objectives of Western policy themselves on the prospects for constitutional change in the Republic? Furthermore, while this question has been explored in the context of the general external pressures on the government to move away from apartheid, relatively little attention has been paid to how outside influences have shaped expectations within the Republic or how they affect the prospects for internal accommodation.

Before the impact of international norms on constitutional change in South Africa can be tackled directly, it is first necessary to outline briefly what these norms are and how they have evolved. It is simplest to approach this question from the assumption of South Africa's near-universal unpopularity that characterises what has been called above the normative, as opposed to strategic, perspective. 'South Africa's unpopularity' needs to be defined more precisely. Useful for this purpose is the concept of international legitimacy, defined by Martin Wight as 'the collective judgement of international society about rightful membership of the family of nations; how sovereignty may be transferred; and how state succession is to be regulated, when large states break up into smaller, or several states combine into one'.[10] It is important to emphasise that international legitimacy is quite distinct from internal legitimacy; that is, the opinions of the inhabitants of a territory as to the rightfulness to rule of the state under which they live. Of course, the two levels of legitimacy may be interrelated, as is evidently so in South Africa's case. However, there is no necessary relationship between these levels of legitimacy.[11] There are regimes with a low degree of internal legitimacy that are nevertheless treated as fully legitimate in international society, and there are a few cases of territories or regimes that enjoy a very high degree of internal legitimacy but lack international legitimacy. Gibraltar and the Falkland Islands are the most obvious examples of the latter.

The reason why South Africa, in particular, lacks international legitimacy is that its political system runs counter to the prevailing interpretation of the principle of self-determination, the international norm that underpins the postwar system of states created by the dismantling of the overseas empires of the European powers. The principle of self-determination has come to be interpreted as the right of the majority to establish an independent state within any area administered as a political entity by a colonial power. In terms of this norm, South Africa constitutes such an entity, to which power was wrongly transferred to a minority at independence, though, of course, this occurred prior to the establishment of the norm. For these purposes, South Africa is not itself a colonial power, except perhaps rather loosely in relation to Namibia, though that territory's boundaries predate South Africa's acquisition of the League of Nations mandate for South West Africa. Thus, according to the prevailing interpretation of the principle of self-determination, the decolonisation of Lesotho constituted a legitimate application of self-determination, while by contrast the creation of the Transkei was an illegitimate denial of the right of the majority within South Africa, notwithstanding resemblances between the two cases. The ethnic basis of the two entities is not relevant to their international legitimacy, however important it may be in practical political terms. The reason is simple. Under what one writer has disparagingly called the 'new UN law of self-determination',[12] the international community has opted to define the 'self' entitled to self-determination in terms of a territorial criterion rather than an ethnic or cultural one. This interpretation, which 'asserts the right of the majority within the frontiers prevailing at a given moment'[13] has dominated political practice since the end of the Second World War, providing the normative basis of decolonisation through much of the Third World.

Two significant features of what can best be called the majoritarian territorial interpretation of self-determination need to be underlined. Firstly, it makes no provision for the rights of minorities, an issue that was prominent in the deliberations of the League of Nations and in the prewar negotiations on the Sudeten German question – an unhelpful precedent for advocates of minority rights after the Second World War. Under the territorial definition of self-determination, the only recourse of minorities is to appeal to the international community for protection of their human rights. Their position as minorities has no special protection. Secondly, the other side of the coin of upholding the territorial integrity of states is the rejection of any right of secession from an independent state, though there has been one major exception to this rule: the emergence of Bangladesh in 1971.[14] Unlike the inhabitants of a colony whose right to self-determination remains an ongoing right which can be exercised in favour of independence at any time, the citizens of an independent state are bound to that state seemingly for all time.[15]

Ali Mazrui has argued that a further factor has played a part in the application of self-determination in Africa. This concerns how the concept of majority rule has been interpreted. While the process of decolonisation resulted in the creation of more than forty independent states in Africa, the demand for self-determination was not couched in terms of separate nationalisms. The people in whose name the right to self-determination was claimed were the 'African people'. Mazrui describes African nationalism as a principle of 'racial sovereignty'.[16] What is illegitimate in terms of this principle is alien rule or white minority rule. In practice, it can be argued that African regimes have had to satisfy a most unexacting test of what constitutes majority rule.[17]

However, Mazrui's argument can be pushed too far. A genuine difficulty exists in judging the legitimacy of a regime that has come to power as a result of the failure or breakdown of democracy, rather than as a clear-cut result of the overthrow of a functioning democracy. In particular, where the military have come to power in the Third World without facing popular resistance to their actions, it has proved difficult to deny legitimacy to the new regimes on the grounds that they constitute a violation of the majority's right to self-determination since the alternative to military rule remains unclear. This is of course not to say that South Africa could satisfy the principle of self-determination through the establishment of military rule in advance of the transition to majority rule. Further, the principle of 'racial sovereignty' has only partially compensated for the absence of legitimising elections at independence in the cases of Angola and Mozambique. It seems unlikely that the two states would be characterised as 'Marxist regimes' and, by implication illegitimate, by the Western media if the governments had come to power through elections, as the very different treatment on the whole accorded Zimbabwe suggests.

It may be objected that the international norm of self-determination as developed through the deliberations of the United Nations is not identical with the Western view of what constitutes the proper exercise of the principle of self-determination, and, further, that there is not a single Western position on this issue. While these arguments have some force at the margin, the West remains committed to the interpretation of self-determination described above and participated fully in its formulation in these terms. For example, the elaboration of the principle of self-determination to provide for the possibility of forms of autonomy for indigenous minorities short of independence has been built on the foundations of the territorial interpretation and is not a challenge to it in any fundamental sense. Indeed, the role of the principle of self-determination in shaping the international order in the post-colonial world has generally been seen and represented as the triumph of Western liberal doctrine, even though its implementation has not always coincided either with Western interests or other Western norms. Further, while there has been some academic criticism of the prevailing interpretation of self-determination and of the consequences of its application,[18] this has had relatively little influence at a political level.

Another objection to this line of argument is that it fails to make apartheid the central reason for South Africa's unpopularity. This argument too has some substance, especially as there is obviously more to Western opposition to apartheid than the failure of the political system to satisfy the criteria of self-determination. The movement within the West towards a norm of racial equality following decolonisation and the desegregation of the South in the United States, has been influential in generating hostility towards apartheid within Western societies independently of the norm of self-determination. However, it also needs to be recognised that hostility towards apartheid arises to a considerable degree from the norm of self-determination. That is, much of international opinion is hostile to apartheid because it is seen as a political system that denies the right of the majority to self-determination. More importantly, the norm of self-determination goes beyond rejection of apartheid to prescribing what would constitute a legitimate outcome to the process of political change in South Africa.

Satisfying the prevailing interpretation of the norm of self-determination therefore presents a greater challenge to the South African state than the adoption of policies that go some way to meeting the norm of racial equality, as it is understood in the West. Current reforms, especially those under the rubric of deracialisation, can be presented as narrowing the gulf between the Republic and Western society as it has developed in the last twenty-five years. Admittedly, considerable difficulties exist even here since some forms of segregation, such as residential and educational apartheid, remain arguably too closely bound up with the survival of white political dominance in South Africa to be dispensable outside the context of radical political change. The essential aspect of the analogy with changes in Western society towards racial equality is that these changes did not entail the abandonment of 'white political supremacy' within the West. By this is meant much more than the obvious point that whites remain an overwhelming majority of Western electorates. Their numerical preponderance would be meaningless if racial categories had lost their political salience. However, that is very far from being the case, as the continuing influence of race and racial issues on voting behaviour shows. This is despite the fact that 'non-whites' constitute relatively small minorities in Western societies. The steps taken to outlaw racial discrimination in Western societies have not eliminated racial prejudice or assumptions of white superiority.

While part of the explanation for the survival of racial prejudice in Western societies is that the movement towards a norm of racial equality is comparatively recent, the political relevance of race within Western societies goes deeper than this. Race remains an implicit element in the definition of what constitutes the West. In particular, the shift towards racial equality has stopped short of dissolving the ethnocentric cultural basis of Western identity. While cultural differences by no means coincide with race, race is frequently seen as a clue to, or indicator of, cultural differences. For example, Margaret Thatcher's controversial interview in 1978 when she spoke of the danger of Britain being 'swamped' by people of an alien culture was widely seen and, indeed, justified as pre-empting growing support within Britain at that time for the explicitly racialist programme of the National Front. The notion of the West, which, admittedly, defies precise definition, is both wider and narrower than the ideological dichotomy between East and West. Membership of the Western alliance against communism, at least formally, is not a precondition of membership of the Western community of nations, as the cases of Sweden, Finland, Switzerland, Ireland, and Austria show. By contrast, identification with the West strategically is not enough for a country to be seen as part of the West, as the examples of Saudi Arabia and Kenya demonstrate. It is quite common for these two countries to be described as 'pro-Western' in a strategic context, but neither would be regarded for that reason as part of the West. While the West also tends to be identified with the capitalist economic system in some form, as a criterion this is as unhelpful as strategic alliances are as a method for suggesting what the boundaries of the West are. Similarly, liberal democracy as a form of government, while associated broadly with the West, does not provide a criterion that accurately identifies which countries form part of the Western community as the system is not confined to the West. For most purposes, the countries of Europe apart from communist states, the United States, Canada, Australia, New Zealand, and Israel are identified as Western countries. However, beyond these cases, the notion seems to be distinctly hazy.

South Africa itself presents a most interesting case of an aspirant or perhaps marginal member of the Western world. In this context, it is far from clear whether apartheid can be regarded as a barrier to the Republic's membership of the Western community of nations or, on the contrary, whether the maintenance of white political domination in some form, remains a reason for the identification of South Africa by the outside world as part of the West. Robert Jackson employs the notion of cultural proximity to describe the closeness of South Africa's identification with the West. On the one hand, this fuels demands within Western societies that the Republic be made to conform to Western standards in relation to racial discrimination. On the other hand, as Jackson points out, 'cultural proximity rules out military intervention by the West in South Africa as it also did in Rhodesia'.[19] Johnson also referred to the close affinity between the West and South Africa and argued that 'there is a possibility that the West (and in practice it comes down to the US) will gradually come to assume, however informally, a "metropolitan" role *vis-à-vis* South Africa'.[20] A comparison with the situation in Afghanistan is instructive in this context. While Soviet intervention has generated relatively little public protest of a mass character in Western societies, neither the British nor the American governments have been inhibited by public opinion in supplying weaponry to the Afghan rebels. By contrast, military assistance to the ANC or, indeed, any other body committed to 'armed struggle' against the South African government would be certain to generate considerable public controversy. At the same time, the extent of mass protests in Western societies over apartheid reflects, at least partly, an assumption of Western responsibility for what is happening in the Republic that is not present in the case of Afghanistan.

For the South African government it is a perpetual dilemma whether to emphasise membership of the Western community of nations or to play down the relevance of Western political models to the country's constitutional development through reference to South Africa's uniqueness as a society. However, the emphasis has generally been more on the former than on the latter, and cultural proximity has been embraced rather than rejected by most South African whites. Afrikaner nationalism has not been isolationist in the way that, for example, Burmese socialism has been. It is worth underlining that one of the most important consequences of cultural proximity is Western hostility to the use of violence as a strategy for overturning apartheid. It forms a central and obvious, if generally unstated, parameter of the debate in the West on sanctions. Unusually, in the case of South Africa, the issues of the legitimacy of the regime and its policies, and of the legitimacy of anti-system violence have been disaggregated. Normally, attitudes towards revolutionary violence against a regime are a function of whether that regime is seen as legitimate or not. In other words, there is generally a high measure of tolerance of, if not support for, violence against a regime that is perceived to be illegitimate for whatever reason, as the Afghan example shows. Indeed, the moral distinction that all societies make internally between the use of force and the use of violence generally hinges more on the issue of the legitimacy of the agent and the role that agent is playing, than on analysis of the intrinsic nature of the action itself. However, South Africa's lack of legitimacy in the West has done little to alter Western inhibitions over the use of violence against South African whites. The contradiction is very evident in Western pleas to the South African government to release 'political prisoners' including those convicted of 'violence', while the West simultaneously denounces the 'armed struggle' as 'terrorism'. Western ambivalence is mirrored inside South Africa by the radical stance against the legitimacy of the regime taken by Archbishop Tutu, while he simultaneously advocates non-violence.

EXTERNAL NORMS AND CONSTITUTIONAL CHANGE

What needs to be drawn out at this point is that the norms of anti-communism, Western cultural ethnocentrism, capitalism, and liberal democracy all play a role in the outside world's judgement both of constitutional change and of South Africa's place in the world. For instance, the first of these has obvious relevance to the strategic perspective on relations between South Africa and the West. Because these norms are so central to the internal debate on constitutional change in South Africa, their external ramifications tend to be obscured. Thus, the demand for one-man-one-vote in a unitary state tends to be viewed primarily from the perspective of the internal legitimacy of the political system rather than that of its international legitimacy. The apparently reasonable assumption underlying this emphasis is that the country's political future will be mainly, if not wholly, determined by the actions of political forces within the country. Its weakness is that it underplays the influence of external norms on the internal political forces themselves. It also underplays the role that external guarantors might play in any resolution of the South African conflict. This has particular relevance to the consociational model of democracy which has attracted a wide measure of interest in South Africa among whites because of its emphasis on power-sharing and on minority rights.

The influence of external norms on the positions of the parties to the conflict in South Africa, is most obviously evident in the appeal that mainstream black opposition to the regime has made to a global constituency for support, latterly in the form of economic sanctions. In particular, the ANC and the United Democratic Front (UDF) are clearly committed to the implementation of the self-determination norm as it has been defined by the international community. Moreover, both bodies have buttressed this case and given it an additional Western slant by drawing on American experience in the Deep South in presenting their case in civil rights terms. It is notable, for example, how much more successful figures such as Winnie Mandela have been in presenting the African nationalist case to the Western media than were any of the African nationalist parties in Zimbabwe prior to independence. At least part of the reason for this success has been that they have used political language that focuses on the racial inequities of the South African system rather than on white rule as alien rule. Non-racialism has been much more to the fore as part of the credo of the main African nationalist grouping in South Africa's case than it has been in that of African nationalist movements elsewhere in Africa, though this issue has also been a divisive one in relation to AZAPO and the Black Consciousness movement. Indeed, this division has cut across the ideological left/right divide and has reduced the political salience for South African blacks of arguments over the role of socialists and communists within the ANC, though that has not of course reassured conservative opinion within the West.

An interesting implication of the civil rights emphasis is that it leaves open the question of South Africa's membership of the Western community of nations after majority rule. Another aspect of the civil rights approach is whether the West's role in the process of change in South Africa is to be conceived as analogous to that of the Federal authorities in the United States in effecting desegregation in the Deep South. That analogy suggests perhaps a conception of majority rule that integrates South Africa more fully into the West. To press the analogy further this casts figures like Archbishop Desmond Tutu and Reverend Allan Boesak in a role rather similar to that of Reverend

Martin Luther King in the United States. Tutu has himself employed the comparison, while identifying significant differences between the two situations, such as the fact that in South Africa's case the law is on the side of the oppressor, and that South African blacks are battling for rights even more basic than those sought by the American civil rights movement.[21] The first of these has some rather obvious, while unstated, implications for the relevance of a strategy of non-violence. While it can be argued that there are too many differences between South Africa and the Deep South for the comparison to provide any sort of guide to the possibilities of constitutional change to majority rule in South Africa, it is clear that in practice the comparison has exerted a considerable influence on perceptions of the conflict, most especially in the United States.

The approach of Chief Buthelezi and Inkatha addresses a rather different set of Western norms in its rhetorical emphasis on opposition to revolutionary violence, anti-communism, and the retention of the free enterprise system. This needs to be seen in the context of Inkatha's much greater readiness to accommodate white interests and white power than the ANC's advocacy of one-man-one-vote in a unitary state and its commitment to 'armed struggle' permit. For example, the proposals of the KwaZulu/Natal Indaba provide for the legal entrenchment of rights both for individuals and for ethnic groups. The far-reaching implications of such guarantees for public expenditure are explored in Chapter 7. Buthelezi's approach addresses a number of Western fears about the consequences of political change in South Africa. Firstly, it offers reassurance that Western strategic and economic interests will be protected. Secondly, in so far as it appears to guarantee a place for whites in any future political dispensation as whites, it addresses Western anxiety that black rule will reduce the influence of Western cultural traditions on the norms of South African society in so far as whites as a group are seen as the principal bearers of these traditions. Thirdly, it appears to offer the prospect of constitutional advance for blacks brought about without massive, and racially polarising, violence that is likely to disturb the commitment within Western societies to racial equality.

Given this appeal, it might seem surprising at first sight that Buthelezi has not proved a more attractive figure to Western political and public opinion. Part of the explanation is the 'tribal' nature of the constituency he is seen as representing. While this means that he is clearly identified as the leader of a section of society, it limits his credibility as a spokesman for blacks in general. It also raises rather starkly the question of whether it is appropriate to treat a majority-ruled South Africa as a potential member of the Western community of nations. Further, 'tribalism' makes Buthelezi appear a much more alien figure to much of Western opinion than either Archbishop Tutu or Reverend Allan Boesak, who appear to be rather more consistent advocates of non-violence than does Buthelezi or Inkatha. In this respect, there is a considerable divergence between Western opinion, especially liberal opinion, and much of white opinion in South Africa.[22] Finally, it is doubtful whether Buthelezi's approach is compatible with the present interpretation of self-determination in so far it entails a readiness to accept limitations on the right of the majority in advance of the achievement of majority rule.

It may be argued that were Buthelezi's political credibility as a spokesman for black aspirations greater, this might matter less, and, further, that he may over time recover the ground he has lost since 1984 to more radical groups. However, even if Buthelezi became a more popular figure among blacks in South Africa, it would do relatively little to enhance the international legitimacy of a settlement that appeared to fall short of one-man-one-vote in a unitary state. Whatever the attractions to the West of a settlement with Buthelezi, even conservative opinion in the West would baulk at the consequences of endorsing unilaterally arrangements that were seen as running counter to the foundations of sovereignty in the Third World. Indeed, it is doubtful that the ANC could accept, were it so minded, an internal settlement that in any way fudged the issue of majority rule without jeopardising its own international support, notwithstanding its current credibility as being representative of a substantial majority of blacks in South Africa.[23] For this reason alone, such a prospect is unlikely, despite indications of ANC interest in a negotiated settlement of the South African conflict.[24] In particular, it is inconceivable that the ANC could accept a consociational settlement that was explicitly presented as running counter to the principle of majority rule. These arguments obviously apply with even greater force to the approach of the government to constitutional change with its emphasis on political rights in the context of imposed group membership, and its initial rejection, for this reason, of the proposals of the KwaZulu/Natal Indaba.

Nonetheless, it is worth emphasising the extent to which the government has gone in attempting to design a constitutional dispensation that accords with Western values. Of particular significance in this context is the government's attempt to adapt the consociational model of liberal democracy to South African circumstances. In principle, the consociational model might appear a quite promising route to international legitimacy for South Africa, for it appears to be compatible both with the norm of self-determination and the maintenance of a measure of white political power under a new constitutional dispensation. In the first place, the consociational model is a well-attested form of liberal democracy. Its inventor, Arend Lijphart, developed the model to explain the mechanisms by which stable democracy was underpinned in a number of the smaller European countries including the Netherlands and Belgium, totally respectable members of the international community. Secondly, the model has particular relevance to divided societies. Indeed, Lijphart has argued that 'if there is to be democracy at all [in South Africa], it will almost certainly have to be of the consociational type'.[25] The failure of majoritarian democratic systems in much of the Third World has helped to buttress the case that special mechanisms, such as power-sharing, are necessary in plural societies if liberal democracy is to be sustained. This view now enjoys quite widespread support among political scientists, as well as ardent critics in South Africa. Further, it may be argued that South Africa's right to choose such arrangements is enshrined in the international norm of non-intervention as enunciated in the United Nations declaration of 1966 on the subject. This states, *inter alia*, that 'every state has an inalienable right to choose its political, economic, social, and cultural system, without interference in any form by another state'.[26] This has usefully been described as 'the right of internal self-determination'.[27] At first sight, therefore, the consociational model would seem to offer considerable attractions to those in South Africa seeking to legitimise the system through a process of evolutionary change, since it would appear to provide a means of fudging the issue of a transition to majority rule.

The South African government's tentative steps in the field of constitutional reform have been much criticised as failing to meet the minimal requirements of the consociational model since they involve cooption rather than genuine power sharing, and because imposed racial classification is the basis of group rights under the new constitution. This is an issue that Adam and Moodley make much of in their book, *South Africa Without Apartheid.* They argue:

> The imposition of an identity on subordinates by the superordinate groups inevitably leads to its rejection. An imposed identity is a stigma, not a source of pride. Any system that imposes identities,

therefore, cannot expect approval even if it guarantees equal rights. If the formation of the group is itself considered an affront to its alleged members, the principle of group rights becomes meaningless.[28]

They suggest that for power-sharing to work it would have to be on the basis of self-chosen groups rather than racial ascription. This problem was recognised in the proposals of the KwaZulu/Natal Indaba. The principle of choice was addressed through the creation of a fifth category for group representation in the second chamber of the legislature. This was a 'South African background group' for those not wishing to be assigned representation on the basis of the four ethnic categories proposed, the African, Afrikaans, Asian, and English 'background groups'.[29]

However, there are many additional reasons for questioning whether the consociational model with its devices of power-sharing, segmental autonomy, minority veto, and proportionality is applicable in South Africa's case. Lijphart himself has listed eight favourable conditions for the functioning of consociationalism.[30] They are: (1) segments of roughly equal size; (2) relative isolation of the segments from each other; (3) a multiple balance of power; (4) presence of some society-wide loyalties; (5) perception of a common external threat; (6) a relatively small population; (7) no extreme inequalities; and (8) prior traditions of political accommodation. They have been derived from the successful experience of consociationalism in Europe, though Lijphart denies that any combination of these is necessary or sufficient for the operation of the model. Nonetheless, it can hardly be encouraging for proponents of a consociational solution that virtually none of the favourable conditions exist in South Africa. The government penchant for describing South Africa as a nation of minorities involves the highly unrealistic assumption that African nationalism can be neutralised as a political force. Almost any constitutional arrangements capable of satisfying the minimum requirements of liberal democracy would seem likely to produce an overall majority for African nationalist parties within the principal chamber of the legislature. Consequently, consociationalism would almost certainly have to operate without the benefit of a multiple balance of power. The extra load placed on decision-making by consociational devices would constitute a further problem in light of the country's relatively large population, while the vast disparity in wealth between white and black in South Africa provides an obvious reason why blacks might find the granting to whites of a minority veto unacceptable. It is of course one of the main attractions of consociationalism to whites.

Of even more fundamental importance is the issue of such a system's external relations, an issue that has wider significance for all forms of internal settlement through constitutional compromise. The ultimate justification of consociationalism in deeply-divided societies is that it reduces the likelihood of inter-community violence. As Adam and Moodley put it: 'Consociationalism amounts to an institutionalized truce; it is neither the reconcilation of differences nor the capitulation of one party to another, but a compromise for coexistence.'[31] It is a truce, moreover, in which external factors usually play an important role, whether negatively or positively. The temporary weakness of interested external powers may be a factor facilitating agreement, as in the Lebanon in 1943. Alternatively, agreement may be seen as a pre-condition for the removal of an unwanted external influence, as in Austria in the 1950s. Finally, the impetus for a truce may come from external powers themselves magnetised by the conflict between communities, as in the agreements reached between Italy and Austria over South Tyrol, and in the establishment of Cyprus as an independent state. The last of these highlights a common danger in deeply-divided societies, which is that external powers are drawn into the conflict on opposite sides through their support for one or other of the parties involved in inter-community violence. Angola is an apposite example in the context of southern Africa.

In South Africa's case, the neutralisation of external powers is not obviously relevant to the prospects of a truce between white and black, nor is it possible to envisage an external threat to South Africa that would be perceived by both sides as wholly divorced from the issue of racial domination. On the contrary, it is reasonable to surmise that there would be considerable support among blacks for almost any form of external intervention as a perceived means of ending white political supremacy. The only external circumstance likely to be favourable to the establishment of consociationalism in South Africa's case therefore would be that of active foreign mediation in the conflict. (Johnson plainly envisaged such mediation as resulting from the assumption by the United States of a metropolitan role in relation to South Africa.) That would entail cooperation between the frontline states of southern Africa and the West to secure an internationally recognised negotiated settlement of the conflict. There have even been suggestions that there might be a role for the Soviet Union in such a process as an external influence on the ANC. In particular, it has been reported that the

United States has directly sought Soviet mediation to persuade the ANC to accept guarantees for the whites in any settlement.[32] This is very far from being the context in which the prospects of consociationalism in South Africa are generally discussed. Rather, consociationalism tends to be seen as a strategy for maintaining a measure of continuing white political influence, if not domination, in the context of an internal settlement. Ideally, the proponents of this strategy hope such a settlement would be supported by most of the countries of the West as a legitimate form of liberal democracy. The fundamental problem of this strategy is that it conflates the processes of external and internal self-determination. Before South Africa can legitimately choose consociationalism or any other form of government in accordance with the principle of internal self-determination, the state requires international legitimacy in terms of the principle of majority rule. This principle might be met through the election of a constitutional convention on the basis of one-man-one-vote, but it could not be bypassed on the grounds that consociationalism in itself met the requirements of majority rule.

This line of argument applies also to all other forms of internal constitutional settlement that deviate from the straightforward application of majority rule. This should not be regarded as a piece of theoretical hair-splitting. It is of real practical significance, as the case of Zimbabwe-Rhodesia showed. The internal settlement between Ian Smith and Bishop Abel Muzorewa went much further in the direction of unadorned majority rule than anything being contemplated by the most *verlig* elements in the South African government, but despite the participation of a majority of the African electorate in the internal elections in 1979 and the favourable report of British Conservative Party observers on the conduct of the poll, the newly elected Conservative government in Britain declined to recognise Zimbabwe-Rhodesia. It did so on the grounds of the constitutional protection given to white privileges. While the Lancaster House Agreement eliminated much of this protection, it also stopped well short of imposing unadorned majority rule on Zimbabwe. The most obvious outward difference between the internal settlement and the Lancaster House Agreement was simply that the former failed to stop the war. But it would be wrong to see this as divorced from the constitutional issue. The lack of international legitimacy of the regime created by the internal settlement was a factor in support for the continuation of the war. More generally, all systems characterised by coercive dominant–subordinate relationships that are no longer able to secure the dominant community's position by force face a problem of how to criminalise political violence from the subordinate community. Concessions to the subordinate community that fail to meet international expectations of what constitutes a legitimate settlement are unlikely to end political violence. Hence external perceptions that the conflict remains unresolved are likely to persist; perceptions that themselves will influence the internal parties.

CONCLUSION

The constitutional strategy of the South African government would appear to be one of hoping that Western ambivalence over the implications of change in the Republic will persuade at least the leading governments in the West to acquiesce in some form of internal settlement, drawing on consociational devices such as power-sharing, though in an attenuated form. Negotiations to this end are likely to be a lengthy process. During the run-up to the South African election for the white House of Assembly in May 1987, government ministers emphasised that the National Party was seeking a mandate to extend the 'power-sharing' principles of the 1983 Constitution Act to the African population but in a way that would retain overall white control of the system. The government's main problem remains finding credible representatives of the African population ready to enter into negotiations on such terms, since all that is directly on offer to African politicians is a place on a national council with a strictly advisory role. While the government's protestations of its willingness to negotiate a new constitutional dispensation may perhaps secure a measure of Western acquiescence, as apartheid itself did at times, there is little reason to suppose that the West would treat any internal settlement that eventually emerged as anything more than transitional or that such a settlement would be capable of ending political violence.

It might fairly be argued that no settlement would be likely to end all political violence in South Africa, given the complexity of the country's divisions. However, what would give additional impetus to such violence in the event of an internal settlement is that it would be perceived by the outside world as an inevitable and enduring consequence of the failure of the settlement to meet fully international norms. Ironically, it would probably be easier to secure special protection for the position of whites in the context of an international settlement of the conflict mediated by the West and the frontline states.

However, it should be emphasised that the frontline states would not have a free hand to buy peace at any price. Their negotiating position would need to be seen as legitimate and be supported by the generality of Third World states before they could force the compliance of different strands of black South African opinion. Further, the frontline states could not fulfil this role if their governments were perceived as operating under the thumb of Pretoria, so the success of South African destabilisation is a potential threat to their mediation.

The scenario of massive bloodshed put forward in the report of the Eminent Persons Group[33] presents the most obvious circumstance in which the West would feel impelled to use all the means at its disposal to get such negotiations off the ground. Johnson predicted that 'the emergence of a real threat to the regime will concentrate minds [in the West] quite wonderfully'.[34] In fact, long before the situation is reached where the regime is in any danger of being overthrown, the prospect of significant numbers of fatalities in inter-racial violence is likely to prompt greater Western involvement in efforts to achieve a political settlement. Even though the situation has not as yet reached the point where there is thought to be an imminent danger of a slide towards uncontrollable inter-community violence, the possibility that such a danger point might be approaching has already begun to exert a powerful influence on Western policy towards southern Africa. It is most clearly reflected in the readiness of right-wing governments in Britain and the United States to enter into negotiations with the ANC at a high political level, and in their support for the frontline states, with the exception of Angola, which still appears to be a target of American destabilisation. In short, the need to find a solution to the South African conflict in accordance with international norms has become a sufficiently pressing concern for Western governments that it has begun to modify the strategic posture of even the most strongly right-wing governments. Pressure from domestic public opinion hostile towards apartheid within countries such as the United States has also contributed to the shift, although the direct influence of the anti-apartheid movement on Western policy has arguably been less important than the indirect influence it has exerted as a result of the encouragement which black opposition in South Africa derived from the campaign for sanctions.

In these circumstances, it seems likely that the contradictions in Western policy towards South Africa will tend to be resolved at the expense of the strategic approach of rewarding Pretoria for its role in the East-West conflict. At the very least, the Western powers will be

MAGDALEN COLLEGE LIBRARY

constrained by the need to ensure that there are as few obstacles as possible to international negotiations over the future of South Africa, given the risks posed by the Republic's internal political instability. In this context, it is the enormity of the consequences for Western societies of racially-polarising bloodshed in South Africa, rather than the degree of probability of such large-scale violence occurring that weighs with Western governments. It would take a very considerable shift in political expectations about South Africa's future before the governments of the main Western powers once again became sufficiently sanguine about Pretoria's capacity to maintain both internal tranquillity and control over the southern African region that they felt able to give priority to strategic and economic interests over the issue of the country's lack of international legitimacy. The strong swing to the right in the white elections in May 1987 has made it more difficult for the South African government to convince the outside world that evolutionary reform from above constitutes a viable way out of the Republic's impasse.

Indeed, the context and the outcome of the May 1987 elections illustrate graphically the failure of constitutional reform on all fronts. The elections were fought against the international background of the imposition of limited economic sanctions by the country's main trading partners and against a domestic background of black protest and violence, notwithstanding the detention of thousands of political activists under the state of emergency. The government hoped that the crisis would lead whites to rally to its support. In the event, almost half the Afrikaner electorate voted for parties of the extreme right. The outcome has compounded the government's problems. However cogently it is argued that sanctions contributed towards the hardening of white opinion against reform, Western governments are bound to come under pressure to extend rather than relax sanctions. While variations among Western countries in the implementation of sanctions are likely to limit their effectiveness, the most likely scenario is of a slow tightening of the operation of sanctions. Only far-reaching constitutional reform is likely to reverse the trend of Western policy. Such a dramatic initiative seems extremely unlikely given the make-up of the new House of Assembly, the imminence of the 1989 general election covering all three Houses of the tricameral parliament (in the absence of a constitutional amendment to extend the life of parliament), and the difficulty the government is likely to encounter in finding credible leaders of African opinion willing to be coopted in circumstances so unpromising for radical reform.

The promise of constitutional reform was an important part of the government's efforts to overcome the crisis of the mid-1970s, which formed the context of Johnson's book. In particular, the prospect of evolutionary change in the South African political system made a favourable impact on conservative opinion in the West and was instrumental in the improvement in relations with the West in the early 1980s. However, of all the steps taken by the government in the aftermath of that crisis, it is the one that has probably done the most to undermine the stability of the system in the mid-1980s. Part of the government's problem was that its efforts to coopt blacks into the system made larger demands on them in terms of requiring or claiming their consent than had the unapologetically exclusionist and racist policies of Verwoerd. Resentment that they were being asked in effect to legitimise their own oppression completely outweighed any amelioration of their social and economic position and prompted black protest on a scale that has plunged the country into an even worse crisis than in 1976. The radicalisation of black opinion has made it much more difficult for the government to find credible black representatives able to endow a process of cooption with a measure of legitimacy. Further, the difficulty the South African government has encountered in suppressing black violence has made Western governments less sanguine about the Republic's future. It is reflected most clearly in their efforts to promote wider negotiations between the South African government and the black opposition, most especially the ANC.

Ironically, the commitment to constitutional reform that helped the government to overcome the earlier crisis, justifying Johnson's predictions, can now be seen to have contained the seeds of a far deeper impasse in the country's political development. The existing constitution deviates so far from the West's conception of the minimum requirements for liberal democracy that even with modification it is incapable of securing limited international approval. At the same time, the changes the government has introduced have proved sufficient to provoke a white backlash powerful enough to deter the government from attempting to find a more radical solution to the political impasse. While superficially the growth of the right appears to strengthen white political supremacy, it limits the government's room for manoeuvre and its capacity to secure Western support through the appearance of flexibility. The counter-argument is that the possibility, even if small, of a more right-wing government makes the West more tolerant of the slow progress of reform under the present government. Nonetheless, overall, there seem to be good grounds for the judgement that constitutional reform has had the opposite effect to that intended by the government. In short, it has weakened rather than strengthened white rule. However, it is a measure of just how entrenched white rule is, that this judgement does not necessitate a revision of Johnson's thesis of the medium-term survival of the system of white supremacy. The most persuasive prediction is that the impasse will remain in the medium term, with no improvement in South Africa's relations with the West, the persistence of domestic political violence, which seems to have become endemic, and the continuation of white political domination, though without the capacity for creating the appearance of political stability.

Notes

1. R. W. Johnson, *How Long Will South Africa Survive?*, London, Macmillan, 1977, p. 326.
2. Ibid., p. 303.
3. Ibid., p. 290.
4. M. Horrell, T. Hodgson, S. Blignaut, and S. Moroney (eds), *A Survey of Race Relations in South Africa: 1976*, Johannesburg, South African Institute of Race Relations, 1977, p. 12.
5. See, for example, J. E. Spence, 'Foreign Policy: Retreat into the Laager', in J. Blumenfeld (ed.), *South Africa in Crisis*, London, Croom Helm and the Royal Institute of International Affairs, 1987, pp. 158.
6. Compare, for example, the perspectives on Western policy in R. I. Rotberg, *Suffer the Future: Policy Choices in Southern Africa*, Cambridge, Massachusetts, Harvard University Press, 1980, and D. E. Albright, *Africa and International Communism*, London, Macmillan, 1980.
7. See, for example, D. Keys, R. Dowden, and P. Pringle, 'US defies African arms embargo', *Independent*, 9 December 1986 and 'S. Africans in Central America', *Southscan* (London), 25 February 1987.
8. This is the apposite title of Joseph Hanlon's book on South Africa's regional policy of destabilisation: J. Hanlon, *Apartheid's Second Front: South Africa's War against its Neighbours*, Harmondsworth, Penguin, 1986.
9. See T. G. Karis, 'South African Liberation: The Communist Factor', *Foreign Affairs*, Winter 1986/87.
10. M. Wight, *Systems of States*, Leicester, Leicester University Press, 1977, p. 153 (edited by Hedley Bull).
11. As well as distinguishing between two levels of legitimacy, it is also useful to distinguish between two types of legitimacy: legitimacy in relation to territory or boundaries, and legitimacy in relation to regimes or political systems. In South Africa's case it is clearly the regime and the political system that lacks legitimacy rather than the territory itself or its boundaries. Indeed, the very legitimacy of the territory has proved an obstacle to

apartheid. The government's partitioning of the territory to create independent Bantustans has not just failed to secure international recognition of the new entities themselves but has ensured that a unitary state has become a precondition for South Africa's international legitimacy scarcely less important than one-man-one-vote. By contrast, the cases of Gibraltar and the Falkland Islands revolve round the issue of territory rather than that of political system. Partition and the border also lie at the heart of Northern Ireland's lack of international legitimacy.

12. M. Pomerance, *Self-Determination in Law and Practice*, The Hague, Martinus Nijhoff, 1982, p. 9.
13. M. Wight, *Systems of States*, op. cit., p. 168.
14. A number of special factors helped to legitimise this single and controversial example of contested secession. Pakistan was itself the product of partition. The two wings of the country were separated geographically, while the people of the East wing, who wished to secede, actually constituted a majority of the population of the whole country. The international consensus on the principle of self-determination is set out in the General Assembly's 1970 *Declaration of Principles of International Law concerning Friendly Relations and Co-operation among States in accordance with the Charter of the United Nations*. There are some examples of secession by mutual agreement between a central and a regional government or between two governments forming a loose confederation. The most important example was Singapore's secession from the Malaysian Federation in August 1965. The Federation was less than two years old at the time. Bangladesh's membership of the United Nations was not uncontested. The People's Republic of China used its newly-acquired veto in the Security Council to hold up Bangladesh's membership until 1974. Thoughout the actual crisis the United States government made constant reference to the UN's position on self-determination in defence of its support for Pakistan. See, for example, K. Knight, 'Bangladesh: The Price of National Unity' in R. E. Johnston (ed.), *The Politics of Division, Partition, and Unification*, New York, Praeger, 1976, pp. 93–5.
15. This is not quite to endorse the jaundiced view of decolonisation among whites in southern Africa in the 1960s that independence meant one-man-one-vote once, since the international legitimacy of a state and its boundaries is not the same as regime legitimacy. Thus, the overthrow of an unpopular regime may legitimately be represented as the exercise of the right to self-determination of the majority and this is the rubric under which the United States has defended support for anti-communist insurgencies under the Reagan Doctrine. However, in practice, it may be difficult to draw a distinction between the state and the regime and a real conflict may arise between a regime's international legitimacy and its internal illegitimacy. This can be illustrated by the case of Zaire. The corrupt and unpopular Mobutu regime has been propped up by the international community at least in part because it has been able to present itself as the custodian of Zaire's territorial integrity and because none of its opponents has succeeded in shaking off the tag of being secessionist.

16. A. Mazrui, *Towards a Pax Africana*, London, Weidenfeld and Nicolson, 1969, p. 21.
17. As an instance, the case of Burundi can be cited where the Tutsi minority controlling the state embarked on a policy of genocide towards the Hutu majority in the early 1970s. The feebleness of the international community's response to this massive violation of human rights can be explained in terms of a reluctance to intervene in a situation where the regime was legitimate in terms of the principle of 'racial sovereignty' and relied on its own resources to implement its policies.
18. See, for example, the writings of Robert Jackson on the consequences of creating states through international norms, especially R. Jackson, 'Negative Sovereignty in Sub-Saharan Africa', *Review of International Studies*, 12, 4, October 1986. See also M. Pomerance, *Self-Determination*, op. cit.
19. R. Jackson, 'Negative Sovereignty', op. cit., p. 260.
20. R. W. Johnson, *How Long Will South Africa Survive?*, op. cit., p. 320.
21. Tutu interviewed on 'Witness to Apartheid', transmitted on Channel 4 (UK Television) on 15 January 1987.
22. See, for example, the view of Buthelezi in B. Buzan and H. O. Nazareth, 'South Africa versus Azania: the implications of who rules', *International Affairs*, Vol. 62, no. 1, Winter 1985/6.
23. 'In a free election in South Africa, the now-outlawed African National Congress could possibly win three-fourths of the black vote as well as some white votes.' T. G. Karis, 'South African Liberation', op. cit., p. 267.
24. See, for example, Allister Sparks, 'Slowly, noisily, the political glacier is starting to shift', *Star Weekly* (Johannesburg), 28 February 1987.
25. A. Lijphart, *Democracy in Plural Societies*, New Haven and London, Yale University Press, 1977, p. 236.
26. UN General Assembly Resolution 2131 (XX) of 1966.
27. See J. E. Spence, 'The Most Popular Corpse in History', *Optima*, 34, 1, March 1986, p. 16.
28. H. Adam and K. Moodley, *South Africa Without Apartheid: Dismantling Racial Domination*, Berkeley, University of California Press, 1986, p. 13.
29. *Sunday Tribune* (Durban), 30 November 1986.
30. A. Lijphart, 'Consociation: The Model and its Application in Divided Societies' in D. Rea (ed.), *Political Cooperation in Divided Societies*, Dublin, Gill and Macmillan, 1982, p. 183.
31. Adam and Moodley, *South Africa Without Apartheid*, op. cit., p. 212.
32. 'US sought Soviet mediation to gain ANC guarantee for Whites', *Southscan* (London), 17 June 1987.
33. *Mission to South Africa: The Commonwealth Report*, Harmondsworth, Penguin, 1986, pp. 139–141.
34. R. W. Johnson, *How Long Will South Africa Survive?*, op. cit., p. 324.

12 Doctrines of 'Change' in South Africa*

Paul B. Rich

INTRODUCTION

A key dimension to the prospect of South Africa surviving in its present form is the degree to which the dominant white political elite is able to make a qualitative conceptual leap away from the hegemonic ideology of racial segregationism, which has dominated the country's politics since Union in 1910. The government's 'reform' policies are seen by its supporters as constituting just such a leap, while most opponents claim that they simply disguise the perpetuation of white political supremacy. In the former view, a change in the distribution of political power has already taken place, while in the latter the system survives because of the government's capacity to employ the rhetoric of change to keep itself in power. The purpose of this chapter is to examine the ideological dimensions to doctrines of political 'change', thus extending the previous discussion of Guelke on the constitutional aspects of reform (Chapter 11). At the same time this chapter will be setting the scene for the more detailed analysis of the structural underpinnings of the issue in the next chapter by Mitchell and Russell.

The chapter will begin by looking at the historical evolution of segregationism since Union, showing the remarkably adaptive manner in which it evolved through the period of South Africa's industrialisation. The chapter will then examine the rise of Afrikaner nationalism and the ideology of apartheid as one very systematised variant of segregationism. This use of historical analysis seeks to show that more recent debates on political 'change', especially discussion of consociationalism, simply adapt segregationism to new political and economic conditions. The consociational debate developed out of a more general discussion that accompanied R. W. Johnson's thesis in *How Long Will South Africa Survive?* that white minority rule had the capacity for survival in the short to medium term and that the function of reformist political analysts was to construct workable models of political reform within the dominant structures of white power.[1] This chapter contends that most of the discourse on political 'change' in South Africa is still being conducted within the ideological framework of segregationism. This implies that the South African ruling elite still has to make a major imaginative leap politically before it can begin to confront an alternative model of South African society. It leads to a paradox which has direct relevance for the Johnson thesis. At the level of ideology, the state's doctrine of 'change' is so limited in its scope that the government is incapable of strengthening its future position through more extensive reform, while current reforms nowhere challenge the system of white political supremacy.

Ruan Maud once argued cogently that reform was the very 'disease for which it purports to be the cure', in that it perpetuated the illusion of a Western-style model of political development in a society which had undergone a very different pattern of political mobilisation.[2] Reformism disguised the essential features of continuing white power. While these arguments described the situation in 1973, they also apply to current reforms. It is important, however, to place this discourse on 'change' in a historical perspective which extends back further, in order to show that more recent phases of debate reflect the continuation of deeply-rooted processes. White South African political discourse has always contained a strongly chameleon quality, drawing on a wider international vocabulary of political debate and in turn trying to adapt towards it in an increasingly opportunistic fashion. Indeed, as we shall see in the following sections, South African racial segregation progressively acquired the trappings of a social theory that could be buttressed by the authority of 'race experts', successfully disguising its racist character through a pseudo-scientific discourse which attracted an educated class of liberals who were far from being simple racist bigots.

SEGREGATION AND THE IDEOLOGY OF WHITE NATIONALISM

The chameleon quality of much official South African political discourse relates to the peculiar position the white settler state has traditionally found itself in during the period since Union in 1910. The South African state has been the sole example this century, apart from that of Israel in 1948, of a minority European cultural fragment achieving political independence as an autonomous nation-state. The politicians and opinion-formers involved in the debate on Closer Union were all too aware of the idiosyncratic nature of the South African state's position and the difficulties in legitimating it, even during the high point of self-confident European imperialism before the First World War. The ideology of racial segregation which began to influence white political discourse at this time, became seen by a number of ideologists as a means of legitimating South African domestic racial policies within an international order increasingly penetrated by ideals of liberal nationalism. In addition, therefore, to its role in perpetuating the pre-capitalist African reserve economies as a means of ensuring a ready supply of cheap black labour power, racial segregationism also appeared to represent a burlesque South African version of the liberal vision of a multinational political order.

South African segregationist thinking in its early phases amounted to a plea for administrative rationalisation based on existing colonial 'native policies' in South Africa, Rhodesia and the Protectorate territories. To writers and spokesmen such as Richard Rose Innes and Howard Pim political segregation seemed to be the means to establish separate African territorial areas under white tutelage which could divert the energies of aspirant African politicians away from the towns and cities of 'white' South Africa.[3] By the time of Union, however, a more sophisticated segregationist ideal emerged, based on a more complex social vision of racial separation. This increasingly drew on a wider body of contemporary social theory whose function was to explain, predict and control the thinking of the various amateur social philosophies of the emergent white settler state.[4]

For a number of recent analysts, the phase of racial segregationism in South African political discourse before 1948 appears marked by a high degree of pragmatism and flexibility compared to the apparently Teutonic thoroughness of its Verwoerdian successor. Andre du Toit, for example, has emphasised the essential conservatism of segregationist ideology, whose programme 'tended to take the form of a number of piecemeal actions aimed at relatively limited goals', in contrast to apartheid, which was characterised by 'the insistence on the consistent application of a few basic principles, primarily that of separation, aimed at ensuring white survival and Afrikaner identity'.[5] This view maintains the conventional stress on the 'Afrikaner' complexion of apartheid despite the fact, as recent revisionist historiography has pointed out, that the implementation of this doctrine depended to a considerable degree on the acquiescence, if not the active collaboration of, English-speaking business and commerce.[6] The ideological sources of apartheid within Afrikaner political thought are clearly crucial, especially in relation to notions of theological separatism within the Dutch Reformed Churches.[7] There is, though, an additional question concerned with the manner in which apartheid was successfully implemented in the period of the 1950s and the 1960s. Apartheid can be seen as the offspring, albeit of a somewhat deviant kind, of a wider political culture of racial segregationism which became entrenched in the South African body politic in the period since Union. This 'culture' still governs debate about political change in South Africa.

In the reconstruction of the South African polity after the Anglo-Boer War, the segregationist doctrine provided both a framework for analysing South African society in terms of the Darwinian struggle of racial groups, as well as an exhortatory appeal to the need for the political cohesion of the nascent white settler nation. Older liberal actions of incorporation of African societies into a single South African polity seemed hard to fix into such a project. As the British writer Archibald Colquhoun observed in 1906, 'we are trying to fit the negro into a scheme of human life which we have elevated into a religion. The scheme seems to be breaking down at several points among ourselves; but, in justice to our theories, we feel bound to go on trying to squeeze him into it, even when our instincts are opposed to such a course'.[8] Some theorists appeared willing even at this stage to cut South Africa off from the mainstream of the Western liberal impulse, even if only for a period. W. F. Bailey, for example, argued the same year that the doctrine of the quality of humankind could not be applied *in toto* to the South African situation and could only be taken up by the 'white community' in that country.[9]

This stress on white national cohesion intensified in the years after 1908 as the prospect of a united country loomed. Some zealous advocates of extreme or 'macro' segregation sought a major programme of ethnic social engineering by the removal of all Africans to 'tropical' regions north of South Africa.[10] In general, a middle position began to be favoured which stood between the older Cape liberal ideal of partial incorporation or assimilation through a qualified franchise, and extreme racial separation. This reflected a need for continuing black labour whilst refusing to grant black workers the same urban citizenship rights as the white working class. Fred W. Bell, for example, as a prominent activist in the Transvaal Native Affairs Society, linked segregation closely with a Social Darwinist philosophy of history, which emphasised the struggle between races and the biological inferiority of the black race through its 'arrested development'.[11]

The importance of such views lay in the strong demand for the political exclusion of blacks from the South African parliament and an attack on the mild liberalism of the qualified Cape African franchise. The arguments of activists like Bell progressively captured the middle ground of white South African opinion and marginalised the older Victorian ideal of a white *mission civilisatrice* in southern Africa. This latter view was most classically stated in 1909 by Lord Selborne at the University of the Cape of Good Hope.[12] Here a case was made for a qualified African franchise on the basis that African societies should not be deprived of access to Western 'civilisation', though 'the more natural and less forced the pace at which that civilisation proceeds, the more sure and better that civilisation will be'.[13] The reserves acted as important 'safety barriers' in the relations of Africans and whites but no impediments should be placed on the 'individual civilised native', from owning land while whites had a responsibility for the evolution of the native.[14] Such sentiments were, however, anathema for segregationists like Bell who condemned Selborne for advocating the eventual black political domination of South Africa.[15] There was a fear of the growth of an educated black intelligentsia, especially if, like the preacher Laputa in John Buchan's novel *Prester John* (1910), they had been educated in the United States and exposed to radical black ideas.[16] The segregationist project was not only designed to preserve white political power for the foreseeable future, but was also concerned at an early stage in establishing a comprehensive pattern of social control over the chances of black educational and political mobility.

In the years after Union, segregationism began progressively to permeate the policy debate of the new South African state. In a recent study, John Cell has seen the ideology functioning in terms of a Leninist model of a vanguard of racist militants acting in advance of the consciousness of their white ethnic and middle-class compatriots in the pursuit of white supremacy and social control in South Africa.[17] The level of ideological cohesion in the early years of the white state, though, suggests that this was a protracted counter-revolution which only began seriously to take off in the late 1930s and 1940s and to find its Lenin in the Verwoerd era of the 1950s and 1960s. What seems more evident for the post Union period from 1910 up to the early 1940s was that segregationists acted as a racist Fabian pressure group which proved surprisingly successful in conquering the commanding heights of political language and vocabulary. At an early stage the segregationists sought out whatever allies they could in both English and Afrikaner circles and, by the 1920s, even a small group of African segregationists. The English press in South Africa was often highly sceptical over the value of the doctrine and the *Transvaal Leader* considered that Bell's ideas might be better suited to other settler territories, such as East Africa.[18]

The segregationists, however, proved remarkably persistent in lobbying central government. They were probably aided in this effort by the fact that some bodies that could have developed as powerful groups in resistance to segregation, such as the Native Affairs Department, remained diffuse and ill-coordinated in the wake of Union. Bell sought to impress General Hertzog with his ideas, writing in 1911 that 'if you tackle the problem you will need all the help possible from those whose heart is fired'.[19] Hertzog, as Minister of Native Affairs in 1912, drew up a draft Land Bill which provided for separate areas of African landholding based on the existing system of reserves. A watered down version of this reached the Statute book as the 1913 Natives Land Act.[20]

Much of the success of the segregationists lay in the fact that from the Edwardian era until the late 1920s, a considerable section of liberal and philanthropic opinion in both South Africa and internationally was favourable to the idea of a benevolent segregation of black African races, partly in reaction to the earlier attempts at assimilationism in nineteenth-century British India.[21] In a general sense, South African segregationism started off by gaining the tacit legitimation, if not fervent support, from an international 'benevolent empire' of missionary and philanthropic opinion.[22]

In South Africa, the proponents of segregation were also successful in becoming, in the years after Union, identified with the scientific study of the native question. Before 1910 some observers, such as Harry Johnstone, had berated the failure to develop a 'scientific' anthropological study in South Africa of its peoples and societies.[23] Over the following years this began to change and the Economic Commission in 1914 (containing two prominent native experts, Maurice Evans and Howard Pim) urged that the 'unbroken study of the native question' was 'imperative' in order to ascertain the 'wants and desires' of black workers and to 'watch the situation continuously and report to the Government as need arises'.[24] The ideology of segregation became linked to a rational policy emphasising African local self-government and avenues for the absorption of the energies of the growing class of educated African intellectuals and political leaders. The segregationist Maurice Evans argued in 1913 that the city was 'a veritable sewer and death trap for the negro',[25] though the strike wave by black workers in 1918–19 and campaign against passes organised by the ANC led Evans to urge the creation of a Native Affairs Council and representation in Parliament.[26] Segregationists, as Cell has pointed out, were important for their capacity to adapt their ideology to changing economic and political circumstances.[27]

This resilient quality of segregationism can be explained through an early recognition in South African governing circles of the need for a cooperative strategy which would incorporate as far as possible liberal spokesmen and analysts into a controlled political consensus on the nature and direction of 'native policy'. By such means potentially troublesome critics, who often had important overseas connections, could be neutralised by being given the impression that through the use of government-created channels they could at least modify if not reverse the direction of policy. The 1920 Native Affairs Act, for instance, established the Native Affairs Commission (NAC), in response to pleas for a panel of 'native experts', and its initial membership included the Natal educationalist Charles T. Loram and the liberal Lovedale missionary Alex Roberts. The NAC proceeded to establish contacts with the Joint Council movement that grew up after 1921 on lines similar to the inter-racial councils in the American South, and a number of English-speaking intellectuals, such as W. M. Macmillan, J. D. Rheinallt Jones, Oliver Schreiner and Howard Pim, felt hopeful that state policy would move in the direction of a benign segregationism that would give a generous territorial provision to African farmers in the reserves in order to avoid the apparent horrors of African urbanisation.

However, the result of the debate on urban 'native policy' was the further entrenchment of urban segregation through the 1923 Natives (Urban Areas) Act, which was rooted in a doctrine enunciated in the 1922 Transvaal (Local Government) Commission Report, chaired by Colonel C. F. Stallard. This urged that Africans should only be in urban areas in order to minister to the needs of the white man. From this time onwards, government policy increasingly moved away from any superficial observance of Victorian philanthropy.[28] Policy now became one of the growing exclusion of Africans from citizenship rights, as further harsher amendments to the Act in 1930 and 1937 attested.[29] In part, this entrenchment of segregationism reflected the growing political cohesion of the white state after 1924, as white labour became successfully incorporated in the wake of the 1922 Rand revolt. The Pact government of the National Party and the South African Labour Party (SALP) entrenched the 'civilised labour' policy through such measures as the Wage Act (1925) and the Mines and Works Act (1926), which reduced the former political opposition of organised white labour to the state of a matter of administrative regulation.[30] This cooptive strategy nullified the hopes of some white radicals for the building of a political base for opposition to segregation through the white trade union movement, and attention turned in communist circles towards harnessing the energies of black radicals through its Night School Movement.[31]

African political leadership in the interwar years, furthermore, found itself continually compelled to accommodate towards racial segregationism. Some moderate spokesmen, such as Selby Msimang and Victor Selope Thema, got drawn into Joint Council circles and wrote for the Chamber of Mines-financed *Umteteli wa Bantu*, where the hope was often guardedly expressed that a just form of segregation might meet African political demands. This leadership was not rooted in a firmly proletarian African urban culture and looked back to the reserves as areas for potential landholding. After a brief phase of radicalism in the ANC under the leadership of Josiah Gumede between 1927 and 1930, the return of a more conservative leadership under Pixley Seme in 1930, led to a renewal of hopes for black self help through industrial training on the lines of Booker T. Washington's Tuskegee Institute in Alabama, rural cooperative production by the African peasantry and speculative land companies in collaboration with friendly white liberal allies.[32] Even the formerly radical ANC paper *Abantu Batho*, which had periodically attacked white liberal manipulation of African politics during the 1920s, now upheld the possibility of collaborating with the state-created segregationist structures for, as Doyle Modiakoatla wrote in 1931, 'segregation is the law of this land and unless we are prepared for bloodshed and misery we have to adapt ourselves to conditions brought about by this policy'.[33]

African hopes for a benevolent segregation became increasingly chimerical during the 1930s as South African industrialisation intensified. This led to an intensification of labour repression. The 1927 Native Administration Act boosted the autocratic powers of tribal chiefs, and the 1932 Native Service Contract Act reduced African farm labour to a semi-serf-like status by making breaches of contract with farmers a criminal offence.[34] To a number of external critics, such as Sidney Olivier, Leonard Barnes and, after his departure from South Africa in 1933, W. M. Macmillan, this course of policy seemed to be taking South Africa increasingly away from the purview of Western liberal thought and to entrench the interests of what Olivier termed 'white capital' at the expense of black labour.[35] Some conservative liberal analysts in South Africa itself, however, continued to stress the apparent rationality of the segregationist doctrine. In 1929 John Kirk, for example, wrote in *The Economic Aspects of Native Segregation in South Africa* that the African reserves provided a subsistence to keep African wages in the urban areas artificially cheap, though he conceded that the urbanised African population would continue to increase.[36] Furthermore, there was the moral dimension that 'with the help of segregation they (the Africans) obtain the chance of discovering and demonstrating to one another advantages in their social order which hitherto they have ignored'.[37] Similarly, for the American Board missionary, Ray Phillips, writing in *The Bantu Are Coming* (1930) the segregationist doctrines of establishing a 'white man's country' in South Africa and allowing Africans to 'develop on their own lines' was 'logical and sound theoretically'.[38]

In the early 1930s, nevertheless, an ideological crisis did occur in the legitimation of the segregationist ideology as the overseas attacks intensified. W. M. Macmillan cogently argued in *Complex South Africa* (1930) that the economic base of African reserves, such as Herschel in the Eastern Cape, was increasingly becoming eroded. There was also a growing emigration of educated Africans which tended to reinforce the 'traditional' conservatism of local headmen.[39] This rebuttal of the idea that segregation could lead to the 'development' or 'uplifting' of the reserves was, nevertheless, met with general indifference among white politicians, especially after the 1932 report of the Native Economic Commission which urged a 'wise, courageous, forward policy of development in the reserves'.[40] A new consensus began to be established in the 1930s based on the continuing extension of territorial segregation, the removal of the remaining legacy of Cape liberalism in the form of the Cape African franchise, and an extended programme of reserve consolidation and economic 'development' based on soil conservation and the teaching of scientific farming techniques through agricultural demonstrators.

The shift to a developmentalist ideology in the 1930s was of long-term significance in that it removed from the central agenda any significant preoccupation with a systematically racist ideology of a Central European variety. After 1933 critics of South African policy tried to make embarrassing analogies with Nazi policy in Germany, but the actual policymakers tended to be either civil servants or committees of politicians with a close eye on external, and especially Commonwealth, reaction. Racial ideologists tended increasingly to be marginalised from the political mainstream, though their continuing importance for shaping white political attitudes was undoubtedly of considerable significance to which historians have paid insufficient attention.[41] But even some of the racists found the resort to 'scientific' arguments to prove permanent black racial inferiority generally unnecessary. As W. A. Russell pointed out in a pamphlet *European Versus Bantu* (1928) American intelligence-testing proving that 25 per cent of a negro sample were of the same standard as whites and 75 per cent were below them, might be of interest, but was too recent to command general confidence. In general Russell referred to the lessons of 'history' to demonstrate the rationality and necessity for segregation.[42]

It thus seemed increasingly apparent by the 1930s that South African segregationism was of a qualitatively different variety to that of the Jim Crow South, there the American negroes were clearly culturally American as their slave ancestry had removed any significantly 'African' attributes of cultural difference. For American racists there had been a strong onus to prove negro inferiority through some form of scientific evidence in a culture geared to respect both the mystique and prestige of the scientific intelligentsia.[43] In South Africa, on the other hand, the overwhelming weight of cultural evidence, especially from the infant subject of Social Anthropology, asserting African difference to whites, seemed enough to demonstrate the necessity for segregation, especially when it became combined with the political manipulation of historical myth to reveal a sacred white frontier tradition based on Calvinist notions of divine historical destiny. As Leonard Thompson has recently shown, one of the strongest inputs into white racial discourse in South Africa in the twentieth century was the reworking of history in order to legitimise the white settler presence in the subcontinent, though his emphasis upon a specifically Afrikaner ethnic presence neglects the wider climate of racist and Darwinist historiography in the tradition of Cory and Theal upon which this ethnic historicism in turn drew.[44] However, both traditions (English Social Darwinist racism and Afrikaner ethnocentrism), shifted the emphasis within white racial discourse significantly towards historical and cultural attributes and away from the scientific racism of Central Europe and America.

Typological racism, influenced by Central European fascism, became, increasingly unfashionable in English intellectual and scientific circles as the horrors of Nazism became manifest.[45] In South Africa too it led to attempts to make the country's segregation policy respectable in international terms by the employment of categories drawn from the discourse of 'race relations'. One of the key ideological figures in the late 1930s engaged in this effort, who straddled the separate worlds of white politics, sugar planting and official political debate, was the chairman of the Native Affairs Commission, George Heaton Nicholls. He particularly championed the goal of 'adaptation' as opposed to 'assimilation', which he saw as shifting the South African system dangerously to a class basis.[46]

Heaton Nicholls's thinking exemplified the climate of political debate in white South African politics in the late 1930s to which conservative liberal opinion sought to adapt. With the removal of W. M. Macmillan as a pivot for the analysis of the economic impact of segregation in the early 1930s, liberal thought inside the South African Institute of Race Relations (formed in 1929) took a lurch in the direction of cultural idealism under the influence of growing study in Social Anthropology and 'Bantu Studies'. In 1939, the President of the Institute, Professor R. F. A. Hoernle, published some Phelps Stokes lectures, *South African Native Policy and the Liberal Spirit*, upholding the possibility of a liberal political solution being realised through 'total separation', though Hoernle admitted that in practice this long-term goal was unlikely to be realised. In a 'heartbreak house' situation, separation in South Africa was to be placed on the central political agenda along with the other options of parallelism and assimilation, though in the context of growing fascist aggression in Europe, Hoernle gloomily thought that there was 'no ultimate hope for the liberal spirit'.[47]

Hoernle's pessimistic *Weltschmerz* acted as a guide for a number of strands of white opinion in the decades ahead and provided intellectual justification for a policy of ethnic separation in a situation where there seemed to be little hope for realising the liberal ideal through the existing parliamentary system, since this would lead in the end to black majority rule.

This became especially evident after the Second World War, when it became increasingly clear that Smuts's faith in the external buttress from Britain and the Commonwealth misread the emerging postwar world of progressive decolonisation, as well as fatally avoided the question of internal domestic political reform in the wake of the 1946 African mine strike.[48] Though plans were afoot for an expansion of the powers of the Natives Representative Council in order to provide political channels for the 'moderate intellectuals', whose sympathies, the deputy Prime Minister Jan H. Hofmeyr felt, were now strained to breaking-point, Smuts felt such discussion could be postponed until after the 1948 election, which he thought he would win. As a consequence, a vital moment for a change of political direction was lost and the composition of the South African governing class was changed with the onset of a National Party government. Though characterised by Leonard Thompson as a 'parting of the ways' in South African politics,[49] the 1948 election should not be over-dramatised by analysts, for the emergence of the new doctrine of 'apartheid' merely confirmed the depth and tenacity of segregationism in white South African vocabulary. Its real significance lay in the employment of a radical segregationism by a more insular governing elite that now relied far less heavily on the external Commonwealth supports, and drove segregationist ideology into an ethnocentric creed to try and fit a new world order of declining European colonial empires and resurgent African nationalism.

APARTHEID AND AFRIKANER NATIONALISM IN SOUTH AFRICA

The advent of the government of Dr D. F. Malan in 1948 led to the adoption of a more specifically Afrikaner ethnic ideology of apartheid. For many observers, this seemed a trek into the past and an anachronistic hope to reverse what seemed to be the inexorable logic toward a multiracial social and political order. However, the importance of apartheid ideology lay in the fact that it represented a political rationalisation of separatist precepts that existed within Afrikaner religious and cultural circles since the middle nineteenth century. In particular, the theology of the Dutch Reformed Church (DRC) systematised local racial prejudices and social practices into a coherent political doctrine.[50] The experience of the Trekker Republics in the nineteenth century acted as vital moral reference points to which nationalist rhetoricians could appeal in the populist mobilisation of the Afrikaner *volk* in the 1930s and 1940s. The constant work, however, of the DRCs in the ordering of social and political life amongst newly urbanised Afrikaners ensured that apartheid had many of the trappings of a moral crusade beyond the more bland social engineering designs of the previous Fabian segregationists.

Nevertheless, when it came to the question of actually implementing the apartheid grand design, it soon became revealed that the nationalist bureaucrats and political entrepreneurs would still be heavily dependent upon the previous experiences of state 'native policy' since Union. Apartheid only marked an intensification of this previous pattern of ethnic social engineering. In September 1948 Dr Verwoerd, at an annual meeting of the Afrikaanse Sakekamer in Cape Town, warned that the doctrine would 'dislocate existing social institutions and create new relations in South Africa. As we progress, we will see our mistakes and rectify them'. Nevertheless, he tried to allay fears that the doctrine would lead to the creation of different racial 'camps' since industry and commerce would still get labour.[51] There was, indeed a strong effort in nationalist political rhetoric to demonstrate a pragmatic strain regarding the implementation of apartheid in the face of strong attacks from the liberal press, such as *The Forum*, that the policy was 'just like Nazi Germany' and would have disastrous results for industry.[52] Despite attempts to show the guiding hand of the Broederbond in National Party policy, the English-speaking press and political establishment proved surprisingly unsuccessful in orchestrating major industrial and commercial opposition to the policies of the state.[53]

This political weakness from commerce and industry reflected its economic dependence upon the state which, since the early 1920s, had taken a prominent role in initiating industrialisation as a safety guard for when the supply of gold eventually ran out.[54] Industry and commerce traditionally lacked strong political leadership and never got involved to any major degree with liberal political circles, which continued to rest upon the churches and academic establishment in the English-speaking universities. The government thus presented its case to secondary industry in terms of progressive bargaining over the labour supply and what the secretary of Native Affairs, Dr W. W. M. Eiselen, termed 'a general revision of attitude towards the available Native labour supply in the country'.[55] While opposition to the state's demand for industrial decentralisation to the border areas around the reserves continued, the more general industrial interest in economic growth throughout the 1950s made the conflict appear more a positive-sum than a zero-sum game of winner takes all.[56]

Furthermore, when it came to the question of legitimising apartheid, the government had a number of ace cards to play. Significantly, not all its apologists proved to be Afrikaners and a number of English-speaking spokesmen could be found to give credence to the doctrine in terms of a more deep-seated segregationist discourse. The Afrikaner rival to the South African Institute of Race Relations (SAIRR), for example, in the form of the South African Bureau of Racial Affairs (SABRA), contained a number of English apologists. Unlike the older model of segregation under the previous Smuts government one of SABRA's proponents, W. E. Barker, argued that apartheid projected 'that horizontal barriers be removed and in its place a vertical division between the races established'. There was still a white role of 'guardianship', however, in order to ensure eventual African self-government in the reserves and the removal of white administration.[57]

In contrast to SABRA's efforts at justifying apartheid ideology, the English liberal intelligentsia were organised around the SAIRR, whose director after 1946, Quintin Whyte, was a strong acolyte of R. F. A. Hoernle. Whyte opposed any one particular strategy through fear of straitjacketing race relations. He considered that 'economic integration' as a consequence of the logic of the market economy was 'essential to the national well being', though he also thought that a measure of 'economic separation' was inevitable on the grounds that 'residential segregation' was considered 'fundamental to harmonious relationships'.[58] This accommodation to some aspects of segregation continued in Institute circles in the 1950s, and in 1955 a prominent Institute member, Ellen Hellmann, strongly urged the partition of South Africa.[59]

The concept of 'partition' appeared to be one that might produce some form of agreement with the conservative liberal establishment. The Government White Paper on the Tomlinson Commission welcomed the Report's rejection of racial 'integration' and 'of any theories of a possible middle course'. The Commission reinforced the apartheid concept by firmly linking it to a programme of 'development' in the reserves which contained a future vision of an approximately equal proportion of whites and Africans in 'European territory' within fifty years.[60] The paper envisaged an expenditure programme of some £25 million in industrial projects in the reserves, which the government now accepted could not remain merely pastoral farming areas; a £30 million agricultural development programme, which included a 40-year forestry programme; and a further £41 million on other projects, including the establishment of 100 towns in the 'African areas'. The programme was seen by the government's critics though as completely inadequate and industry tried to resist attempts to diversify to the reserves.[61] There was however no major business or industrial revolt against government policy, though as the 1950s progressed, government policy did become sensitive to the labour needs of industry.[62]

Apartheid took on some of the features of state-directed and *dirigiste* economic planning which did not appear so substantially different to state interventionism in the mixed economies of other Western states. On the political level, though, the government of Dr Verwoerd began to initiate a veritable counter-revolution during the critical phase of African decolonisation. Segregationism was expanded to new frontiers way beyond the limited and repressive system of Jim Crow segregation in the US South. The 1959 Promotion of Bantu Government Act and the creation of self-government in the Transkei in 1963 took apartheid some way towards the original vision of the racist idealists like Fred Bell. However, if this was a period in which state policy was considerably informed by apartheid racist ideology, it was not shaped by a single blueprint, such as Dr G. Cronje's *'n Tuiste vir die Nageslag* (A Home for Posterity), as Leonard Thompson has recently suggested.[63] The influence of the SABRA ideologists on the forging of government policy was for the most part tangential and transitory, and by the late 1950s it began to decline in importance as state policy became increasingly directed by a politicised civil service and, from the middle 1960s, a burgeoning security policy and military apparatus. Racial ideology in its purest form began to give way before the exigencies of praetorianism in South African politics.[64]

When it came to the question of the moral legitimation of policy, it also became clear that the South African government was unable to seal off internal political debate from surrounding global concern on the implications of apartheid. This had been evident from at least the early 1950s as Church opinion became increasingly vocal in its criticism of government policy. In 1956 Trevor Huddleston, in an important book *Naught for your Comfort*, questioned not only the entire ethical basis of apartheid and its support from the Dutch Reformed Churches, but the moral right of whites to decide the future of South African society.[65]

The sources within Afrikaner nationalism, furthermore, were diverse, consisting of Scottish Presbyterianism, Kuyperian neo-Calvinism and romantic or 'neo-Fichtean' nationalism.[66] If the latter had tended to predominate in Afrikaner politics by the Verwoerd era, it was still the hope of many conservative South African liberals that a dialogue could be formed with liberal members of the DRCs in order to wean them away from a slavish justification of state policies. When it came to the actual implementation of policy, too, it became apparent by the late 1950s that the chief terrain of victory of the Afrikaner nationalist ideologues was in the field of education. In large areas of economic policy it still seemed feasible that the government preferred to place pragmatism before ideology.

This attempt at promoting dialogue focused on the SAIRR, especially as some SAIRR members had been involved in the holding of a Multi-Racial Conference at the University of the Witwatersrand in November 1957, which had called for 'inter-racial talks' in order to draw up a new constitution guaranteeing civil rights and equal rights of citizenship and universal suffrage on a common roll.[67] The conference tried to spell out the nature of economic, social and political duties in a common society for, as Z. K. Matthews remarked in a paper, 'Political Arrangements in a Multi-Racial Society', South Africa was 'as good a laboratory as can be found anywhere for the testing out of political arrangements in a real multi-racial society'. There was in this endeavour a similar element of experimentalism as in that of the apartheid ideologues, though Matthews went on significantly to warn that 'even if we succeed in getting beyond thinking of people in terms of race, we may fall into the similar error of looking at them in terms of groups such as the white and non-white, the Afrikaans-speaking and the English-speaking, the Indian or the Coloured, and think of their political rights in terms of the groups to which they belong'.[68] This cautioning against the allurements of 'ethnicity', as it would now be termed, was congruent with the sentiments of many at the conference that the chief political task in the reconstruction of South African society was not the intricate balancing of ethnic or group rights but the passage from white minority rule to 'non racial democracy'.[69] There was a recognition that group interests had emerged in South African politics, but as Govan Mbeki pointed out in a paper 'Economic Rights and Duties in a Multi-Racial Society', these were largely defensive, such as African group interests forged in reaction to the 1913 Natives Land Act or coloured and Indian interests created as a result of the 1950 Group Areas Act. 'Unless these groups assert their right to live', he poignantly concluded, 'they will be exterminated.'[70]

The thinking of many black and white South African liberals in the late 1950s was thus radically counter to the sociology of ethnogenesis. The treason trial tended to reinforce this trend towards either multiracialism or non-racialism, and Quintin Whyte was surprised to find in an interview with Albert Luthuli and Z. K. Matthews that the leadership of the ANC felt there was little African nationalism in its ranks, for 'if anyone got up and spoke in these terms at an ANC meeting, they would get short shrift'. At a time when the ANC had come under growing attack from the Africanists, who broke away to form the PAC in 1959, it appeared that an alliance with the liberals was still seen as eminently desirable as a means of acting as 'negotiators' with the government.[71]

The suppression of the ANC in 1960, the move towards violent struggle with the formation of *Umkonto we Sizwe*, and the entrenchment of apartheid after the passage of the Transkei constitution in 1963, altered the South African political landscape radically. Indeed the period 1960–64 can be considered more of a watershed than that of 1948, for it reinforced the nomenclature of group rights and interests in South African political discourse and initiated a pattern of 'top down' cooption and reform, which by the late 1970s had occupied the middle ground of debate over the nature and direction of 'change' in the society.

THE MANUFACTURE OF 'POLITICAL CHANGE'

Despite the South African state's clampdown on political opposition after 1960, there were important ideological and theological pressures at work to undermine the cohesion of the dominant apartheid doctrine. Many DRC ministers in the course of the 1950s became increasingly concerned to move apartheid away from 'tribal' domination by Afrikanerdom, towards radical racial and geographical separation. In part, this reflected a generational cleavage between older ministers who had been engaged in battles for the recognition of Afrikaans in the 1920s and 1930s, and a younger generation which had emerged since the late 1940s and was becoming worried by external pressures against apartheid. By 1958 the younger group was estimated to form some 25 per cent of pastors in the Transvaal and their sentiments became expressed through the writings of theological critics such as B. B. Keet and Ben Marais.[72]

These divisions came to a head with the attendance of the Dutch Reformed Churches at the Cottesloe Consultation in December 1960, where a memorandum from the Cape DRC formed the basis for discussion with six representatives from the World Council of Churches (WCC). Though the delegates of the Nederduitsch Hervormde Kerk distanced themselves from the findings of Cottesloe, the involvement of the Cape DRC produced a powerful counter-attack from such pillars as *Die Transvaler*, *Die Kerbode* and Dr Verwoerd. In 1962, the synodical meeting of the DRCs condemned Cottesloe and left the WCC the following year. The theological dilemma still remained, for, as a moderate critic like Ben Marais recognised, it was no longer possible to isolate South African history from a wider global history. He optimistically hoped, though, that South African policies would be 'accepted as a great contribution to the development of Africa and for multinational societies everywhere'.[73]

For some radical critics in the 1960s, however, apartheid was an abomination which required a more fundamental restructuring of the society. These radical rumblings grew in a variety of quarters including sections of the Christian Institute (CI), which had been founded by Beyers Naude in 1963 in despair at the DRC's willingness to kowtow to government pressure. By 1969, the CI, along with the South African Council of Churches, decided to formulate a more radical position in contrast to the conservative liberals in the Institute of Race Relations, some of whose members, such as Quintin Whyte, had begun to move in the 1960s towards accepting the political realities of Bantustan development and to work in collaboration with this policy in the hope of undermining it from within.[74] The result was the Study Project on Christianity in Apartheid Society (Spro-Cas).

Spro-Cas tried to link a strategy for political change with firm ethical principles following a period when the impact of apartheid seemed to have undermined and demoralised many of its former liberal critics. The project was concerned to include a number of 'pragmatic liberals' who were not merely concerned with drawing up utopian revolutionary plans from an exile setting but to debate feasible changes.[75] Six commissions were established to investigate the law, churches, economics, social change and politics, though they were dominated by academic social scientists. In part, this reflected the emergence of universities and the academic establishment in the West as the new priesthood of modern capitalist societies which, as C. W. de Kiewiet has pointed out, may not directly exercise political power but certainly influences its form, location and goals.[76]

In South Africa the growing secularisation within Afrikanerdom tended to exacerbate this trend as the older theological debates received new social scientific form, especially as conventional apartheid discourse appeared increasingly unable to cope with the strains of a rapidly industrialising society. By the late 1960s a division had occurred within Afrikanerdom between *verkramptes* and *verligtes*, with the latter favouring a more pragmatic and flexible approach to apartheid and sceptical of the Verwoerdian vision of total racial separation. For some analysts, this period has become crucial for sowing the seeds of what has now come to be termed the philosophy of 'new apartheid'.[77] Others, however, have stressed the emergence of a genuine commitment to reform, but one based on what Kogila Moodley has termed 'technocratic liberation' infused with a firm commitment to the tenets of 'messianic scientism'.[78] In a period when the faith in the power of the social sciences was in decline in many Western states, South African political debate remained unique in its commitment to the power of social science analysis to point to the way to a 'political solution', based on both a dispersal of power away from the state and various models of ethnic federalism which would meet the demands for group as well as individual rights. To some degree, the employment of this social science became subject to the more general phenomenon of 'deviousness, manipulation and control' that Joseph Lelyveld has observed as a general feature of contemporary South African politics.[79]

Certainly, social scientists in South Africa were not alone in pointing to the apparent deficiencies of older concepts in political theory which stressed the primacy of individual rights and duties to the exclusion of group ones. If there had been a debate on group rights among groups of English pluralists, it had never encountered the more general post-colonial phenomenon of 'ethnic' group rights. This lacuna in traditional Western political thought meant, as Vernon Van Dyke pointed out, that 'a doctrine accepting both individuals and communities as right-and-duty bearing units is susceptible to universal application, whereas a doctrine focussing on individuals is not'.[80] The more orthodox liberals in South Africa were driven increasingly on to the institutionalisation of ethnic groups in the emergent 'homelands', which made the more conventional hope for 'non-racial democracy' increasingly difficult to realise.

Furthermore, it was clear by the early 1970s that the new black intelligentsia that had been educated in segregated 'bush universities' was more committed to black group rights, through the Black Consciousness political creed, compared to its ANC predecessor of the 1950s. This was not a reification of African tribal culture as the apartheid theorists had sought, but an amorphous pattern of beliefs of a new political generation finding its feet. While Black Consciousness could develop in a more conservative direction and infuse ethnic movements such as Inkatha, it could also act as a radicalising doctrine in an industrial class struggle, with ethnicity reinforcing black working-class consciousness, as became apparent by the time of the 1973 Durban strikes.[81] The impact of such upsurges, especially the Soweto revolt of June 1976, was to force South Africa into a more sophisticated cooptive strategy than had seemed apparent at the time of the Spro-Cas deliberations six years earlier. The granite face of apartheid of the Verwoerd era has thus come to be replaced by the more absorbent, sponge-like years of P. W. Botha.

In this respect, the work of Spro-Cas may be judged to have acted in an unforeseen manner, working if anything to modify the South African political agenda and stabilise government policy rather than transform it. The report of the Political Commission, *South Africa's*

Political Alternatives, was notable for stressing the need for a devolution of power away from the state on a pluralistic basis to local, regional or 'communal' levels. The Report stressed the need for an 'open pluralism' which was not defined by a rigid ideology but reflected the voluntary nature of group attachments, of which ethnicity was a major defining variable. To this extent, the Report sought to shift thinking away from any form of imposed ethnic classification, as in the South African government's homelands policy.[82] But as part of this approach the Commission did recommend the need for 'creative change' through the use of the 'representative authorities' created by government policy without accepting the assumptions of separate development. A two-stage model of transition would thus ensue, first opening up the existing separate development system to a pluralistic devolution of powers and then in the second stage the establishment of a federal multiracial system of government.[83] The Report has given strong credence to the idea that the separate development policy contains strong enough internal dynamics for the South African political system to be moved, through a process of mutual bargaining, towards a more liberal model of federalism and multi-racial government. The logic of social science and rational bargaining had replaced the earlier faith in a Whig theory of progressive devolution of parliamentary liberties, which had governed much liberal thought until the end of the 1950s.

For the Afrikaner political establishment in South Africa such notions of open pluralism provided a valuable new injection of thought in the wake of the crises of the middle 1970s, when white political self-confidence had become considerably eroded at the time of the ignominious troop withdrawal from Angola in early 1976 and the Soweto revolt of June the same year.[84] In one respect, the decade had opened with an increased commitment to separate development, for the 1970 Bantu Homelands Citizenship Act made every African who was not a 'citizen' of a self-governing territory become a 'citizen' of the territorial authority area to which he was attached. But the coherence of the apartheid doctrine was starting to crumble in the late 1970s, with the Muldergate crisis confirming long-held suspicions in many white circles on the disarray of the government. For some analysts, 'survival politics' had begun to take over and it appeared possible that the drowning state might clutch at any straw.[85]

The debate on pluralism quickly became incorporated into the vocabulary of *verligtheid* as it appeared feasible that policy was moving in the direction of 'deracialisation'. The pluralist thesis became combined with an extensive debate on the merits of consociationalism. Arend Lijphart defined this in terms of executive power-sharing among the representatives of all 'significant groups', a high degree of internal autonomy for groups that wish it, proportional representation and proportional allocation of civil service positions and a minority veto on vital issues. Such a consociational strategy could, Lijphart urged, be recommended with 'reasonable confidence' for South Africa, though the attraction for some analysts, such as Lawrence Schlemmer, lay in the fact that consociational democracy was a 'normative concept'.[86] As a 'multi-racial model', the idea, suggested W. F. de Klerk, should be 'properly marketed among whites and non-whites, both in South Africa and overseas. All interested parties should know that this is a new concept and that there is much potential for evolutionary progress in this programme'.[87]

In some respects, the pluralist and devolutionary concept was not especially new, since it acted as a reworking of older notions of cooption of elite political groups. In the event of a breakdown in the strategy, Lijphart suggested the Hoernlean solution of radical partition, though consociational democracy was seen as the only likely model to ensure a degree of democracy in South Africa, given that it was a 'plural society with extremely deep cleavages dividing the different segments of the population'.[88] There is no real manner, however, by which the consociational democracy model can be falsified since it contains both analytical and normative elements: if the model fails, therefore, this is because the leaders have not tried hard enough (just as for rainmakers, the failure of the skies to open is always due to an insufficient effort to placate the gods):

> The theory does not claim that consociational solutions will always work; if they fail, it will be because segmental leaders are unable or unwilling to manage the inherently difficult inter and intra-segmental balancing act.[89]

Critics of consociational democracy had often pointed out that it was substantially West European in its orientation and Lijphart's comparative analysis is often anchored around the Dutch, Swiss, Austrian and Belgian examples. But none of these societies has a history remotely comparable to that of South Africa, with a legacy of violent colonial conquest and a rapid industrialisation organised on the basis of a monopoly capitalism.[90] For the most part, the consociational democracy model fails to incorporate class categories or to understand the inter-relationship of 'ethnic' or 'communal' sentiments with class ones. The model is thus very weak in being able to explain how the various elite leaderships can deliver consociational democracy to their own followers. Only five pages before the end of Lijphart's *Power Sharing in South Africa* is the 'crucial role' of political leadership recognised.[91] The model is really offered up to the ruling white political apparatus and little account is taken of the interests or ideas of black political leadership, especially the UDF and ANC. The pretensions of this social science 'model' thus become revealed as conservative political ideology.

Even Lijphart proved disappointed by the government's eventual constitutional dispensation of 1983, which tended to reinforce the basic structures of apartheid. This constitution in some respects tightens up separate development given that Indians and coloureds do not have homelands, though the consociational features of the new parliament are very weak with the minority chambers able to delay but not veto legislation, which is divided on apartheid lines between 'general' and 'own' affairs. The doctrines of segregationism have continued to dominate the working of the South African political system, with even the reforms in petty apartheid and mixed marriages legislation congruent with the drive towards macro segregation. As Hoernle had predicted in the 1930s, the extension of segregation on the macro plane would make micro segregation less necessary given the compartmentalisation of the society into self-contained 'segments'.[92] The politics of 'change' in South Africa still needs to address key issues germane to the 'core values' of the ruling white group: the abolition of the Group Areas Act, the abolition of segregation in schools, health care and the civil service; the abolition of the homelands; the legalisation of the black political parties, including the ANC; and the lifting of security legislation. These measures determine to a considerable degree the commitment of the white state to move towards a genuine policy of deracialisation and a move away from the dominant ideology of segregationism which has dominated its thinking since the creation of the Union in 1910.

Some analysts, such as Adam and Moodley, have berated the 'slow pseudo-reform policies of Pretoria', and suggest that the model of industrial bargaining may be more viable than veto rights and 'sham coalitions'.[93] Theodor Hanf and colleagues have gone as far as to admit that 'sham consociationalism' can be used to bolster up the white minority regime for 'the mechanism which maintains an equilibrium between the groups in a consociational democracy also entrenched the status quo in South Africa's minority democracy'.[94] It is this factor which forces political scientists, like social scientists and historians generally, to observe more fully the consequences of their own research and to be aware of the potential for the political manipulation of their work. In the South African context, the 'scientific method', Lelyveld has cogently pointed out, 'as [Afrikaner] pedagogues practice it, has reduced itself to a technique of selective quotation. There is a giddy enthusiasm, even innocence, about the strenuous efforts they make to isolate old racial doctrines into current academic jargon that will advance the "international marketing of this country"'.[95] Strong doubts thus remain on the degree to which the debate on political reform represents any significant conceptual break with the dominant ideology of the past rooted in racial segregation.

CONCLUSION

The foregoing discussion has sought to focus on the ideological aspects to the contemporary debate on 'change' in South African politics, and has suggested that it has been strongly hidebound by a more general burden of the past. The domination of segregationist ideology since the foundation of the South African state, has ensured an entrenchment of ideas of racial and cultural 'otherness' within white South African political discourse. While this ideology was able to free itself from a close attachment to scientific racist ideas since at least the early 1930s, the adoption of a set of more protean 'cultural' and 'ethnic' arguments ensured its survival in the post Second World War era.

In practice, the debate on 'change' and 'reform' since the middle 1970s needs to be seen within a longer trajectory of white South African politics, which, as Alf Stadler has recently pointed out, led to periods of unrest and political mobilisation (such as those after both the First and Second World Wars) being accompanied by a two-pronged policy of both reform and increased racial segregation. In the debate on urban 'native policy' between 1920 and 1923, for example, there were the alternative strategies of cooption, represented by the Godley Report of 1923, which recommended the abolition of the pass laws and the incorporation of an urban black elite into the local government of the urban areas, and the rival report of the 1922 Stallard Commission, which argued for the extension of urban segregation and the marginalisation of educated Africans from what were seen as 'white' urban politics. This two-pronged approach was repeated to some extent after the Second World War when the rival Fagan and Sauer reports marked rival approaches of accommodation towards urban black political leadership and the rechanneling of their political energies towards the reserves.[96] In both instances, the segregationist strategy eventually prevailed.

In some respects, contemporary South African debate over reform is at a similar impasse, with the white election of May 1987 confirming a considerable increase in political support among the white electorate for the extreme right and the Conservative Party's commitment to return to the original Verwoerdian vision of apartheid. The initially optimistic climate of thinking amongst *verligte* Afrikaner intellectuals on the intentions of the P. W. Botha administration in the early 1980s, has been replaced by a growing pessimism. With an increasing number of South African military incursions into neighbouring states, the South African government has been forced to subordinate its professed policy of reform to the exigencies of counter-insurgency strategy. The input from the civilian *verligte* intellectuals, or 'critical moralists' as they have been termed, has therefore tended to decline.[97] This is not to say that the military itself does not favour a political reform agenda, but it is one substantially on its own terms, and the resulting frustration felt by a number of the formerly hopeful *verligtes* was probably best expressed by the active participation of the so-called 'New Nationalists' in the May election and the prominent Stellenbosch academics who resigned from the National Party. This development, though, can be seen as, in part, a reaction to their growing exclusion from political influence due to the militarisation of the South African state machine.

Thus it can be concluded that the debate on reform in the early 1980s has been to a considerable degree pre-empted by the growth in military power in the workings of the South African state. This has led some analysts to see the emergence of an alternative system of government under the control of the State Security Council.[98] The National Security Management System has effectively stymied the input from the civilian intellectuals and the pace of reform has come to be dictated by the logic of counter-insurgency strategy. As Philip Frankel has pointed out, the South African military does not as yet have a very sophisticated group of intellectuals, who have tended to draw in a very derivative fashion on an eclectic group of counter-insurgency theorists from Britain, France and the United States.[99] While the military probably favours some new political initiatives, they tend to lack any coherent programme and their domination also provides an umbrella for the protection of highly conservative groups who stand to lose from too hasty a reform programme, such as middle-ranking civil servants and state personnel. Even before the May 1987 election, government ministers had been vocal in condemning projects such as the proposed Natal Indaba: for Stoffel Botha, the Home Affairs Minister, this represented the 'domination' of the Zulu over the minorities.[100] This attempt to appease far right-wing opinion was further reinforced by P. W. Botha's backtracking on earlier hints at reform of the Group Areas Act. He committed himself in November 1986 to the continuation of the principle of separate residential areas in cities for different racial groups.[101]

In many ways, therefore, the South African state and its bureaucratic-military apparatus has strengthened the ideological tenets of apartheid. Far from leading to a major break with the past, the debate on 'change' in the early 1980s was much in keeping with previous fluid periods in South African politics. It has not led to a new political strategy which breaks with the dominant pattern of racial segregation, but to its entrenchment, with a rigid authoritarian resistance to any political reform which would undermine white power and privilege.

This suggests a number of points which are relevant to the Johnson thesis. First, ideological ferment amongst whites does not on its own bring South Africa to a Rubicon, for political debate about 'change' fails to break substantially with the dominant paradigm of racial segregationism. At the level of ideological discourse, therefore, the system of white political supremacy is not being impugned by political reform, even if it is by other factors. At the structural level, the state has the capacity to survive for a long time yet. However, paradoxically, given the variety of forces pushing toward a qualitative shift in the distribution of political power, the state is also incapable of strengthening itself via reform. This chapter has shown that the ideological framework within which the state conceives of reform simultaneously strengthens and weakens the system of white political supremacy. The state's doctrines of 'change' protect it from engaging in sufficient reform to threaten white control of political power, while also denying it the capacity to implement reforms of such vision that they will dampen the pressure for fundamental change in South Africa.

Notes

* I am grateful to the British Academy and the Leverhulme Trust for providing grants for the research on which this chapter is based.

1. London, Macmillan, 1977.
2. Ruan Maud, 'The Future of an Illusion: The Myth of White Meliorism

in South Africa', in Adrian Leftwich (ed.), *South Africa*, London, Allison and Busby, 1974, p. 309.

3. See, for instance, R. W. Rose-Innes, *The Glen Grey Act and the Native Question*, Lovedale, 1903, pp. 33–4; Howard Pim, *The Question of Race*, Johannesburg, 1906.
4. John Dunn, 'Social Theory, Social Understanding and Political Action', in Christopher Lloyd (ed.), *Social Theory and Social Practice*, Oxford, Clarendon Press, 1983, pp. 109–35.
5. Andre du Toit, 'Ideological Change, Afrikaner Nationalism and Pragmatic Racial Domination in South Africa', in Leonard Thompson and Jeffrey Butler (eds), *Change in Contemporary South Africa*, Berkeley, University of California Press, 1975, p. 38.
6. See, for example, Martin Legassick, 'Legislation, Ideology and Economy in Post 1948 South Africa', *Journal of Southern African Studies*, I, 1974, pp. 5–35.
7. Susan Rennie Ritner, 'The Dutch Reformed Church and Apartheid', *Journal of Contemporary History*, 2, 4, October 1967, pp. 17–37; Brian M. du Toit, 'Missionaries, Anthropologists and the Policies of the Dutch Reformed Church', *The Journal of Modern African Studies*, 22, 4, 1984, pp. 617–32.
8. Archibald Colquhoun, *The Afrikaner Land*, London, 1906, p. 10.
9. W. F. Bailey, 'Native and White in South Africa', *The Nineteenth Century*, February 1906, p. 329.
10. A. F. H. Duncan, 'British South Africa and the Native Problem', *The African Monthly*, March 1908, p. 383.
11. Fred W. Bell, *The South African Native Problem: A Suggested Solution*, Transvaal, Central News Agency, 1909, p. 9. For an analysis of this debate on the Witwatersrand, see Martin Legassick, 'The Making of South African "Native Policy", 1903–1923: The Origins of Segregation', London, ICS seminar paper, 1972; 'British Hegemony and the Origins of Segregation, 1900–1914', ibid., 1973.
12. Lord Selborne, Address delivered at the University of the Cape of Good Hope, 27 February 1909, Cape Town, 1909, p. 10.
13. Ibid., p. 18.
14. Ibid., p. 17.
15. Fred W. Bell, *The Black Vote: South Africa's Greatest Problem*, Johannesburg, 1909.
16. Paul B. Rich, 'Milnerism and a Ripping Yarn: Transvaal Land Settlement and John Buchan's novel *Prester John*, 1901–1910', in Belinda Bozzoli (ed.), *Town and Countryside in the Transvaal*, Johannesburg, Ravan Press, 1983, pp. 412–13.
17. John Cell, *The Highest Stage of White Supremacy: The Origins of Segregation in South Africa and the American South*, Cambridge, Cambridge University Press, 1984. See also Saul Dubow, 'Race, Civilisation and Culture: the elaboration of segregationist discourse in the inter-war years' in Shula Marks and Stanley Trofido (eds) *The Politics of Race, Class and Nationalism in Twentieth Century South Africa*, London, Longman, 1987, pp. 71–94.
18. *The Transvaal Leader*, 15 October 1909. Howard Pim was also critical of

Bell's views, having been in 1903–5 an enthusiast of strict segregation. He argued that Bell's ideal would mean a diminution of the black labour supply and there could be no 'fixed solution' to the 'native question'. 'In human affairs', he went on, '"all is flux", and to settle once and for all a society and a form of government which will meet for all time the needs of two widely differing races passes the wit of man', *The State*, January 1910, p. 30.

19. F. W. Bell Papers, Church of the Province Archives, University of the Witwatersrand, F. W. Bell to J. B. M. Hertzog, 19 September 1911.
20. J. R. H. Davenport, *South Africa: A Modern History*, Johannesburg, Macmillan, 1977, p. 332.
21. Paul B. Rich, *Race and Empire in British Politics*, Cambridge, Cambridge University Press, 1986, pp. 29–33.
22. Richard Elphick, 'Mission Christianity and Interwar liberalism', unpublished paper presented to a Conference on South African Liberalism, Houws Hoek, Cape Town, April 1986.
23. H. H. Johnston, 'South African Interest in South Africa', *The African Monthly*, 1, V, February 1907, pp. 259–65.
24. *Report of the Economic Commission*, UG-21, 1914, pp. 38–9.
25. Maurice Evans, *Black and White in the Southern States*, 1913, p. 235.
26. *The Star*, 14 April 1919. See also Peter Walshe, *The Rise of African Nationalism in South Africa*, London, C. Hurst, 1970.
27. *The Highest Stage of White Supremacy*, p. 18.
28. Gareth Stedman Jones, *Outcast London*, Harmondsworth, Penguin, 1976.
29. Rodney Davenport, 'The Triumph of Colonel Stallard: The Transformation of the Natives (Urban Areas) Act between 1923 and 1937', *South African Historical Journal*, LXXI, 1972, pp. 360–88.
30. David Yudelman, *The Emergence of Modern South Africa*, Cape Town, David Philip, 1984, p. 261.
31. Adrienne Bird, 'The Adult Night School Movement for Blacks on the Witwatersrand, 1920–1980', in Peter Kollaway (ed.), *Apartheid and Education*, Johannesburg, Ravan Press, 1984, pp. 192–221.
32. *The Rise of African Nationalism in South Africa*, pp. 230–1; R. Morrell, 'Nipping a Little Game in the Bud: Pixley Ka Izaka Seme, Land Purchase and Rural Differentiation in the Eastern Transvaal, c. 1910–1920', History Workshop Paper, University of the Witwatersrand, 9–13 February 1987.
33. *Abantu Batho*, 26 May 1931.
34. Michael L. Morris, 'The Development of Capitalism in South African Agriculture: Class Struggle in the Countryside', *Economy and Society*, 5, 1979, pp. 292–343.
35. *Race and Empire in British Politics*, pp. 72–73; Paul B. Rich, 'Industrialisation, Fabianism and Race: Sydney Olivier and the liberal critique of South African segregation', London, ICS, seminar paper, 1984.
36. John Kirk, *The Economic Aspects of Native Segregation in South Africa*, London, P. S. King and Sons, 1929, pp. 82–3.
37. Ibid., pp. 122–3.
38. Ray E. Phillips, *The Bantu are Coming*, London, SCM, 1930, p. 76.

39. W. M. Macmillan, *Complex South Africa*, London, Faber and Faber, 1930; Paul B. Rich, 'W. M. Macmillan, South African Segregation and Commonwealth Race Relations, 1919–1938', in Shula Marks and Hugh Macmillan (eds), *W. M. Macmillan: Historian, Thinker and Social Activist*, London, M. Temple Smith (forthcoming).
40. *Report of the Native Economic Commission*, UG22-1932, p. 13; Paul B. Rich, *White Power and the Liberal Conscience: Racial Segregation and South African Liberalism, 1921–1960*, Manchester, Manchester University Press, 1984, pp. 58–63.
41. See, for example, H. R. Abercrombie, who argued for a strategy of major racial engineering since, 'In Africa the Nordics may yet renew themselves and reverse for some considerable time the decadence which is apparent in some quarters. This can be done by physical efficiency and scientific planning', H. R. Abercrombie, *Africa's Peril: the Colour Problem*, London, Marsham Simpkin (1938?), p. 216. The author was a former president in the Transvaal Agricultural Union.
42. W. A. Russell, *European Versus Bantu*, Cape Town, Marshall Miller (1928?), p. 6.
43. Stephen Jay Gould, *The Mismeasurement of Man*, New York, W. W. Norton, 1981.
44. Leonard Thompson, *The Political Mythology of Apartheid*, New Haven, Yale University Press, 1985.
45. *Race and Empire in British Politics*, pp. 114–19.
46. *Heaton Nicholls Papers*, MS Nic. 2.08 1 f.3 unpub ms. n.d., cited in Shula Marks, *The Ambiguities of Dependence in South Africa*, Johannesburg, Ravan Press, 1986, pp. 40–1.
47. R. F. A. Hoernle, *South African Native Policy and the Liberal Spirit*, Cape Town, Oxford University Press, 1939, p. 168; *White Power and the Liberal Conscience*, pp. 66–9.
48. Paul B. Rich, 'Liberalism and Ethnicity in South African Politics, 1921–1948', *African Studies*, 34, 3–4, 1976, pp. 167–80.
49. Leonard Thompson, 'The Parting of the Ways in South Africa', in P. Clifford and R. Louis (eds), *The Transfer of Power in Africa: Decolonization, 1940–60*, New Haven, Yale University Press, 1982, pp. 417–45.
50. Ken Jubbe, 'The Prodigal Church: South Africa's Dutch Reformed Church And Apartheid Policy', *Social Compass*, 2–3, 1985, p. 281.
51. *Natal Mercury*, 28 September 1948.
52. *The Forum*, 22 April 1950.
53. *The Forum*, 1 April 1950. See Paul B. Rich, 'Liberalism and Ethnicity in South African Politics'.
54. *The Emergence of Modern South Africa*, pp. 240–43.
55. *The Manufacturer*, October 1950. See also Legassick, 'Legislation, Ideology and Political Economy'.
56. *The Manufacturer*, July 1954. It is thus hard to accept Herman Giliomee's assertion in 1982 that in the early 1980s a 'new ideology of growth' had now replaced apartheid 'as the dominant panacea', *The Parting of the Ways*, Cape Town, David Philip, 1982, p. 103.
57. W. E. Barker, 'Apartheid: The Only Solution', *Journal of Racial Affairs*, 1, 1, September 1948, pp. 24–38. See also L. E. Neame, *White Man's*

Africa, Stewart, 1952, p. 62, arguing for a similar idea of 'Separation' on the basis of R. F. A. Hoernle's arguments.

58. Quintin Whyte, *Apartheid and Other Policies*, Johannesburg, SAIRR, 1948, p. 20. See also Q. Whyte, *Go Forward in Faith*, Johannesburg, SAIRR, 1954.
59. Ellen Hellman, *In Defence of a Shared Society*, Johannesburg, SAIRR, 1956, p. 3; 'The Racial Problem in South Africa', *The Listener*, 12 July 1956.
60. *The Government's White Paper on the Development of Bantu Areas*, Fact Paper No. 10, Pretoria, 1956, p. 2.
61. See *The Manufacturer*, May 1956.
62. *Report of the Department of Native Affairs, 1954–1957*, UG14-'59, p. 48.
63. 'The Parting of the Ways', pp. 427–9. Thompson admits though that 'the utopian vision that had inspired Afrikaner intellectuals in the first flush of their 1948 victory had faded by 1960' (p. 429).
64. Philip Frankel, *Pretoria's Praetorians*, Cambridge, Cambridge University Press, 1984.
65. Trevor Huddleston, *Naught For Your Comfort*, London, Collins, 1956.
66. Jaap Durand, 'Afrikaner Piety and Dissent', in Charles Villa-Vicencio and John W. de Gruchy (eds), *Resistance and Hope: South African Essays in honour of Beyers Naude*, Cape Town, David Philip, 1985, pp. 39–51; See also Dunbar T. Moodie, *The Rise of Afrikanerdom*, Berkeley, University of California Press, 1975.
67. *Report of the Multi-Racial Conference*, University of the Witwatersrand, 3–5 December 1957, Johannesburg, The Planning Committee, 1957.
68. Z. K. Matthews, 'Political Arrangements in a Multi-Racial Society', paper presented to Multi-Racial Conference, pp. 1–4.
69. Alan Paton, 'Civil Rights in a Multi-Racial Society', paper presented to Multi-Racial Conference.
70. G. A. Mbeki, 'Economic Rights and Duties in a Multi-Racial Society', paper presented to Multi-Racial Conference.
71. *Quintin Whyte Papers*, Church of the Province Archives, University of the Witwatersrand, AD 1502/Bb3, Notes of Meeting with Chief Luthuli, Professor Z. K. Matthews, Mr Joe Matthews and Mr Ncwana, n.d.
72. *F. van Wyk Papers*, Church of the Province Archives, University of the Witwatersrand, AD 1752/3Bo42, Lex Van Wijk to F. van Wyk, 25 May 1960, encl 'Notes on thinking about race problems in the Ned Geref. Kerk' (marked 'confidential'); Ben Marais to F. Van Wyk, 31 October 1960 encl 'Further Notes by Prof. B. Marais'.
73. Ben Marais, *The Two Faces of Africa*, Pietermaritzburg, Shuter and Shooter, 1964, p. 37. For the divisions over Cotteslsoe see David Bosch, 'The Fragmentation of Afrikanerdom and the Afrikaner Churches', in *Resistance and Hope*, pp. 68–71.
74. AD1502, Ba5, Quintin Whyte, 'The Relevance of Transkeian Development to Race Relations in South Africa', Johannesburg, SAIRR, paper No. 94/63, 1963.
75. The term 'pragmatic liberalism' comes from Charles Simkins, *Reconstructing South African Liberalism*, Johannesburg, SAIRR, 1984. For the development of Spro-Cas see Peter Walshe, *Church versus State in South*

Africa: The Case of the Christian Institute, London, C. Hurst, 1983, pp. 102–23.

76. C. W. de Kiewiet, 'The World and Pretoria', *Virginia Quarterly Review*, 45, 1, Winter 1969, p. 5.
77. 'Unmasking Neo-Apartheid', *Third World Quarterly*, 83, July 1986.
78. Kogila Moodley, 'The Legitimation Crisis of the South African State', *The Journal of Modern African Studies*, 24, 2, 1986, pp. 188–90.
79. Joseph Lelyveld, *Move Your Shadow: South Africa, Black and White*, New York, Times Books, 1985, p. 37.
80. Vernon Van Dyke, 'The Individual, the State and Ethnic Communities in Political Theory', *World Politics*, 29, 3, April 1979, p. 367.
81. This is the general argument of Merle Lipton who has suggested that 'neither the dry class categories of the Marxists, nor the tortuous race categories of the pluralists, seem able to contain the force and complexity – and yet instability – of this combination of ethnicity, class and kinship', *Capitalism and Apartheid*, London, Wildwood House, 1985, p. 290. Later, though she argues, in the light of the ethnic mobilisation of groups like Inkatha that 'ethnicity . . . remained a powerful force which could not simply be manipulated by the SA government nor ignored by black nationalists' (p. 359).
82. Spro-Cas, *South Africa's Political Alternatives*, Johannesburg, Ravan Press, 1981 (first edition 1973), p. 217.
83. Ibid., p. 221–42.
84. Heribert Adam, 'Outside Influences on South Africa: Afrikanerdom in Disarray', *The Journal of Modern African Studies*, 21, 1, 1983, pp. 235–51.
85. Heribert Adam, 'Survival Politics: Afrikanerdom in Search of a New Ideology', *The Journal of Modern African Studies*, 16, 4, 1978, pp. 657–69; 'When the chips are Down: Confrontation and Accommodation in South Africa', *Contemporary Crises*, 1, 1977, pp. 417–35. 'Mere survival ideology', remark Adam and Moodley, 'represents the lowest common denominator of a divided ruling class in crisis', Heribert Adam and Kogila A. Moodley, *South Africa Without Apartheid*, Berkeley, University of California Press, 1986, p. 72.
86. Arend Lijphart, 'Majority Rule Versus Democracy in Deeply Divided Societies', in Nic Rhoodie (ed.), *Intergroup Accommodation in Plural Societies*, London, Macmillan for the Institute for Plural Societies, University of Pretoria, 1978, p. 35; L. Schlemmer, 'The Plural Devolution of Power' in ibid.
87. Ibid., W. F. de Klerk, 'South Africa's Domestic Politics: Key Questions and Options'.
88. Arend Lijphart, 'Federal, Confederal and Consociational Options for the South African Plural Society', in Robert I. Rotberg and John Barratt (eds), *Conflict and Compromise in South Africa*, Cape Town, David Philip, 1980, p. 51.
89. Arend Lijphart, *Power Sharing in South Africa*, Berkeley, Institute of International Studies, 1985, p. 106. Elsewhere, though, we are told that 'it is important to understand that consociationalism deals with the

potential problems of a plural society not by trying to make the society less plural, but by making it more plural – at least initially' (p. 106).

90. Much of Lijphart's analysis is weakened by a shallow knowledge of South African history and politics. Thus we read that 'In South Africa the Tswanas and Ndebeles have fellow ethnics (*sic*) in Botswana and Zimbabwe respectively', thus revealing an understanding of South African 'ethnicity' little different to the present government spokesmen, ibid., p. 124. Similarly we are told that 'In comparison with Lebanon and Malaysia, the political leadership in South Africa is more instead of less culturally homogeneous because it is largely Westernised', ibid., p. 129. Apart from begging the question of the meaning of being 'Westernised' this fatuous statement overlooks the role of the Afrikaner extreme right in mobilising Afrikaner 'ethnic' opinion as well as the question of black political leadership groupings such as Inkatha.
91. Ibid., p. 130.
92. Paul B. Rich, 'R. F. A. Hoernle, Idealism and the Liberal Response to South African Segregation', paper presented to South African History Workshop, Wesleyan University, April 1986.
93. Heribert Adam and Kogila Moodley, "A Plural or a Common Society in South Africa', *Queens Quarterly*, 92, 1985, p. 697; *South Africa Without Apartheid*, pp. 207–10.
94. Theodor Hanf, Heribert Weiland and Gerda Vierdag, *South Africa: The Prospects of Peaceful Change*, London, Rex Collins, p. 411.
95. *Move Your Shadow*, p. 65.
96. Alf Stadler, *The Political Economy of Apartheid*, London, Croom Helm, 1987, pp. 88–93.
97. *South Africa Without Apartheid*, pp. 73–76.
98. *Guardian*, 3 October 1986.
99. Philip Frankel, *Pretoria's Praetorians*, op. cit.
100. *Independent*, 2 December 1986.
101. *Independent*, 24 November 1986.

13 Political Impasse in South Africa: State Capacities and Crisis Management*

Mark Mitchell and Dave Russell

INTRODUCTION

Any reassessment of Johnson's arguments must address the issue of the capacity of a state to survive. However, political research into the policies and activities of the South African state has consistently failed to offer any detailed 'balance sheet' of the strengths and weaknesses displayed by the state in its fight for survival. We believe that there is an urgent need to re-route research on the South African state in this direction. A better understanding of the South African state and its future prospects requires a much closer examination of the capabilities and resources of the state itself. In the past there has been insufficient consideration given to the reasons for the increasing incapacity of the South African state to implement effectively its own 'strategy for survival'. There is a need to focus on those factors that limit the ability of the South African state to formulate and pursue policies necessary for effective 'crisis-management'; only then will it be possible to assess the state's capacity to deal with these factors. This would appear to be a necessary prerequisite for understanding the current political impasse in South Africa, an impasse brought about through the inability of the state to re-impose control from above and the failure of the opposition forces to seize power from below.

STATE THEORY AND THE SOUTH AFRICAN STATE

Since the 1970s, when the concept of the state re-emerged from the shadows in social science, an increasing number of researchers have rejected grand theorising about 'the capitalist state' in favour of a more grounded approach anchored in the empirical examination of different states in their own historical settings.[1] This kind of reorientation in state theory and research, principally based on a welcome rapprochement between neo-Marxism and more traditional Weberian political sociology, has developed from a growing awareness of a number of serious deficiencies in various established approaches to the analysis of the state. We believe that many analyses of policy-making and social change in South Africa are similarly deficient, including Johnson's. Therefore, any attempt to provide a more adequate account of the unique South African state–society relationship, must move beyond the current limitations of research on the South African state.

Much of the standard literature on the state in South Africa and elsewhere appears to be deficient in four crucial respects. Firstly a great deal of work on the state is based on a 'society-centred' approach to state activities and policies which in practice accords little or no autonomy to the state itself. The customary analytical ploy is to view the state, and all that it does, either as the product of societal needs or as a reflection of the competing demands of social groups or classes. Such an approach is, of course, rife within most variants of pluralism and in all varieties of Marxism, where the common tendency is to overlook or even deny the potential that all states possess for genuine autonomous action. Secondly, society-centred theories are generally inclined to operate with an 'internalist' conception of the state which fails to recognise that the activities of any state are also rooted in international pressures and conditions.[2] Simple internalist accounts seriously neglect the extent to which the organisation and power of any state is shaped by its relations with other nation states and by its geopolitical position within an international system of competing states.

Thirdly, many recent contributions to state theory and research have tended to play down the key role performed by the state's coercive apparatuses in the establishment and maintenance of state power. Instead, right across the theoretical spectrum, the emphasis has been on the consensual dimensions of political rule, in which the authority or legitimacy of the state is seen as the cornerstone of state power. In this way, recent state theory has emphasised the 'problem of legitimacy' at the expense of giving due consideration to the state's vitally important coercive capabilities. Fourthly, in much of the literature, the state tends to appear as a kind of 'black box', that reorganises and processes 'inputs' of various kinds in an invisible and ultimately mysterious manner. Little attention is paid to the specific organisational structures of particular states or to the different capacities and resources states

MAGDALEN COLLEGE LIBRARY

possess for exercising authoritative political rule. Furthermore, such an approach appears to be premised upon the dubious implicit assumption that states necessarily exhibit a high degree of internal organisational unity. This fails to recognise that the level of institutional coherence inside any state is both a highly contingent matter, and something that is critically important in determining the state's political effectiveness.[3]

It is our contention that most explanations of the policies and activities of the South African state have been predominantly society-centred, although some writers have been more willing in the recent past to shift in the direction of state-centred analytical strategies.[4] Without doubt, deep-rooted society-centred assumptions have underlain much of the social science debate about South Africa. For example, such assumptions are in essence held in common by both camps in the long-running argument over whether the apartheid state has been shaped by economic and class interests, or whether it is the product of the mobilisation of ethnic power.[5] Furthermore, both sides have continued to emphasise the societal determinants of the recent policy shifts forced upon the South African state. That is, despite the fact that much more complex, sophisticated analyses are now available (analyses that look in part at the internal structure and operation of the South African state system), relatively little systematic attention has been given to the study of the state's ability to formulate and pursue its own policies in a hostile domestic and international environment. Recent analyses of the process of 'reform from above' in South Africa have paid relatively little attention to the question of whether political rulers in Pretoria possess the resources necessary to secure their official goals in the face of economic crisis and against the mounting opposition of an array of social groups. Instead the primary focus of research has been on the manner in which changing state policy and practice have been the outcome of societal pressures exerted by a variety of class and ethnic forces.[6] In departing from prevailing society-centred approaches, we insist that more needs to be understood about the patterns of organisation through which demands are shaped, and more knowledge is required of the institutional structures through which policy is formulated and implemented. The analysis of the interplay of ethnic and class interests remains vital but it must be expanded to incorporate a systematic investigation of the institutional structures through which demands are shaped and power is determined. What follows is an attempt to show how such an analysis can provide the basis for an understanding of the current political impasse in South Africa.

BRINGING THE SOUTH AFRICAN STATE BACK IN

It is time for the problem of 'state autonomy' to be taken far more seriously in the debate about South Africa. This theoretical innovation must start from the neo-Weberian assumption that all states have some potential for the pursuit of autonomous action.[7] In the South African context, this means that more attention should be given to the ability of state controllers and bureaucratic officials to pursue goals at odds with those of both the dominant classes and the subordinate social groups.

In effect the South African state – or at least key parts within it – has been able to formulate strategic objectives not only against the wants and demands of a subordinate black population but also at variance with the wishes of key economic interests within the privileged white minority. Furthermore the evidence suggests that the autonomous power traditionally located in the coercive and administrative apparatuses of the state has been vitally enhanced in the present atmosphere of crisis in South Africa. The overwhelming need to preserve internal order and political stability has initiated an all-out drive to secure the state's own military-inspired strategic objectives. It is the rise of military power and influence, together with the militarisation of policy processes, that constitute the decisive feature of the autonomous state action now being taken in the pursuit of domestic order and national security – currently the government's highest political goals.

This concern with the question of the state's ability to impose itself on South African society, taken in conjunction with our support for Skocpol's plea to 'bring the state back in', may well be viewed with some irony by sceptical critics who remember the place of the state in 'plural society' theory in days gone by. It will be recalled that earlier theorists like Kuper placed an emphasis on the primary and independent role of the state in structuring ethnic relations in so-called plural societies like South Africa.[8] However, whilst we do wish to emphasise the potential of any state for independent action, we are also anxious to avoid the pitfalls of state-centric theory.[9] Simply to argue that the state is responsible for political outcomes ignores important questions about why and how particular strategies and policies are formulated. Moreover state-centric theories also fail to consider the factors affecting whether or not any particular state is capable of achieving the implementation of its declared aims.

The way to avoid the shortcomings of both state-centred and society-centred approaches is to focus on the dynamic nature of the state-society relationship. We advocate the adoption of a relational approach which is founded upon the assumption that all states are constrained and shaped to some extent by the social relations that surround them, and by the specific constellation of international and national pressures which confront any state.[10] In turn, state power may always be utilised to organise and intervene in different areas of socioeconomic life. State power therefore often needs to be mobilised – with varying degrees of success – against the opposition of powerful social groups and in the face of adverse international and national conditions. However the empirical study of specific states in their own socioeconomic contexts cannot be advanced simply by emphasising the relational nature of states. Rather, satisfactory progress can most effectively be made by pursuing three specific lines of inquiry. Firstly, we need to introduce the notion of 'state capacities'.[11] The formulation and pursuit of strategic objectives, together with the success or failure of various policy initiatives, depends to an important extent on the state's own capacities, and in particular on its own institutional resources and internal organisation.

Secondly, proper weight must be given in the study of state capacities to the nature and character of institutional structures beyond the confines of the state. As one writer puts it, 'the capacities of a state to implement a programme tend to depend as much on the configuration of society as of the state'.[12] Applied to South Africa, this approach demands something more than a consideration of the constraints imposed by dominant collectivities (for example the recalcitrance of the big corporations with respect to the decentralisation programme), and by political opponents (most obviously, spiralling black protest since 1976). It also points to the relevance of examining the organisational and ideological character of the assorted intermediary organisations representative of particular economic interests.[13] (For example 'peak associations' of capital and labour acting as intermediaries between their members and the state.) Research in this direction might provide some answers to questions about the quality and effectiveness of the state's extensive economic interventions in the economy.

For example, the state appears to lack access to an institutional network appropriate for the growth of new corporatist forms of economic intervention based on the incorporation of independently-formed organised producer interests. This assessment applies both to the 'new wave' black trade unions which the Botha government has so far been unable to coopt or regulate, and also to those employers' organisations still firmly set apart from the governing institutions of the state. The inability of the South African state to develop corporatist arrangements for the implementation of economic policies has in effect served to perpetuate – to its own cost – a reliance on structurally deficient modes of bureaucratic intervention.[14]

Thirdly, following on from this, a critical examination must be undertaken of the important ways in which political forces and a variety of social struggles in South African society are themselves partly an outcome of the institutional structures of the state.[15] Over the years the South African state has, of course, prohibited and actively discouraged the authentic representation of subordinate group interests in its policy processes and political decision-making. In this way the state's own structures and activities have shaped a political culture of black politics that is itself inimical to the success of the new collaborative machinery being created for the co-optation of black politicians and trade union leaders. The failure of the Botha government's attempt to impose control over the emerging black trade unions via its controversial labour reforms is not surprising.[16] Thus in certain crucial respects, the South African state is a prisoner of its own history, since many of the political impediments to the development of new forms of economic intervention and representation have long been of its own making.

Any assessment of the prospects for the survival of white rule in South Africa for the foreseeable future must focus on the capacities and weaknesses of the South African state.[17] The enduring strength of the South African state is strikingly evident in the development of its formidable coercive and administrative powers to organise the population along 'racial' lines and to secure the compliance of many groups and individuals within the dominated sectors of society. In fact, Pretoria has been increasingly ready and able to turn to an expanding set of military/security apparatuses in order to safeguard the political domination of the beleaguered South African state. It is because of the military resources and coercive capabilities of the well-armed South African state that we have previously concluded that it is a mistake to over-exaggerate the vulnerability of the South African state at this point in time.[18] The coercive apparatuses appear thus far to be capable of imposing political rule and preserving white security. Indeed recent developments tend to confirm the view that the South African state possesses a capacity for much greater repression than has been evident in the past.

Nevertheless, the survival capacities of the South African state do not – and cannot – depend on coercive strength and military might alone. Consideration must also be given to the economic and political resources at the disposal of the South African state. In terms of economic strength, it is apparent that South Africa's political rulers have the ability to mobilise significant economic resources – both internally and regionally – in pursuance of their strategic objectives. Internally the South African state has developed over the years important instruments for controlling some of the 'commanding heights' of the economy. These include the existence of a large 'parastatal' sector, as well as a galaxy of economic controls designed to aid the state's search for greater national economic self-sufficiency. Regionally, South Africa's great economic strength in relation to neighbouring southern African countries continues to be of immense significance. The regional power of the South African state to exploit and expand its economic superiority over competing states in the region is undoubtedly a vital economic weapon in its armoury. Furthermore Pretoria's capacity to make political capital out of this regional dependency on the South African economy by concluding 'non-aggression pacts' and ceasefire agreements in exchange for economic aid and co-operation, constitutes another very important resource.

However, any appraisal of South African state power must highlight some of its crucial weaknesses. First, and foremost, state power in South Africa is marked by its chronic and complete inability to generate any widespread popular consent for its political rule. Any hopes that the economic and political reforms of the 'total strategy' might provide a basis for generating wider internal support for the state have by now been effectively dashed. The South African state is capable of securing sustained legitimation only from those privileged minority groups that it benefits directly and, given the balance of political forces inside South Africa, it appears to have little capacity to effect a dramatic transformation in this situation. But whilst the incapacities of the South African state tend to revolve around this fundamental structural weakness – the 'institutionalisation of legitimation crisis' – we believe that other peculiar weaknesses also need to be recognised.[19]

The capacity of any state to initiate and implement its plans and policies is dependent on three interrelated factors. In the first place it depends upon the extent to which the state can coordinate its organisational resources in a relatively coherent and unified manner in the pursuit of realistic goals that command a high level of support inside the state. Secondly, it is dependent on the organisational configuration of social and political forces in the wider society, forces which in turn are partly shaped and conditioned by the policies and practices of the state itself. Thus the implementation of policy initiatives depends crucially on the ability of the state to enlist at least the tacit support of a range of strategically significant groups in society and to mobilise *their* organisational resources in the pursuit of the state's own objectives. Thirdly, this relational interplay between state and society in the policy process necessarily takes place within the framework of a wider international context whose effects may seriously circumscribe the ability of any state to secure its goals. To some extent states are inevitably 'hemmed in' by a range of transnational pressures and forces over which they can exercise only limited control. Below we attempt to assess the relative significance of these three factors in the South African context in order to arrive at an overall assessment of the capacities of the South African state for policy formation and implementation, and hence its capacity for survival.

THE INTERNAL ORGANISATION OF THE SOUTH AFRICAN STATE

The effective exercise of state power is always influenced by the extent to which there is internal unity within any state system.[20] We agree with Johnson that the National Party regime in South Africa has been characterised by a relatively high degree of internal unity and that this has enhanced its ability to impose white minority rule. However, there have been some important changes in the means by which this relative unity has been preserved since 1948, as has been shown in an earlier chapter.

The onset in the mid-1970s of the current crisis facing the South African state precipitated a reorganisation of its machinery. The subsequent militarisation of the state since 1978, and the emergence of a highly autonomous executive exercising an increased level of direction and control over state activities, represents a profoundly important development that has changed the face of state power in South Africa.[21] This reorganisation of the state and other innovations in state activities flow from a dominant political logic which calls for a 'total war' to be waged against 'national enemies' and hostile forces inside and outside South Africa's borders. In our opinion these developments have affected the capacities of the South African state in a least two important ways. Firstly, they have increased the autonomous power of the state to initiate and pursue its own policies. Rather than political decision-making becoming more sensitive to key economic interests, the state's structures and activities have in some important ways become more insulated from societal pressures. This trend towards increasing 'state autonomy' has been marked by a significant loosening of the longstanding ties between the state and the various organised ethnic interests of white labour and capital. It has also been characterised by the failure of the Botha government's economic and political reforms to build effective institutional 'pathways' through which other organised interests could be drawn into vital economic policy processes. Instead the cultivation of a garrison-state mentality has served to enhance the power and influence of the military establishment. Further, these organisational changes have reinforced the South African state's traditional capacity for strategic planning. However the increasing subordination of policy formulation to military-bureaucratic needs has so far failed to guarantee either the coherence or the successful implementation of new policy initiatives. In practice therefore the so-called total strategy has turned out to be more of a total shambles![22]

It should be stressed that certain basic aspects of the internal organisation of the South African state have been characterised by a high degree of continuity since 1948. Thus the relative unity inside the state has been maintained and the National Party has managed to retain overall control of the state itself. Nevertheless at the same time there has been a substantial reorganisation of the institutional structures and activities of the state – especially since P. W. Botha came to power in September 1978.[23] In turn this recasting of the state has significantly accelerated changes in the established organisational relationships between an assortment of ethnically mobilised Afrikaner groups inside and outside the state.

The ruling National Party no longer dominates the state machine in the same way nor does the bureaucracy perform the unifying role that it once did. For most of the post-1948 period an 'elective dictatorship' of the National Party, together with a high degree of cohesion within the political executive, were the decisive features of Afrikaner state control. In addition the government traditionally enjoyed the fruits of a close, collaborative relationship with a like-minded, ideologically-reliable state bureaucracy. Also the existence of close links between the government and certain Afrikaner producer groups in an ethnically-exclusive form of sectoral corporatism had the important effect of blurring some of the lines between the state and society.[24] These were smudged even more by the 'trafficking of top personnel' between different organisations inside and outside the state, and by the operation of a less formal organisational network of Afrikaner structures in and around the state.[25] In the favourable economic conditions of the 1950s and 1960s, this organisational configuration managed to produce a coherent set of official policy initiatives – deeply imprinted with the ideology of Afrikaner nationalism – that were then effectively implemented by a combination of coercive and legal-bureaucratic mechanisms.

However, since 1978 the nationalist strategy for survival has increasingly emphasised a process of militarisation in which the demands of 'total war' have been paramount. The development of a siege culture and the growing preoccupation with national security have in turn precipitated some very important changes inside the South African state. These have been characterised above all by the emergence of an invigorated, highly autonomous executive at the summit of a militarised South African state. In effect the restructuring of state power has shifted the focus of political decision-making away from the cabinet and the National Party towards new centralised state structures in which key military/security personnel play a crucial role.[26] One important outcome of this rationalisation programme has been the establishment of a new all-embracing 'national security management system' to guide the formulation and execution of wide areas of state policy.

At the peak of this stands the powerful State Security Council (SSC) which nowadays is the supreme decision-making institution inside the state. The SSC meets regularly under the chairmanship of President Botha and amongst its most important participants are senior representatives from the police, the military, and the security forces. It is responsible for the initiation of all strategic policies and in addition it coordinates and supervises the work of virtually all other departments of state through its chain of fifteen interdepartmental committees. Increasingly, the SSC has assumed responsibility for crucial issues like security, foreign policy, economic affairs and the formulation of the constitutional reform programme.[27] More specifically, the SSC is said to have been instrumental in the imposition of the states of emergency against the wishes of some leading members of the cabinet.[28] The SSC also directs and funds a nationwide network of Joint Management Centres (JMCs) charged with the coordination of security matters at the local and regional levels.[29] Each of the JMCs is composed of military and police leaders together with civil servants and representatives from local business, although the precise composition and functioning of these secret committees remains unclear.[30] Together with the concentration of power in the Presidential office itself and in key departments, like the Department of Constitutional Development and Planning, there has been a decisive shift of power towards the executive arm of the state. The restructuring process has produced what appears to be a much stronger, militarised political directorate that is more immune to political pressures from both inside and outside Afrikanerdom.

It would be wrong to conclude that this 'strengthening' of the state will necessarily ensure a more efficient administration and a tighter system of political control. Such a conclusion would merely reproduce the assumptions and beliefs of the South African military strategists themselves. Whilst it is true that the streamlining of state machinery has enhanced the state's coercive and administrative capabilities in vital ways, it has conspicuously failed to provide effective mechanisms for securing the successful implementation of the various policy initiatives that have come from above. Despite the reformist rhetoric, the new institutional structures of the state fail to provide any real channels for the sort of policy bargaining with organised producer interests that is the hallmark of economic policy-making in many other capitalist countries.[31] Indeed it can be argued that the reorganisation of the South African state has rendered it more rather than less insensitive to key organised interests which remain outside the state. Although a growing number of business representatives have been directly coopted into the state, and President Botha has attempted to engage in a dialogue with both the English-speaking and Afrikaans-speaking business communities, there has been an absence of corporatist arrangements for implementing the economic policies made within the new circles of power. The rationalisation of state structures has in effect redrawn the boundaries between the state and society in ways which have increased rather than eroded the autonomy of the state. In the final analysis the recent changes have served to reinforce rather than to diminish the South African state's lack of political and organisational resources for dealing with key strategic groups in its ailing economy.

Above all the 'survival politics' practised by the government are based on its steely determination to maintain white control of the state apparatuses at all costs. It is this that has led to the mobilisation of white South Africans for war, the militarisation of policy processes and intensified military activities inside and outside South Africa's borders. In this process the tendency has been for military/security priorities to win out over the needs of the economy. As a result the different parts of the state system are now held together less by the old 'tribal glue' and more by a new, Afrikaner version of command politics.

STATE–SOCIETY RELATIONS IN SOUTH AFRICA

Despite the fact that the South African state continues to exhibit a high degree of cohesion amongst its specific ensemble of institutions and organisations, this internal unity in and of itself is not a sufficient condition for effective political rule. The strength and effectiveness of any state depends not only upon internal factors but also on the interplay between internal and external circumstances, each of which conditions the other. Thus the South African state, largely because of its own history of exclusion and repression, lacks the societal resources that are necessary if the state is to intervene in society to secure its policy objectives. Consequently, despite a growing recognition of the need for new policy initiatives over a wide range of areas, the South African state has to a large extent been crippled by the degree of institutional and organisational incongruity underlying state–society relations in South Africa. As a result the state remains structurally remote from a number of strategically significant social groups and is restricted to bureaucratic and authoritarian modes of state intervention, since it lacks the mechanisms necessary for the deployment of more selective and sensitive interventionist strategies.[32] This 'lack of fit' between state and society has been intensified by the relentless drive to Afrikanerise the South African state, which has served to isolate government ministers and their senior advisers still further. Paradoxically, therefore, the ethnic exclusivity of the South African state is at one and at the same time both a source of strength and a source of weakness; for although it has sustained the high level of internal unity inside the state, it has also contributed to the state's relative isolation from those groups and interests with which it must engage if it is to develop effective policy responses to the Republic's economic and political problems.

The exclusive nature of 'insider' politics in South Africa and the limitations that have resulted from the largely self-imposed isolation of the state are in part counteracted by the peculiar form of 'commission politics' that is a central feature of South African political life.

Successive governments since 1948 have responded to the need for policy innovations by establishing commissions of enquiry which in effect serve to broaden the basis of political debate beyond the narrow confines of the National Party. However the autonomy and effectiveness of these commissions is severely limited in a number of ways. In the first place, politically reliable Afrikaners still dominate the membership of these commissions and invariably act as their chair. Secondly the membership of those commissions appears to be characterised by a relative absence of producer interests, in particular representatives of organised labour. Thirdly, as these commissions are only advisory, the government can choose to ignore their advice if the recommendations should prove to be unacceptable, as was shown in the case of the De Lange Commission in 1981.[33] Commission politics, therefore, does little to extend or deepen the basis of policy initiation and formulation in South Africa.

In recent years it is the area of economic policy that has been most obviously and adversely affected by the asymmetrical nature of state–society relations in South Africa. Since the early 1970s successive governments have attempted to introduce a range of new economic initiatives in an effort to revive the flagging fortunes of the South African economy. However, the state has been hampered in its attempts to advance policies for economic growth by the absence of strong unified organisations representing the interests of capital and labour. The lack of such centralised 'peak associations' has tended to undermine the effectiveness of these policy initiatives. In effect the state has lacked a set of clear and unambiguous 'pathways' via which producer groups can represent their interests to the state and by means of which the state can attempt to extend its own formal boundaries.

As far as business interests are concerned, the South African state is confronted by an array of ethnically divided organisations claiming to represent the interests of different fractions of capital, as well as by several traditionally powerful sectoral interest groups representing particular industries.[34] This has made it much more difficult for the state to develop close 'insider' links with such groups and to engage in formal and informal bargaining with their representatives.

In addition, important features of central economic management and planning have been persistently motivated by political rather than economic considerations, and largely retained in the face of strong opposition from various sectors of white capital. This is still the case despite moves towards new modes of economic management in recent years. With the support of financial and banking interests in particular the South African state has advanced new monetarist-type economic policies.[35] However South African-type free market policies have involved only a selective rolling-back of the state's economic interventions. The adoption of a 'market-orientated monetary strategy' has led to freer markets in money, finance and foreign exchange but has left intact crucial areas of apartheid state intervention. The contradictions and limitations of the much-vaunted 'return to free enterprise' are thus readily apparent. In turn these reflect the incapacity of the state to formulate and implement economic policies which can successfully reverse the downward trend in the economy and at the same time help to secure popular quiescence and political control. In fact it can be argued that the limited range of free market policies that have been applied so far have had disastrous economic and political effects.[36] In short 'monetarist' policy innovations not only exacerbated the post-1982 recession, they also failed to deal with the restrictions and regulations that are deeply embedded in the apartheid system.

To an important extent this inability to roll back state economic intervention is a consequence of the political priority given to national security and the need to re-impose political order. The escalating military/strategic demands of 'total war', for instance, have made it increasingly unrealistic for the state to surrender control over the 'commanding heights' of the economy. Indeed with 60 per cent of fixed capital assets in South Africa in the hands of the state or state corporations it has always been unlikely that the rhetoric of 'freeing' free enterprise could be effectively translated into reality in this respect.[37] Furthermore the new economic policies have seriously failed to control the spiralling fiscal costs of maintaining the apartheid system.[38] Sustained black political resistance has dramatically forced up the cost of maintaining apartheid. As a consequence state spending on repression and political control has escalated but so too has 'social expenses' expenditure aimed at supporting the living standards of the population.[39] In turn attempts by the state to limit 'social costs' by reducing subsidies or raising rents/fares have had the effect of fuelling further black protest.

Without doubt the state's inability to contain the high costs of preserving the apartheid system has been detrimental to economic growth.[40] Altogether we see little evidence to support Adam's contention that both Afrikaner and English capital share a common interest in 'growth at any cost' and that this is leading to 'bureaucratically unrestricted market exploitation' and to the 'ideologically unrestricted use of all available labour'.[41] Instead, politically-motivated economic policies remain which are strongly opposed by white capital. For example the industrial decentralisation policy, providing substantial incentives to those firms willing to relocate their businesses away from the traditional centres of economic growth and towards the Bantustans, remains deeply unpopular with the representatives of white business interests.[42]

Similarly, the influx control system has long been opposed by organised industry. However, both the industrial decentralisation and influx control policies have been significantly modified in recent years. To some extent these changes represent a more economically-orientated approach to problems of urbanisation and regional development, but economic considerations are still not paramount. The changes are in effect a response to the state's incapacity to stem the flow of industry and population to South Africa's metropolitan and commercial centres.[43] As a result, the traditional apartheid division between 'white' and Bantustan areas has been seriously eroded.

These developments are acknowledged by the state's new urban and regional strategy in which the traditional premises of 'grand apartheid' have been replaced by the concept of 'planned urbanisation'.[44] Acknowledging the inevitability of African urbanisation and the failure of the Riekert strategy to control it, the new initiatives officially accept the settlement of sections of the burgeoning African population in and around the cities. Crucially, the Regional Services Council Act has created new metropolitan areas with their own administrative and fiscal resources and which include African townships *within* Bantustans adjacent to 'white' areas. At the same time the state is trying to encourage the dispersal of capital and population in new ways. Firstly, within the highly industrialised metropolitan centres the state has created deconcentration areas. These areas are in the metropolitan peripheries and often straddle borders between Bantustans and 'white' areas. The aim is to relieve population pressures in the established townships within the core metropolitan areas by relocating homeless township families, squatter families and the like to these places. In order to provide employment opportunities in such areas industry and commerce are being tempted by a South African version of the 'enterprise zone' concept in which deconcentration points are exempt from the usual tax, wage and health regulations. Secondly, the industrial decentralisation policy has been adapted so as to offer inducements for capital to disperse to fewer, more favourable regional 'growth points'. Decentralisation no longer scatters industry to a wide range of border areas adjoining the Bantustans. Rather, the policy is now focused more selectively on designated towns with proven economic growth potential. The objective is better balanced regional development and the regime is attempting to secure this by attracting investment away from the established, highly industrialised regions towards newly-expanding ones based on selected major towns as the chosen 'growth points'. Significantly, the eight declared development regions correspond to changes in geographical patterns of capital location and labour settlement that have been developing since the late 1960s, rather than the politically-created Bantustan boundaries of traditional apartheid.

It should be noted that the state's urban and regional strategy only partially breaks with past political and ideological goals.[45] Neither has it achieved the desired positive response from the private sector. There is some truth in the official claim that since 1982 a stronger economic-related and market-directed approach has been applied but political/security considerations are still paramount. South Africa's political rulers are still primarily concerned to control the movement and settlement of the African population. The drive to promote 'orderly urbanisation' has not been dictated primarily by economic considerations but by the need to control the escalating migration of blacks to the urban areas and more specifically by the requirement to arrest the townships crisis. The previous Riekert strategy for dealing with the urbanisation problem – tightening up influx controls and dividing African 'urban insiders' from Bantustan 'outsiders' – palpably failed. Like Riekert, the new policy for 'planned urbanisation' inevitably involves strategies of exclusion: it remains to be seen whether it will afford the state any greater capacity for social control.

However, significant opposition to these policy initiatives has already emerged from within the ranks of industry and in general the private-sector response to the regional development programme has been mixed. Whilst some firms have responded to the decentralisation incentives, representatives of business interests have voiced strong criticism of the initiatives. The Federated Chamber of Industries (FCI), for instance, has argued the merits of free inter-regional competition over the induced dispersal policies.[46] The new fiscal controls designed to strengthen the tax base of the Regional Services Councils are also said to have 'elicited a howl of protest from organised commerce and industry'.[47] Altogether the evidence suggests that the updated industrial decentralisation and influx control policies have been devised and implemented with limited reference to organised capitalist interests.

Thus the recent history of state-capital relations in South Africa is complicated by a recurring tendency for the 'needs of the economy' to be subordinated to political/strategic requirements, a trend that has been accentuated by the growing militarisation of the South African state. However, parallel developments in state–labour relations, are if anything, even more complex and contradictory, since the state is confronted by a bewildering variety of trade union federations claiming to represent workers' interests.[48] An earlier chapter has shown how the introduction of union reforms in the late 1970s totally failed to incorporate and neutralise the 'new wave' black unions. Indeed, these reforms had the net effect of making an already difficult situation much worse for the Nationalist government. Here too, in the field of labour relations, the capacity of the South African state to realise its political objectives has been severely limited by the intractable problems of state–society relations in South Africa.

THE SOUTH AFRICAN STATE AND THE INTERNATIONAL ORDER

The policy processes of any state are conditioned not only by its internal organisation and its societal resources but by a complex of geopolitical and economic factors that arise from its specific location within the wider international system of states. It follows that the capacity of the South African state to engage in effective crisis-management depends to some degree upon the impact of these trans-national pressures.

We have already noted that regionally the South African state is in a powerful position since it is able to display a lethal combination of military and economic resources to maintain its dominance over the whole of southern Africa. Nevertheless regional domination exacts its price, and the growing involvement of South Africa in the economic destabilisation of the frontline states, together with the extensive deployment of the SADF in Namibia, has added considerably to the escalating costs of defending the Republic from its enemies. Most obviously the military have absorbed an increasing share of GNP with the defence budget increasing by more than 50 per cent in real terms between 1977 and 1982.[49] But in addition the very considerable growth in the size of the SADF has drawn an increasing number of white males into the military for ever-greater periods of national service, and this in turn has distorted still further a labour market already suffering from severe shortages of skilled and professional employees. The preparation for total war has therefore had the effect of intensifying the South African state's economic problems.

The ability of the South African state to engage in effective 'crisis-management' has been further restricted by the fact that the Republic, as a major exporter of certain primary commodities, occupies a peculiarly unique position within world markets.[50] This is a source both of strength and of weakness for the economy. On the one hand South African mineral exports are of strategic significance to the West since the Republic is the major supplier of a range of metals – chromium, vanadium, manganese, antimony and the platinum-related metals – that are extensively used in the defence and aerospace industries to produce high strength alloys. Apart from South Africa, the other major world producer of these metals is the USSR. On the other hand, overdependence on the mining sector renders the South African economy potentially vulnerable to fluctuations in demand and changes in the prices of these primary commodities. This is particularly true in relation to gold which in recent years has contributed between one-third and one-half of the Republic's foreign exchange earnings. In 1980 when the price of gold on the international market averaged over $600 an ounce, the mining sector contributed over 22 per cent towards South Africa's GDP. In 1984 when the average price fell to $360 an ounce this share was reduced to under 14 per cent.[51] Thus, as the South African Reserve Bank itself has noted, 'short-run prospects for the South African economy necessarily remain tied to a significant extent to the vagaries of the gold price in the international market',[52] which in turn contributes to the marked fluctuations in the Republic's balance of payments figures, as an earlier chapter has shown.

Economic problems have been further exacerbated by the periodic collapses in business confidence that have followed successive political crises in South Africa. The Sharpeville shootings of 1960, the Soweto riots of 1976, and the widespread uprising in the black townships during 1985 all resulted in a massive 'flight' of capital out of the country, together with associated losses of foreign exchange reserves and an effective devaluation of the rand. We may agree with Gavin that 'in each case, when the political disturbance was quelled, the capital flight ceased'.[53] Nevertheless, this additional element of economic uncertainty has undoubtedly made the difficult task of crisis-management much more problematic.

CONCLUSION

In this chapter we have tried to show that an understanding of the current political impasse in South Africa must start from an analysis of the contradictory nature of state power. It is our contention that, paradoxically, the South African state is at one and the same time both relatively strong and relatively ineffective. Its continuing organisational unity together with its formidable and expanding military power are undoubted sources of strength; yet at the same time these very strengths have generated a set of structural and organisational impediments to effective policymaking since they have served to distance the state from key strategic groups and interests in the wider society.

It is now apparent that the brief reformist interlude of the late 1970s and early 1980s has come to an abrupt and bloody end and that the 'total national strategy for survival' has all but collapsed. Indeed, the reforms themselves have had profoundly negative consequences for the South African state, in that they have led to an intensification and politicisation of conflicts throughout South Africa. There are three reasons why the total strategy itself has tended to amplify the escalating spiral of violence and repression. Firstly the reforms themselves created a new set of political opportunities which, though limited in nature, allowed oppositional forces to organise in new ways. This was the case with the 1983 constitutional changes which gave birth to the United Democratic Front and the post-Wiehahn trade union reforms which enabled black unions to operate more effectively than in the past. As a result of these reforms the opposition has become much more broadly-based and much better-organised than before. Secondly, the creation of a highly militarised form of command politics, with its interlocking network of national, regional and local bodies able to bypass the traditional institutions of political rule, has had the effect of magnifying the structural incongruities between state and society in South Africa. As a result there is now an unbridgeable structural divide between the political/military directorate at the head of the garrison state and the multiple centres of resistance and opposition in the factories, schools, churches and communities throughout South Africa. Thirdly the strategic priorities of this militarised state have been singularly inappropriate for meeting the needs of a variety of organised producer interests in South African society. The dysfunctional consequences that have followed the rise of military-bureaucratic policymaking in South Africa suggest that the existence of a strong, centralised, authoritarian state executive is itself no guarantee of effective, rational policies.

The combined effects of the restructuring of the state together with the 'top-down' imposition of a set of ineffective reforms, has tended to magnify the nature of the crisis in South Africa. The demise of the total strategy has engendered a significant degree of 'policy-paralysis' within the South African state and there must now be serious doubts over whether the state is any longer capable of reimposing 'law and order' or a sufficient degree of popular quiescence. But if the state can no longer secure compliance and has lost the capacity for effective political rule, neither are the subordinate groups strong enough to mount a decisive challenge to the might of the South African state. It is this situation that has given rise to the current political impasse in the Republic. If the black communities throughout South Africa are increasingly ungovernable, the militarised apartheid state remains as yet unassailable. In the medium term, therefore, the South African state seems likely to survive in its present form.

Notes

* We are indebted to Geoff Berridge and Terence Moll for their comments on an earlier draft.

1. P. Evans, D. Rueschemeyer and T. Skocpol, *Bringing The State Back In*, Cambridge, Cambridge University Press, 1985; D. Held, 'Central Perspectives on the Modern State', in D. Held et al. (eds), *States and Societies*, Oxford, Martin Robertson, 1983; D. Held, 'Power and Legitimacy in Contemporary Britain', in G. McLennan, D. Held and S. Hall (eds), *State and Society in Contemporary Britain*, Cambridge, Polity Press, 1984.
2. D. Held et al., *States and Societies*, op. cit.; T. Skocpol, 'Bringing the State Back In: Strategies of Analysis in Current Research', in P. Evans et al., *Bringing the State*, op. cit.
3. B. Jessop, *The Capitalist State*, Oxford, Martin Robertson, 1982.
4. S. Greenberg, *Race and State in Capitalist Development*, New Haven and London, Yale University Press, 1980; R. Davies, D. O'Meara and S. Dlamini, *The Struggle for South Africa Vol 2*, London, Zed Press, 1984; H. Adam and K. Moodley, *South Africa Without Apartheid*, Berkeley, University of California Press, 1986.
5. H. Adam and H. Giliomee, *Ethnic Power Mobilised: Can South Africa Change?*, New Haven, Yale University Press, 1979; H. Adam and K. Moodley, *South Africa Without Apartheid*, op. cit.; H. Wolpe, 'Towards an Analysis of the South African State', *International Journal of the Sociology of Law*, 8, 1980, pp. 399–421; H. Wolpe, 'Apartheid's Deepening Crisis', *Marxism Today*, January 1983, pp. 7–11; R. Davies and D. O'Meara, 'Total Strategy in Southern Africa: An Analysis of South African Regional Strategy Since 1978', *Journal of Southern African Studies*, 11, 2, 1985, pp. 183–211; M. Lipton, *Capitalism and Apartheid*, London, Wildwood House, 1986.

6. H. Adam and K. Moodley, *South Africa Without Apartheid*, op. cit.; M. Lipton, *Capitalism and Apartheid*, op. cit.; R. Davies and D. O'Meara, 'Total Strategy', op. cit.
7. T. Skocpol, 'Bringing the State Back In', op. cit.
8. Kuper maintains that in plural societies like South Africa, 'the state precedes and constitutes society; it is the state that is primary and imposes some measure of ordered relations on otherwise hostile or dissociated groups'. L. Kuper, 'Plural Societies: Perpectives and Problems', in L. Kuper and M. G. Smith (eds) *Pluralism in Africa*, Berkeley, University of California Press, 1971, p. 17–18.
9. State-centric theory tends to argue that state policies and activities are not primarily an outcome of pressure from competing groups, but are the outcome of autonomous state action. E. Nordlinger, *On The Autonomy of the Democratic State*, Cambridge, Massachusetts, Harvard University Press, 1981.
10. S. Hall, 'The State In Question', in G. McLennan, D. Held and S. Hall (eds), *The Idea of the Modern State*, Milton Keynes, Open University Press, 1984; D. Held, 'Power and Legitimacy', op. cit.
11. T. Skocpol, 'Bringing the State Back In', op. cit.
12. P. A. Hall, *Governing the Economy: The Politics of State Intervention in Britain and France*, Cambridge, Polity Press, 1986, p. 21.
13. 'Intermediation' is a key concept in recent accounts of 'societal corporatism'. It refers to the capacity of organised interests to negotiate agreements with the state and with each other. In this process the role of 'intermediary groups' is seen as crucial since they must have enough control over their own members to deliver their part of any bargain.
14. Offe has offered some important insights into the deficiencies of the bureaucratic mode of state intervention in capitalist societies. C. Offe, 'The Theory of the Capitalist State and the Problem of Policy Formulation', in L. Lindberg et al. (eds), *Stress and Contradiction in Modern Capitalism*, Lexington, D. C. Heath, 1975 and *Contradictions of the Welfare State*, London, Hutchinson, 1984. See also A. Cawson, *Corporatism and Welfare*, London, Heinemann Educational Books, 1982.
15. B. Jessop, *The Capitalist State*, op. cit.; T Skocpol, 'Bringing the State Back In', op. cit.
16. See Chapter 10 in this book and M. Mitchell and D. Russell, 'South Africa in Crisis: The Role of the Black Trade Unions' in W. Brierley (ed.), *Trade Unions and the Economic Crisis of the 1980s*, Aldershot, Gower, 1987; H. Adam and K. Moodley, *South Africa Without Apartheid*, op. cit.
17. H. Adam, 'Survival Politics: Afrikanerdom in Search of a New Ideology', *Journal of Modern African Studies*, 16, 1978, pp. 657–69.
18. M. Mitchell and D. Russell, 'Militarisation and the South African State', in C. Creighton and M. Shaw (eds), *The Sociology of War and Peace*, London, Macmillan, 1987.
19. The idea that 'legitimation crisis' has been institutionalised in South Africa is put forward by H. Adam and K. Moodley, *South Africa Without Apartheid*, p. 129.
20. B. Jessop, *The Capitalist State*, op. cit.
21. M. Mitchell and D. Russell, 'Militarisation and the South African State',

op. cit.; G. Cawthra, *Brutal Force*, London, International Defence and Aid Fund for Southern Africa, 1986; P. Frankel, *Pretoria's Praetorians: Civil Military Relations in South Africa*, Cambridge, Cambridge University Press, 1984.

22. We have taken the idea of 'total strategy/total shambles' from S. Friedman who in turn states that he acquired the phrase from J. Kane-Berman. See S. Friedman, 'Political Implications of Industrial Unrest in South Africa', in D. Hindson (ed.), *Working Papers in Southern African Studies, Vol. 3*, Johannesburg, Ravan Press, 1983, p. 134.
23. R. Davies and D. O'Meara, 'Total Strategy', op. cit.; M. Mitchell and D. Russell, 'Militarisation and the South African State', op. cit.
24. 'Sectoral corporatism' is a term introduced by Lembruch. He makes a distinction between it and 'corporatist concertation', which involves tripartite political bargaining about the overall management of the economy. 'Sectoral corporatism' in contrast is limited to specific sectors of the economy and above all involves a special relationship between the government and particular organised interests who enjoy privileged access to the policy-making process. See G. Lembruch, 'The Logic and Structural Conditions of Neo-Corporatist Concertation', in J. H. Goldthorpe (ed.), *Order and Conflict in Contemporary Capitalism: Studies in the Political Economy of Western European Nations*, Oxford, Oxford University Press, 1984.
25. The term 'trafficking of top personnel' originates from F. Van Zyl Slabbert, 'Afrikaner Nationalism, White Politics and Political Change in South Africa', in L. Thompson and J. Butler (eds), *Change in Contemporary South Africa*, Berkeley, University of California Press, 1975, p. 9.
26. G. Cawthra, 'Brutal Force', op. cit.; M. Mitchell and D Russell, 'Militarisation and the South African State', op. cit.
27. W. Cobbett, D. Glaser, D. Hindson and M. Swilling, 'South Africa's Regional Political Economy: A Critical Analysis of Reform Strategy in the 1980s', *South Africa Review 3,* Johannesburg, Ravan Press, 1986, p. 163; J. Brewer, 'The Police in South African Politics', in S. Johnson (ed.), *South Africa: No Turning Back*, London, Macmillan, 1988.
28. J. Brewer, 'The Police in South African Politics', op. cit.
29. In 1986 the SSC had established 12 JMCs in the large conurbations and another 60 in smaller towns. In addition a further 348 mini-JMCs were operating at the local level under the control of the larger committees. J. Brewer, 'The Police in South African Politics', op. cit., and G. Cawthra, *Brutal Force*, op. cit., pp. 37–8.
30. G. Cawthra, *Brutal Force*, op. cit., pp. 37–8.
31. A. Cawson, *Organised Interests and the State: Studies in Meso-Corporatism*, London, Sage, 1986; P. A. Hall, *Governing the Economy*, op. cit.
32. M. Mitchell and D. Russell, 'Restructuring Apartheid', unpublished paper presented to the Annual Conference of the British Sociological Association, University College, Cardiff, April 1983.
33. The modest proposals made by the De Lange Commission on black education were diluted very considerably by the government. In particular the central principle of 'equal quality' of educational provision to be administered by a single education department was rejected. For discus-

sion of the De Lange proposals, see L. Chisholm and P. Christie, 'Restructuring in Education', *South Africa Review* 1, Johannesburg, Ravan Press, 1983, pp. 254–63.

34. There are four major organisations claiming to represent business interests in South Africa. The Federated Chambers of Industry and the Association of Chambers of Commerce are organisations representing mainly 'non-Afrikaner' capital. The Afrikaanse Handelsinstituut is the Afrikaner business equivalent, while the much smaller National African Federated Chambers of Commerce represents black capital. The two most powerful sectoral capitalist groupings are the South African Chamber of Mines and the South African Agricultural Union. For details on these organisations, see R. Davics, D. O'Meara and S. Dlamini, *The Struggle for South Africa*, op. cit., pp. 105–21.
35. The influence of financial capital in offering support to 'monetarist' free market economic policies was apparent in the De Kock Commission of Inquiry into the Monetary System and Monetary Policy in South Africa, which reported in 1984. According to Moll this commission was packed with representatives of 'highly sectional financial and banking interests'. See T. Moll, 'Microeconomic Policy and Poverty in South Africa: The Crucial Issues', *Post-Carnegie Working Paper*, Cape Town, Department of Economics, University of Cape Town, 1987, p. 23.
36. Ibid.
37. M. Gavin, 'The High Cost of Reform', in M. Uhlig (ed.), *Apartheid in Crisis*, Harmondsworth, Penguin, 1986, p. 227.
38. T. Moll, 'Microeconomic Policy', op. cit., pp. 10–11.
39. Ibid.
40. Ibid.
41. H. Adam, 'Minority Monopoly in Transition: Recent Policy Shifts in the South African State', *Journal of Modern African Studies*, 18, 4, 1980, pp. 617–18.
42. M. Lipton, *Capitalism and Apartheid*, op. cit., pp. 153–6.
43. W. Cobbett et al., 'South Africa's Regional Political Economy', op. cit.
44. Ibid.
45. In particular the urban and regional strategy breaks with established 'homeland' policy and the commitment to Bantustan development. Importantly, it departs from some crucial 'political and territorial premises of apartheid'. See W. Cobbett et al., 'South Africa's Regional Political Economy', op. cit., p. 138. However, race/ethnicity still remains paramount in the political economy of South Africa.
46. Ibid, p. 148.
47. Ibid, p. 150.
48. For further details, see our chapter on trade unions in this volume.
49. The published figures seriously underestimate the true size of the defence budget. For these and other statistics documenting the expansion of the SADF, see M. Mitchell and D. Russell, 'The Militarisation of the South Africa State', op. cit., p. 104, and G. Cawthra, *Brutal Force*, op. cit., p. 259.
50. In spite of its relatively high levels of economic growth and its ability to attract foreign investment, it has been argued by some writers that South

Africa is a 'peripheral' economy. See M. Bienefeld and D. Innes, 'Capital Accumulation in South Africa', *Review of African Political Economy*, 7, 1976, pp. 31–55.

51. M. Gavin, 'The High Cost of Reform' op. cit., p. 256.
52. This quotation is taken from an advertisement placed by the South African Reserve Bank in *The Economist* 21 June 1980.
53. M. Gavin, 'The High Cost of Reform', op. cit., p. 241.

14 Five Minutes to Midnight*

John D. Brewer

It is a commonplace in the sociology of knowledge that ideas are a direct or indirect reflection of their social context. Writings on South Africa have always seemed to me to be a good illustration of this general point.[1] Ten years after Johnson outlined his thesis on the tenacity of apartheid, some commentators thought the situation had changed sufficiently in South Africa for them to begin to think about what the country will be like without it. In 1987, for example, Adam and Moodley published a study they entitled *South Africa Without Apartheid*,[2] and international conferences were able to attract participants to discuss views on the nature of the post-apartheid economy. Two prestigious study groups met in that year to consider South Africa's future. The one sponsored by the Anglo-American Corporation was established in order to address the issue of South Africa beyond apartheid, a remit which formed the title of its report, while the report of the group organised under the auspices of the David Davies Memorial Institute of International Studies used the metaphor of an onward journey, believing there now to be no turning back for South Africa.[3]

Another important theme which represents the reality of South Africa, and therefore which dominates the literature on the country, is that of crisis. The presentation of South Africa as a society in crisis had become almost ubiquitous amongst academics by 1987, as reflected in the titles of their published work.[4] The interlocking problems facing apartheid are widely documented, and while crisis can be an overused word, the South African state does face ideological disunity and political disaffection among whites, civil unrest, economic problems which are compounded by high demands on state expenditure, and international pressure. But 'crisis' and 'change' are not the only terms to feature in political discourse about South Africa, for the notion of 'time' rivals these in prominence. Political rhetoric is replete with references to the idea that time is pressing and about to run out. This terminology formed the title of the influential Rockefeller report on South Africa, and self-consciously governed the deliberations of the

Commonwealth Eminent Persons Group and the earlier Buthelezi Commission. The belief that time is pressing permeated the discourse of groups as diverse as South African businessmen, reformist politicians, international critics, and the African National Congress (ANC), who all at one time or other employed the allegory for political effect. Hence the subtitle of Murray's study of modern South Africa was *Time of Agony, Time of Destiny*.[5]

In this context it seems appropriate to halt this trend, dispiriting though it is, and reconsider Johnson's claims about the medium-term stability of the system of white political supremacy and its relative protection from fundamental change and crisis. In Johnson's usage, time was not running out for South Africa but had stood still, with the clock stuck steadfastly at five minutes to midnight.

Reluctantly, any such review must conclude that while things change in South Africa, they also stay very much the same. The change in circumstances since the publication of *How Long Will South Africa Survive?* in 1977 has not weakened apartheid to any great extent. However, while Berger and Godsell, a decade on, were correct to complain of what they called the fantasies about South Africa's future,[6] the society is unstable to the extent that there are deep-seated social, political and economic conflicts, and widespread coercion and violence, which justify attention being focused on the system which replaces it. But South Africa is not in crisis to the extent that it faces an imminent and apocalyptic rebellion. This is why one recent visitor to South Africa, new to the country, could write: 'The first thing that struck me was that when I was leaving, my secretary said to me, "Good luck!", as if I were off to Beirut. What struck me when I arrived was that I felt more physically safe than when I march around Manhattan .. [T]his society is not on the brink of disintegration. I mean, its a well-functioning society.'[7] The problems South Africa has to confront are embedded deep in underlying structural conditions and are not so apparent to tourists as they walk the bustling streets of Durban, Cape Town or Johannesburg. But the intractable problems are there, even though they may not be visible. One commentator coined an apt phrase to describe this when he said that neither revolution nor resolution is at hand;[8] Johnson's allegory of the motionless clock, stuck just before the final hour, remains symbolic of South Africa's situation. However, the chapters in this volume show that the hands are beginning to waver.

The contributors have outlined in detail the reasons why this is so, and here I will only draw out some of the salient features of their arguments, looking first at the factors which make the regime's immediate overthrow unlikely. A theme running throughout many chapters is how the South African state is becoming militarised as a response to internal instability, a threat which it expresses in law and order terms. As Mitchell and Russell emphasise, this militarisation is simultaneously a strength and a weakness. It gives the state organisational unity and military power, but in the process isolates it from key groups within South African society, both white and black. But as Giliomee shows, there is little evidence of opposition among whites to this encroaching totalitarianism. Nor it there any loss of morale among whites, so that the loyalty of the major components of the militarised state, such as the army and police, is not in dispute. Whites still seem willing to pay higher taxes and conscript their sons in order to maintain this level of militarisation.

Lodge argues that militarisation has been the strategy through which the state has been able to quell black protest in the townships. Black protest subsided following the second state of emergency and the organisational structure of the United Democratic Front (UDF) has been damaged, and in February 1988 the state proscribed it from engaging in political activity, along with sixteen other political and humanitarian organisations. The UDF's momentary high profile, therefore, has to be seen as a product of the government's tolerance of open opposition, something that proved to be quite temporary. Moreover, as I show, black opposition is fissile and disunited over matters of strategy, tactics and ideology, which is a problem which restricts the political effectiveness of the black trade union movement as well. The government reinforced controls on political unionism in February 1988 when it proscribed the largest and most radical trade union organisation, the Congress of South African Trade Unions, from engaging in politics. Mitchell and Russell also discuss some of the other constraints on the black unions. To some extent it seems that government reforms have been effective in strengthening the system of white political supremacy, if only by provoking division amongst opponents in how they respond to the initiatives. Trade union reforms and constitutional change are two examples discussed here which illustrate this point.

However, irrespective of this opposition disunity, internal rebellion is never capable alone of bringing down apartheid because of the realities of military power, contrary to the rhetoric of the state's opponents in the heady days before the states of emergency. Black South Africans have few military resources to match those of the state and sabotage depends for its effectiveness on a loss of morale among whites and a consequent disaffection among the armed forces, neither of which is likely in South Africa. This military imbalance can only be corrected by military intervention by the regional states or the superpowers. Braun shows, however, that South Africa's destabilisation policies have thoroughly intimidated the neighbouring states, while Berridge argues that superpower interests in the region have not changed since 1977 and that both superpowers are decidedly against military intervention. Indeed, he claims there is a compatibility between their respective interests and agreement between them to prevent the issue interfering in wider superpower relations. If anything, southern Africa is a less important issue for the superpowers now than it was at the time of Johnson's writing.

Yet it is not military intervention but sanctions which is the most widely canvassed measure for applying Western pressure on South Africa. But Berridge sees no evidence today of the West manipulating the gold market to pressurise South Africa, as Johnson documented in 1977, and increases in the gold price as a result of the uncertainty in the stock market toward the end of 1987 made it even less conceivable that the United States would try to force the price down to put pressure on Pretoria. However, some economic sanctions have been applied. While it is the case that sanctions have a ratchet effect, so that once imposed they are unlikely ever to be discontinued, the current measures are largely symbolic: a simple matter of the West's placebo politics, as Braun and Weiland describe it. Holland argues that, in fact, the very decision-making structure of the European Economic Community prevents more effective sanction policies being introduced. The emphasis upon consensus allows individual member states to use their veto against more effective policies when this conflicts with their national interest. Guelke believes that the West will intervene only when interracial violence leads to an escalation in the number of fatalities, the prospect of which is far off, although he shows how political violence in South Africa during the period 1984 to 1986 did encourage Western countries to adopt the placebo strategy.

But even if more effective sanctions could be agreed upon and applied by the West, Moll argues that the system of white political supremacy could survive in the short term by retreating into a laager or siege economy. As he points out, while there are strains within the economy (which is the factor leading most commentators to apply the description of crisis to South Africa), there are no signs of immediate collapse, and the economy can well fund further militarisation, especially if it becomes a laager or siege type.

However, the main thrust of the chapters is to demonstrate how the balance of forces in South Africa is shifting against the system of white political supremacy, although not to the extent of threatening its immediate prospects of survival. Contributors have identified numerous factors which explain why the hands of the clock have moved, if only to marginally nearer midnight. Again I will merely emphasise some of the central points from their detailed arguments.

The dynamics of internal politics have changed since 1977. In relation to black politics, Lodge and I make clear that the states of emergency and the restrictions imposed in February 1988 will have only a superficial effectiveness in quelling black protest because the underlying base of black politics is now stronger. Lodge emphasises how black politics has become internationalised, so that repression has wider ramifications, and how black political culture has simultaneously matured and become militant. In my chapter I show how black protest has been strengthened despite the fissures within it. For example, there are new and important ideological and class alliances, armed struggle is being coordinated with political mobilisation, and the labour and trade union movement is being used as a powerful force pushing for political change, even if not as effectively as it could. This radicalism is shown in an extension of the strategies by which opposition is pursued, some of which are more resistant to state repression, and an expansion in political goals. I believe that long-term tactical and strategic breakthroughs have been made which make black protest more capable of weakening the system of white political supremacy when combined with other pressures. Moreover, this strength is divorced from the organisations which happen to give expression to it, for it reflects broad structural changes and realignments in black politics. Therefore, new organisations are likely to replace those that are proscribed or prohibited from engaging in politics and be equally capable of drawing on the strength these realignments provide.

In terms of the dynamics of white politics, Giliomee shows how the ideological disunity among whites has facilitated the search for alternatives to apartheid, which has given legitimacy to the idea and rhetoric of reform. Amongst most Afrikaners apartheid is a discredited ideology, and those that disagree are currently excluded from the political elite. Giliomee sees little prospect of the more right-wing Conservative Party ever extending its power base sufficiently to assume political power, especially given support for the National Party amongst English-speaking South Africans. Were the Conservative Party ever to do so, Giliomee believes that the government would suspend elections and rule through referenda and by decree. Contrary to Johnson's claim, Giliomee does not see history to be on the side of the *verkramptes*, although the Conservative Party and the semi-fascist movements close to it will constrain the government's ability to modernise the regime through reform.

But if the future lies with the *verligtes*, reform is still likely to be restricted to economic and social apartheid rather than abolishing white political supremacy. There is a view that no external pressure should be applied to South Africa in order to give every encouragement to the 'reformers' within the government. This rather presupposes that *verligtes* are capable of dismantling political apartheid. As Rich shows with respect to constitutional change, at the level of ideology the debate about political change amongst 'reformers' is still conducted in terms of segregationist-type models. At the structural level of the state, Giliomee, and Mitchell and Russell describe current policy as a combination of reform and repression within a centralised state which risks becoming isolated, although Rich, and Mitchell and Russell argue that reform has temporarily been halted. However, both elements of this duality pose problems for the system of white political supremacy. The reforms, so called, can develop a momentum of their own, in such a way that the state loses control over the process of change, as occurred with both constitutional and trade union reforms. Giliomee argues that in the long run repression risks alienating many whites, who have to face the fiscal burden of militarised policing and who would have difficulty in reconciling themselves to a totalitarian state. Excessive repression would also be incompatible with South Africa's advanced industrialised infrastructure and the need for a minimally cooperative labour force. The repressive aspect of the state's dual strategy also ensures that the state is incapable of proceeding with sufficient fundamental change to strengthen its position via reform.

Demography is also on the side of change. In the year 2000 South Africa is expected to have a population of 45 millions, the white proportion of which grows smaller and smaller as the millennium approaches, which requires the unlikely possibility of more and more black South Africans being willing to cooperate in their own repression. But demographic considerations are more important for their economic implications. The growing black population will need to be fed, housed, educated and employed somewhere in South Africa, and the demands of the South African economy will not be met by the diminishing number of whites. The logic of demography and capitalist development in South Africa is in favour of residential, educational and housing reform. But even if one disputes the view that industrialisation encourages reform (and there is a body of literature which argues it does, even though this does not extend to political reform),[9] the balance of the economy has shifted to grant blacks economic power as consumers and producers. This economic power is being used to demand a redistribution of political power. On this argument, placing blacks in employment provides just as much potential for change as massive black unemployment.

While the South African economy is not in a state of immediate collapse, both Moll and Nattrass see its health as too precarious to fund the demands that are likely to be made on it in the future. Nattrass especially emphasises how this is true as much for expensive reform as for expensive repression, but the inability to do either weakens the system of white political supremacy in the long term. There are economic constraints on the state which prevent it from both spending its way out of trouble by reform and spending to keep itself in power through continued repression. Thus, Moll argues that while theoretically the South African state could finance further militarisation, this would be at the cost of a high fiscal burden, and expenditure on black education, housing, and welfare, the political implications of which are destabilising. This was shown in 1984 when economic recession caused rent and service charge increases to be levied in the black townships, provoking considerable political opposition and violence, the immediate consequences of which temporarily worsened South Africa's economic situation.

In this regard, even the placebo sanctions the West imposed have had some economic bite. In the long run placebo-type measures will have a cumulative effect, but current sanctions had an immediate effect in the withdrawal of capital from South Africa and a permanent increase in the costs of capital to South African businessmen. From 1984 South Africa has been a net exporter of capital, although this was not entirely due to disinvestment and sanctions, but also to the conditions imposed by the international banking community. The Chairman of the Anglo-American Corporation, Gavin Relly, said in a speech during 1987 that in his view the economy needed to be a net importer of capital, in order to meet all necessary domestic demands and to allow South Africa to play her role in the region.[10] But the attention focused on the question of whether or not more effective sanctions will be imposed, tends to obscure the fact that even without this increased pressure, the South African economy is not strong. South Africa has only an average GNP, and her position relative to those with a similar GNP is declining, irrespective of sanctions.

Overall, it seems that ten years on from Johnson's *How Long Will South Africa Survive?*, the balance of forces in South Africa still excludes a revolutionary overthrow of the government, but the government's capacity to maintain the present pattern of political power has weakened. If the militarised and centralised state is as yet unassailable, the system is becoming more ungovernable. So while the clock is still at five minutes to midnight, it is no longer riveted in this position.

However, it is hardly appropriate to describe this as constituting stability. The system of white political supremacy may survive in the short term but it is not stable. A term used in many chapters in this volume to describe the current situation in South Africa is 'impasse'. Impasse means deadlock and stalemate, and while some situations of impasse seem permanent, there is always a pressure toward flux and change which is absent in situations of amicable (as distinct from enforced) stability. This is because impasse reflects disagreement and incompatibility between opposites, rather than the capitulation of one to the other, and the inability by one to impose on the other. Impasse arises when neither side can force their wishes on the other and when neither will surrender, irrespective of the logic of the situation. When the logic of the situation favours one side over the other, even if this is in the medium term, the failure to concede and bow to logic makes the stalemate fragile as a real shift in the balance of forces inevitably occurs over time. For the reasons outlined in the preceding chapters, South Africa's impasse is not of the permanent variety, for the logic of the situation supports black South Africans. This is not to say that in the short term South Africa will become more unstable than at present – stalemates can persevere for a long time. But the current impasse reflects a shift in the balance of forces in favour of black South Africans, and the scales will continue to tip, if crescively, in their direction, so that the debate about the future of South Africa must now begin from different premises than Johnson's.[11] We might not at present be much nearer the hour, but in these circumstances it is more conceivable than ever before that we will reach the other side of midnight.

Notes

* I wish to thank Adrian Guelke and Geoff Berridge for comments on an earlier draft. The latter's 'aggressive red pen' was a special source of improvement to the arguments contained here.

1. For example see J. D. Brewer, 'The Concept of Political Change and the

Language of Change in South Africa', *Africa Quarterly*, 21, 1981, p. 5; J. D. Brewer, *After Soweto: An Unfinished Journey*, Oxford, The Clarendon Press, 1987, p. 9.

2. H. Adam and K. Moodley, *South Africa Without Apartheid*, Berkeley, University of California Press, 1987.
3. See S. Johnson (ed.), *South Africa: No Turning Back*, London, Macmillan, 1988.
4. For a selection see: J. Blumenfeld (ed.), *South Africa in Crisis*, London, Croom Helm, 1997; R. Cohen, *Endgame in South Africa*, London, James Currey, 1986; F. Parker, *South Africa: Lost Opportunities*, Aldershot, Gower, 1984; M. Murray, *South Africa: Time of Agony, Time of Destiny*, London, Verso, 1987; J. Saul and S. Gelb, *The Crisis in South Africa*, London, Zed Press, 1986; M Ulig (ed.) *Apartheid in Crisis*, Harmondsworth, Penguin, 1986; H. Wolpe, 'Apartheid's Crisis, *Marxism Today*, January 1983.
5. Murray, *South Africa: Time of Agony, Time of Destiny*, op. cit.
6. P. Berger and B. Godsell, 'Fantasies About South Africa', *Optima*, 35, 1987, pp. 126–33.
7. P. Berger in interview with Simon Barber, reported in Simon Barber, 'South Africa Beyond Apartheid', ibid., p. 123.
8. Address at The Hague, Netherlands, 10 September 1987.
9. See Merle Lipton, *Capitalism and Apartheid*, London, Wildwood House, 1986, who argues that these reforms are in the interests of the dominant fraction of capitalism in South Africa, but that this fraction will remain opposed to political reform.
10. Address at The Hague, Netherlands, 10 September 1987.
11. A similar point was made by Robert Rotberg, *Suffer the Future*, London, Harvard University Press, 1980, p. 159.

Index